TExES

GENERALIST EC-6 191 ESSENTIALS EDITION

By: Sharon Wynne, M.S.

XAMonline, INC.
Boston

XAMonline, Inc.
25 First Street, Suite 106
Cambridge, MA 02141
Toll Free 1-800-509-4128
Email: info@xamonline.com
Web: www.xamonline.com
Fax: 1-617-583-5552

Library of Congress Cataloging-in-Publication Data

Wynne, Sharon A.

TExES Generalist EC-6 191 Essentials Edition / Sharon A. Wynne. 1st ed
ISBN 978-1-60787-113-2
1. TExES Generalist EC-6 191
2. Study Guides
3. TExES
4. Teachers' Certification & Licensure
5. Careers

Printed in the United States of America œ-1

TExES Generalist EC-6 191 Essentials Edition
ISBN: 978-1-60787-113-2

Table of Contents

DOMAIN II

DOMAIN III

DOMAIN IV

DOMAIN V

SAMPLE TEST

Available Boost chapters of the TExES Generalist EC-6 191 Teacher Certification Study Guide: in-depth review of each Domain of the Generalist EC-6 Essentials Edition

Domain I: English Language Arts and Reading
ebook ISBN: 978-1-60787-659-5
Book ISBN: 978-1-60787-102-6

Domain II: Mathematics
ebook ISBN: 978-1-60787-658-8
Book ISBN: 978-1-60787-103-3

Domain III: Social Studies
ebook ISBN: 978-1-60787-657-1
Book ISBN: 978-1-60787-104-0

Domain IV: Science
ebook ISBN: 978-1-60787-656-4
Book ISBN: 978-1-60787-105-7

Domain V: Fine Arts, Health, and Physical Education
ebook ISBN: 978-1-60787-655-7
Book ISBN: 978-1-60787-106-4

DOMAIN I
ENGLISH LANGUAGE ARTS AND READING

PERSONALIZED STUDY PLAN

ORAL LANGUAGE

Phonemes

A **PHONEME** is the smallest contrastive unit in a language system and the representation of a sound. The phoneme has been described as the smallest meaningful psychological unit of sound. The phoneme is said to have mental, physiological, and physical substance: our brains process the sounds; the sounds are produced by the human speech organs; and the sounds are physical entities that can be recorded and measured. Consider the English words *pat* and *sat*, which appear to differ only in their initial consonants. This difference, known as opposition, is adequate to distinguish these words, and therefore the *p* and *s* sounds are said to be different phonemes in English. A pair of words, identical except for such a sound, is known as a minimal pair, and the two sounds are separate phonemes.

PHONEME: the smallest contrastive unit in a language system and the representation of a sound

Phonemic awareness

PHONEMIC AWARENESS is the acknowledgement of sounds and words; for example, a child's realization that some words rhyme. Onset and rhyme, for example, are skills that might help students learn that the sound of the first letter, *b*, in the word *bad* can be changed with the sound *d* to make it *dad*. The key in phonemic awareness is that when you teach it to children it can be taught with the students' eyes closed. In other words, it's all about sounds, not about ascribing written letters to sounds.

PHONEMIC AWARENESS: the acknowledgement of sounds and words; for example, a child's realization that some words rhyme

To be phonemically aware means that the reader or listener can recognize and manipulate specific sounds in spoken words. The majority of phonemic awareness tasks, activities, and exercises are oral.

Since the ability to distinguish between individual sounds, or phonemes, within words is a prerequisite to the association of sounds with letters and manipulating sounds to blend words (a fancy way of saying "reading"), the teaching of phonemic awareness is crucial to emergent literacy. Children need a strong background in phonemic awareness in order for phonics instruction to be effective.

PHONOLOGICAL AWARENESS: the reader's ability to recognize the sound of spoken language, including how sounds can be blended together, segmented, and manipulated

Phonics

PHONOLOGICAL AWARENESS refers to the reader's ability to recognize the sound of spoken language, including how sounds can be blended together, segmented (divided up), and manipulated (switched around). This awareness then leads to **PHONICS**, a method for teaching children to read. It helps students "sound out words."

PHONICS: a method for teaching children to read

Development of phonological skills may begin during pre-K years. Indeed, by the age of 5, a child who has been exposed to rhyme can recognize a rhyme. Such a child can demonstrate phonological awareness by filling in the missing rhyming word in a familiar rhyme or rhymed picture book.

Phonological awareness skills include:

1. Rhyming and syllabification
2. Blending sounds into words—such as *pic-tur-bo-k*
3. Identifying the beginning or starting sounds of words and the ending or closing sounds of words
4. Breaking words down into sounds—also called "segmenting" words
5. Recognizing other smaller words in a big word by removing starting sounds, e.g., *hear* to *ear*

Morphology, Syntax, and Semantics

MORPHOLOGY: the study of word structure

SYNTAX: the rules or patterned relationships that correctly create phrases and sentences from words

SEMANTICS: the meaning expressed when words are arranged in a specific way

MORPHOLOGY is the study of word structure. When readers develop morphemic skills, they are developing an understanding of patterns they see in words. For example, English speakers realize that *cat, cats,* and *caterpillar* share some similarities in structure. This understanding helps readers to recognize words at a faster and easier rate, since each word doesn't need individual decoding.

SYNTAX refers to the rules or patterned relationships that correctly create phrases and sentences from words. When readers develop an understanding of syntax, they begin to understand the structure of how sentences are built, and, eventually, the beginning of grammar.

SEMANTICS refers to the meaning expressed when words are arranged in a specific way. This is where connotation and denotation of words eventually has a role with readers.

Pragmatics

Pragmatics is concerned with the difference between the writer's meaning and the literal meaning of the sentence based on social context. When someone is competent in pragmatics, he or she is able to understand the writer's intended meaning. In a simpler sense, pragmatics can be considered the social rules of language.

Assessment of Oral Language Skills

Assessment information should be used to provide performance-based criteria and academic expectations for all students in evaluating whether students have learned the expected skills and content of the subject area. By analyzing the various types of assessments, teachers can gather more definitive information on projected student academic performance. Instructional strategies for teachers would provide learning targets for student behavior, cognitive thinking skills, and processing skills that can be employed to diversify student learning opportunities.

Assessment drives the instruction. Some of the methods teachers can employ to assess for learning involve both formative and summative evaluation. Formative assessment consists of testing; however, teachers can make summative assessment part of their daily routine by using such measures as:

- Anecdotal records
- Portfolios
- Listening to children read
- Oral presentations
- Checklists
- Running records
- Samples of work
- Self-evaluation

Informal assessment

For informal assessment, teachers can observe students during their everyday classroom activities. Teachers should make a point to evaluate a student multiple times at different times of the day and during different types of tasks. They can keep records, notes, or checklists of the child's oral skills. This type of assessment can include other students, for example, in cooperative learning environments. This type of assessment is often particularly authentic because the student will display typical oral skills while at ease. Students in higher grades can learn how to assess themselves using checklists, journals, portfolios, and other types of self-evaluation.

Formal assessment

Formal assessments take more planning. The teacher typically targets certain oral skills utilizing specific tasks and assessment methods. A formal assessment can be an oral interview that is recorded in some manner; picture-cued description/stories; oral prompts; text retelling; or role playing. There are also formal assessment tests teachers can obtain to formally record a student's oral skill development.

Speech or Language Delays

Speech or language delays in children can be cause for concern or intervention. Understanding the development of language in young children can provide information on delays or differences. Parents and teachers must understand the difference between developmental speech, word development, and language delays/differences that may prevent oral language acquisition. The ability to differentiate between the natural development of children's language patterns and the delayed development of those patterns should be the focus of the adult caregivers who provide the environmental stimulis and language experiences for children.

Age/language acquisition guidelines

- Children at the age of 2 should have speech patterns that are about 70 percent intelligible.
- Children at the age of 3 should have a speech pattern that is about 80 percent intelligible.
- Children at the age of 4 should have a speech pattern that is about 90 percent intelligible.
- Children at the age of 5 should have a speech pattern that is 100 percent intelligible.
- Children over the age of 5 will develop speech patterns that continue at 100 percent intelligibility with increased vocabulary.

Teachers and parents who have concerns about a child's language development should be proactive in addressing them. Early intervention is critical. Effective steps in addressing language delays or differences include: contacting a speech pathologist to evaluate a child's speech, an auditory specialist to test for hearing disorders, a pediatrician to test for motor-function delays, and utilizing other assessment resources for evaluation.

Stimulating Development of Children's Oral Language Skills

In order to stimulate the development of their oral language skills, children should be exposed to a challenging environment that is rich in opportunities. Teachers should remain focused on oral language skills throughout the day, even while teaching other subjects.

Activities that encourage development of oral language skills

- Encourage meaningful conversation
- Allow dramatic playtime
- Let children share personal stories
- Sing the alphabet song
- Teach the art of questioning
- Read rhyming books
- Play listening games
- Encourage sharing of information

If an educational program is child-centered, it will surely address the developmental abilities and needs of the students because it will take its cues from students' interests, concerns, and questions.

Scaffolding Theory

Most language skills need to have layers of information gathered and stored to ensure a sound basis for continued learning. Scaffolding is a metaphorical term that illustrates the process of gathering knowledge of concepts. Some ingredients of scaffolding are predictability, playfulness, focus on meaning, role reversal, modeling, and nomenclature.

Instructional scaffolding is the provision of sufficient supports to promote learning when concepts and skills are first being introduced to students. These supports may include:

- Resources: The teacher provides supportive materials such as recommended readings, documents, or storyboards.
- A compelling task: The student or group is given an extensive task to perform, which requires them to learn and master successive and continually more difficult facets of a particular language skill.
- Templates and guides: The teacher provides outlines, language-use templates, and study guides. Initially, these supports explain the skill to the student and provide examples to allow the student to model the communicative task.
- Guidance on the development of cognitive and social skills: Each layer of language scaffolding should call for increased development of cognitive thinking. With young students, in particular, activities should include development of progressively more advanced socially acceptable patterns and norms.

Strategies for Enhancing Language Development

The act of simulating the sounds and words in his or her environment provides the child with language enhancement and acquisition. The promotion of language development should include repetition and language engagement.

Children's toys, games, and books can be used to further language development. Providing language simulation activities that model how to ask questions or put words into sentences are effective instructional strategies.

Providing children with instructional language cues can facilitate learning and language development. Using strategic tools such as rephrasing sentences (e.g., "dada goed") into questions (e.g., "Is daddy going?") can provide children with correct sentence formats and other ways of looking at oral meaning. When children are given labels for objects, they can use word association in developing language acquisition.

Teachers and evaluators of children's language development must work effectively with families. Fostering collaborative efforts to provide a community approach to promoting children's oral development is both pragmatic and necessary if children are to become effective communicators.

When parents and teachers understand that children have individualized language foundations that are valid communication systems, a child can develop beginning speech patterns without the stereotype of an adult's perception of language delay or differences. Children reflect their environments and their cultural and familial identifications.

Engaging children in conversations with teachers and parents can provide nonverbal and verbal clues about how conversations work and what visual cues or body cues can be used to express nonverbal meaning.

Relationship Between Oral and Written Language

A "balanced literacy" curriculum focuses on the use of oral and written language skills in various instructional contexts.

- Independent reading: Students independently choose books that are at their reading levels.
- Guided reading: Teachers work with small groups of students to help them with their particular reading problems.
- Whole-group reading: The entire class reads the same text, and the teacher incorporates activities to help students learn phonics, comprehension, fluency, and vocabulary.

In addition to these components of balanced literacy, teachers incorporate writing so that students can learn the structures of communicating through text.

Role of oral development

In 2000, the National Reading Panel released its now well-known report on teaching children to read. The report's "big five" critical areas of reading instruction are:

- Phonemic awareness: The acknowledgement of sounds and words
- Phonics: The connection between the sounds and letters on a page
- Fluency: Reading connected pieces of text

- Comprehension: The reader's ability to ascribe meaning to text
- Content-area vocabulary: The specific vocabulary related to the particular concepts of various academic disciplines

Role of vocabulary

Teachers need to help students learn strategies to figure out the meanings of difficult words when they encounter them on their own. They can do this by teaching students how to identify the meanings of words in context (usually through activities in which the word is taken out of the sentence and the students have to figure out a way to make sense of the sentence). In addition, dictionary skills must be taught in all subject areas. Teaching vocabulary is not just the teaching of words: it is the teaching of complex concepts, each with histories and connotations.

Explicitly teaching vocabulary works best when teachers connect new words to words, ideas, and experiences with which students are already familiar. Finally, students need plenty of exposure to the new words.

Read alouds

Read alouds can be used to teach the student listener while developing background knowledge, increasing comprehension skills, and fostering critical thinking.

Teaching Public Speaking Skills

In public speaking, not all speeches require the same type of speaking style. For example, when delivering a humorous speech, it is important to utilize body language to accent humorous points. However, when giving instructions, it is extremely important to speak clearly and slowly, carefully noting the mood of the audience, so that if there is confusion on peoples' faces, the speaker can go back and review something. In group discussions, speakers must be sure to listen to other speakers carefully and tailor their messages to fit the general mood of the discussion at hand. The speaker should focus on covering the content, while also relating to audience members as much as possible.

As students practice these skills, they can receive guidance and modeling by watching videos of speeches similar to those they are giving themselves. Also, the various attributes of each type of oral speaking strategy should be discussed with students so that they clearly hear the differences.

The skills needed to write an essay are helpful when trying to prepare a presentation, participate in a discussion about literature, or orally retell a story. Non-written genres and traditions that include literary elements have systematic organizational structures. Such genres and traditions include, but are not limited to, oral narratives, persuasive rhetoric, research presentations, poetry recitations, and responses to literature.

Persuasive pieces

When working to persuade an audience about a particular issue, a speaker often presents many scenarios or examples rather than explaining the issue in full detail. This method ensures that people are emotionally and logically persuaded without making it seem as if the speaker's opinion is being forced on people.

Research presentations

Research presentations often present a thesis or overarching claim or argument. Then they explicate, or explain, the thesis or argument with examples and details. The point of a research presentation is to provide an audience with enough details that they will: (a) remember the presentation, and (b) believe the argument, but not so many details that they will become bored with the presentation.

Poetry

Poetry recitation involves the reading aloud of written poetry. It requires a careful understanding of the poetry before reciting it, as the meaning often changes the way it is read out loud. Good poetry recitation involves drama, persona, and charisma.

Discussion

Responding to literature, particularly in discussions, involves making claims about the literature and then defending those claims with specific details from the text or personal experience.

Teaching Listening Skills

For young children, listening discrimination aids their learning and further oral development. Games that encourage students to distinguish between animal sounds or that ask students to match a sound with the picture that makes the sound are two excellent activities teachers can use with students to practice listening discrimination. Phoneme games that, for example, ask students to circle the letter that is the beginning sound or a rhyming sound also aid listening skills. In addition, music games that encourage children to pat a beat, hear a rhyme, or follow an instruction (e.g., Simon Says) all allow children to practice listening in a fun environment.

For older students, two aspects of listening warrant attention:

1. Comprehension: Understanding what someone says, the purposes behind the message, and the contexts in which it is said
2. Purpose: When we understand the purpose of listening in various contexts, comprehension becomes much easier. Furthermore, when we know the purpose of listening, we can better adjust our comprehension strategies.

First, when complex or new information is provided to us orally, we must analyze and interpret it. Second, the purpose of listening is often simply enjoyment. We like to listen to stories; we enjoy poetry; we like radio dramas and theater. Listening to literature can also be a great pleasure.

Finally, listening in large- and small-group conversation requires more than just listening. It involves feedback and active involvement. Students need to learn how listening carefully to others in discussions actually promotes better responses on the part of subsequent speakers. One way teachers can encourage this in both large- and small-group discussions is to encourage students to respond *directly* to the previous student's comments before moving ahead with their new comments.

Strategies for active listening

As soon as we start listening to something new, we can tap in to our prior knowledge to attach new information to what we already know. This not only helps us understand the new information more quickly, it also assists us in remembering the material.

We can also look for transitions between ideas. Sometimes, in oral speech, the speaker's tone of voice or body language changes when he or she is beginning to talk about a new idea. Listeners should take advantage of this and notice how the speaker changes character and voice in order to signal a transition between ideas.

Listeners can also better comprehend the underlying intent of a speaker when they notice nonverbal cues. The expression on the face of a speaker can do more to signal irony, for example, than actual words.

One good way to follow oral speech is to take notes and outline major points.

Other classroom methods can help students learn good listening skills. For example, teachers can have students practice following complex directions. They can also have students orally retell stories or retell (in writing or in oral speech) oral presentations of stories or other materials.

Effective listening

- Associate: Listeners relate ideas to each other
- Visualize: Listeners try to see pictures in their minds as they read
- Concentrate: Listeners have a specific purpose for reading
- Repeat: Listeners keep telling themselves important points and associating details with these points

Evaluating Effectiveness of Spoken Messages

Responding to messages

In addition to the words, messages are transferred by eye contact, physical closeness, tone of voice, visual cues, and overall body language.

In addition to the words, messages are transferred by eye contact, physical closeness, tone of voice, visual cues, and overall body language. Language employs symbols—gestures, visual clues, or spoken sounds—to represent communication between the teacher and the student.

A straight message is one in which words, vocal expression, and body movements are all congruent.

Evaluating messages

Analyzing the speech of others is a good technique for helping students to improve their own public speaking abilities. Video is a useful tool for this purpose.

Students should pay attention to:

- Volume: A speaker should use an appropriate volume—not so loud as to be annoying, but not so soft as to be inaudible.
- Pace: The rate at which words are spoken should be appropriate—not so fast as to make the speech impossible to understand, but not so slow as to put listeners to sleep.
- Pronunciation: A speaker should make sure words are spoken clearly. Listeners do not have a text to go back to so they can reread things they didn't catch.
- Body language: While animated body language can help a speech, too much of it can be distracting. Body language should help convey the message but not detract from it.
- Word choice: The words speakers choose should be consistent with their intended purpose and the audience.

- Visual aids: Visual aids, like body language, should enhance a message. Many visual aids can be distracting and detract from the message.

English-Language Learners

The teacher needs to assess the ELL students to determine how cultural, ethnic, and linguistic experiences can affect the students' learning. The teacher should work with students to:

- Promote cross-cultural understanding: Providing personal communication with another person from a different cultural environment can help promote understanding.
- Challenge stereotypes, intolerance, and racism: Some expressions and behaviors normal or common in the ELL's home culture may be considered unacceptable in an English-language culture.
- Explain and clarify typical English-language cultural views, morals, and societal norms: This helps give context to ELL beliefs in English-language culture.

Language development in children develops in an efficient manner, so the focus should be on allowing the child to create his or her own language scenarios in constructing language repertoires.

Technology for Developing Oral Communication Skills

Using technology to create computerized versions of books that emulate oral language patterns can engage children in endless hours of structured learning activities.

Technologies that provide children with tools to practice language patterns can include instructional content that increases vocabulary of high-frequency words, irregular words, and age-appropriate words. Tape recorders and educational software can encourage children with opportunities to develop word comprehension and meaning along with automatic recall and usage.

Today's market offers a wealth of language development tools, including computer software programs, books on tape, word games, hardcopy textual and pictorial books, and independent lesson assignments.

PHONOLOGICAL AND PHONEMIC AWARENESS

Phonics involves studying the rules and patterns found in language. By age 5 or 6, children can typically begin to use phonics to understand the connections between letters, their patterns, vowel sounds (i.e., short vowels, long vowels), and the collective sounds they all make.

Phonemic awareness is the ability to break down and hear separate and/or different sounds and distinguish between the sounds one hears. Phonemic awareness is required to begin studying phonics, when students will need to be able to break down words into the smalls units of sound, or phonemes, to later identify syllables, blends, and patterns. Phonological awareness is a broader term that includes phonemic awareness.

Instructional Methods

Since the ability to distinguish between individual sounds, or phonemes, within words is a prerequisite to association of sounds with letters and manipulating sounds to blend words (a fancy way of saying "reading"), the teaching of phonemic awareness is crucial to emergent literacy. Children need a strong background in phonemic awareness in order for phonics instruction to be effective.

Methods for teaching phonemic awareness

- Clapping syllables in words
- Distinguishing between a word and a sound
- Using visual cues and movements to help children understand when the speaker goes from one sound to another
- Incorporating oral segmentation activities which focus on easily distinguished syllables rather than sounds
- Singing familiar songs (e.g., "Happy Birthday," "Knick-Knack, Paddy Wack") and replacing key words in them with words with a different ending or middle sound (oral segmentation)
- Dealing children a deck of picture cards and having them sound out the words for the pictures on their cards or calling for a picture by asking for its first and second sound

Five types of phonemic awareness tasks

Theorist Marilyn Jager Adams, who researches early reading, has outlined five basic types of phonemic awareness tasks:

- Task 1: The ability to hear rhymes and alliteration
- Task 2: The ability to do oddity tasks (recognize the member of a set that is different, or odd, among the group)
- Task 3: The ability to orally blend words and split syllables
- Task 4: The ability to orally segment words
- Task 5: The ability to do phonics manipulation tasks

For English-language learners, the phonology of English is an important component. Phonographemic differences between words in English are a common source of confusion and thus need to be taught explicitly with plenty of learning activities to enable learners to acquire them sufficiently.

Phonemic awareness for ELL classroom

Some areas of focus for the ELL classroom include:

- Homonyms: A general term that describes word forms that have two or more meanings
- Homographs: Two or more words that have the same spelling or pronunciation but different meanings, e.g., *stalk* (part of a plant)/*stalk* (follow)
- Homophones: Two or more words that have the same pronunciation but different meanings and spelling, e.g., *wood/would, cite/sight*
- Heteronyms: Two or more words that have the same spelling but different pronunciation and meaning, e.g., *Polish/polish*

Some useful activities for instruction would be to identify misspelled words, to recognize multiple meanings of words and sentences, to spell words correctly, and to match words with their meanings.

Phonological Assessment

Phonological assessment should focus on a student's ability to listen for, distinguish between, and identify sounds. Assessments that consider rhyme and syllable awareness are key to assessing phonological development. Students should also be able to identify and distinguish beginning (initial), middle, and ending sounds of simple words in the early childhood and elementary classrooms.

Once the basics of phonics are understood, phonological assessments should move on to consider a student's grasp of sound blends and ability to pull apart and manipulate sounds and sound blends. Teachers can evaluate a student's invented spelling to see how he or she understands and identifies sounds. They can also have students match words to the same words or to rhyming words to evaluate this skill. A third possibility is to have students play sound games in which they isolate the sounds they hear, showing they are able to identify them.

Promoting Phonological and Phonemic Awareness

English has approximately forty phonemes. Language games that encourage phonological and phonemic awareness help students understand that language is a series of sounds that form words, and, ultimately, sentences.

- Listening games sharpen a student's ability to hear selective sounds.
- Counting syllables games help students discover that many words are made of smaller chunks.
- Rhyming games draw students' attention to the sound structure of words.
- Word and sentence-building games help students understand that language consists of words connected to form sentences.

Daily reading sessions with the students (one-on-one or in a group) help develop their understanding of print concepts.

Structured computer programs can also help teach or reinforce these skills.

When families are asked to participate in a reading program by reading, discussing stories, and writing with their children, teachers are encouraging the family to reinforce the development of students' reading awareness skills.

Activities that parents can practice with students at home:

- Playing games with words that sound alike as you experience them in every-day home activities
- Demonstrating how sounds blend together in familiar words
- Playing a game in which the goal is to find objects with names that begin with a certain initial sound
- Playing clapping games in which you clap with each distinct sound

ALPHABETIC PRINCIPLE

The **ALPHABETIC PRINCIPLE**, sometimes called graphophonemic awareness, describes the understanding that written words are composed of patterns of letters that represent the sounds of spoken words.

ALPHABETIC PRINCIPLE: sometimes called graphophonemic awareness, describes the understanding that written words are composed of patterns of letters that represent the sounds of spoken words

The alphabetic principle has two parts:

- Words are made up of letters and each letter has a specific sound.
- The correspondence between sounds and letters leads to phonological reading.

Since the English language is dependent on the alphabet, being able to recognize and sound out letters is the first step for beginning readers. Decoding is essential.

Basic features of the alphabetic principle

1. Students need to be able to take spoken words apart and blend different sounds together to make new words.
2. Students need to apply letter sounds to all of their reading.
3. Teachers need to use a systematic, effective program in order to teach children to read.
4. The teaching of the alphabetic principle usually begins in kindergarten.

Patterns of Alphabetic Skill Development

Critical skills that students need to learn are:

- Letter-sound correspondence
- How to sound out words
- How to decode text to make meaning

Students who are first learning to read need appropriate instruction in understanding, learning, and using the correct spelling-sound conventions of the English writing system.

Instruction must be adapted to account for children's differences. For those children with previous knowledge of the alphabetic principle, instruction extends their knowledge as they learn more about the formal features of letters and their sound correspondences. Students with fewer prior experiences have to be taught the beginning alphabetic principle: that a limited set of letters makes up the alphabet and that these letters stand for the sounds that make up spoken words. These students will require more focused and direct instruction.

Literacy Development for Children From Non-English-Speaking Cultures

The nasal phonetics of French differ vastly from the sharp, nasal phonetics of Asian languages that are based on a combination of symbols and vowel sounds used both in singular and combination patterns to create meaningful dialogue for the speaker and the person interpreting the meaning of those sounds.

American English oral language consists of phonological components that create rules for combining sounds where words have beginnings and endings, unlike some words in other languages that have long-sounding tones and shorter interpretations. Semantic components are the smallest combination of words and letters to produce different words. The syntactic component uses rules that allow for semantic inclusions into complex sentences.

For English-language learners from a variety of language backgrounds that include cultural and familial inflections and language use, the ability to transcend the foundational boundaries that are imposed by the English standards of language can be insurmountable, both short- and long-term. Effective instructional design should include language constructions that recognize the importance of cultural language acquisition as a more pragmatic approach to teaching children the English alphabet.

Strategies for Teaching the Alphabetic Principle

Multisensory structured language education uses visual, auditory, and kinesthetic cues simultaneously to enhance memory and learning.

Multisensory structured language education uses visual, auditory, and kinesthetic cues simultaneously to enhance memory and learning.

- Quilt book: Students can piece together pictures of objects whose names begin with the same letter of the alphabet.
- Rhyme time: Students participate in reciting a rhyme and identifying the words that all begin with the same sound.
- Letter path: Use masking tape to outline a large letter on the floor. As the students follow the path of the letter, have them name words that begin with that letter.
- Shape game: Call out a letter. Have the students arrange themselves to form the shape of that letter.

Teachers should promote independent reading outside of school by providing enjoyable and easy-to-implement activities for home use. Teachers should also strive for frequent home-school communication. Parents can also be encouraged to spend time in the classroom observing and helping the teacher.

To foster positive parental and community involvement, teachers can implement a variety of programs:

- Home reading journals
- Telephone calls
- Informal notes
- Parent-teacher meetings
- Literacy newsletters

Formal and Informal Assessments for Alphabetic Skills

Teachers should closely monitor the development of each individual student's language acquisition skills.

Assessment tools

- Checklists
- Observations/surveys
- Portfolio collections

LITERACY DEVELOPMENT

EMERGENT LITERACY is the concept that young children are emerging into reading and writing with no real beginning or ending point. This stage of reading is when the reader understands that print contains a consistent message.

EMERGENT LITERACY: the concept that young children are emerging into reading and writing with no real beginning or ending point

Characteristics of emerging readers:

1. Can attend to left-to-right directionality and features of print
2. Can identify some initial sounds and ending sounds in words

3. Can recognize some high-frequency words, names, and simple words in context

4. Can use pictures to predict meaning

Areas of Emerging Evidence

1. Experiences with print (through reading and writing) help preschool children develop an understanding of the conventions, purpose, and functions of print.

2. Phonological awareness and letter recognition contribute to initial reading acquisition by helping children develop efficient word recognition strategies.

3. Storybook reading affects children's knowledge about, strategies for, and attitudes toward reading.

Design Principles In Emergent Literacy

Conspicuous strategies can be incorporated in beginning reading instruction to ensure that all learners have basic literacy concepts.

- Conspicuous strategies: A sequence of teaching events and teacher actions used to help students learn new literacy information and relate it to their existing knowledge. Conspicuous strategies can be incorporated in beginning reading instruction to ensure that all learners have basic literacy concepts.
- Mediated scaffolding: A systematic transition from fully teacher-directed instruction to more student-directed learning. Teachers can act as scaffolds during storybook-reading activities by adjusting their demands (e.g., asking increasingly complex questions or encouraging children to take on portions of the reading) or by reading more complex text as students gain knowledge of beginning literacy components.
- Strategic integration: Many children have difficulty making connections between old and new information. Strategic integration can be applied to help link old and new learning.
- Primed background knowledge: Teachers can utilize children's background knowledge to help children link their personal literacy experiences to beginning reading instruction, while also closing the gap between students with rich literacy experiences and those with poorer literacy experiences.
- Emergent literacy: Strong support is found in the literature for the important contribution that early childhood exposure to oral and written language makes to the facility with which children learn to read.

Developing Students' Awareness of Print

The structure of the English language consists of rules of grammar, capitalization, and punctuation. For younger children, this means being able to recognize letters and form words. For older children, it means being able to recognize different types of text, such as lists, stories, and signs, and knowing the purpose of each type.

Reid (1988, p. 165) described three metalinguistic abilities that young children acquire through early involvement in reading activities:

1. Word consciousness: Children who have access to books can tell the story through the pictures first. Gradually, they begin to realize the connection between the spoken words and the printed words. The beginning of letter and word discrimination begins in the early years.
2. Language and conventions of print: During this stage, children learn how to hold a book, where to begin to read, the left-to-right motion, and how to continue from one line to another.
3. Functions of print: Children discover that print can be used for a variety of purposes and functions, including entertainment and information.

Instructional strategies

- Big books in the classroom: Gather the children around you in a group with the big book placed on a stand. As you read, point to each word.
- A classroom rich in print: There should be plenty of books in the classroom for children to read on their own or in small groups.
- Word wall: Each of the letters of the alphabet is displayed with words under it that begin with that letter.
- Sounds of the letters: In addition to learning the letter names, students should learn the corresponding sound of each letter.
- Book-handling skills
  - Practicing how to handle a book: How to turn pages, find the top and bottom of pages, and tell the difference between the front and back covers
  - Book organization: Students demonstrate an understanding of the organization of books by being able to identify the title, cover, author, left-to-right progression, top-to-bottom order, and one-to-one correspondence. Students may learn these skills individually as they become more familiar with books.

Distinguishing letters from numbers and text from pictures

Children should understand that pictures show words in action. Pictures can have one or multiple meanings, depending on the reader or the teacher creating the instruction.

Types of Literature for Different Developmental Stages

From being read to by parents and caregivers from the earliest ages, toddlers can handle board books with sturdy pages. Children ages 2 and 3 enjoy what are called toy books, i.e., those that have flaps to lift up, textures to touch, or holes to peek through. From ages 3 to 7, children enjoy a variety of nonfiction concept books. These books combine language and pictures to show concrete examples of abstract concepts.

Another category of concept books is alphabet books, *popular with children from preschool through grade 2.*

In grades K-2, when children are becoming early readers, two other genres of literature become salient: wordless picture books and easy-to-read books. Wordless picture books accommodate readers and nonreaders alike because there is no text.

From the preschool years onward, picture books, characterized by illustrations and a plot that are closely interrelated (one usually cannot exist independently of the other), are suitable for children.

Chapter books are appropriate for readers in grades 2, 3, and 4 and beyond. They are characterized by occasional illustrations, relatively short chapters, and interesting plots that appeal to children ages 8 and up.

WORD ANALYSIS AND IDENTIFICATION SKILLS

A root word is the primary base of a word. A prefix is an affix (a morpheme that attaches to a base word) that is placed at the start of a root word but can't make a word on its own. A suffix follows the root word to which it attaches.

Word Recognition Skills

WORD ANALYSIS (also called phonics or decoding) is the process readers use to figure out unfamiliar words based on written patterns. **WORD RECOGNITION** is the process of automatically determining the pronunciation and some degree of the meaning of an unknown word. In other words, fluent readers recognize most written words easily and correctly, without consciously decoding or breaking them down.

WORD ANALYSIS: the process readers use to figure out unfamiliar words based on written patterns

WORD RECOGNITION: the process of automatically determining the pronunciation and some degree of the meaning of an unknown word

DECODING refers to the ability to sound out a word by translating different letters or groups of letters (graphemes) into sounds (phonemes).

DECODING: the ability to sound out a word by translating different letters or groups of letters (graphemes) into sounds (phonemes)

Reading comprehension requires the reader to learn the code in which a message is written and to be able to decode it to get the message. **ENCODING** involves changing a message into symbols.

ENCODING: changing a message into symbols

Tasks for assessing word-analysis and decoding skills can be grouped into three categories:

- Comparing sounds
- Blending phonemes into words
- Segmenting words into phonemes

Sight-word vocabulary

Sight words, or high-frequency words, are words that appear frequently in reading, and are thought to make up approximately 50 percent of elementary textbook reading. For example, some basic sight words for kindergartners include: *the*, *a*, *here*, *to*, *in*, *and*, *is*, *be*, *it*, *go*, *you*, *be*, *he*, *she*, *him*, *her*, *for*, and *are*. Because these words have little actual meaning on their own, they derive their meaning from the surrounding context, and most students learn to immediately recognize them on sight.

Context clues

When people read, they use four sources of background information to comprehend the meaning behind the literal text (Reid, pp.166-71):

1. Word knowledge: One's knowledge of word meanings is *lexical knowledge*—a sort of dictionary. Knowledge of spelling patterns and pronunciations is *orthographic knowledge*.
2. Syntax and contextual information: When children encounter unknown words in a sentence, they rely on their background knowledge to choose a meaning that makes sense.

3. Semantic knowledge: This encompasses the reader's background knowledge of a topic, which is combined with information from the text as the reader tries to comprehend the material.
4. Text organization: Good readers are able to differentiate types of text structure (e.g., narrative, exposition, compare-contrast, or time sequence). They use their knowledge of text to build expectations and to construct a framework of ideas on which to build meaning.

Contextual redefinition

This strategy supports children in using the context more effectively by presenting them with sufficient context *before* they begin reading. It models the use of contextual clues to make informed guesses about word meanings.

Identification of Vowel Sounds

Children who understand and have memorized the vowel-sound essentials increase their decoding of new words by a higher percentage than children who base comprehension on predictable text of known words and usage.

Applying vowel sounds to syllabic words increases reading ability and word usage. Children who understand and have memorized the vowel-sound essentials increase their decoding of new words by a higher percentage than children who base comprehension on predictable text of known words and usage.

The vowel-sound essentials include the following vowel-letter combinations:

- Short vowels: *a*, *e*, *i*, *o*, and *u*
- Long vowels: *a*, *e*, *i*, *o*, and *u*
- Diagraphs (two letters that produce one sound): *ai*, *ee*, *ie*, *oa*, *ay*, *au*, and *aw*
- Diphthongs (two letters with two sounds): *ou*, *oo*-long/short, *ew*, *ow*-long/short, *oi*
- R vowels: *ar*, *er*, *ir*, *or*, *ur*

The phonetics of syllabic words includes a core nucleus of vowel sounds that can be viewed in common words as a "consonant-vowel-consonant" sequence of letters and sounds. Longer syllabic words such as *imagination* have stress and tone on each part of the syllabic segments that includes a phonetic emphasis on the core nucleus of the word.

Students will be better at comprehension if they have a strong working vocabulary.

Students will be better at comprehension if they have a strong working vocabulary. Research has shown that students learn more vocabulary when it is presented in context, rather than in vocabulary lists, for example.

Auditory games and drills during which students recognize and manipulate the sounds of words, separate or segment the sounds of words, take out sounds, blend sounds, add in new sounds, or take apart sounds to recombine them in new formations are a good way to foster phonological awareness.

Identification of Common Morphemes, Prefixes, and Suffixes

Key structural analysis components include:

- Root words: Words from which other words are developed.
- Base words: Stand-alone linguistic units that cannot be deconstructed or broken down into smaller words. For example, in the word *retell*, the base word is *tell*.
- Contractions: Shortened forms of two words in which a letter or letters have been deleted. The deleted letters have been replaced by an apostrophe.
- Prefixes: Beginning units of meaning that can be added, or *affixed*, to a base word or root word.
- Suffixes: Ending units of meaning that can be *affixed*, or added, to the ends of root or base words.
- Compound words: Words that are formed when two or more base words are connected to form a new word. The meaning of the new word is in some way connected with that of the base words.
- Inflectional endings: Types of suffixes that impart a new meaning to the base or root word. These endings change the gender, number, tense, or form of the base or root words. Like other suffixes, they are also called "bound morphemes."

SYNTAX refers to the rules or patterned relationships that correctly create phrases and sentences from words. When readers develop an understanding of syntax, they begin to understand the structure of how sentences are built, and, eventually, the beginning of grammar.

SYNTAX: the rules or patterned relationships that correctly create phrases and sentences from words

SEMANTICS refers to the meaning expressed when words are arranged in a specific way. This is where connotation and denotation of words eventually has a role with readers.

SEMANTICS: the meaning expressed when words are arranged in a specific way

The Value of Dictionaries, Glossaries, and Other References

Dictionary

The uses of a dictionary include:

- Word spelling
- Word pronunciation
- Syllable breakdown
- Definition or definitions
- Part of speech
- Synonyms/antonyms
- Word origin
- Use in a sentence/context/connotation

Every word in the dictionary is an **entry word**. The words at the top of each page are called **guide words**, and they identify the first word on the page (upper left) and the last word on a page (upper right). These words help users find their entry words more efficiently.

Glossary

A **glossary** is similar to a dictionary in that it provides definitions of words; however, a glossary is typically a collection of difficult, unfamiliar, or new words located in one section of a reading.

Thesaurus

A **thesaurus** helps people locate synonyms and antonyms of words.

READING FLUENCY

Reading Rates

One way to evaluate reading fluency is to look at student accuracy, and a good way to do this is to keep **running records** of students during oral reading.

Results of running record informal assessment can be used for teaching based on text accuracy. If a child's accuracy rate is from 95 to100 percent, the child is ready for independent reading. If a child's rate is from 92 to 97 percent, the child is ready for guided reading. If a child's rate is below 92 percent, he or she needs a read aloud or shared reading activity.

Reading rate guidelines by grade level

The following general guidelines can be applied for reading lists of words with a speed drill and a one-minute timing:

- 30 correct words per minute (wpm) for first- and second-grade children
- 40 correct wpm for third-grade children
- 60 correct wpm for mid-third-grade children
- 80 wpm for students in fourth grade and higher

Techniques to help students with decoding

- Students listen to text as they follow along with the book
- Students follow the print using their fingers as guides
- Reading materials are used that students would be unable to read independently

Experts recommend that a beginning reading program should incorporate partner reading, practice reading difficult words prior to reading the text, timings for accuracy and rate, opportunities to hear books read, and opportunities to read to others.

Prosody

PROSODY concerns versification of text and involves such matters as which syllable of a word is accented. It is that aspect which translates reading into the same experience as listening in the reader's mind. It involves intonation and rhythm through such devices as syllable accent and punctuation.

PROSODY: concerns versification of text and involves such matters as which syllable of a word is accented

Importance of Word Identification Skills and Reading Fluency to Reading Comprehension

Fluency in reading depends on automatic word identification, which assists the student in achieving comprehension. Automatic reading involves the development of strong orthographic representations, which allows fast and accurate identification of whole words made up of specific letter patterns.

Examples of the Six Types of Syllables

One of the most useful devices for developing automaticity in young students is the visual pattern provided in the six syllable types.

1. **NOT** (closed)

   Closed in by a consonant—vowel makes its **short** sound

2. **NO** (open)

   Ends in a vowel—vowel makes its **long** sound

3. **NOTE** (silent "e")

   Ends in vowel consonant "*e*"—vowel makes its **long** sound

4. **NAIL** (vowel combination)

   Two vowels together make the sound

5. **BIRD** ("*r*" controlled)

   Contains a vowel followed by the letter r—vowel sound is changed by the r

6. **TABLE** (consonant "*l*"-"*e*")

   Applied at the end of a word

These orthographic (letter) patterns signal vowel pronunciation to the reader. Students must learn to apply their knowledge of these patterns to recognize the syllable types and to see the patterns automatically, and ultimately, to read words as wholes. The move from decoding letter symbols to identifying recognizable terms to automatic word recognition is a substantial move toward fluency.

Students must learn to apply their knowledge of these patterns to recognize the syllable types and to see the patterns automatically, and ultimately, to read words as wholes.

Four Types of Words

English orthography is made up of four basic word types:

1. Regular for reading and spelling (e.g., *cat, print*)
2. Regular for reading but not for spelling (e.g. *float, brain*—could be spelled *flote* or *brane*, respectively)
3. Rule-based (e.g., *canning*—doubling rule, *faking*—drop *e* rule)
4. Irregular (e.g., *beauty*)

Opportunities to Read Various Literary Genres

Reading specialists need to have a large amount of material available to be able to meet the needs of the various students they may encounter. There are various accepted methods of organizing material. In most cases, the texts should be leveled according to some standards. Many people use the Fountas and Pinnell leveling system or the developing readers assessment system. They both provide lists of books and their corresponding levels; in fact, most major publishing companies provide this information for all of their materials.

Fictional genres that may appeal to students in kindergarten through twelfth grade include:

- Mystery
- Fantasy
- Drama
- Historical fiction
- Fable
- Mythology
- Fairy tale
- Poetry
- Folklore
- Legends
- Realistic fiction
- Tall tales
- Science fiction

Nonfiction genres include:

- Essays
- Narrative nonfiction
- Biography
- Speech
- Autobiographies

Reference materials include:

- Dictionaries
- Thesauruses
- Encyclopedias
- Almanacs

Fostering Collaboration to Promote Literacy

Regardless of the positive or negative impacts on students' education from outside sources, it is the teacher's responsibility to ensure that all students in the classroom have an equal opportunity for academic success. This begins with the teacher's statement of high expectations for every student, and develops through the planning, delivery, and evaluation of instruction that provides for inclusion and ensures that all students have equal access to the resources necessary to acquire the academic skills being taught and measured in the classroom.

Involvement among families, teachers, libraries, principals, and other school professionals should be viewed as a partnership in which everyone actively strives to create and promote an enriching environment for children to develop their reading skills. Many schools are instituting school-wide computer programs and using other technology to aid in the ongoing reading development of their students.

Schools can collaborate with local libraries to create summer reading programs. Teachers can also form literacy programs to involve the community and families in the students' reading curriculum.

Teachers, family members, and other professionals should utilize the following reading fluency instructional strategies:

- Model fluent oral reading (read aloud) followed by student reading
- Model reading with expression followed by student reading with expression
- Guided oral repeated readings
- Audio-assisted reading
- Partner reading

READING COMPREHENSION

National Reading Panel Vocabulary Guidelines

1. There is a need for direct instruction of vocabulary items required for a specific text.
2. Repetition and multiple exposures to vocabulary items are important. Students should be given items that will be likely to appear in many contexts.
3. Learning in rich contexts is valuable for vocabulary learning. Vocabulary words should be those that the learner will find useful in many contexts. When vocabulary items are derived from content learning materials, the learner will be better equipped to deal with specific reading matter in content areas.
4. Vocabulary tasks should be restructured as necessary. It is important to be certain that students fully understand what is asked of them in the context of reading rather than focusing only on the words to be learned.

5. Vocabulary learning is most effective when it entails active engagement in learning tasks.

6. Computer technology can be used effectively to help teach vocabulary.

7. Vocabulary can be acquired through incidental learning. Much of a student's vocabulary will have to be learned in the course of doing things other than explicit vocabulary learning. Repetition, richness of context, and motivation may also add to the efficacy of incidental learning of vocabulary.

8. Dependence on a single vocabulary instruction method does not result in optimal learning. A variety of methods can be used effectively, with emphasis on multimedia, richness of context in which words are to be learned, and the number of exposures to words that learners receive.

Only two or three words should require explicit teaching. If the number is higher than that, the children need guided reading and the text needs to be broken down into smaller sections for teaching. When broken down, each text section should only have two to three words that need explicit teaching.

Literal Comprehension

The topic of a paragraph or story is what the paragraph or story is about.

The main idea of a paragraph or story states the important idea(s) that the author wants the reader to know about a topic.

The topic sentence indicates what the passage is about. It is the subject of that portion of the narrative.

A paragraph is a group of sentences about one main idea. Paragraphs usually have two types of sentences: a topic sentence, which contains the main idea, and two or more detail sentences, which support, prove, provide more information, explain, or give examples.

Inferential Comprehension

In order to draw inferences and make conclusions, a reader must use prior knowledge and apply it to the current situation. A conclusion or inference is never stated.

Conclusions are drawn as a result of a line of reasoning. Inductive reasoning begins with particulars and reasons to a generality.

Deductive reasoning begins with a generalization, such as "Green apples are sour," and supports that generalization with specifics.

A common fallacy in reasoning is the *post hoc ergo propter hoc* ("after this, therefore because of this"), or the false-cause fallacy. These occur in cause/effect reasoning, which may go either from cause to effect or effect to cause. They occur when an inadequate cause is offered for a particular effect, when the possibility of more than one cause is ignored, or when a connection between a particular cause and a particular effect is not made.

Interpretive and Evaluative Comprehension

STYLE: the artful adaptation of language to meet various purposes

TONE: the attitude an author takes toward his or her subject.

POINT OF VIEW: an author's perspective

STYLE is the artful adaptation of language to meet various purposes. TONE is the attitude an author takes toward his or her subject. The author's choice of words helps the reader determine the overall tone of a statement or passage.

POINT OF VIEW is an author's perspective. While most of us think of point of view in terms of first- or third-person (or even the points of view of various characters in stories), point of view also helps explain a lot of language and the presentation of ideas in nonfiction and fiction.

Transition From "Learning to Read" to "Reading to Learn"

At points in the learning-to-read process, teachers can help students understand that people read for a variety of reasons. Sometimes people read for pleasure, in which case they can decide whether to skim quickly for the content or read slowly to savor ideas and language. Other times, people simply want to find information quickly, in which case they skim or scan. In some texts, rereading is necessary to fully comprehend information.

Skimming is when readers read quickly while paying little attention to specific words. This is often done when readers want a full picture of a text, but do not want to focus on the details. Skimming can be done as a preview or a review.

Scanning is a bit different from skimming. In scanning, readers go straight to specific ideas, words, sections, or examples. They pick and choose what to read in a text. This is done when the reader does not need to know everything in a text.

In-depth reading is done when readers want to enjoy a text or learn from it thoroughly. For the most part, in this type of reading, readers move forward quickly and do not stop to focus on a specific word or idea, although sometimes this is necessary. The main idea of this type of reading is that readers do not skip over or read quickly to get information. They read everything carefully and thoroughly.

The final type of reading is rereading. Sometimes, whole texts must be reread for the concepts. This is usually the case when the text is difficult. A word, concept, or a few ideas may need to be reviewed before the reader can go on. Another method of rereading is rereading a whole text months or years after reading it the first time.

Strategies for Facilitating Comprehension

Making predictions

One theory or approach to the teaching of reading that gained currency in the late sixties and early seventies was the importance of asking inferential and critical-thinking questions that would challenge and engage the reader in the text. This approach went beyond the literal level of what was stated in the text to an inferential level of using text clues to make predictions and then to a critical level of involving the child in evaluating the text. While this approach is still used, it is currently only considered to be one component of the teaching of reading.

Questioning

As the word implies, students answer questions regarding a text, either out loud, in small groups, or individually on paper. The best questions are those that require students to think about the text (rather than just find an answer in the text).

Although questioning tends to be overused in many classrooms, it is still a valid method of teaching students to comprehend.

Graphic organizers

Graphic organizers are graphical representations of content in a text. Graphic organizers solidify a visual relationship among various reading and writing ideas, including: sequence, timelines, character traits, fact and opinion, main idea and details, and differences and similarities (generally done using a Venn diagram of interlocking circles, KWL chart, etc).

KWL charts

KWL charts are exceptionally useful for reading comprehension by outlining what students **K**now, what they **W**ant to know, and what they've **L**earned after reading. Students are asked to activate prior knowledge and further develop their knowledge about a topic using this organizer. Teachers often display and maintain KWL charts throughout the study of a text to continually record pertinent information about students' reading.

Elements of Literary Analysis

Children's literature is a genre of its own and emerged as a distinct and independent form in the second half of the eighteenth century.

COMMON FORMS OF CHILDREN' S LITERATURE.	
Traditional literature	Traditional literature opens up a world in which right wins out over wrong, hard work and perseverance are rewarded, and helpless victims find vindication. Children are introduced to fanciful beings, humans with exaggerated powers, talking animals, and heroes who will inspire them.
Folktales/fairy tales	Adventures of animals or humans and the supernatural characterize these stories. The hero is usually on a quest and is aided by otherworldly helpers. More often than not, the story focuses on good and evil and reward and punishment.
Fables	Animals that act like humans are featured in these stories and usually reveal human foibles or sometimes teach a lesson.
Myths	These stories about events from the earliest times, such as the origin of the world, are often considered true in the societies of their origin.
Legends	These are similar to myths except that they tend to deal with events that happened more recently.
Poems	The only requirement of poetry is rhythm. Subgenres include fixed types of literature such as the sonnet, elegy, ode, pastoral, and villanelle. Unfixed types of literature include blank verse and dramatic monologue.
Tall tales	These are purposely exaggerated accounts of individuals with superhuman strength.
Modern fantasy	The stories start out based in reality, which makes it easier for the reader to suspend disbelief and enter worlds of unreality. These tales often appeal to children's ideals of justice and address issues having to do with good and evil; because children tend to identify with the characters, they are more likely to retain the message in the story.
Science fiction	Robots, spacecraft, mystery, and civilizations from other ages often appear in these stories. Most presume advances in science on other planets or in a future time. Most children like these stories because of their interest in space and the "what if" aspect of the stories.

Continued on next page

Modern realistic fiction	These stories are about real problems that real children face. By discovering that their hopes and fears are shared by others, young children can find insight into their own problems.
Historical fiction	Historical fiction tells a story set in the past, often in a significant or notable period of time. The events or backdrop to the story are based on actual historical events but told from the perspective of a fictional character living during the time period being portrayed.
Biography	A biography is the story of a person's life, as written by someone other than that person.

Reading Comprehension Skills In K-6 Statewide Curriculum and Grade-Level Expectations for Those Skills

Kindergarten

Students use a flexible range of metacognitive reading skills in both assigned and independent reading to understand an author's message. Students will continue to apply earlier standards with greater depth in increasingly more complex texts as they become self-directed, critical readers. The student is expected to: (a) discuss the purposes for reading and listening to various texts (e.g., to become involved in real and imagined events, settings, actions, and to enjoy language), (b) ask and respond to questions about text, (c) monitor and adjust comprehension (e.g., using background knowledge, creating sensory images, rereading a portion aloud), (d) make inferences based on the cover, title, illustrations, and plot, (e) retell or act out important events in stories, and (f) make connections to his or her own experiences, to ideas in other texts, and to the larger community, and discuss textual evidence.

Information in this section is taken from Reading/ Comprehension Skills, Kindergarten-Grade 5, Beginning with School Year 2009-2010 at:

http://ritter.tea.state.tx.us /rules/tac/chapter110 /19_0110_0010-1.pdf

First grade

Students use a flexible range of metacognitive reading skills in both assigned and independent reading to understand an author's message. Students will continue to apply earlier standards with greater depth in increasingly more complex texts as they become self-directed, critical readers. The student is expected to: (a) establish purposes for reading selected texts based upon desired outcome to enhance comprehension, (b) ask literal questions of text, (c) monitor and adjust comprehension (e.g., using background knowledge, creating sensory images, rereading a portion aloud), (d) make inferences about text and use textual evidence to support understanding, (e) retell or act out important events in stories in logical order, and

(f) make connections to his or her own experiences, to ideas in other texts, and to the larger community, and discuss textual evidence.

Second grade

Students use a flexible range of metacognitive reading skills in both assigned and independent reading to understand an author's message. Students will continue to apply earlier standards with greater depth in increasingly more complex texts as they become self-directed, critical readers.

Students use a flexible range of metacognitive reading skills in both assigned and independent reading to understand an author's message. Students will continue to apply earlier standards with greater depth in increasingly more complex texts as they become self-directed, critical readers. The student is expected to: (a) establish purposes for reading selected texts based upon content to enhance comprehension, (b) ask literal questions of text, (c) monitor and adjust comprehension (e.g., using background knowledge, creating sensory images, rereading a portion aloud, generating questions), (d) make inferences about text using textual evidence to support understanding, (e) retell important events in stories in logical order, and (f) make connections to his or her own experiences, to ideas in other texts, and to the larger community, and discuss textual evidence.

Third grade

Students use a flexible range of metacognitive reading skills in both assigned and independent reading to understand an author's message. Students will continue to apply earlier standards with greater depth in increasingly more complex texts as they become self-directed, critical readers. The student is expected to: (a) establish purposes for reading selected texts based upon his or her own or others' desired outcome to enhance comprehension, (b) ask literal, interpretive, and evaluative questions of text, (c) monitor and adjust comprehension (e.g., using background knowledge, creating sensory images, rereading a portion aloud, generating questions), (d) make inferences about text and use textual evidence to support understanding, (e) summarize information in text, maintaining meaning and logical order, and (f) make connections (e.g., thematic links, author analysis) between literary and informational texts with similar ideas and provide textual evidence.

Fourth grade

Students use a flexible range of metacognitive reading skills in both assigned and independent reading to understand an author's message. Students will continue to apply earlier standards with greater depth in increasingly more complex texts as they become self-directed, critical readers. The student is expected to: (a) establish purposes for reading selected texts based upon his or her own or others' desired outcome to enhance comprehension, (b) ask literal, interpretive, and evaluative questions of text, (c) monitor and adjust comprehension (e.g., using background knowledge, creating sensory images, rereading a portion aloud, generating questions), (d) make inferences about text and use textual evidence to support understanding, (e) summarize information in text, maintaining meaning and logical order, and (f) make connections (e.g., thematic links, author analysis) between literary and informational texts with similar ideas and provide textual evidence.

Fifth grade

Students use a flexible range of metacognitive reading skills in both assigned and independent reading to understand an author's message. Students will continue to apply earlier standards with greater depth in increasingly more complex texts as they become self-directed, critical readers. The student is expected to: (a) establish purposes for reading selected texts based upon his or her own or others' desired outcome to enhance comprehension, (b) ask literal, interpretive, evaluative, and universal questions of text, (c) monitor and adjust comprehension (e.g., using background knowledge, creating sensory images, rereading a portion aloud, generating questions), (d) make inferences about text and use textual evidence to support understanding, (e) summarize and paraphrase texts in ways that maintain meaning and logical order within a text and across texts, and (f) make connections (e.g., thematic links, author analysis) between and across multiple texts of various genres, and provide textual evidence.

Sixth grade

Students use a flexible range of metacognitive reading skills in both assigned and independent reading to understand an author's message. Students will continue to apply earlier standards with greater depth in increasingly more complex texts as they become self-directed, critical readers. The student is expected to: (a) establish purposes for reading selected texts based upon his or her own or others' desired outcome to enhance comprehension, (b) ask literal, interpretive, evaluative, and universal questions of text, (c) monitor and adjust comprehension (e.g., using background knowledge; creating sensory images; rereading a portion aloud; generating questions), (d) make inferences about text and use textual evidence to support understanding, (e) summarize, paraphrase, and synthesize texts in ways that maintain meaning and logical order within a text and across texts, and (f) make connections (e.g., thematic links, author analysis) between and across multiple texts of various genres, and provide textual evidence.

The following information is taken from Reading/Comprehension Skills, Grades 6-8, Beginning with School Year 2009-2010 at:

http://ritter.tea.state.tx.us/rules/tac/chapter110/19_0110_0017-1.pdf

READING, INQUIRY, AND RESEARCH

Interpreting Information In Various Formats

Quantitative data is often easily presented in graphs and charts in many content areas.

Students should be taught to evaluate all of the features of a graph, including the main title, what the horizontal axis represents, and what the vertical axis represents. Also, students should locate and evaluate the graph's key (if there is one) in the event there is more than one variable represented on the graph. For example, line graphs are often used to plot data from a scientific experiment. If more than one variable was used, a key or legend would indicate what each line on the graph represents. Then, once students have evaluated the axes and titles, they can begin to assess the results of the experiment.

Study Skills

Because good comprehension the goal of all reading, teachers can help their students by teaching them specific features of texts that they can use to clarify or enhance their understanding.

Using specific textual features, students can begin to find information more easily, which allows them to create their own schema. Using this schema, they can analyze and organize the information in a manner that ties it directly to their own personal experience and prior knowledge. Once it is connected, it will be easier to recall.

Most texts provide brief introductions, which readers can use to determine if the information they are seeking is located in the passage to be read. By reading a short passage, a student can quickly ascertain whether a complete reading is necessary or if a quick skim will suffice.

When searching for information, students can become much more efficient if they learn to use a glossary and index.

Charts, graphs, maps, diagrams, captions, and photos in text can be as helpful as looking up unknown words in the glossary. They can provide more insight into and clarification of concepts and ideas the author is conveying.

Highlighting is a difficult strategy for students to master. Even at the college level, students seem to have a hard time determining what is important. Key ideas and vocabulary are a good place to start with highlighting. Teaching students to highlight less information rather than more is also important.

Outlining is a skill many teachers use to help students understand the important facts.

Mapping involves using graphics, pictures, and words to represent the information in the text. The students can personalize their maps and use colors and pictures that have meaning to them. This provides a natural bridge to prior knowledge and frames the information in a more personal way.

Note-taking skills also require direct instruction.

Test taking is another area in which students sometimes lag in skill development. Teaching students to eliminate automatic wrong answers first, then narrow down the choices is a start. In open-ended questions, students need to be able to restate the question in their answer and understand that they need to answer all parts of the question being asked.

WRITING CONVENTIONS

Stages In Development of Writing Skills

Learning to write is generally a sequential process and can be broken down into five stages:

- Readiness: The first stage includes scribbling, showing interest in writing tools, marking paper, enjoying stories, and noticing print and pictures in the environment.
- Drawing and exploring: The second stage includes shape and early letter writing, connecting pictures to expressions, associating letters with sounds, and playing with letters, sounds, and pictures.
- Confident experimentation: The third stage includes writing more, experimenting with words, print, and pictures more, and shows early conventions of print such as word spacing and punctuation, and attempting longer words.
- Moving toward independence: The fourth stage includes keen observation of print in the environment, expanding oral stories, writing words and phrases independently, and increased conventions of print.
- Expanding and adding detail: The final, fifth stage includes writing sentences and paragraphs, experiments with sharing writing and journaling,

increased details and use of writing conventions, and showing expanding vocabulary and use of writing with pictures.

—From *http://www.learningtowrite.ecsd.net/stages percent20of percent20writing.htm*

Development of fine-motor skills for writing

In order for children to write correctly, they must first develop their fine-motor skills. These hands-on activities are excellent for practicing fine-motor skills:

- Tearing: Tear newspaper into strips and then crumple them into balls. Use the balls to stuff a Halloween pumpkin or other art creation.
- Cutting: Cut pictures from magazines. Cut a fringe on the edge of a piece of construction paper.
- Puzzles: Have children put together a puzzle with large pieces. This will help to develop proper eye-hand coordination.
- Clay: Manipulating playdough into balls strengthens a child's grasp. Let the children explain what they created from their playdough objects.
- Finger painting: If a child has not developed fine-motor skills yet, it helps to trace a pattern with the child's finger before he or she tries it with a pencil. Have the child trace a pattern in sand, cornmeal, finger paint, etc.
- Drawing: Draw at an easel with a large crayon. Encourage children to practice their name or letters of the alphabet.

Strategies for Teaching Pencil Grip

- The primary grip: Beginning writers with undeveloped fine-motor skills should be taught the primary grip. First, have the child join the tips of the thumb and middle finger. Then place the pencil in the space between them. Finally, have the child lay the index finger on top of the pencil. This way, the index finger pushes against the thumb and middle finger. As children grow, the proportions of their hands change. This allows them to hold the pencil or pen differently and write faster.
- Paper position: Right-handed children should place the paper directly in front of them and hold it in place with the left hand. The light should come from the left. Otherwise, the child's hand will cast a shadow just where the child needs to see what he or she is writing. With the paper slightly to the right of the writer, the line of vision is clear. Teachers should check to see if students are sitting upright. Make sure they are not gripping the pen too hard, and that the paper is in the right position.

- Beginning strokes: A teacher may need to teach a student the direction of the pencil strokes. A good word to practice with is the student's first name. Identify one letter at a time. Show the beginning point right on the top line and the ending point on the bottom line. Slowly write the child's name on one line, one letter at a time, so he or she can clearly see it. Have the child write directly under your sample, not to the side. Write your sample in straight, easy-to-copy letters.

Potential problems

- Gripping the pencil too tightly: A common problem for all young children learning to write is gripping the pencil too tightly, which makes writing tiresome. Usually, students learn to relax their grip as their writing skills develop, but teachers can remind students to hold the instrument gently.
- Holding the pencil incorrectly: If the child tends to hold the pencil too close to the point, make a mark on the pencil at the correct spot to remind him or her where to grip it.
- Left-handed writers: A right-handed student writes away from his or her body and pulls the pencil, while a left-handed student must write toward his or her body and push the pencil. Left-handed students should place the paper at an angle and to the left.

In languages that are written from left to right, like English, it is more difficult to write with the left hand.

Developmental Stages of Spelling

Like writing, spelling develops in stages. The developmental stages of spelling are:

1. Pre-phonemic spelling: Children know that letters stand for a message but they do not know the relationship between spelling and pronunciation.
2. Early phonemic spelling: Children are beginning to understand spelling. They usually write the beginning letter correctly but write consonants or long vowels for the rest.
3. Letter-name spelling: Some words are consistently spelled correctly. The student is developing a sight vocabulary and a stable understanding of letters as representing sounds. Long vowels are usually used accurately, but silent vowels are omitted. The child spells unknown words by attempting to match the name of the letter to the sound.
4. Transitional spelling: This phase is typically entered in late elementary school. Short vowel sounds are mastered and some spelling rules known. Children are developing a sense of which spellings are correct and which are not.

5. Derivational spelling: This stage is usually reached between high school and adulthood. This is the stage when spelling rules are being mastered.

Rules and Conventions of Punctuation, Capitalization, and Spelling

Spelling

Most plurals of nouns that end in hard consonants or hard consonant sounds followed by a silent *e* are made by adding *s*. Some words ending in vowels only add *s*.

fingers, numerals, banks, bugs, riots, homes, gates, radios, bananas

Nouns that end in soft consonant sounds *s*, *j*, *x*, *z*, *ch*, and *sh*, add *es*. Some nouns ending in *o* add *es*.

dresses, waxes, churches, brushes, tomatoes, potatoes

Nouns ending in *y* preceded by a vowel just add *s*.

boys, alleys

Nouns ending in *y* preceded by a consonant change the *y* to *i* and add *es*.

babies, corollaries, frugalities, poppies

Some nouns' plurals are formed irregularly or remain the same.

sheep, deer, children, leaves, oxen

Some nouns derived from foreign words, especially Latin, may make their plurals in two different ways, one of them Anglicized. Sometimes the meanings are the same; other times, the two plurals are used in slightly different contexts. It is always wise to consult the dictionary in these cases.

appendices, appendixes	*criterion, criteria*
indexes, indices	*crisis, crises*

Make the plurals of closed (solid) compound words in the usual way except for words ending in *ful*, which make their plurals on the root word.

timelines, hairpins, cupsful

Make the plurals of open or hyphenated compounds by adding the *s* to the word that changes in number.

fathers-in-law, courts-martial, masters of art, doctors of medicine

Make the plurals of letters, numbers, and abbreviations by adding *s*.

fives and tens, IBMs, 1990s, ps *and* qs *(note that letters are italicized)*

Capitalization

Capitalize all proper names of persons (including specific organizations or agencies of government); places (countries, states, cities, parks, and specific geographical areas); things (political parties, structures, historical and cultural terms, and calendar and time designations); and religious terms (deities, revered persons or groups, and sacred writings).

Capitalize proper adjectives and titles when they are used with proper names.

California gold rush, President John Adams, French fries, Homeric epic, Romanesque architecture, Senator John Glenn

Capitalize all main words in titles of works of literature, art, and music.

Note: *Some words that represent titles and offices are not capitalized unless used with a proper name.*

Punctuation

In a quoted statement that is either declarative or imperative, place the period inside the closing quotation marks.

"The airplane crashed on the runway during takeoff."

If the quotation is followed by other words in the sentence, place a comma inside the closing quotations marks and a period at the end of the sentence.

"The airplane crashed on the runway during takeoff," said the announcer.

In most instances in which a quoted title or expression occurs at the end of a sentence, the period is placed before either the single or double quotation marks.

"The middle-school readers were unprepared to understand Bryant's poem 'Thanatopsis.'"

Early book-length adventure stories like Don Quixote *and* The Three Musketeers *were known as "picaresque novels."*

There is an instance in which the final quotation mark would precede the period—if the content of the sentence were about a speech or quote so that the meaning might be obscured by the placement of the period.

The first thing out of his mouth was "Hi, I'm home."

but

The first line of his speech began "I arrived home to an empty house".

In sentences that are interrogatory or exclamatory, the question mark or exclamation point should be positioned outside the closing quotation marks if the quote itself is a statement or command or cited title.

Why was Tillie shaking as she began her recitation, "Once upon a midnight dreary..."?

In declarative sentences that include a quotation that is a question or an exclamation, place the question mark or exclamation point inside the quotation marks.

Commas

Separate two or more coordinate adjectives modifying the same word and three or more nouns, phrases, or clauses in a list.

Maggie's hair was dull, dirty, and lice-ridden.

Dickens portrayed the Artful Dodger as skillful pickpocket, loyal follower of Fagin, and defender of Oliver Twist.

Use commas to separate antithetical or complementary expressions from the rest of the sentence.

The veterinarian, not his assistant, would perform the delicate surgery.

The more he knew about her, the less he wished he had known.

Semicolons

Use semicolons to separate independent clauses when the second clause is introduced by a transitional adverb. (These clauses can also be written as separate sentences, preferably by placing the adverb within the second sentence.)

The Elizabethans modified the rhyme scheme of the sonnet; thus, it was called the English sonnet.

Use semicolons to separate items in a series that are long and complex or have internal punctuation.

The Italian Renaissance produced masters in the fine arts: Dante Alighieri, author of the Divine Comedy*; Leonardo da Vinci, painter of* The Last Supper*; and Donatello, sculptor of the* Quattro Coronati, *the four saints.*

Colons

Place a colon at the beginning of a list of items.

The teacher directed us to compare Faulkner's three symbolic novels: Absalom, Absalom*;* As I Lay Dying*; and* Light in August.

Do not use a colon if the list is preceded by a verb.

Three of Faulkner's symbolic novels are Absalom, Absalom*;* As I Lay Dying, *and* Light in August.

Subject-verb agreement

A verb agrees in number with its subject. Making them agree depends on one's ability to properly identify the subject.

One of the boys was playing too aggressively.

No one in the class, not the teacher or the students, was listening to the message from the intercom.

The candidates, including a grandmother and a teenager, are debating some controversial issues.

If two singular subjects are connected by *and*, the verb must be plural.

A man and his dog were jogging on the beach.

If two singular subjects are connected by *or* or *nor*, a singular verb is required.

Neither Dot nor Joyce has missed a day of school this year.

Either Fran or Paul is missing.

If one singular subject and one plural subject are connected by *or* or *nor*, the verb agrees with the subject nearest to the verb.

Neither the coach nor the players were able to sleep on the bus.

If the subject is a collective noun, its sense of number in the sentence determines the verb. It is singular if the noun represents a group or unit and plural if the noun represents individuals.

The House of Representatives has adjourned for the holidays.

The House of Representatives have failed to reach agreement on the subject of adjournment.

Verbs (tense)

Present tense is used to express that which is currently happening or is always true.

Randy is playing the piano.

Randy plays the piano like a pro.

Past tense is used to express action that occurred in a past time.

Randy learned to play the piano when he was six years old.

Future tense is used to express action or a condition of future time.

Randy will probably earn a music scholarship.

Present perfect tense is used to express action or a condition that started in the past and is continued or completed in the present.

Randy has practiced piano every day for the last ten years. Randy has never been bored with practice.

Past perfect tense expresses action or a condition that occurred as a precedent to some other action or condition.

Randy had considered playing clarinet before he discovered the piano.

Future perfect tense expresses action that started in the past or the present and will conclude at some time in the future.

By the time he goes to college, Randy will have been an accomplished pianist for more than half of his life.

Indicative mood is used to make unconditional statements; subjunctive mood is used for conditional clauses or wish statements that refer to conditions that are possible or wished for but not real.

Verbs (mood)

Indicative mood is used to make unconditional statements; subjunctive mood is used for conditional clauses or wish statements that refer to conditions that are possible or wished for but not real. Verbs in subjunctive mood are plural with both singular and plural subjects.

If I were a bird, I would fly.

I wish I were as rich as Donald Trump.

Verb conjugation

The conjugation of verbs follows the patterns used in the discussion of tense, above. However, the most frequent problems in verb use stem from the improper formation of past and past participial forms.

Regular verbs:	*believe, believed, (have) believed*
Irregular verbs:	*run, ran, run; sit, sat, sat; teach, taught, taught*

Other problems stem from the use of verbs that are the same in some tenses but have different forms and meanings in other tenses.

I lie on the ground. I lay on the ground yesterday. I have lain down.

I lay the blanket on the bed. I laid the blanket there yesterday. I have laid the blanket there every night.

The sun rises. The sun rose. The sun has risen.

He raises the flag. He raised the flag. He had raised the flag.

I sit on the porch. I sat on the porch. I have sat in the porch swing.

I set the plate on the table. I set the plate there yesterday. I had set the table before dinner.

Pronouns

A pronoun used as a subject of predicate nominative is in nominative case.

A pronoun used as a direct object, indirect object, or object of a preposition is in objective case.

Common pronoun errors occur from misuse of reflexive pronouns:

Singular:	*myself, yourself, herself, himself, itself*
Plural:	*ourselves, yourselves, themselves*
Incorrect:	*Jack cut hisself shaving.*
Correct:	*Jack cut himself shaving.*
Incorrect:	*They backed theirselves into a corner.*
Correct:	*They backed themselves into a corner.*

Adjectives

An adjective should agree with its antecedent in number.

Those apples are rotten. This one is ripe. These peaches are hard.

Comparative adjectives end in *-er* and superlatives in *-est*, with some exceptions like *worse* and *worst*. Adjectives that cannot easily make comparative inflections are preceded by *more* or *most*.

Ms. Carmichael is the better of the two basketball coaches.

That is the hastiest excuse you have ever contrived.

When comparing one thing to others in a group, exclude the thing under comparison from the rest of the group.

Incorrect:	*Joey is larger than any baby I have ever seen. (Since you have seen him, he cannot be larger than himself.)*
Correct:	*Joey is larger than any other baby I have ever seen.*

Include all necessary words to make a comparison clear in meaning.

I am as tall as my mother. I am as tall as she (is).

My cats are better behaved than those of my neighbor.

WRITTEN COMMUNICATION

When teaching writing, teachers must provide many opportunities for children to write. Writing should be a daily activity in the classroom, just as reading is.

Students must understand that writing is a process and typically involves many steps.

Stages of Writing

Writing is an iterative process. As students engage in the various stages of writing, they develop and improve not only their writing skills but their thinking skills as well.

Stages of the writing process:

- Prewriting: Students gather ideas before writing. Prewriting may include clustering, listing, brainstorming, mapping, free writing, and charting.
- Drafting: Students compose the first draft. Students should follow their notes/writing plan from the prewriting stage.
- Revising and editing: Revision is probably the most important step in the writing process. In this step, students examine their work and make changes in wording, details, and ideas.
- Proofreading: Students proofread the draft for punctuation and mechanical errors.
- Publishing: Students may have their work displayed on a bulletin board, read aloud in class, or printed in a literary magazine or school anthology.

Writing for Various Audiences

There are four main forms of discourse: persuasion, exposition, narration, and description.

PERSUASION is a piece of writing—a poem, a play, a speech—the purpose of which is to change the minds of readers or listeners or to get them to do something. This can be achieved in many ways:

- The credibility of the writer/speaker might lead the listeners/readers to a change of mind or a recommended action.
- Reasoning is important in persuasive discourse. No one wants to believe that he or she accepts a new viewpoint or goes out and takes action just because he or she likes and trusts the person who recommended it. Logic comes into play in persuasive reasoning.
- The third and most powerful force that leads to acceptance or action is emotional appeal.

PERSUASION: a piece of writing—a poem, a play, a speech—the purpose of which is to change the minds of readers or listeners or to get them to do something

EXPOSITION is discourse intended to inform. Expository writing is not focused on changing anyone's mind or getting anyone to take a certain action. Its purpose is to give information. Examples include driving directions to a particular place or the instructions for putting together a toy that arrives unassembled.

EXPOSITION: discourse intended to inform

NARRATION is discourse that is presented chronologically—something happened, and then something else happened, and then something else happened. It is also called a story. News reports are often narrative in nature, as are records of trips, etc.

NARRATION: discourse that is presented chronologically

DESCRIPTION is discourse intended to make an experience available through one of the five senses—seeing, smelling, hearing, feeling (as with the fingers), and

DESCRIPTION: discourse intended to make an experience available through one of the five senses

tasting. Descriptive words allow the reader to "see" with her mind's eye, hear through her mind's ear, smell through her mind's nose, taste with her mind's tongue, and feel with her mind's fingers.

A paraphrase is the rewording of a piece of writing. The result is not necessarily shorter than the original. It uses different vocabulary and possibly a different arrangement of details.

A summary is a distillation of the elements of a piece of writing or a speech. A summary is much shorter than the original. A summary does not make judgments about the original; it simply reports the original in condensed form.

Letters are often expository in nature—their purpose is to provide information. However, letters are also often persuasive—the writer wants to persuade or get the recipient to do something. They are also sometimes descriptive or narrative—the writer shares an experience or tells about an event.

Research reports are a special kind of expository writing. A topic is researched—explored by searching the literature, interviewing experts, or even conducting experiments—and the findings are written up to convey what was discovered to a particular audience. Research reports can be simple, such as delving into the history of an event, or complex, such as a report on a scientific phenomenon that requires complicated testing and reasoning to explain. A research report often suggests several alternative conclusions but highlights one as the best answer to the question that originally inspired the research, which becomes the thesis of the report.

Clarifying Writing

Writing introductions

It's important to remember that in the writing process, the introduction should be written last. Until the body of the paper has been determined, it's difficult to make strategic decisions regarding the introduction. The basic purpose of the introduction, then, is to lead the audience into the discourse. It lets the reader know the purpose of the discourse and it conditions the audience to be receptive to what the writer wants to say. It can be very brief or it can take up a large percentage of the total word count.

The most important thing to remember is that the purpose and structure of the introduction should be deliberate if it is to serve the purpose of "leading the reader into the discussion."

The introduction often ends with the thesis, the point or purpose of the paper. However, this is not set in stone. The thesis may open the body of the discussion, or it may conclude the discourse. The most important thing to remember is that the purpose and structure of the introduction should be deliberate if it is to serve the purpose of "leading the reader into the discussion."

Writing Conclusions

Aristotle taught that the conclusion of a piece of writing should strive to do five things:

1. Inspire the reader with a favorable opinion of the writer
2. Amplify the force of the points made in the body of the text
3. Reinforce the points made in the body of the text
4. Rouse appropriate emotions in the reader
5. Restate in a summary way what has been said

Literacy Skills for English-Language Learners

- Knowledge of the subject matter
- Processes of sequencing letters/sounds to build words and units of meaning
- Knowledge of text structure
- Use of context clues to predict meaning
- Awareness that text may be written for different purposes
- Reading strategies such as defining author's purpose, predicting, skimming, scanning, guessing vocabulary from context, making inferences, etc.
- Thinking processes involved in decoding text
- Positive experiences with first-language literacy

VISUALS

Comparing and Contrasting Print, Visual, and Electronic Media

A print message has positive and negative features. Positive features include longevity and portability. Print messages appeal almost exclusively to the mind, and allow students to recursively read sections that warrant more thought. A negative feature of print messages is that they are not accessible to nonreaders.

A graphic message gives a quick overview of a quantifiable situation. Some learners find that graphic information is easier to understand than print, and many struggling readers find graphic messages more helpful, too. However, compared to print, graphic messages convey a much smaller range of information.

An audio message allows for messages delivered with attention to prosody. Students who can't read can still access the material. Audio messages invite the listener to form mental images consistent with the topic of the audio. Audio messages allow learners to close their eyes for better mental focus. Listening to an audio message is a more passive activity than reading a print message.

An audiovisual message offers the greatest accessibility for learners. It has the advantages of both media, the graphic and the audio. Learners' eyes and ears are engaged. Nonreaders get significant access to content. On the other hand, viewing an audiovisual presentation is an even more passive activity than listening to an audio message because information is coming to learners effortlessly through two senses.

Interpreting and Evaluating Visual Images

Political cartoons

The political, or editorial, cartoon presents a message or point of view about people, events, or situations using caricature and symbolism to convey the cartoonist's ideas, sometimes subtly, sometimes brashly, but always quickly. A good political cartoon has wit and humor, which is usually obtained by slick exaggeration and not used merely for comic effect. It also has a foundation in truth; that is, the characters must be recognizable to the viewer and the point of the drawing must have some basis in fact even if it has a philosophical bias. The third requirement is a moral purpose.

Using political cartoons as a teaching tool enlivens lectures, prompts classroom discussion, promotes critical thinking, develops multiple talents and learning styles, and helps prepare students for standardized tests. It also provides humor.

Using political cartoons as a teaching tool enlivens lectures, prompts classroom discussion, promotes critical thinking, develops multiple talents and learning styles, and helps prepare students for standardized tests. It also provides humor. However, it may be the most difficult form of literature to teach. Many teachers who choose to include cartoons in their social studies curricula caution that, while students may enjoy them, they may not always understand the cartoonists' messages.

The best strategy for teaching such a unit is through a subskills approach that leads students step by step to higher orders of critical thinking. For example, the teacher can introduce caricature and use cartoons to illustrate the principles. Students are able to identify and interpret symbols if they are given the principles for doing so and get plenty of practice, and cartoons are excellent for this. It can cut down the time it takes for students to develop these skills, and many of the students who might not learn to identify symbols may overcome the roadblocks through the analysis of political cartoons. Many political cartoons exist for the teacher to use in the classroom.

Analyzing Data Presented In Visuals

Visuals are an effective and dynamic way to add meaning to a text. Some possibilities for the analysis of data, whether presented in tables, charts, graphs, maps, or other illustrations, include:

- Qualitative descriptions: Would drawing conclusions about the quality of a particular treatment or course of action be revealed by the illustration?
- Quantitative descriptions: How much do the results of one particular treatment or course of action differ from another, and is that variation significant?
- Classification: Is worthwhile information derived from breaking the information down into classifications?
- Estimations: Is it possible to estimate future performance on the basis of the information in the illustration?
- Comparisons: Is it useful to make comparisons based on the data?
- Relationships: Are relationships between components revealed by scrutiny of the data?
- Cause-and-effect relationships: Do the data suggest that there are cause-and-effect relationships that were not previously apparent?
- Mapping and modeling: If the data were mapped and a model drawn up, would the point of the document be demonstrated or refuted?

Choosing the appropriate graphic form depends on the type of information and data with which one is working. For example, a pie chart that shows parts of a whole would not be useful for showing trends over time. A line chart, rather than a bar chart, is more effective when showing the interaction of two variables.

- Tables: Tables depict exact numbers and other data in rows and columns.
- Graphs: Graphs depict trends, movements, distributions, and cycles more clearly than tables. While graphs can present statistics in a more interesting and comprehensible form than tables, they are less accurate.
- Maps: While the most obvious use of maps is to locate places geographically, they can also show specific geographic features such as roads, mountains, and

rivers. Some maps show information according to geographic distribution such as population, housing, or manufacturing centers.

- Illustrations: A wide range of illustrations, such as photographs, drawings, and diagrams, can be used to illuminate the text in a document. Illustrations can also be part of a graphic layout designed to make a page more attractive.

Technology for Producing Teaching Material

MULTIMEDIA: a technology for presenting material in both visual and verbal forms

MULTIMEDIA refers to a technology for presenting material in both visual and verbal forms. This format is especially conducive to classroom use since it reaches both visual and auditory learners.

Software programs for producing teaching material

- Adobe Acrobat
- PC Paintbrush
- Microsoft Word
- Microsoft Excel
- Microsoft Visio
- Microsoft PowerPoint

ASSESSMENT OF LITERACY

ASSESSMENT: the practice of collecting information about something

EVALUATION: the process of judging the children's responses to determine how well they are achieving particular goals or demonstrating certain skills

ASSESSMENT is the practice of collecting information about something from children's responses, and **EVALUATION** is the process of judging the children's responses to determine how well they are achieving particular goals or demonstrating certain skills.

There are two broad categories of assessment:

- Informal assessment utilizes observation and other nonstandardized procedures to compile evidence of children's progress. Informal assessments include but are not limited to: checklists, observations, and performance assessments/tasks.
- Formal assessment consists of standardized tests and procedures carried out under circumscribed conditions. Formal assessments include state tests, standardized achievement tests, NAEP tests, etc.

Key Terms

- **Formative testing** sets targets for student learning and creates an avenue to provide data on whether students are meeting the targets.
- **Diagnostic testing** is used to determine students' skill levels and current knowledge.
- **Normative testing** establishes rankings and comparatives of student performance against an established norm of achievement.
- **Alternative testing** is a nontraditional method of helping students construct responses to problem solving.
- **Authentic testing** refers to real-life assessments that are relevant and meaningful in a student's life (e.g., calculating a 20 percent discount on an iPod for a student learning math percentages creates a more personalized approach to learning).
- **Performance-based testing** judges students according to pre-established standards.
- **Traditional testing** refers to the variety of teacher assessments that either come with the textbooks or are directly created from the textbooks.

Criterion-Referenced and Norm-Referenced Tests

Criterion-referenced tests

CRITERION-REFERENCED TESTS are tests that measure children against criteria or guidelines that are uniform for all of the test takers. Therefore, by definition, no special questions, formats, or considerations are given for the test taker who is either from a different linguistic/cultural background or is already identified as a struggling reader/writer. On a criterion-referenced test, it is possible that a child can score 100 percent if he or she has been exposed to and mastered all of the concepts on the test. A child's score on such a test indicates which of the concepts have already been taught and what the child needs additional review or support in mastering.

CRITERION-REFERENCED TESTS: tests that measure children against criteria or guidelines that are uniform for all of the test takers

Norm-Referenced Tests

NORM-REFERENCED TESTS are tests that measure children against one another. Scores on these tests are reported in percentiles. Each percentile indicates the percentage of the testing population whose scores were lower than or the same as a particular child's score. Standardized norm-referenced tests are being used in many districts today. They foster unhelpful and invalid comparisons between young readers, which do not help individual readers progress in reading development,

NORM-REFERENCED TESTS: tests that measure children against one another

but rather track and stigmatize them. Of course, this type of test does not take into account special linguistic, cultural, socioeconomic, or special needs concerns.

Characteristics of an Effective Assessment

1. Assessment should be an ongoing process, with the teacher making some kind of an informal or formal assessment almost every time the child speaks, listens, reads, writes, or views something in the classroom. The assessment should be a natural part of the instruction and not intrusive.

2. The most effective assessment is integrated into ongoing instruction. Throughout the teaching and learning day, the child's written, spoken, and reading contributions to the class, or lack thereof, need to be continually assessed.

3. Assessment should reflect the actual reading and writing experiences for which classroom learning has prepared the child. The child should be able to show that he or she can read and explain or react to a similar literary or expository work.

Assessment needs to be a collaborative and reflective process. Teachers can learn from what the children reveal about their own individual assessments.

4. Assessment needs to be a collaborative and reflective process. Teachers can learn from what the children reveal about their own individual assessments. Children, even as early as grade 2, should be supported by their teacher to continually and routinely ask themselves questions assessing their reading (and other skill) progress. They might ask: "How have I done in understanding what the author wanted to say?", "What can I do to improve my reading?", and "How can I use what I have read to learn more about this topic?" Teachers need to be informed by their own professional observation *and* by children's comments as they assess and customize instruction for children.

5. High-quality valid assessment is multidimensional and may include, but is not limited to: samples of writings, student retellings, running records, anecdotal teacher observations, self-evaluations, and records of independent reading. From this multidimensional data, the teacher can derive a consistent level of performance and design additional instruction to enhance the level of student performance.

6. Assessment must take into account children's ages and ethnic/cultural patterns of learning.

7. Assessment should be performed in order to teach children from their strengths, not their weaknesses. Teachers should find out what reading behaviors children demonstrate well and then design instruction to support those behaviors.

8. Assessment should be part of children's learning process, and not done *on* them but, rather, *with* them.

Validity, Reliability, and Bias in Testing

VALIDITY is how well a test measures what it is supposed to measure. **RELIABILITY** is the consistency of the test. This is measured by whether the test indicates the same score for the child who takes it twice.

VALIDITY: how well a test measures what it is supposed to measure

RELIABILITY: the consistency of the test

Bias in testing occurs when the information in the test or the information required to respond to a multiple-choice question or constructed response (essay question) is not available to test takers who come from a different cultural, ethnic, linguistic, or socioeconomic background than the majority of the test takers.

Determining Students' Reading Levels

Reading levels consist of a combination of a word accuracy percentage and a comprehension percentage.

Independent

This is the level at which the child can read text totally on his or her own. When reading books at the independent level, students are able to decode between 95 and 100 percent of the words and comprehend the text with 90 percent or better accuracy. Much of the research indicates that about 98 percent accuracy makes for a good independent reader; however, other research uses figures as low as 95 percent accuracy.

Instructional

This is the level at which the student should be taught. Materials at the instructional level provide enough difficulty to increase the student's reading skills without providing so much that it becomes too cumbersome to finish the selection. Typically, the acceptable range for accuracy is between 85 and 94 percent, with 75 percent or greater comprehension. Some standards rely on the number of errors made instead of the accuracy percentage, with no more than one error out of twenty words read being the acceptable standard.

Frustrational

Books at a student's frustrational level are too difficult for that child and should not be used. The frustrational level is any text with less than 85 percent word accuracy and/or less than 75 percent comprehension.

Literacy Portfolios

Portfolios should include the following categories of materials:

- Work samples: These can include children's story maps, webs, KWL charts, pictures, illustrations, storyboards, and writings about the stories they have read.
- Records of independent reading and writing: These can include the children's journals, notebooks, or logs of books read with the names of the authors, titles of the books, date completed, and pieces related to the book completed or in progress.
- Checklists and surveys: These include checklists designed by the teacher for reading development, writing development, ownership checklists, and general interest surveys.
- Self-evaluation forms: These are the children's own evaluations of their reading and writing process framed in their own words. They can be simple templates with starting sentences such as: "I am really proud of the way I..."

Some teachers and schools advocate having the child include formal test results and questions in the portfolio.

Reading Stages for English-Language Learners

- Stage 1 readers: These readers have developed a phonological awareness of the second language and are becoming familiar with the letter-sound correlations. They are comfortable with the direction of English print and have begun to acquire some basic vocabulary in the language. They recognize a few sight words.
- Stage 2 readers: These readers have a good grasp of the phonological aspects of the language and their vocabulary is growing. They are beginning to recognize many of the high-frequency words as sight words, without having to decode the sounds. They are able to understand the main idea of simple text, and they are starting to use meaningful patterns of intonation when they read aloud.
- Stage 3 readers: These readers are reading more difficult texts with better fluency. They have developed some reading strategies, such as predicting and using context clues for meaning. They are able to read for information, with less attention to the decoding process. They are able to read for different purposes, such as to find answers to questions or to summarize.
- Stage 4 readers: These readers are fluent. They have a well-developed vocabulary and they use all sources of information for interpreting the text, including grammatical and syntactic structures. They are efficient users of reading strategies and they are able to analyze the text and respond to it in different ways. They are able to read for pleasure as well as for practical reasons.

Self-Assessment in Writing

Holistic scoring gives an overall assessment of the student work by assigning an overall or combined grade to the work that takes all of the component parts of a task into consideration. Holistic scoring involves assessing a child's ability to construct meaning through writing. It uses a scale called a rubric, which ranges from 0 to 4.

Holistic scoring gives an overall assessment of the student work by assigning an overall or combined grade to the work that takes all of the component parts of a task into consideration.

Record of Reading Behavior

There are specific steps for taking the record of reading behavior and analyzing its results:

1. Select a text: If you want to see if the child is reading on instructional level, choose a book that the child has already read. If the purpose of the test is to see whether the child is ready to advance to the next level, choose a book from that level which the child has not yet seen.
2. Introduce the text: If the book is one that has been read, you do not need to introduce the text other than by saying the title. However, if the book is new to the child, you should briefly share the title and tell the child a bit about the plot and style of the book.
3. Take the record: Generally with emergent readers in grades 1-2, there are only 100-150 words in a passage used to take a record. Make certain that the child is seated beside you so that you can see the text as the child reads it.

You may want to photocopy the text in advance for yourself so you can make direct notations on your text while the child reads from the book.

After you introduce the text, make certain that the child has the chance to read the text independently. Be certain that you do not "teach" or help the child with it, other than to supply an unknown word that the child requests. The purpose of the record is to see what the child does on his or her own. As the child reads the text, you must be certain to record the reading behaviors the child exhibits.

Comprehension check

A comprehension check should be done by inviting the child to retell the story. This retelling can then be used to ask further questions about characters, plot, setting, and purpose, which allow you to observe and record the child's level of comprehension.

Calculating the reading level and the self-correction rate

Calculating the reading level lets you know if the book is at the level the child can read independently, comfortably with guidance, or at a level that frustrates the child.

Generally, an accuracy score of 95-100 percent suggests that the child can read the text and other books or texts on the same level independently.

An accuracy score of 90-94 percent indicates that the text will probably present challenges for the child, but with guidance from you, a tutor, or parent, the child will be able to master these texts and enjoy them. This is instructional level.

However, an accuracy score of 89 percent or less tells you that the material you have selected for the child is too hard for the child to control alone. Material at this level needs to be shared with the child in a shared reading situation or read to the child.

Keeping score on the record

Insertions, omissions, substitutions, and teacher-told responses all count as errors. Repetitions are not scored as errors. Corrected responses are scored as self-corrections.

No penalty is given for a child's attempts at self-correction that result in a finally incorrect response, but the attempts should be noted. Multiple unsuccessful attempts at a word score as one error only.

The lowest score for any page is zero. If a child omits one or more lines, each word omitted is counted as an error. If the child omits a page, deduct the number of words omitted from the total number of words that you have used for the record.

Calculating the reading level

Note the number of errors made on each line on the Record of Reading Behavior in the column marked E (for Error).

Total the number of errors in the text and divide this number into the number of words that the child has read. This will give you the error rate.

If a child read a passage of 100 words and made 10 errors, the error rate would be 1 in 10. Convert this to an accuracy percentage, or 90 percent.

Calculating the self-correction rate

Total the number of self-corrections.

Next, add the number of errors to the number of self-corrections and divide by the number of self-corrections.

A self-correction rate of 1 in 3 to 1 in 5 is considered good. This rate indicates that the child is able to help him- or herself as problems are encountered in reading.

Analyzing the record

As you review the errors, consider whether the child made an error because of semantics (cues from meaning), syntactics (language structure), or visual information difficulties.

This record should assist the educator in developing a detailed, date-specific picture of the child's progress in reading behavior. It should be used to help the educator individualize instruction for the specific child.

As you analyze self-corrections, consider what led the child to make that self-correction. Consider which cues the child uses effectively and which ones the child does not use well.

DOMAIN II
MATHEMATICS

PERSONALIZED STUDY PLAN

MATHEMATICS INSTRUCTION

Theories and Principles of Learning Math

Situated learning theory: Students learn more easily from instruction involving relevant, real-world situations and applications than from abstract concepts.

Constructivism: Prior knowledge greatly influences the learning of math, and learning is cumulative and vertically structured. Thus, it is important for teachers to be aware of the knowledge and ideas that students already have about a subject.

Instructional strategies building on diversity

Students of certain ethnic and racial groups that emphasize expressiveness and communication may benefit from an interactive learning environment. Conversely, students of ethnic groups that emphasize personal learning and discipline may benefit from a more structured, traditional learning environment. As is always the case when considering ethnic differences, however, one must be careful to avoid making inappropriate generalizations.

The cultural and ethnic background of a student greatly affects his or her approach to learning mathematics. In addition, factors such as socioeconomic status can affect student learning styles.

Low-income students may not have had the same early educational background and exposure to traditional educational reasoning strategies and techniques that other students have. Thus, they may initially require a more application-based curriculum until they develop sufficient abstract reasoning skills.

Sequence of Instruction

When introducing a new mathematical concept to students, teachers should utilize the concrete-to-representational-to-abstract sequence of instruction. The first step of the progression is the introduction of a concept modeled with concrete materials. The second step is the translation of concrete models into representational diagrams or pictures. The third and final step is the translation of representational models into abstract models using only numbers and symbols.

Manipulatives and Other Tools

The use of supplementary materials in the classroom can greatly enhance the learning experience by stimulating student interest and satisfying different learning styles. Manipulatives, models, and technology are examples of tools available to teachers.

MANIPULATIVES: materials that students can physically handle and move

MODELS: means of representing mathematical concepts by relating the concepts to real-world situations

MANIPULATIVES are materials that students can physically handle and move. They allow students to understand mathematical concepts by allowing them to see concrete examples of abstract processes. **MODELS** are means of representing mathematical concepts by relating the concepts to real-world situations.

Other tools available to help students learn math:

- Counters: Can be used to help students understand number sense from basic counting to algebra.
- Rulers: Help students learn about measurement, the length of an object, or distance. Understanding measurement helps students to understand perimeter, circumference, and area in geometry.
- Measuring containers: Teach students about fractions and the relationships between standard units (pint, quart, gallon) and metric units (milliliter, liter). Students also learn about the volume of available space in different-size containers.
- Protractors: Teach students about angles.
- Scales: A good tool to teach the concept of equality in equations.
- Money: Helps them understand the value associated with each denomination. Students learn the basic concepts of money management and personal finances using their addition and subtraction skills.
- Software: Math programs can enhance the teaching and learning of mathematical concepts.

Methods of Instruction

Successful teachers select and implement instructional delivery methods that best fit the needs of a particular classroom format. Individual, small-group, and large-group classroom formats require different techniques and methods of instruction.

Individual instruction allows the teacher to interact closely with the student.

Small-group instruction requires the teacher to provide instruction to multiple students at the same time. Because the group is small, instructional methods that encourage student interaction and cooperative learning are particularly effective. For example, group projects, discussion, and question-and-answer sessions promote cooperative learning and maintain student interest. In addition, working problems as a group or in pairs can help students learn problem-solving strategies from each other.

> *It is important to be aware that not all students learn the same way and, therefore, alternative instructional strategies may be appropriate.*

Lecture is a common instructional method for teaching large groups. In addition, demonstrating methods of problem solving and allowing students to ask questions about homework and test problems is an effective strategy for teaching large groups.

Alternative methodologies include the use of:

- Simulations
- Toolkits
- Strategy and role-playing games
- Peer tutoring
- Group, cooperative, and collaborative learning
- Learning by design
- Multimedia
- Storytelling structures
- Coaching and scaffolding
- Case studies
- Encouraging mathematical discourse

The **questioning technique** is a mathematic process skill in which students devise questions to clarify the problem, eliminate possible solutions, and simplify the problem-solving process. By developing and attempting to answer simple questions, students can tackle difficult and complex problems.

Sometimes, the teacher can guide the discourse by asking questions to generate discussion. Other times, the students can be encouraged to generate their own discussions, sharing their questions and thoughts among themselves. A third type of discourse takes place in small groups when the students work both independently and collaboratively.

Teachers can ask the following types of questions to encourage higher-order thinking:

- Questions that require manipulation of prior knowledge
- Questions that require students to state ideas or definitions in their own words
- Questions that require students to solve a problem
- Questions that require observation and/or description of an object or event
- Questions that call for comparison and contrast

It is also recommended that teachers give a student enough time to attempt to answer a question before calling on another student. When a student is having trouble responding to a question, a teacher should ask probing questions; for example:

- Asking for clarification
- Rephrasing the question

- Asking related questions
- Restating the student's ideas (Ornstein, 1995)

Assessment

State standardized testing is an important tool for curriculum design and modification. Most states have stated curriculum standards that mandate what students should know. Teachers can use the standards to focus their instruction and curriculum planning.

When an assessment does not provide the expected results, the teacher must reflect on the method of instruction and make modifications so the students learn the material. To avoid this, the teacher may want to incorporate informal assessments into the instruction to check students' understanding along the way

Teachers should use a variety of assessment procedures. In addition to the traditional methods of performance assessment like multiple-choice, true/false, and matching tests, many other methods are available to teachers.

Types of assessment

An alternative assessment is any type of assessment in which students create a response rather than choose an answer. This type of assessment is sometimes called formative assessment, due to the emphasis on feedback and the flow of communication between teacher and student. It is the opposite of summative assessment, which occurs periodically and consists of temporary interaction between teacher and student.

Alternative assessment includes:

- Short-response and essay questions
- Student portfolios
- Projects, demonstrations, and oral presentations

One type of alternative assessment is bundled testing, the grouping of different question formats for the same skill or competency. For example, a bundled test of exponential functions may include multiple-choice questions, short-response questions, word problems, and essay questions. The variety of questions tests different levels of reasoning and expression.

Scoring methods

Scoring methods are an important, and often overlooked, part of effective assessment. Teachers can use a simple three-point scale for evaluating student responses.

No answer or an inappropriate answer that shows no understanding scores zero points. A partial response showing a lack of understanding, a lack of explanation, or major computational errors scores one point. A somewhat satisfactory answer that answers most of the question correctly but contains simple computational errors or minor flaws in reasoning receives two points. Finally, a satisfactory response displaying full understanding, adequate explanation, and appropriate reasoning receives three points.

When evaluating student responses, teachers should look for common error patterns and mistakes in computation. Teachers should also incorporate questions and scoring procedures that address common error patterns and misconceptions into their methods of assessment.

Assessment for English-language learners

Mathematic assessments may understate the abilities of English-language learners because poor test scores may stem from difficulty in reading comprehension, not a lack of understanding of mathematic principles. Uncharacteristically poor performance on word problems by English-language learners is a sign that reading comprehension, not mathematic understanding, is the underlying problem.

Math in the Workplace

Teachers can increase students' interest in math by relating mathematical concepts to familiar events in their lives and using real-world examples and data whenever possible. Relating math to various careers and professions shows students why math is relevant and helps them in the career exploration process.

The use of math in various disciplines

Artists, musicians, scientists, social scientists, and business people use mathematical modeling to solve problems in their disciplines. Mathematics is a key aspect of visual art. Artists use the geometric properties of shapes, ratios, and proportions in creating paintings and sculptures. For example, mathematics is essential to the concept of perspective. Artists must determine the appropriate lengths and heights of objects to portray three-dimensional distance in two dimensions.

The uses of mathematics in science are endless. Physical scientists use vectors, functions, derivatives, and integrals to describe and model the movement of objects. Biologists and ecologists use mathematics to model ecosystems and study DNA. Chemists use mathematics to study the interaction of molecules and to determine proper amounts and proportions of reactants.

Examples in the classroom

Teachers can be creative in showing how math is used in different professions. Here are just a few examples:

- Learning about math in different professions can begin as early as kindergarten. When teaching the basics of addition and subtraction, teachers can set up a "bank" in the classroom.

- Math is used in the construction industry. Teachers can set up their classrooms as work zones. Students can use measurement and shapes in constructing or designing a building or playground.
- A lesson about tessellations include students designing a floor or wallpaper.
- A lesson on fractions can lead to discussions of how they are used in cooking and baking.

WHOLE NUMBER: one of the counting numbers

INTEGER: a positive or negative number

RATIONAL NUMBER: the quotient $\frac{a}{b}$ of two integers, where $b \neq 0$

REAL NUMBER: a member of the set of all numbers, rational and irrational

IRRATIONAL NUMBER: any real number that cannot be expressed as the quotient $\frac{a}{b}$ of two integers, where $b \neq 0$

PRIME NUMBER: a number with exactly two factors, itself and one

COMPOSITE: a number with more than two factors

NUMBER CONCEPTS AND OPERATIONS

Whole Numbers, Integers, Rational Numbers, and Real Numbers

A **WHOLE NUMBER** is one of the counting numbers. There are only ten of them:
0, 1, 2, 3, 4, 5, 6, 7, 8, 9

An **INTEGER** is a positive or negative number.

An odd number is an integer that is not a multiple of two, e.g., -5, -17, 7, 111.

An even number is an integer that is a multiple of two, e.g., -24, -2, 36, 2004.

A **RATIONAL NUMBER** is the quotient $\frac{a}{b}$ of two integers, where $b \neq 0$. Since an integer can be written as a fraction with a denominator of 1, integers are included in the set of rational numbers. The set of rational numbers is also infinite. Rational numbers include all of the whole numbers, integers, and fractions whose decimal equivalents terminate.

A **REAL NUMBER** is a member of the set of all numbers, rational and irrational. The set of real numbers is also infinite. An **IRRATIONAL NUMBER** is any real number that cannot be expressed as the quotient $\frac{a}{b}$ of two integers, where $b \neq 0$.

A **PRIME NUMBER** has exactly *two* factors, itself and one. A **COMPOSITE** number has more than two factors. Zero and 1 are *neither* prime nor composite.

Divisibility Rules

- Rule 1: A number is **divisible by 2** if it is an even number (which means the last digit is 0, 2, 4, 6, or 8).
- Rule 2: A number is **divisible by 3** if the sum of its digits is evenly divisible by 3.
- Rule 3: A number is **divisible by 4** if the last two digits of the number are evenly divisible by 4.

Number Properties

The three basic number properties are distributive, commutative, and associative. These number properties are the rules of number operations.

1. Distributive property of multiplication over addition: $x(y + z) = xy + xz$.
2. Commutative property of multiplication and addition: The order of numbers does not matter. In other words, $a + b = b + a$ and $ab = ba$.
3. Associative property of addition and multiplication: The grouping of numbers does not matter. In other words, $(a + b) + c = a + (b + c)$ and $a(bc) = (ab)c$.

Rational- and Real-Number Algorithms

ALGORITHMS are methods or strategies for solving problems. In general, algorithms make use of number properties to simplify mathematical operations.

ALGORITHMS: methods or strategies for solving problems

Addition

The partial sums method of integer addition relies on the associative property of addition. Consider the partial sum algorithm of the addition of 125 and 89. We first sum the columns from left to right and then add the results.

125	
+ 89	
100	Hundreds column sum
+ 100	Tens column sum
+ 14	Ones column sum
214	

The associative property of addition shows why this method works. We can rewrite 125 plus 89 as follows:

$(100 + 20 + 5) + (80 + 9)$

Using the associative property to group the terms:

$(100) + (20 + 80) + (5 + 9) = 100 + 100 + 14 = 214$

Rational number addition relies on the distributive property of multiplication over addition and the understanding that multiplication of any number by one yields the same number. Consider the addition of $\frac{1}{4}$ to $\frac{1}{3}$ by means of common denominator.

$\frac{1}{4} + \frac{1}{3} = \frac{3}{3}(\frac{1}{4}) + \frac{4}{4}(\frac{1}{3}) = (\frac{3}{12}) + (\frac{4}{12}) = \frac{7}{12} \rightarrow$ Recognize that $\frac{3}{3}$ and $\frac{4}{4}$ both equal 1.

A common error in rational number addition is the failure to find a common denominator and adding both numerators and denominators.

A common error in rational number addition is the failure to find a common denominator and adding both numerators and denominators.

Subtraction

The same-change rule of substitution takes advantage of the property of addition of zero. The addition of zero does not change the value of a quantity.

$289 - 97 = 292 - 100$ because

$289 - 97 = (289 + 3) - (97 + 3) = (289 - 97) + (3 - 3)$

$= 289 - 97 + 0$

Note the use of the distributive property of multiplication over addition, the associative property of addition, and the property of addition of zero in proving the accuracy of the same-change algorithm. A common mistake when using the same-change rule is adding from one number and subtracting from the other. This is an error in reasoning resulting from misapplication of the distributive property (e.g., failing to distribute -1).

Multiplication

The partial products algorithm of multiplication decomposes each term into simpler numbers and sums the products of the simpler terms.

$$\begin{array}{r} 84 = 80 + 4 \\ \times\ 26 = 20 + 6 \end{array}$$

$$\begin{array}{lcr} 80 \times 20 & \rightarrow & 1600 \\ 80 \times 6 & \rightarrow & 480 \\ 20 \times 4 & \rightarrow & 80 \\ 6 \times 4 & \rightarrow & \underline{24} \\ & & 2184 \end{array}$$

We can justify this algorithm by using the **foil method** of binomial multiplication and the distributive property of multiplication over addition.

$$(80 + 4)(20 + 6) = (80)(20) + (4)(20) + (6)(80) + (6)(4)$$

Common errors in partial product multiplication result from mistakes in binomial multiplication and mistakes in pairing terms of the partial products (e.g., multiplying incorrect terms).

Division

We can justify the partial quotients algorithm for division by using the distributive property of multiplication over division. Because multiplication is the reverse of division, we can check the result by multiplying the divisor by the partial sums.

```
18)1440 |
  − 900 | 50
    540 |
  − 360 | 20
    180 |
   − 90 |  5
     90 |
   − 90 |  5
      0   80 → final quotient = 80 with no remainder
```

Check:

$$18\,(50 + 20 + 5 + 5) = (18)(50) + (18)(20) + (18)(5) + (18)(5) = 1440$$

Common errors in division often result from mistakes in translating words to symbols, for example, misinterpreting 10 divided by 5 as $\frac{5}{10}$. In addition, when using the partial quotients algorithm, errors in subtraction and addition can produce incorrect results.

The Fundamental Theorem of Arithmetic

Any integer $n > 1$ that is divisible by at least one positive integer that is not equal to one or n is called a composite number. A natural number n that is only divisible by one and n is called a prime number.

According to the fundamental theorem of arithmetic, every integer greater than 1 can be written uniquely in the form:

$$p_1^{e_1} p_2^{e_2} \cdots p_k^{ek}.$$

where the p_i are distinct prime numbers and the e_i are positive integers.

Greatest Common Factor

GREATEST COMMON FACTOR: the largest number that is a factor of all of the numbers given in a problem

Note: There can be other common factors besides the GCF.

GCF is the abbreviation for the **GREATEST COMMON FACTOR**. The GCF is the largest number that is a factor of all of the numbers given in a problem. The GCF can be no larger than the smallest number given in the problem. If no other number is a common factor, then the GCF is the number 1. To find the GCF, list all possible factors of the smallest number given (include the number itself). Starting with the largest factor (which is the number itself), determine whether it is also a factor of all of the other given numbers. If so, that is the GCF. If that factor does not work, try the same method on the next smallest factor. Continue until a common factor is found. This is the GCF.

Example: Find the GCF of 12, 20, and 36.

The smallest number in the problem is 12. The factors of 12 are 1, 2, 3, 4, 6, and 12. Twelve is the largest factor, but it does not divide evenly into 20. Neither does 6, but 4 will divide into both 20 and 36 evenly. Therefore, 4 is the GCF.

Least Common Multiple

LEAST COMMON MULTIPLE: the smallest number that all of the given numbers will divide into

LCM is the abbreviation for **LEAST COMMON MULTIPLE**. The least common multiple of a group of numbers is the smallest number that all of the given numbers will divide into. The least common multiple is always the largest of the given numbers or a multiple of the largest number.

Example: Find the LCM of 20, 30, and 40.

The largest number given is 40, but 30 will not divide evenly into 40. The next multiple of 40 is 80 (2×40), but 30 will not divide evenly into 80 either. The next multiple of 40 is 120. 120 is divisible by both 20 and 30, so 120 is the LCM (least common multiple).

Different Representations of Rational Numbers

Rational numbers can be written using several different representations, including fractions, decimals, percents, and exponents.

In order to express a fraction as a decimal or percentage, convert it into an equivalent fraction with a denominator that is a power of 10 (for example, 10, 100, or 1000).

Example: $\frac{1}{10} = 0.10 = 10\%$

Alternatively, a fraction can be converted into a decimal by dividing the numerator by the denominator.

Example: $\frac{3}{8} = 8\overline{)3.000}^{\,0.375} = 37.5\%$

A decimal can be converted to a percentage by multiplying by 100, or merely moving the decimal point two places to the right, as shown in the examples above.

A percentage can be converted to a decimal by dividing by 100, or moving the decimal point two places to the left.

A percentage can be converted to a fraction by placing it over 100 and reducing to simplest terms.

The exponent form is a shortcut way of writing repeated multiplication. The base is the factor. The **EXPONENT** tells how many times that number is multiplied by itself.

EXPONENT: a number that tells how many times the base is multiplied by itself

Example: $3^4 = 3 \times 3 \times 3 \times 3 = 81$
where 3 is the base and 4 is the exponent.

When 10 is raised to any power, the exponent indicates the number of zeroes in the product.

When 10 is raised to any power, the exponent indicates the number of zeroes in the product.

Example: $10^7 = 10{,}000{,}000$

Different Representations of Real Numbers

Real numbers can be represented in a variety of formats. Some of these formats are more amenable to certain situations than others, and it is important to be able to select the proper representation of a real number for a given situation.

For instance, if exact calculations are required, decimal representations (or percent representations, which are simply the decimal representation multiplied by 100) of irrational numbers are not appropriate. The use of a decimal necessarily requires use of a finite representation; thus, the decimal form of an irrational number must be rounded to some digit, leading to inaccuracies in calculations. In other cases, such as when calculating with very large or very small numbers, an exponential form such as scientific notation is useful.

Visual Representations of Numbers and Algorithms

Numbers need not be represented exclusively as standard Arabic numerals. They can be represented by:

- Shaded regions (to represent either a whole number or a fraction)
- Fraction strips

Concrete and visual representations can help demonstrate the logic behind operational algorithms.

- Number lines
- Diagrams (one type of diagram involves a particular number of objects of the same type to represent a number)

Concrete examples are real-world applications of mathematical concepts. For example, measuring the shadow produced by a tree or building is a real-world application of trigonometric functions; acceleration or velocity of a car is an application of derivatives; and finding the volume or area of a swimming pool is a real-world application of geometric principles.

Blocks or other objects modeled on the base-ten system are useful concrete tools. Base-ten blocks represent ones, tens, and hundreds.

Tiles, blocks, or other countable manipulatives such as beans can also be used to demonstrate numbers in base ten or in other bases. Each stack represents a place, with the number of blocks in the stack showing the place value.

Tiles, pattern blocks, or geoboards can be used to demonstrate geometry algorithms for the calculation of quantities such as area and perimeter.

Stacks of blocks representing numbers are useful for teaching basic statistics concepts such as mean, median, and mode. Rearranging the blocks to make each stack the same height demonstrates the mean or average value of the data set.

Percentage calculations can be visualized using two parallel number lines, one showing the actual numbers, the other showing percentages.

Multiplication can be shown using arrays. For instance, 3×4 can be expressed as 3 rows of 4 each.

□□□□
□□□□
□□□□

Fractions can be represented using pattern blocks, fraction bars, or paper folding.

Diagrams of arithmetic operations can present mathematical data in visual form. For example, a number line can be used to add and subtract, as illustrated below.

This number line represents five added to negative four on the number line, or $-4 + 5 = 1$.

Counting Techniques

Counting sequences of numbers

It is easy enough to count a list of numbers that starts with one and increases in increments of one (e.g., 1, 2, 3, … 18), but how about a list such as 12, 13, 14, … 34 or 4, 8, 12, … 68? How can one determine how many numbers there are in each of those lists without actually counting each one of them?

In the first case, try subtracting 11 from each number in the list:

$12 - 11, 13 - 11, 14 - 11, \ldots. 34 - 11$

This leads to the list 1, 2, 3, … 23 and it is clear that the number of terms in that list is 23.

In general, for a list of numbers that goes from x to y, subtract $x - 1$ from each number. Thus, the total number of items in the list is $y - (x - 1) = y - x + 1$.

In the second case, try dividing each number in the list by 4. Thus 4, 8, 12, … 68 becomes 1, 2, 3, …17 and it is obvious that there are seventeen numbers in that list.

Counting overlapping lists

The classic method for solving problems with overlapping lists is using Venn diagrams that make it easy to visualize the overlapping and nonoverlapping parts.

The classic method for solving problems with overlapping lists is using Venn diagrams that make it easy to visualize the overlapping and nonoverlapping parts.

Counting multiple independent events

A familiar type of counting problem is one in which the total number of possibilities of combining independent events is counted.

Example: Emma has 7 skirts, 5 tops, and 12 scarves. How many different outfits can she create using combinations of one skirt, one top, and one scarf?

Emma can select a skirt in 7 ways, a top in 5 ways, and a scarf in 12 ways.

Hence, the total number of possible combinations is the product of the possible choices in each category: $7 \times 5 \times 12 = 420$.

Permutations and combinations

A **PERMUTATION** is one of a number of possible selections of items, without repetition, where order of selection is important.

PERMUTATION: one of a number of possible selections of items, without repetition, where order of selection is important

COMBINATION: one of a number of possible selections, without repetition, where order of selection is not important

A **COMBINATION** is one of a number of possible selections, without repetition, where order of selection is not important.

Example: If any two numbers are selected from the set {1, 2, 3, 4}, list the possible permutations and combinations.

Combinations	**Permutations**
12, 13, 14, 23, 24, 34	12, 21, 13, 31, 14, 41,
	23, 32, 24, 42, 34, 43,
(six combinations)	(twelve permutations)

The formula for $_nP_r$, the number of possible permutations of r objects selected from n objects, is:

$$_nP_r = n(n-1)(n-2)\ldots(n-r+1) = \frac{n!}{(n-r)!}$$

The formula for the number of possible combinations of r objects selected from n, $_nC_r$, is:

$$_nC_r = \frac{_nP_r}{r!} = \frac{n!}{(n-r)!r!}$$

The number of permutations of n objects in a ring is given by $(n-1)!$.

Place Value

Whole-number place value

Consider the number 792. We can assign a place value to each digit. There are 7 sets of 100, plus 9 sets of 10, plus 2 ones in the number 792.

Decimal place value

More complex numbers have additional place values to both the left and right of the decimal point. Consider the number 374.8. The number after the decimal (8) is in the tenths place and tells us that the number contains 8 tenths.

Place value for older students

Each digit to the left of the decimal point increases progressively in powers of ten. Each digit to the right of the decimal point decreases progressively in powers of ten.

Each digit to the left of the decimal point increases progressively in powers of ten. Each digit to the right of the decimal point decreases progressively in powers often.

Example: 12345.6789 occupies the following powers-of-ten positions:

10^4	10^3	10^2	10^1	10^0	0	10^{-1}	10^{-2}	10^{-3}	10^{-4}
1	2	3	4	5	.	6	7	8	9

Rounding Numbers

Whole numbers

To round whole numbers, first find the place value to which you want to round (the rounding digit) and look at the digit directly to its right. If the digit is less than five, do not change the rounding digit and replace all numbers after the rounding digit with zeroes. If the digit is greater than or equal to five, increase the rounding digit by one and replace all numbers after the rounding digit with zeroes.

Example: Round 517 to the nearest ten.
1 is the rounding digit because it occupies the tens place.
517 rounded to the nearest ten = 520; because $7 > 5$, we add one to the rounding digit.

Decimals

Rounding decimals is the same as rounding whole numbers except that you simply drop all of the digits to the right of the rounding digit.

Example: Round 417.3621 to the nearest tenth.
3 is the rounding digit because it occupies the tenths place.
417.3621 rounded to the nearest tenth = 417.4; because $6 > 5$, we add one to the rounding digit.

PATTERNS AND ALGEBRA

Visual Representations of Functions

The relationship between two or more variables can be analyzed using a table, graph, written description, or symbolic rule. The function $y = 2x + 1$ is written as a symbolic rule. The same relationship is also shown in the table below:

x	0	2	3	6	9
y	1	5	7	13	19

A relationship could be written in words by saying the value of y is equal to two times the value of x, plus one. This relationship could be shown on a graph by plotting given points, such as the ones shown in the table above.

Representation of a linear function

LINEAR FUNCTION: a function defined by the equation $y = mx + b$

A **LINEAR FUNCTION** is a function defined by the equation $y = mx + b$. It is determined by m, the slope of the line, otherwise known as the rate of change. The slope is constant everywhere on the line.

Example: Consider the function $y = 2x + 1$. This function can be represented as a table of values as well as a graph, as shown below.

x	y
-2	-3
-1	-1
0	1
1	3
2	5

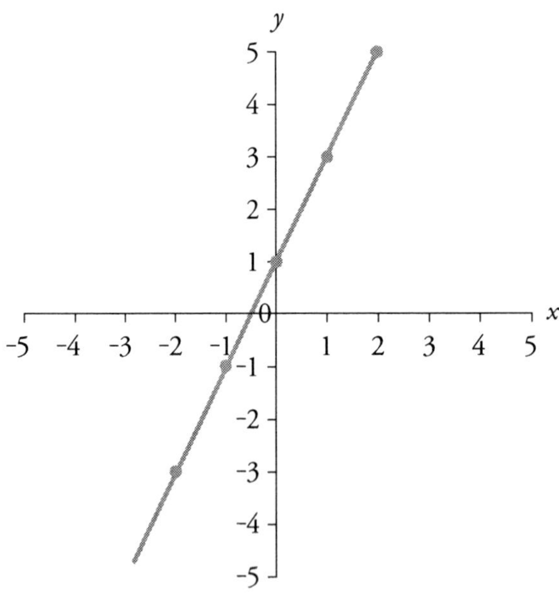

Using Algebra to Make Predictions

Algebraic concepts and reasoning can be used to investigate patterns, make generalizations, formulate models, make predictions, and validate results by providing an organized system by which to display the data. The data can be displayed in various formats, such as tables and graphs, to help define the pattern.

Example: The following table represents the number of problems Mr. Rodgers is assigning his math students for homework each day, starting with the first day of class.

Day	1	2	3	4	5	6	7	8	9	10	11
Number of Problems	1	1	2	3	5	8	13				

If Mr. Rodgers continues this pattern, how many problems will he assign on the eleventh day?

Day 2 = 1 + 0 = 1
Day 3 = 1 + 1 = 2
Day 4 = 2 + 1 = 3
Day 5 = 3 + 2 = 5
Day 6 = 5 + 3 = 8
Day 7 = 8 + 5 = 13

Therefore, Day 8 would have 21 problems; Day 9, 34 problems; Day 10, 55 problems; and Day 11, 89 problems.

Constructing Sequences

A **SEQUENCE** is a pattern of numbers or symbols arranged in a particular order. Examining a sequence sometimes reveals a particular rule that governs the pattern. For instance, the sequence 1, 4, 9, 16, ... consists of the squares of the natural numbers. Using this rule, the next term in the series, 25, can be found by squaring the next natural number, 5.

SEQUENCE: a pattern of numbers or symbols arranged in a particular order

Other patterns can be created using algebraic variables. Patterns can also be pictorial. In each case, one can predict subsequent terms or find a missing term by first discovering the rule that governs the pattern.

In sequences defined with implicit governing rules, the rules have not been stated but can be discovered by studying the patterns. The task in each of the examples is to uncover the explicit rule that governs the sequence.

The most common numerical patterns based on explicit rules are arithmetic sequences and geometric sequences. In an arithmetic sequence, each term is separated from the next by a fixed number (e.g., 3, 6, 9, 12, 15, ...). In a geometric sequence, each term in the series is multiplied by a fixed number to get the next term (e.g., 3, 6, 12, 24, 28, ...)

Arithmetic sequences

ARITHMETIC SEQUENCE: a set of numbers with a common difference between the terms

An **ARITHMETIC SEQUENCE** is a set of numbers with a common difference between the terms. Terms and the distance between terms can be calculated using the following formula:

$a_n = a_1 + (n - 1)d$, where
a_1 = the first term
a_n = the nth term (general term)
n = the number of the term in the sequence
d = the common difference

Example: Find the eighth term of the arithmetic sequence 5, 8, 11, 14, ...

$a_n = a_1 + (n - 1)d$	
$a_1 = 5$	identify the first term
$d = 8 - 5 = 3$	find d
$a_8 = 5 + (8 - 1)3$	substitute
$a_8 = 26$	

Geometric sequences

GEOMETRIC SEQUENCE: a series of numbers in which a common ratio can be multiplied by a term to yield the next term

A **GEOMETRIC SEQUENCE** is a series of numbers in which a common ratio can be multiplied by a term to yield the next term. The common ratio can be calculated using the formula:

$r = \frac{a_{n+1}}{a_n}$, where r = common ratio and a_n = the nth term

The ratio is then used in the geometric sequence formula:

$a_n = a_1 r^{n-1}$

Example: Find the eighth term of the geometric sequence 2, 8, 32, 128, ...

$r = \frac{a_{n+1}}{a_n}$	use common ratio formula to find the ratio
$r = \frac{8}{2}$	substitute $a_n = 2$, $a_{n+1} = 8$
$r = 4$	
$a_n = a_1 \times r^{n-1}$	use $r = 4$ to solve for the eighth term
$a_8 = 2 \times 4^{8-1}$	
$a_8 = 32{,}768$	

Identifying and Creating Patterns

Models

Models are a means of representing mathematical concepts by relating the concepts to real-world situations.

When introducing a new mathematical concept to students, teachers should utilize the concrete-to-representational-to-abstract sequence of instruction. The first step is the introduction of a concept modeled with concrete materials. The second step is the translation of concrete models into representational diagrams or pictures. The third and final step is the translation of representational models into abstract models using only numbers and symbols.

When introducing a new mathematical concept to students, teachers should utilize the concrete-to-representational-to-abstract sequence of instruction.

Example: Kepler discovered a relationship between the average distance of a planet from the Sun and the time it takes the planet to orbit the Sun.
The following table shows the data for the six planets closest to the Sun:

	Mercury	**Venus**	**Earth**	**Mars**	**Jupiter**	**Saturn**
Average distance, x	0.387	0.723	1	1.523	5.203	9.541
x^3	0.058	0.378	1	3.533	140.852	868.524
Time, y	0.241	0.615	1	1.881	11.861	29.457
y^2	0.058	0.378	1	3.538	140.683	867.715

Looking at the data in the table, we see that $x^3 = y^2$. We can conjecture the following function for Kepler's relationship: $y = \sqrt{x^3}$.

Using Algebra to Solve Real-World Problems

Many real-world situations involve linear relationships. One example is the relationship between distance and time traveled when a car is moving at a constant speed. The relationship between the price and quantity of a bulk item purchased at a store is also linear, assuming that the unit price remains constant. These relationships can be expressed using the equation of a straight line, and the slope often describes a constant or average rate of change, expressed in miles per hour or dollars per item, for example.

Example: A man drives a car at a speed of 30 mph along a straight road. Express the distance, d, traveled by the man as a function of the time, t, assuming the man's initial position is d_0. The equation relating d and t is expressed by:

$$d = 30t + d_0$$

Notice that this equation is in the familiar slope-intercept form $y = mx + b$. In this case, the time, t (in hours) is the independent variable, and the distance, d (in miles) is the dependent variable. The slope is the rate of change of distance with time, i.e., the speed (in mph). The y-intercept, or intercept on the distance axis, d_0, represents the initial position of the car at the start time, $t = 0$.

The above equation is plotted below with $d_0 = 15$ miles (the point on the graph where the line crosses the y-axis).

$$d = 30t + 15$$

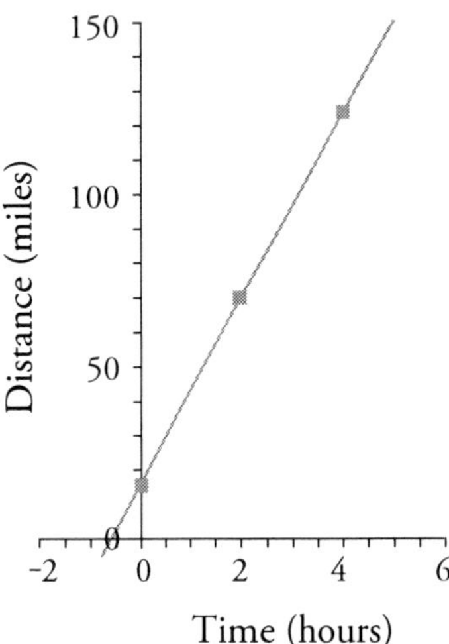

The x-intercept, or intercept on the time axis represents the time at which the car would have been at $d = 0$, assuming it was traveling at the same speed before $t = 0$. This value can be found by setting $d = 0$ in the equation:

$$0 = 30t + 15$$

$$30t = -15$$

$$t = \frac{-15}{30} = -\frac{1}{2} \text{ hr}$$

This simply means that if the car was at $d = 15$ miles when we started measuring the time ($t = 0$), it was at $d = 0$ miles half an hour before that.

Example: A cubic container is modified so that its length is increased by 4 inches and its width is shortened by 2 inches. The height of the container remains unchanged. If the volume of the container is 16 cubic inches, what is its height?

Let the side of the original cube be x inches.

The volume of the modified container is given by

$$x(x + 4)(x - 2) = 16$$

Distributing and rearranging, we get

$$x(x^2 + 2x - 8) = 16$$

$$\rightarrow x^3 + 2x^2 - 8x - 16 = 0$$

The third-order polynomial equation above can be grouped and factored as follows:

$$x^2(x + 2) - 8(x + 2) = 0$$
$$\rightarrow (x + 2)(x^2 - 8) = 0$$

The solutions to the equation are, therefore, $x = -2, \pm 2\sqrt{2}$.

Since the height of the box must be a positive number, we choose the positive solution. Thus the height is $2\sqrt{2}$ inches.

Using proportions to solve problems

A **PROPORTION** is an equation in which a fraction is set equal to another. To solve the proportion, multiply each numerator by the other fraction's denominator. Set these two products equal to each other and solve the resulting equation. This is called cross-multiplying the proportion.

PROPORTION: an equation in which a fraction is set equal to another

Proportions can be used to solve word problems whenever relationships are compared; for example, in situations involving scale drawings and maps, similar polygons, speed, time and distance, cost, or comparison shopping.

Example: Which is the better buy, six items for $1.29 or eight items for $1.69?

Find the unit cost.

$\frac{6}{1.29} = \frac{1}{x}$	$\frac{8}{1.69} = \frac{1}{x}$
$6x = 1.29$	$8x = 1.69$
$x = 0.215$	$x = 0.21125$

Thus, eight items for $1.69 is the better buy.

Using linear systems of equations and inequalities

Problems with more than one unknown quantity can be modeled and solved using linear systems of equations and inequalities. Some examples are given below.

Example: Farmer Greenjeans bought four cows and six sheep for $1700. Mr. Ziffel bought three cows and twelve sheep for $2400. If all of the cows were the same price and all of the sheep were another price, find the price charged for a cow and the price charged for a sheep.

Let x = price of a cow
Let y = price of a sheep

Farmer Greenjeans's equation would be: $4x + 6y = 1700$

Mr. Ziffel's equation would be: $3x + 12y = 2400$

To solve by addition-subtraction:

Multiply the first equation by -2: $-2(4x + 6y = 1700)$

Keep the other equation the same: $(3x + 12y = 2400)$

By doing this, the equations can be added to each other to eliminate one variable and solve for the other variable.

$$
\begin{array}{rcl}
-8x - 12y &=& -3400 \\
\underline{3x + 12y} &=& \underline{2400} \\
-5x &=& -1000 \\
x &=& 200
\end{array}
$$

Add these equations.

$x = 200 \leftarrow$ the price of a cow was \$200.

Solving for y, $y = 150 \leftarrow$ the price of a sheep was \$150

LINEAR PROGRAMMING: the optimization of a linear quantity that is subject to constraints expressed as linear equations or inequalities

LINEAR PROGRAMMING is the optimization of a linear quantity that is subject to constraints expressed as linear equations or inequalities.

Example: Sharon's Bike Shoppe can assemble a 3-speed bike in 30 minutes and a 10-speed bike in 60 minutes. The profit on each bike sold is \$60.00 for a 3-speed bike and \$75.00 for a 10-speed bike. How many of each type of bike should the shop assemble during an 8-hour day (480 minutes) to maximize its possible profit? Total daily profit must be at least \$300.00.

Let x be the number of 3-speed bikes and y be the number of 10-speed bikes. Since there are only 480 minutes to use each day, the first inequality is the following:

$$30x + 60y \leq 480$$
$$x + 2y \leq 16$$

Since the total daily profit must be at least \$300.00, then the second inequality can be written as follows, where P is the profit for the day.

$$P = \$60x + \$75y \geq \$300$$
$$4x + 5y \geq 20$$

To visualize the problem, plot the two inequalities and show the potential solutions as a shaded region.

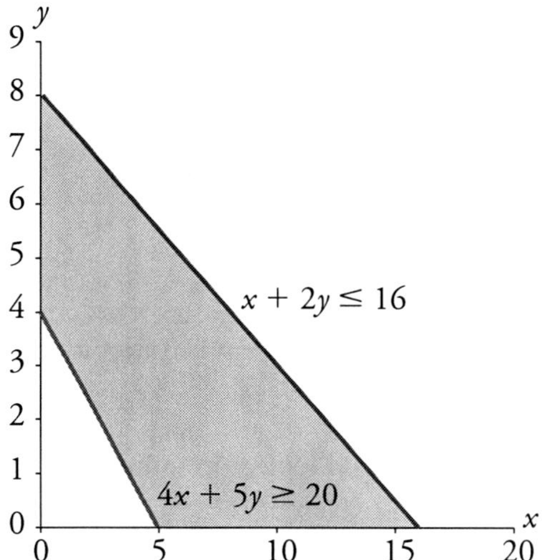

The solution to the problem is the ordered pair of whole numbers in the shaded area that maximizes the daily profit. The profit curve is added as shown below.

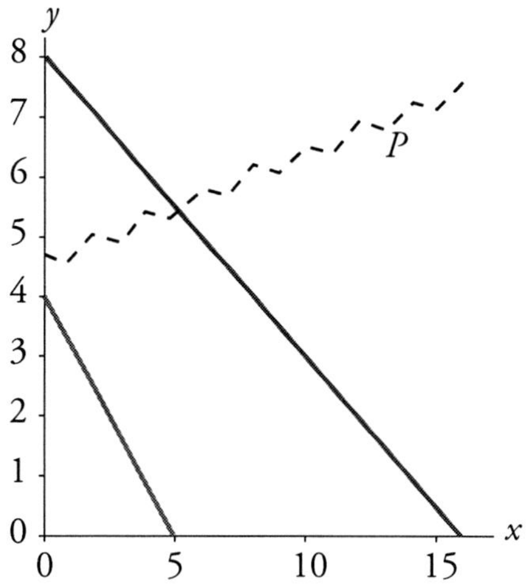

Based on the plot, it is clear that the profit is maximized for the case in which only 3-speed bikes (corresponding to x) are assembled. Thus, the correct solution can be found by solving the first inequality for $y = 0$.

$$x + 2(0) \leq 16$$
$$x \leq 16$$

Assembling sixteen 3-speed bikes (and no 10-speed bikes) maximizes profit to $960.00 per day.

GEOMETRY AND MEASUREMENT

Spatial Concepts

The five regular solids, or **polyhedra**, *are the cube, tetrahedron, octahedron, icosahedron, and dodecahedron.*

The union of all points on a simple closed surface and all points in its interior form a space figure called a **solid**.

NET: a two-dimensional figure that can be cut out and folded up to make a three-dimensional solid

A **NET** is a two-dimensional figure that can be cut out and folded up to make a three-dimensional solid.

Cube 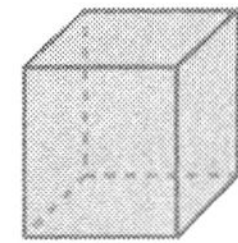 6 squares 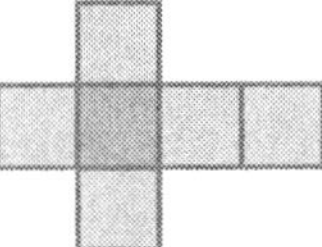

Tetrahedron 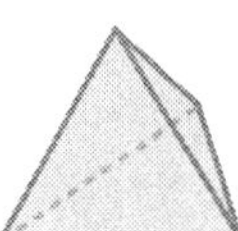 4 equilateral triangles 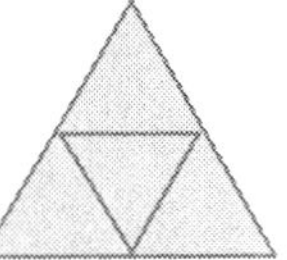

CONGRUENT FIGURES: figures that have the same size and shape

CONGRUENT FIGURES have the same size and shape. The symbol for congruence is ≅.

Polygons (pentagons) *ABCDE* and *VWXYZ* are congruent. They are exactly the same size and shape.

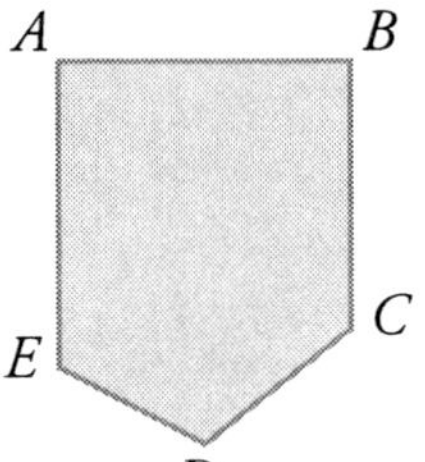

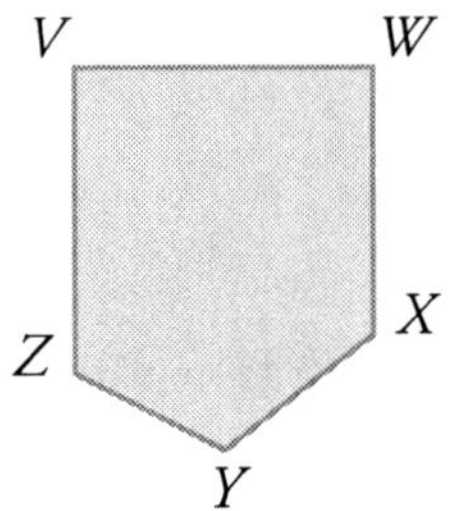

Perimeter, Area, and Volume

PERIMETER: the sum of the lengths of the sides of the figure

AREA: the number of square units covered by the figure

Perimeter and area

The **PERIMETER** of any polygon is the sum of the lengths of the sides of the figure. The **AREA** of a polygon is the number of square units covered by the figure.

Figure	Area Formula	Perimeter Formula
Rectangle	LW	$2(L + W)$
Triangle	$\frac{1}{2}bh$	$a + b + c$
Parallelogram	bh	sum of lengths of sides
Trapezoid	$\frac{1}{2}h(a + b)$	sum of lengths of sides

Example: Find the area of this trapezoid.

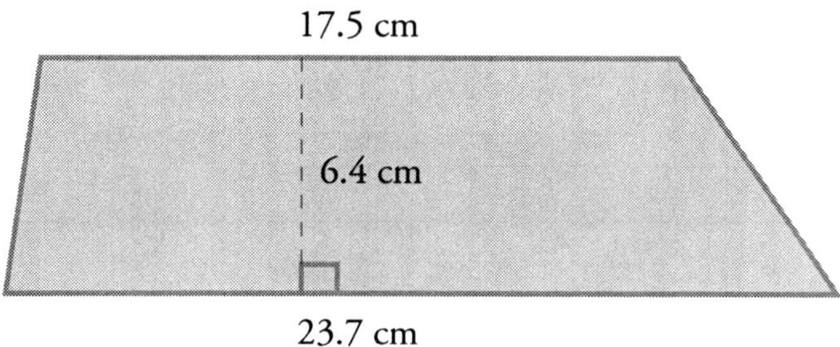

The area of a trapezoid equals one-half the sum of the bases times the altitude.

$$\begin{aligned} Atrapezoid &= \tfrac{1}{2}h(b_1 + b_2) \\ &= 0.5(6.4)(17.5 + 23.7) \\ &= 131.84 \text{ cm} \end{aligned}$$

Volume and surface area

Figure	Volume	Total Surface Area
Right cylinder	$\pi r^2 h$	$2\pi rh + 2\pi r^2$
Right cone	$\frac{\pi r^2 h}{3}$	$\pi r\sqrt{r^2 + h^2} + \pi r^2$
Sphere	$\frac{4}{3}\pi r^3$	$4\pi r^2$
Rectangular solid	LHW	$2LW + 2WH + 2LH$

Figure	Lateral Area	Total Area	Volume
Regular pyramid	$\frac{1}{2}Pl$	$\frac{1}{2}Pl + B$	$\frac{1}{3}Bh$
P = perimeter, h = height, B = area of base, l = slant height			

Example: How much material is needed to make a basketball that has a diameter of 15 inches? How much air is needed to fill the basketball?
Draw and label a sketch:

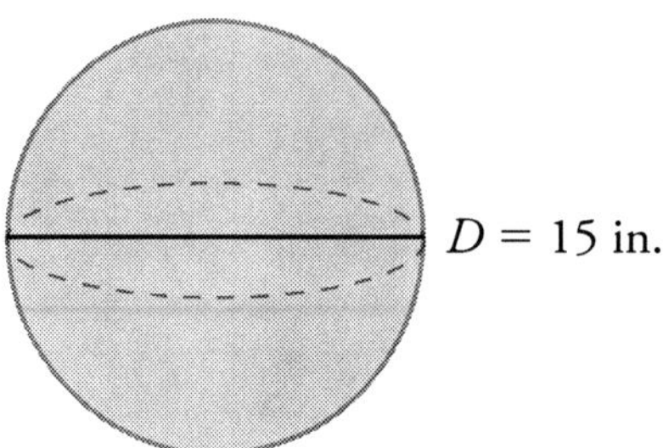

Total Surface Area	Volume	
$\text{TSA} = 4\pi r^2$	$V = \frac{4}{3}\pi r^3$	1. Write formula
$= 4\pi(7.5)^2$	$= \frac{4}{3}\pi(7.5)^3$	2. Substitute
$= 706.8 \text{ in}^2$	$= 1767.1 \text{ in}^3$	3. Solve

Properties of Congruent Triangles

Two triangles are congruent if each of the three angles and three sides of one triangle correspond in a one-to-one fashion with the angles and sides of the second triangle.

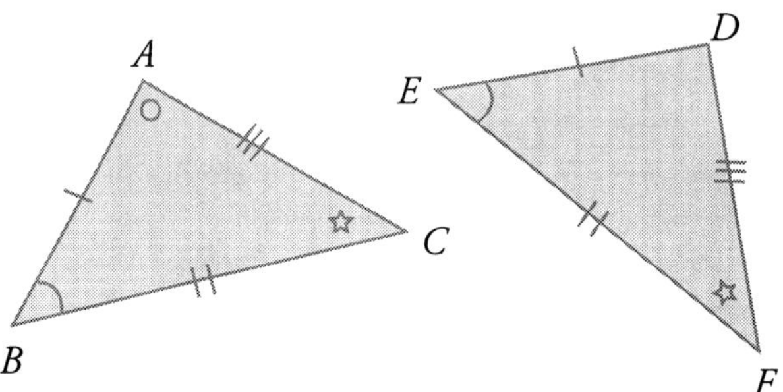

In the example above, the two triangles *ABC* and *DEF* are congruent if these six conditions are met:

1. $\angle A \cong \angle D$
2. $\angle B \cong \angle E$
3. $\angle C \cong \angle F$
4. $\overline{AB} \cong \overline{DE}$
5. $\overline{BC} \cong \overline{EF}$
6. $\overline{AC} \cong \overline{DF}$

SAS Postulate

SAS Postulate (side-angle-side): If two sides and the included angle of one triangle are congruent to two sides and the included angle of another triangle, then the two triangles are congruent.

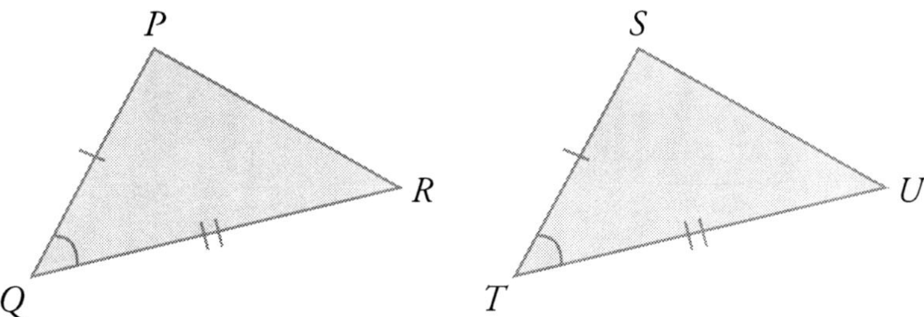

SSS Postulate

SSS Postulate (side-side-side): If three sides of one triangle are congruent to three sides of another triangle, then the two triangles are congruent.

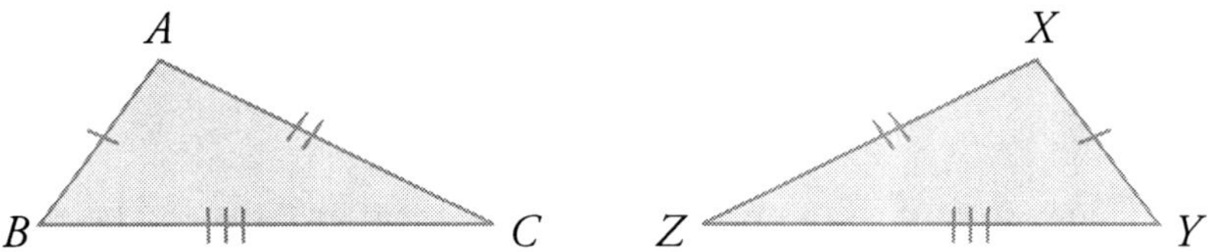

Since $AB \cong XY$, $BC \cong YZ$, and $AC \cong XZ$, then $\Delta ABC \cong \Delta XYZ$.

ASA Postulate

ASA Postulate (angle-side-angle): If two angles and the included side of one triangle are congruent to two angles and the included side of another triangle, the triangles are congruent.

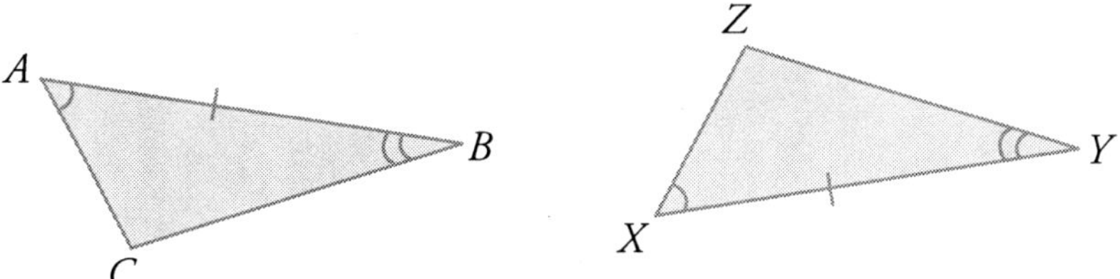

Since $\angle A \cong \angle X$, $\angle \mathrm{B} \cong \angle Y$, $AB \cong XY$, then $\Delta ABC \cong \Delta XYZ$.

HL Theorem

HL Theorem (hypotenuse-leg): A congruence shortcut that can only be used with right triangles. According to this theorem, if the hypotenuse and leg of one right triangle are congruent to the hypotenuse and leg of another right triangle, then the two triangles are congruent.

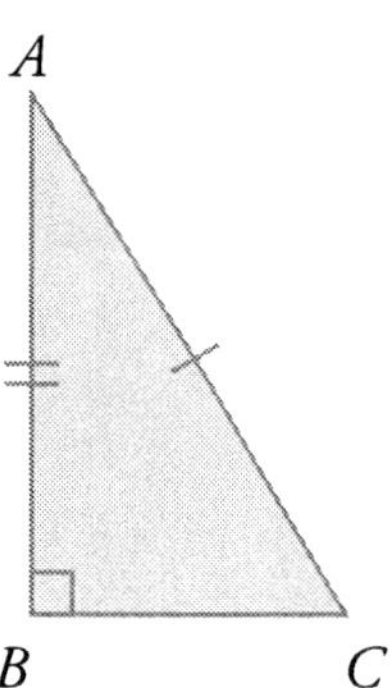

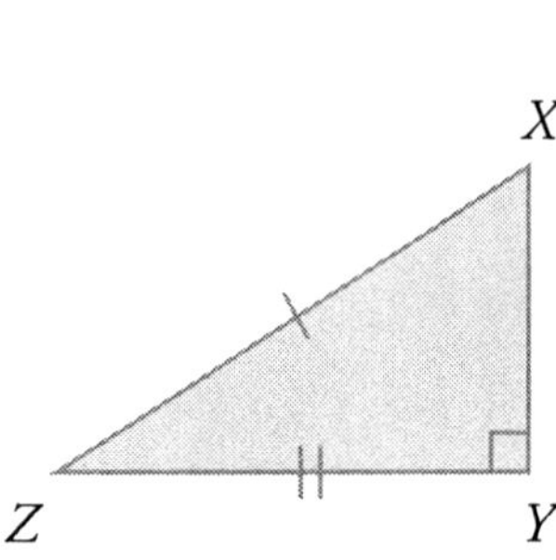

If $\angle B$ and $\angle Y$ are right angles and $AC \cong XZ$ (hypotenuse of each triangle), then $AB \cong YZ$ (corresponding leg of each triangle), and $\Delta ABC \cong \Delta XYZ$.

Points, Lines, Angles, and Planes

POINT: a dimensionless location with no length, width, or height

LINE: connects a series of points and continues "straight" infinitely in two directions

LINE SEGMENT: a portion of a line

RAY: a portion of a line that has only one end point and continues infinitely in one direction

A **POINT** is a dimensionless location with no length, width, or height.

A **LINE** connects a series of points and continues "straight" infinitely in two directions.

A **LINE SEGMENT** is a portion of a line. Because line segments have two end points, they have a defined length or distance.

A **RAY** is a portion of a line that has only one end point and continues infinitely in one direction.

An **angle** is formed by the intersection of two rays.

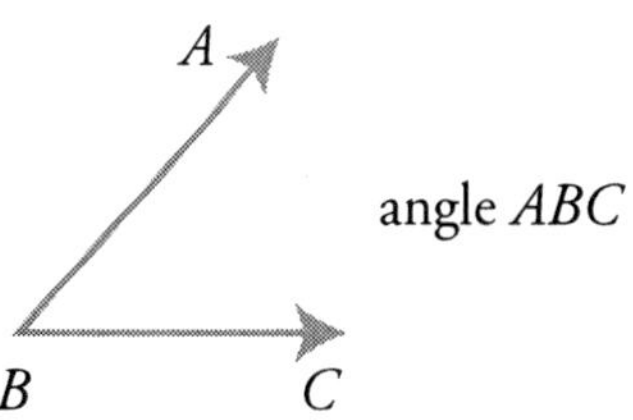

angle *ABC*

Angles are measured in degrees. $1° = \frac{1}{360}$ of a circle.

A **right angle** measures 90°.

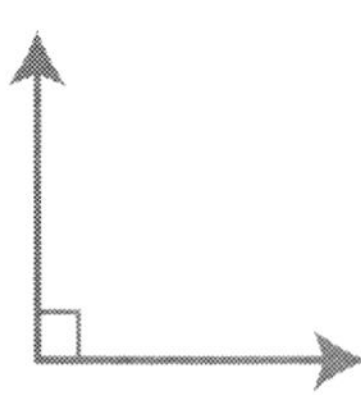

An **acute angle** measures more than 0° and less than 90°. An **obtuse angle** measures more than 90° and less than 180°. A straight angle measures 180°. A **reflexive angle** measures more than 180° and less than 360°.

A **PLANE** is a flat surface defined by three points. Planes extend indefinitely in two dimensions.

PLANE: a flat surface defined by three points; planes extend indefinitely in two dimensions

Parallel and perpendicular lines

PARALLEL LINES in two dimensions can be defined as lines that do not intersect.

PARALLEL LINES: lines that do not intersect

Two lines are **PERPENDICULAR** in two or three dimensions if they intersect at a point and form 90° angles between them.

PERPENDICULAR LINES: lines that intersect at a point and form 90° angles

Properties of parallel lines

The parallel postulate in Euclidean planar geometry states that if a line, *l*, is crossed by two other lines, *m* and *n* (where the crossings are not at the same point on *l*), then *m* and *n* intersect on the side of *l* where the sum of the interior angles α and β is less than 180°.

This implies that if α and β are both 90° and, therefore, $\alpha + \beta = 180°$, then the lines do not intersect on either side. This is illustrated below.

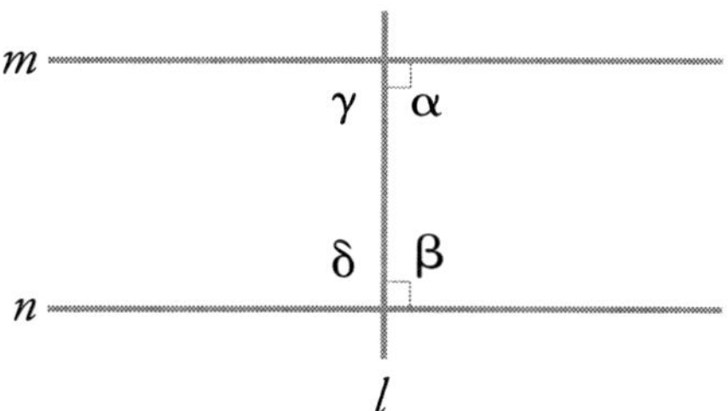

Let the nonintersecting lines *m* and *n* used in the above discussion remain parallel, but adjust *l* such that the interior angles are no longer right angles.

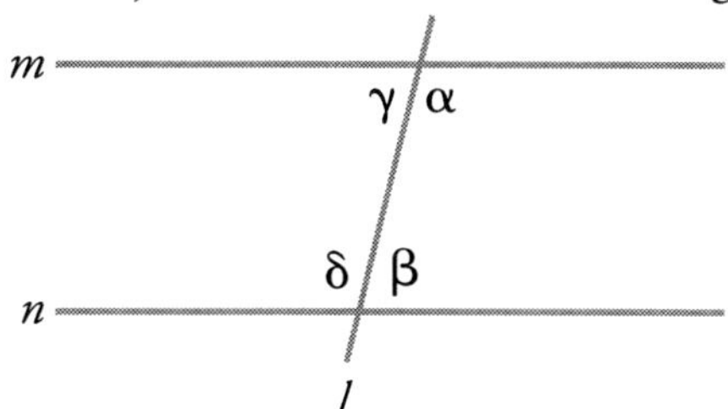

The parallel postulate still applies, and it is therefore still the case that $\alpha + \beta = 180°$ and $\gamma + \delta = 180°$. Combined with the fact that $\alpha + \gamma = 180°$ and $\beta + \delta = 180°$, the alternate interior angle theorem can be justified. This theorem states that if two parallel lines are cut by a transversal, the alternate interior angles are congruent.

One of the consequences of the parallel postulate, in addition to the alternate interior angle theorem, is that corresponding angles are equal. If two parallel lines are cut by a transversal line, then the corresponding angles are equal. The diagram

If two parallel lines are cut by a transversal line, then the corresponding angles are equal.

below illustrates one set of corresponding angles (α and β) for the parallel lines m and n cut by l.

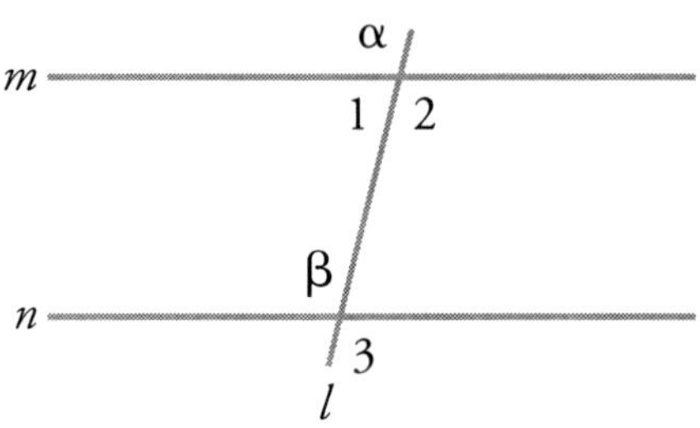

Polygons

POLYGON: a simple closed figure composed of line segments

A **POLYGON** is a simple closed figure composed of line segments. A regular polygon is one for which all sides are the same length and all interior angles are the same measure.

The sum of the measures of the interior angles of a polygon can be determined using the following formula, where n represents the number of angles in the polygon.

Sum of $\angle s = 180(n - 2)$

The sum of the measures of the exterior angles of a polygon, taken one angle at each vertex, equals 360°.

QUADRILATERAL: a polygon with four sides

A **QUADRILATERAL** is a polygon with four sides. The sum of the measures of the angles of a convex quadrilateral is 360°.

TRAPEZOID: a quadrilateral with *one* pair of parallel sides

A **TRAPEZOID** is a quadrilateral with *one* pair of parallel sides.

The two parallel sides of a trapezoid are called the bases, and the two nonparallel sides are called the legs.

In an isosceles trapezoid, the nonparallel sides are congruent.

PARALLELOGRAM: a quadrilateral with *two* pairs of parallel sides

A **PARALLELOGRAM** is a quadrilateral with *two* pairs of parallel sides and has the following properties:

1. The diagonals bisect each other.
2. Each diagonal divides the parallelogram into two congruent triangles.

3. Both pairs of opposite sides are congruent.
4. Both pairs of opposite angles are congruent.
5. Two adjacent angles are supplementary.

Circles

The distance around the perimeter of a circle is the **CIRCUMFERENCE**. The ratio of the circumference to the diameter is represented by the Greek letter pi (π), where $\pi \cong 3.14$. The circumference of a circle is expressed by the formula $C = 2\pi r$ or $C = \pi d$, where r is the radius of the circle and d is the diameter. The area of a circle is expressed by the formula $A = \pi r^2$.

CIRCUMFERENCE: The distance around the perimeter of a circle

If you draw two radii in a circle, the angle they form with the center as the vertex is a central angle. The measure of an arc is equal to the measure of the central angle that forms the arc.

Given two points on a circle, the two points form two different arcs. The arc that measures less than 180° is a minor arc and the arc that measures more than 180° is a major arc.

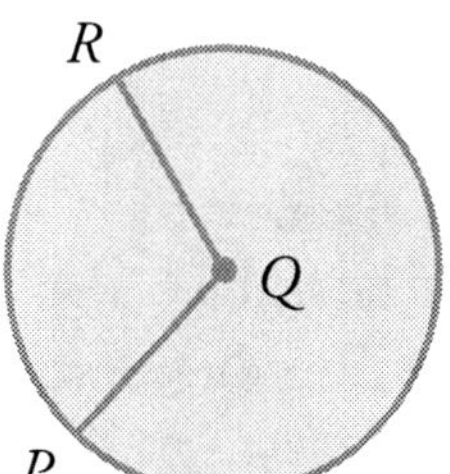

$$\frac{\angle PQR}{360°} = \frac{\text{length of arc } RP}{\text{circumference of circle}} = \frac{\text{area of sector } PQR}{\text{area of circle}}$$

Three-Dimensional Figures

Similar solids share the same shape but are not necessarily the same size. The ratio of any two corresponding measurements of similar solids is the scale factor. For example, the scale factor for two square pyramids, one with a side measuring 2 inches and the other with a side measuring 4 inches, is 2:4.

If the scale factor of two similar solids is $a{:}b$, then

ratio of base perimeters $= a{:}b$
ratio of areas $= a^2{:}b^2$
ratio of volumes $= a^3{:}b^3$

Tessellations

TRANSFORMATIONAL GEOMETRY: the study of manipulating objects by flipping, twisting, turning, and scaling

SYMMETRY: exact correspondence between two parts or halves, as if one were a mirror image of the other

TESSELLATION: an arrangement of closed shapes that completely covers a plane without overlapping or leaving gaps

A transformation is a change in the position, shape, or size of a geometric figure. **TRANSFORMATIONAL GEOMETRY** is the study of manipulating objects by flipping, twisting, turning, and scaling. **SYMMETRY** is exact correspondence between two parts or halves, as if one were a mirror image of the other.

A **TESSELLATION** is an arrangement of closed shapes that completely covers a plane without overlapping or leaving gaps. Unlike tilings, tessellations do not require the use of regular polygons. In art, the term *tessellation* is used to refer to pictures or tiles, mostly in the form of animals and other life forms, that cover the surface of a plane in a symmetrical way without overlapping or leaving gaps. M.C. Escher is known as the "father" of modern tessellations. Tessellations are used for tiling, mosaics, quilts, and other art forms.

There are four basic transformational symmetries that can be used in tessellations:

- Translation
- Rotation
- Reflection
- Glide reflection

A translation is a transformation that "slides" an object a fixed distance in a given direction. An example of a translation in architecture would be stadium seating. The seats are the same size and the same shape and face in the same direction.

A rotation is a transformation that turns a figure around a fixed point called the center of rotation.

An object and its reflection have the same shape and size, but the figures face in opposite directions. The line where a mirror can be placed is called the line of reflection.

A glide reflection is a combination of a reflection and a translation.

Dilation is a transformation that shrinks a figure or makes it bigger.

Estimation and Measurement

One must be familiar with the metric and U.S. customary systems in order to estimate measurements.

COMMON EQUIVALENTS		
ITEM	**APPROXIMATELY EQUAL TO**	
	Metric	**Imperial**
Large paper clip	1 gram	1 ounce
1 quart	1 liter	
Average-size man	75 kilograms	170 pounds
1 yard	1 meter	
Math textbook	1 kilogram	2 pounds
1 mile	1.6 kilometers	
1 foot	30 centimeters	
Thickness of a dime	1 millimeter	0.1 inches

Estimating height: The most effective method of estimating height is to compare the height of an object to an object of known height.

Estimating distance: An effective method of estimating short distances is "stepping off," or "pacing."

Estimating perimeter: We can estimate the perimeter of geometric shapes by estimating the length of one portion of the shape (e.g., the side of a polygon).

Any measurement you get with a measuring device is approximate.

Precision and accuracy

PRECISION is an indication of how exact a measurement is, without reference to a true or real value. If a measurement is precise, it can be made again and again with little variation in the result.

ACCURACY is a measure of how close the result of measurement comes to the true value.

If you are throwing darts, the true value is the bull's eye. If all three darts land on the bull's eye, the dart thrower is both precise (all land near the same spot) and accurate (the darts all land on the true value).

PRECISION: an indication of how exact a measurement is, without reference to a true or real value

ACCURACY: a measure of how close the result of measurement comes to the true value

Metric system

The basic unit of **length** is the meter. One meter is approximately one yard.

The basic unit of **weight** or mass is the gram. A paper clip weighs about one gram.

The basic unit of **volume** is the liter. One liter is approximately one quart.

MOST COMMONLY USED UNITS	
1 m = 100 cm	1000 mL = 1 L
1 m = 1000 mm	1 kL = 1000 L
1 cm = 10 mm	1000 mg = 1 g
1000 m = 1 km	1 kg = 1000 g

U.S. system

UNITS OF LENGTH ARE INCHES, FEET, YARDS, AND MILES		
12 inches (in.)	=	1 foot (ft.)
36 in.	=	1 yard (yd.)
3 ft.	=	1 yd.
5,280 ft.	=	1 mile (mi.)
760 yd.	=	1 mi.

To change from a larger unit to a smaller unit, multiply.

To change from a smaller unit to a larger unit, divide.

UNITS OF WEIGHT ARE OUNCES, POUNDS, AND TONS		
16 ounces (oz.)	=	1 pound (lb.)
2,000 lb.	=	1 ton (T.)

UNITS OF CAPACITY ARE FLUID OUNCES, CUPS, PINTS, QUARTS, AND GALLONS		
8 fluid ounces (fl. oz.)	=	1 cup (c.)
2 c.	=	1 pint (pt.)
4 c.	=	1 quart (qt.)
2 pt.	=	1 qt.
4 qt.	=	1 gallon (gal.)

Conversions Between Measurement Systems

CONVERSION OF LENGTH FROM ENGLISH TO METRIC		
1 inch	≈	2.54 centimeters
1 foot	≈	30 centimeters
1 yard	≈	0.9 meters
1 mile	≈	1.6 kilometers

CONVERSION OF WEIGHT FROM ENGLISH TO METRIC		
1 ounce	≈	28 grams
1 pound	≈	0.45 kilogram ≈ 454 grams

CONVERSION OF VOLUME FROM ENGLISH TO METRIC		
1 teaspoon (tsp.)	≈	5 milliliters
1 fluid ounce	≈	15 milliliters
1 cup	≈	0.24 liters
1 pint	≈	0.47 liters
1 quart	≈	0.95 liters
1 gallon	≈	3.8 liters

Proving Geometric Relationships

THEOREMS: mathematical statements that can be proven to be true based on postulates, definitions, algebraic properties, given information, and previously proved theorems

THEOREMS are mathematical statements that can be proven to be true based on postulates, definitions, algebraic properties, given information, and previously proved theorems.

The following algebraic postulates are frequently used as reasons for statements in two-column geometric properties:

Addition Property	If $a = b$ and $c = d$, then $a + c = b + d$.
Subtraction Property	If $a = b$ and $c = d$, then $a - c = b - d$.
Multiplication Property	If $a = b$ and $c \neq 0$, then $ac = bc$.
Division Property	If $a = b$ and $c \neq 0$, then $\frac{a}{c} = \frac{b}{c}$.
Reflexive Property	$a = a$
Symmetric Property	If $a = b$, then $b = a$.
Transitive Property	If $a = b$ and $b = c$, then $a = c$.
Distributive Property	$a(b + c) = ab + ac$
Substitution Property	If $a = b$, then b can be substituted for a in any other expression (a can also be substituted for b).

PROBABILITY AND STATISTICS

Displaying Data in Different Formats

Basic statistical concepts can be conveyed without the need for computation. For example, inferences can be drawn from a graph or statistical data.

Example: Graph the following information using a line graph.
The number of National Merit finalists in each school year.

	90–91	91–92	92–93	93–94	94–95	95–96
Central	3	5	1	4	6	8
Wilson	4	2	3	2	3	2

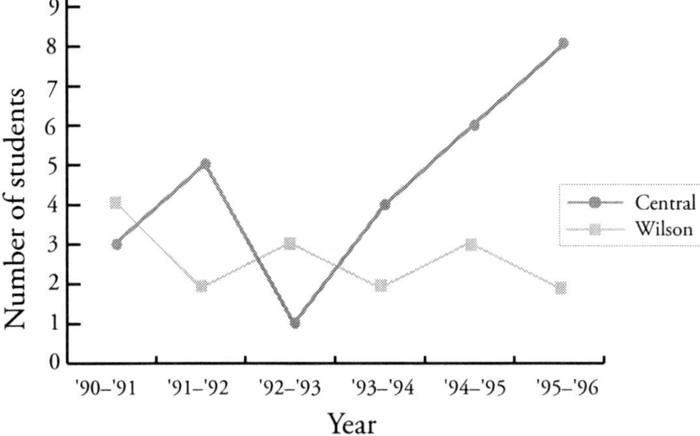

Scatter plots compare two characteristics of the same group of things or people and usually consist of a large body of data. They show how much one variable is affected by another. The relationship between the two variables is their correlation. The closer the data points come to making a straight line when plotted, the closer the correlation.

Measures of Central Tendency and Spread

Measures of central tendency define the center of a data set, and measures of dispersion define the amount of spread.

MEAN: the average value of a data set

MEDIAN: the middle value of a data set

MODE: the value that appears most often in a data set

The most common measures of central tendency that define the center of a data set are mean, median, and mode. The **MEAN** is the average value of a data set; the **MEDIAN** is the middle value of a data set; and the **MODE** is the value that appears most often in a data set. The mean is the most descriptive value for tightly clustered data with few outliers. Outlier data, values in a data set that are unusually high or low, can greatly distort the mean. The median, on the other hand, may better describe widely dispersed data and data sets with outliers because outliers and dispersion have little effect on the median value.

RANGE: the difference between the highest and lowest values in a data set

VARIANCE: the average squared distance from each value of a data set to the mean

STANDARD DEVIATION: the square root of the variance

The most common measures of spread that define the dispersion of a data set are range, variance, standard deviation, and quantiles. The **RANGE** is the difference between the highest and lowest values in a data set. The **VARIANCE** is the average squared distance from each value of a data set to the mean. The **STANDARD DEVIATION** is the square root of the variance. A data set clustered around the center has a small variance and standard deviation, while a dispersed data set with many gaps has a large variance and standard deviation. Quantiles or percentiles divide a data set into equal sections.

Data Collection, Experiments, and Simulations

SAMPLE STATISTICS: important generalizations about the entire sample, such as mean, median, mode, range, and sampling error (standard deviation)

SAMPLE STATISTICS are important generalizations about the entire sample, such as mean, median, mode, range, and sampling error (standard deviation).

Sample size is one important factor in the accuracy and reliability of sample statistics. As sample size increases, sampling error (standard deviation) decreases. Sampling error is the main determinant of the size of the confidence interval. Confidence intervals decrease in size as sample size increases. A confidence interval gives an estimated range of values, which is likely to include a particular population parameter.

The law of large numbers states that the larger the sample size, or the more times we measure a variable in a population, the closer the sample mean will be to the population mean.

The central limit theorem states that as the number of samples increases, the distribution of sample means (averages) approaches a normal distribution.

Basic Principles of Probability

PROBABILITY: the chance of an event occurring

PROBABILITY measures the chance of an event occurring. The probability of an event that must occur, a certain event, is one. When no outcome is favorable, the probability of an impossible event is zero.

$$P(\text{event}) = \frac{\text{number of favorable outcomes}}{\text{number of total outcomes}}$$

A simple event is one that describes a single outcome, whereas a compound event is made up of two or more simple events. The following discussion uses the symbols $\cap$ to mean "and," $\cup$ to mean "or," and $P(x)$ to mean "the probability of x."

Probability of events A and B occurring

If A and B are independent events, then the probability that both A and B will occur is the product of their individual probabilities.

$$P(A \cap B) = P(A)P(B)$$

Example: Given two dice, the probability of tossing a three on each of them simultaneously is the probability of a three on the first die, or $\frac{1}{6}$, times the probability of tossing a three on the second die, also $\frac{1}{6}$.

$$\tfrac{1}{6} \times \tfrac{1}{6} = \tfrac{1}{36}$$

When the outcome of the first event affects the outcome of the second event, the events are dependent. Any two events that are not independent are dependent. This is also known as conditional probability.

$$P(A \cap B) = P(A)P(B|A)$$

Example: Two cards are drawn from a deck of 52 cards, without replacement; that is, the first card is not returned to the deck before the second card is drawn. What is the probability of drawing a diamond?

$A =$ drawing a diamond first

$B =$ drawing a diamond second

$P(A) = \frac{13}{52} = \frac{1}{4}$ $\qquad$ $P(B) = \frac{12}{51} = \frac{4}{17}$

$P(A \cap B) = \frac{1}{4} \times \frac{4}{17} = \frac{1}{17}$

Probability of event A or B occurring

For arbitrary events,

$$P(A \cup B) = P(A) + P(B) - P(A \cap B)$$

For mutually exclusive events,

$$P(A \cup B) = P(A) + P(B)$$

Example: A card is selected from a deck of playing cards. What is the probability that it is a king or a spade?

Since the two outcomes (king or spade) are not mutually exclusive, we use the formula:

$$P(A \cup B) = P(A) + P(B) - P(A \cap B)$$

The probability of selecting a king $= \frac{4}{52} = \frac{1}{13}$.

The probability of selecting a spade $= \frac{13}{52} = \frac{1}{4}$.

The probability of selecting both a king and a spade $= \frac{1}{52}$.

Therefore, the probability that the selected card is a king or a spade is $\frac{1}{13} + \frac{1}{4} - \frac{1}{52} = \frac{16}{52} = \frac{4}{13}$.

Fundamental counting principle

In a sequence of two distinct events in which the first one has n number of outcomes or possibilities and the second has m number of outcomes or possibilities, the total number of possibilities of the sequence will be:

$$n \times m$$

Example: A car dealership has three Mazda models and each model comes in a choice of four colors. How many different Mazda cars are available at the dealership?

Number of available Mazda cars = (3)(4) = 12

The Addition Principle of Counting states:

If A and B are events, $n(A \text{ or } B) = n(A) + n(B) - n(A \cap B)$.

The Addition Principle of Counting for Mutually Exclusive Events states:

If A and B are mutually exclusive events, $n(A \text{ or } B) = n(A) + n(B)$.

The Multiplication Principle of Counting for Dependent Events states:

Let A be a set of outcomes of Stage 1 and B a set of outcomes of Stage 2. Then the number of ways $[n(A \text{ and } B)]$, that A and B can occur in a two-stage experiment is given by:

$$n(A \text{ and } B) = n(A)n(B|A),$$

where $n(B|A)$ denotes the number of ways B can occur, given that A has already occurred.

The Multiplication Principle of Counting for Independent Events states:

Let A be a set of outcomes of Stage 1 and B a set of outcomes of Stage 2. If A and B are independent events, then the number of ways $[n(A \text{ and } B)]$, that A and B can occur in a two-stage experiment is given by:

$$n(A \text{ and } B) = n(A)n(B).$$

Geometric probability (probability as the ratio of two areas)

GEOMETRIC PROBABILITY: describes situations that involve shapes and measures

GEOMETRIC PROBABILITY describes situations that involve shapes and measures. For example, given a 10-inch string, we can determine the probability of cutting the string so that one piece is at least 8 inches long.

Other geometric probability problems involve the ratio of areas. For example, to determine the likelihood of randomly hitting a defined area of a dartboard (pictured below), we determine the ratio of the target area to the total area of the board.

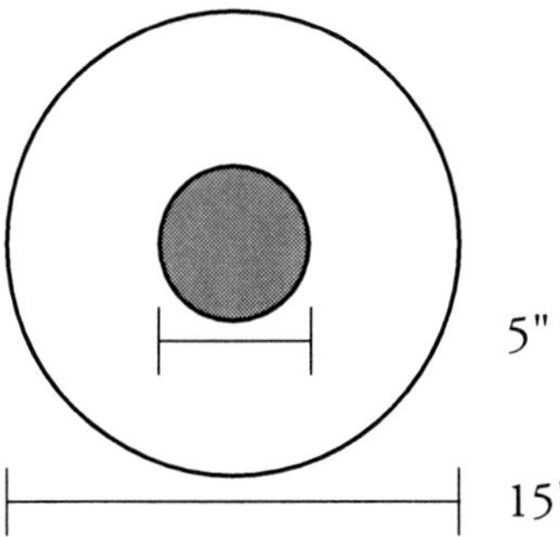

Given that a randomly thrown dart lands somewhere on the board, the probability that it hits the target area is the ratio of the areas of the two circles. Thus, the probability, P, of hitting the target is

$$P = \frac{(2.5)^2 \pi}{(7.5)^2 \pi} \times 100 = \frac{6.25}{56.25} \times 100 = 11.1\%$$

Using probability to draw conclusions

Some probability-related questions to ask about events being observed include:

- Are the events equally likely?
- Are the events independent?
- Are the events mutually exclusive?

The law of large numbers is a useful concept to keep in mind while making observations.

STATISTICAL HYPOTHESIS TESTING is a method of determining, to within a certain confidence level, whether a particular conclusion can be accepted according to a certain set of data.

STATISTICAL HYPOTHESIS TESTING: a method of determining, to within a certain confidence level, whether a particular conclusion can be accepted according to a certain set of data

The first step of hypothesis testing is to formulate the so-called null hypothesis, which is assumed to be true unless sufficient evidence warrants its rejection.

The next step involves computation of a test statistic using the associated sample data. Comparison of this data with a critical value for the test statistic (which is a threshold value for a given confidence) allows one to determine whether to accept or reject the null hypothesis. Common test statistics include the t-test, the z-test, and the X^2 (chi-square) goodness-of-fit test.

Probability models

There are three common probability distributions or models used to represent situations: the normal distribution, the binomial distribution, and the geometric distribution.

There are three common probability distributions or models used to represent situations: the normal distribution, the binomial distribution, and the geometric distribution. The first type, the normal distribution, would be covered in an EC-6 classroom.

Normal distribution

NORMAL DISTRIBUTION: the distribution associated with most sets of real-world data

A **NORMAL DISTRIBUTION** is the distribution associated with most sets of real-world data. It is frequently called a bell curve. A normal distribution has a random variable X with mean μ and variance σ^2.

Example: Albert's Bagel Shop's morning customer load follows a normal distribution, with mean (average) 50 and standard deviation 10. The standard deviation is the measure of the variation in the distribution. Determine the probability that the number of customers tomorrow will be less than 42.

Z-SCORE: a measure of the distance in standard deviations of a sample from the mean

First, convert the raw score to a **Z-SCORE**. A z-score is a measure of the distance in standard deviations of a sample from the mean.

The z-score $= \frac{X_i \times \bar{X}}{s} = \frac{42 - 50}{10} = -\frac{8}{10} = -.8$

Next, use a table to find the probability corresponding to the z-score. The table gives us .2881. Since our raw score is negative, we subtract the table value from .5.

$.5 - .2881 = .2119$

We can conclude that $P(x < 42) = .2119$. This means that there is about a 21% chance that there will be fewer than 42 customers tomorrow morning.

Statistics in the Real World

Statistical experiments are used to study real-world phenomena that involve a large number of observations with multiple possible outcomes when the outcome of a particular observation depends on chance.

In the classroom, statistical analysis can be done using a variety of real-world examples:

- Comparing temperature: Students can use the measures of central tendency, mean, mode, and range to compare temperatures in their area to temperatures in another state or country.
- Sampling: Students can create a survey to use with students in different grades. The results can be displayed with a graph, histogram, or line plot.
- Tracking populations in the wild: Students can determine the population of an animal, tree, or plant in a region by taking a sampling of a small area and using that to determine the population in a larger area.
- Sports: Statistics are widely used in sports. Most of the statistics are centered around the mean, or average.

MATHEMATICAL PROCESSES

Deduction and Induction

There are two kinds of logical reasoning that students can use when learning mathematical concepts:

- **INDUCTION** is the process of finding a pattern from a group of examples. The pattern is the conclusion that the set of examples seems to indicate. It may be a correct conclusion or an incorrect conclusion due to the fact that other examples may not follow the predicted pattern.
- **DEDUCTION** is the process of arriving at a conclusion based on statements that are known to be true, such as theorems, axioms, or postulates. Conclusions found using deductive thinking based on true statements will always be true.

INDUCTION: the process of finding a pattern from a group of examples

DEDUCTION: the process of arriving at a conclusion based on statements that are known to be true

HYPOTHESIS: the information that is assumed to be true

CONCLUSION: what must be proven true

Conditional statements are frequently written in if-then form. The *if* clause of the statement is known as the **HYPOTHESIS**, and the *then* clause is known as the **CONCLUSION**. In a proof, the hypothesis is the information that is assumed to be true whereas the conclusion is what must be proven true. A conditional is considered to be in the form:

If p, then q.

P is the hypothesis. Q is the conclusion.

Example: If an angle has a measure of 90 degrees, then it is a right angle.

In this statement, "an angle has a measure of 90 degrees" is the hypothesis. "It is a right angle" is the conclusion.

Conditional: If p, then q.

P is the hypothesis. Q is the conclusion.

Inverse: If ~ p, then ~ q

Negative of both the hypothesis (if not p, then not q) and the conclusion from the original conditional.

Converse: If q, then p.

Reverse of the two clauses. The original hypothesis becomes the conclusion. The original conclusion then becomes the new hypothesis.

Contrapositive: If ~ q, then ~ p.

Reverse the two clauses. The "If not q, then not p" original hypothesis becomes the conclusion. The original conclusion now becomes the new hypothesis. *Then* both the new hypothesis and the new conclusion are negated.

Suppose the following statements were given to you, and you were asked to reach a conclusion:

All rectangles are parallelograms.
Quadrilateral *ABCD* is not a parallelogram.

In if-then form, the first statement would be:

If a figure is a rectangle, then it is also a parallelogram.

Note that the second statement is the negation of the conclusion of the first statement (remember also that the contrapositive is logically equivalent to a given conditional). That is, If ~ q, then ~ p. Since "*ABCD* is *not* a parallelogram" is like saying, "If ~ q," then you can come to the conclusion, "then ~ p."

Therefore, the conclusion is that *ABCD* is not a rectangle.

Connections and Equivalent Representations in Math

We can represent any two-dimensional geometric figure in the Cartesian or rectangular coordinate system.

In order to find the distance from a given point to another given line, the perpendicular line that intersects the point and line must be drawn and then the equation of the other line written. From this information, the point of intersection can be found. This point and the original point are used in the distance formula given below:

$$D = \sqrt{(x_2 - x_1)^2 + (y_2 - y_1)^2}$$

Example: Find the perimeter of a figure with vertices at (4, 5), (-4, 6) and (-5, -8).

The figure being described is a triangle. Therefore, the length for all three sides must be found. Carefully identify all three sides before beginning.

Side 1 = (4, 5) to (-4, 6)

Side 2 = (-4, 6) to (-5, -8)

Side 3 = (-5, -8) to (4, 5)

$$D_1 = \sqrt{(-4 - 4)^2 + (6 - 5)^2} = \sqrt{65}$$

$D_2 = \sqrt{((-5 - (-4))^2 + (-8 - 6)^2} = \sqrt{197}$

$D_3 = \sqrt{((4 - (-5))^2 + (5 - (-8)^2))} = \sqrt{250}$ or $5\sqrt{10}$

Perimeter $= \sqrt{65} + \sqrt{197} + 5\sqrt{10}$

Parabola

A **PARABOLA** is a set of all points in a plane that are equidistant from a fixed point (focus) and a line (directrix).

PARABOLA: a set of all points in a plane that are equidistant from a fixed point (focus) and a line (directrix)

FORM OF EQUATION $y = a(x - h)^2 + k$ $x = a(y - k)^2 + h$

Ellipse

FORM OF EQUATION $\frac{(x-h)^2}{a^2} + \frac{(y-k)^2}{b^2} = 1$ $\frac{(x-h)^2}{b^2} + \frac{(y-k)^2}{a^2} = 1$

for ellipses where $b^2 = a^2 - c^2$ where $a^2 > b^2$.

Hyperbola

FORM OF EQUATION $\frac{(x-h)^2}{a^2} - \frac{(y-k)^2}{b^2} = 1$ $\frac{(y-k)^2}{a^2} - \frac{(x-h)^2}{b^2} = 1$

where $c^2 = a^2 + b^2$ where $c^2 = a^2 + b^2$

To write the equation given the center and the radius, use the standard form of the equation of a circle:

$$(x - h)^2 + (y - k)^2 = r^2$$

Selecting a Strategy to Solve a Problem

The guess-and-check strategy calls for making an initial guess about the solution, checking the answer, and using the outcome of this check to inform the next guess. With each successive guess, one should get closer to the correct answer.

Another indirect approach to problem solving is working backwards. If the result of a problem is known (for example, in problems that involve proving a particular result), it is sometimes helpful to begin from the conclusion and attempt to work backwards to a particular known starting point.

Between identification of known information and identification of a solution to the problem is a somewhat gray area that, depending on the problem, could potentially involve a myriad of different approaches.

Estimation

Estimation and approximation can be used to get a rough idea of the result of a calculation or to check the reasonableness of an answer. A simple check for reasonableness is to ask whether the answer expected is more or less than a given number. For instance, when converting 20 km to meters, ask yourself whether you are expecting a number greater or less than 20.

The most common estimation strategies taught in schools involve replacing numbers with numbers that are simpler to manipulate. These methods include rounding off, front-end digit estimation, and compensation. While rounding off is done to a specific place value (e.g., nearest ten or hundred), front-end estimation involves rounding off or truncating to whatever place value the first digit in a number represents.

Compensation involves replacing different numbers in different ways so that one change can more or less compensate for the other.

Example: $32 + 53 = 30 + 55 = 85$

Early History of Mathematics

Mathematics predates recorded history. Prehistoric cave paintings that use geometrical figures and slash counting have been dated prior to 20,000 BCE in Africa and France.

The early history of mathematics is found in Mesopotamia (Sumeria and Babylon), Egypt, Greece, and Rome. Noted mathematicians from these times include Euclid, Pythagoras, Apollonius, Ptolemy, and Archimedes.

Islamic culture from the sixth through the twelfth centuries acquired knowledge of math from areas of the globe ranging from Africa and Spain to India. Contacts in India provided additional influences from China. This mixture of cultures and ideas brought about many developments, including the concept of algebra, our current numbering system, and the concept of zero. India was the primary source of many of these developments. Notable scholars of this era include Omar Khayyam and Muhammad al-Khwarizmi.

Important figures in history of math

The growth of mathematics since 1800 has been enormous and has affected nearly every aspect of life. Some names significant in the history of mathematics since 1800 and the work they are most known for include:

- Joseph-Louis Lagrange (theory of functions and of mechanics)
- Pierre-Simon Laplace (celestial mechanics, probability theory)
- Joseph Fourier (number theory)
- Lobachevsky and Bolyai (non-Euclidean geometry)
- Charles Babbage (calculating machines, origin of the computer)
- Lady Ada Lovelace (first known program)
- Florence Nightingale (nursing, statistics of populations)
- Bertrand Russell (logic)
- James Maxwell (differential calculus and analysis)

- John von Neumann (economics, quantum mechanics, and game theory)
- Alan Turing (theoretical foundations of computer science)
- Albert Einstein (theory of relativity)
- Gustav Roch (topology)

DOMAIN III
SOCIAL STUDIES

PERSONALIZED STUDY PLAN

PAGE		KNOWN MATERIAL/ SKIP IT
115	Social science instruction	☐
124	History	☐
146	Geography and culture	☐
159	Economics	☐
166	Government and citizenship	☐

SOCIAL SCIENCE INSTRUCTION

The mission of the Texas Education Agency is to provide leadership, guidance, and resources to help schools meet the educational needs of all students. The Texas Essential Knowledge and Skills Web site contains the information needed for each grade level necessary knowledge and skills.

For further details see:

www.tea.state.tx.us

For specific details on social studies see:

www.tea.state.tx.us/rules/tac/chapter113/index.html.

See Chapter 113, TEKS for Social Studies, at:

ritter.tea.state.tx.us/rules/tac/chapter113/index.html

Terminology

A complete social studies glossary would be too lengthy to include here. Instead, here are two online sources for your reference:

PDF document:
http://www.michigan.gov/documents/10-02Glossary_48851_7.pdf

HTML Web page:
http://www.whitehall.k12.mi.us/curriculum/socialstudies/glossaryofterms.htm

—Compiled by Karen R. Todorov, Social Studies Education Consultant for the Michigan Department of Education

Effect of Developmental Stages on Learning

Teachers must understand how children learn best during each period of development. The most important premise of child development is that all domains of development (physical, social, and academic) are integrated. Development in each domain is influenced by the other domains. Moreover, today's educator must also have knowledge of exceptionalities and how these exceptionalities affect all domains of a child's development.

The stimulus of the classroom can promote learning or evoke behavior that is counterproductive for both students and teachers. Students are social beings who normally gravitate to action in the classroom, so teachers must create engaging classroom environments that provide focus and maximize learning opportunities.

Physical development

Factors determined by the physical stage of a child's development include:

- Ability to sit and attend
- Need for activity
- Relationship between physical skills and self-esteem
- Degree to which physical involvement in an activity (as opposed to being able to understand an abstract concept) affects learning

Cognitive (academic) development

Children demonstrate patterns of learning beginning with preoperational thought processes and moving to concrete operational thoughts. Eventually they begin to acquire the mental ability to think about and solve problems in their head because they can manipulate objects symbolically. Children of most ages can use symbols such as words and numbers to represent objects and relationships, but they sometimes need concrete reference points. It is essential that children be encouraged to use and develop these thinking skills to solve problems that interest them. The content of the curriculum must be relevant, engaging, and meaningful to them.

Social development

Children progress through a variety of social stages. Beginning with an awareness of peers but a lack of concern for their presence, young children engage in "parallel" activities (playing alongside their peers without directly interacting with them). During the primary years, children develop an intense interest in peers. They establish productive, positive social and working relationships with one another. This stage of social growth continues to increase in importance throughout the child's school years. The teacher should provide opportunities and support for cooperative small-group projects that not only develop cognitive ability but also promote peer interaction. The ability to work and relate effectively with peers is of major importance and contributes greatly to the child's sense of confidence.

Developmentally Appropriate Instructional Practices

A child-centered educational program will take its cues from students' interests, concerns, and questions. Making an educational program child-centered involves building on the natural curiosity children bring to school and asking them what they want to learn.

Teachers help students identify their own questions, puzzles, and goals, and then structure widening circles of experience for them to investigate those topics. Teachers must infuse all of the skills, knowledge, and concepts that society mandates into a child-driven curriculum. Teachers should also draw on their understanding of children's developmental needs and enthusiasms to design experiences that lead them into areas they might not otherwise choose but that engage them and that they do enjoy. Teachers can also bring their own interests and enthusiasms into the classroom to motivate children.

Implementing such a child-centered curriculum is the result of careful and deliberate planning.

Good planning includes:

1. Specifying behavioral objectives
2. Specifying students' entry behavior (knowledge and skills)
3. Selecting and sequencing learning activities to move students from entry behavior to objective behavior
4. Evaluating the outcomes of instruction in order to improve planning

Goal of Diversity Education

The teaching of diversity is a quest for equality, social justice, and the pursuit of democracy. The foremost goal of diversity education is to reorganize schools so that all students gain an understanding of the attitudes and skills needed to function in a culturally and ethnically diverse nation and world. Diversity education is consistent with the principles outlined in the U.S. Constitution and the Bill of Rights. These documents guarantee basic human rights, civil liberties, and equality, democracy, freedom, and justice to individuals from all cultural, language, and social groups.

Research Tools and Technology

The computer also offers abundant opportunities as a teaching tool and resource. The Internet provides a wealth of information on all topics, including material suitable for any age group. Children enjoy playing games, so presenting material in a game-like format is also a good teaching tool. Making puzzles for vocabulary, letting students present information in the form of a story or even a play, and using other engaging activities helps the students learn and retain various concepts.

Teachers need a toolkit of instructional strategies, materials, and technologies to encourage and provide students with problem-solving and critical-thinking skills about subject content.

These days almost all libraries have electronic search systems to assist students in finding information on almost any subject. And, using the Internet, with powerful search engines like Google, students can retrieve information that can be difficult to find in the local library.

Students can utilize **spreadsheets, graphing programs, graphic arts programs**, and **web design software** to present research findings for both small and large projects. Teachers can also set up web searching "games" such as **WebQuests** to quiz or reinforce material with students.

Social Science Skills and Vocabulary

There are many social science skills required to promote learning in the social science classroom:

- Acquiring information
- Organizing and using information
- Communicating information
- Social participation
- Content-area vocabulary development

As students study concepts, themes, and events, they continually encounter content-area vocabulary. Students should be taught and encouraged to use resources such as word walls, glossaries, online resources, KWL charts, textbooks, and teammates to reinforce and internalize terms and concepts relevant to understanding content material.

Teachers should vary the methods used to introduce content vocabulary as well as continue to revisit terms taught in the past so that students develop strong working vocabularies throughout their study of the social sciences. Teachers should also monitor and differentiate this instruction so that no student is left behind when content terms are being introduced, since understanding the terms is part of the vital foundation of learning the higher concepts.

Major Disciplines in the Social Sciences

The disciplines within the social sciences, sometimes referred to as social studies, include anthropology, geography, history, sociology, economics, and political science.

The disciplines within the social sciences, sometimes referred to as social studies, include anthropology, geography, history, sociology, economics, and political science. Some programs include psychology, archaeology, philosophy, religion, law, and criminology. The subjects of civics and government may also be a part of an educational curriculum.

- **Anthropology:** The scientific study of human culture and the relationship between humans and culture. Anthropologists study different groups and how they relate to other cultures in their patterns of behavior, similarities, and differences. Their research is twofold: cross-cultural and comparative. The major method of study is referred to as **participant observation**. The anthropologist studies and learns about people by living among them and participating with them in their daily lives.

- Archaeology: The scientific study of past human cultures by examining the remains they left behind—objects such as pottery, bones, buildings, tools, and artwork. Archaeologists locate and examine evidence to help explain the way people lived in the past. They use special equipment and techniques to gather the evidence and keep detailed records of their findings because much of their research causes destruction of the remains being studied.
- Civics: The study of the responsibilities and rights of citizens, with emphasis on such subjects as freedom, democracy, and individual rights. Students study local, state, national, and international government structures, functions, and problems. Related to this topic are other social, political, and economic institutions.
- Economics: The study of how goods and services are produced and distributed. It also includes the ways people and nations choose what and from whom they buy. Some of the methods of study include research, case studies, analysis, statistics, and mathematics.
- Geography: The study of places and the way living things and Earth's features are distributed. It includes where animals, people, and plants live and the effects of their relationship with Earth's physical features. Geographers also explore the locations of Earth's features, how they got there, and why this is important.
- History: The study of the past, especially the human past, its important political and economic events, and its cultural and social conditions. History is generally divided into three main categories: time periods, nations, and specialized topics. Study is accomplished through research, reading, and writing.
- Political science: The study of political life and various aspects of government, including elections, political parties, and public administration. In addition, political science examines values such as justice, freedom, power, and equality. There are six main fields of political study in the United States:
  - Political theory and philosophy
  - Comparative governments
  - International relations
  - Political behavior
  - Public administration
  - American government and politics

- Psychology: The study of behavior and mental processes by observing and recording the ways people and animals relate to each other. Psychologists scrutinize specific patterns, enabling them to discern and predict certain behaviors, and use scientific methods to verify their ideas. In this way, they have been able to learn how to help people fulfill their individual potentials and to strengthen understanding between individuals as well as between groups, nations, and cultures. The results of psychological research have deepened our understanding of the reasons for people's behavior
- Sociology: The study of human society: the individuals, groups, and institutions that make up society. It includes every feature of the human social condition. It deals with the predominant behaviors, attitudes, and types of relationships within a society, defined as a group of people with a similar cultural background living in a specific geographical area.

Social Science Concepts

- Causality: The reason something happens—its cause—is a basic category of human thinking. We want to know the causes of a major event in our lives. In the study of history, causality is the analysis of the reasons for change. The question we ask is why and how a particular society or event developed in the particular way it did, given the context in which it occurred.
- Conflict: Conflict in history is the opposition of ideas, principles, values, or claims. Conflict may take the form of internal clashes of principles, ideas, or claims in a society or group, or it may take the form of opposition between groups or societies.
- Bias: Bias is a prejudice or predisposition either toward or against something. In the study of history, bias can refer to the persons or groups studied, in terms of a society's bias toward a particular political system, or it can refer to the historian's predisposition to evaluate events in a particular way.
- Interdependence: This is a condition in which two things or groups rely on one another, as opposed to independence, in which each thing or group relies only on itself.
- Identity: Identity is the state or perception of being a particular thing or person. Identity can also refer to the understanding or self-understanding of groups or nations.
- Nation-state: This is a particular type of political entity that provides a sovereign territory for a specific nation in which other factors also unite the citizens (e.g., language, race, or ancestry).

- Culture: Culture refers to the civilization, achievements, and customs of the people of a particular time and place.
- Socialization: This is the process by which humans learn the expectations their society has for their behavior in order that they might successfully function within that society

Assessment

Assessment methods are ways to determine if a student has sufficiently learned the required material. The test is the usual method, where the student answers questions on the material he or she has studied. Other methods involve writing essays on various topics. Verbal reports can accomplish the same goal.

Today's emphasis on educational accountability by the public and the legislature is a mandate for effective teaching and assessment of student learning outcomes. Performance-based assessments are being used exclusively for state testing of high school students in ascertaining student learning outcomes based on individual processing and presentation of academic learning.

Effective classroom assessment can provide educators with a wealth of information on student performance and teacher instructional practices. Assessment can provide teachers with data to use in planning student learning to increase academic achievement and success for students.

Assessment of ESL students

Teaching students who are learning English as a second language poses some unique challenges, particularly in a standards-based environment. The key is realizing that no matter how little English a student knows, the teacher should teach with the student's developmental level in mind. This means that instruction should not be "dumbed-down" for ESL students. Different approaches should be used, however, to ensure that ESL students (a) get multiple opportunities to learn and practice English, and (b) still learn content.

Many ESL approaches are based on social learning methods. When they are placed in mixed-level groups or paired with a student of a different level of ability, students get a chance to practice English in a natural, nonthreatening environment.

In teacher-directed instructional situations, visual aids such as pictures, objects, and video are particularly effective at helping students make connections between words and items with which they are already familiar.

ESL students may need additional accommodation with assessments, assignments, and projects. For example, teachers may that find written tests provide little information about an ESL student's understanding of the content. Therefore, an oral test may be better suited to ESL students. When students are somewhat comfortable and capable with written tests, a shortened test may be preferable to a longer one. Note that students may need extra time for translation.

For further details, refer to:

www.tea.state.tx.us

For specifics on social studies, see:

www.tea.state.tx.us/rules/tac/chapter113/index.html

Practical Applications of Social Science Issues and Trends

Current research shows ten trends in social studies:

- Study more history
- Study more geography
- Use literature
- Focus on multiculturalism
- Renew attention to Western civilization
- Emphasize ethics and values
- Renew attention to religion
- Study contemporary and controversial issues
- Cover issues in depth
- Write, write, write

—From "Trends in K-12 Social Studies: Educational Resources: ADD, ADHD, Literacy, ESL, Special" at: *http://www.apples4theteacher.com/resources/*

Use of Maps and Graphics

An idea presented visually is often easier to understand than an idea presented verbally, that one hears or reads. Among the more common illustrations used are various types of maps and graphs.

A **map** can provide information that might take hundreds of words to explain.

Bar graphs and **line graphs** are the types of graphs used most often. Two major reasons graphs are used are:

- To present a model or theory visually to show how two or more variables interrelate
- To present real-world data visually to show how two or more variables interrelate

Charts are similar to graphs. It depends on the type of information you want to illustrate the choice of a graph chart. One of the most common types of chart is the **pie chart** because it is the easiest to read and understand. Pie charts are used often, especially when one is trying to illustrate the differences in percentages among various items, or when one is demonstrating a whole divided into parts.

Photographs and globes are useful as well, but because they are limited in the kind of information they can show, they are rarely used. An exception to this would be the case of a photograph of a particular political figure or a time that one wishes to visualize.

Fostering Collaboration with Parents and the Community

Students no longer only need to memorize dates or locations on a map but must learn to apply critical thinking skills to the challenges and issues in our nation and world.

Teachers need to communicate to parents, colleagues, and the community that the field of social studies education is shifting in order to meet the challenges of today's complex world.

There are several strategies that can be implemented by teachers to communicate the value of a social studies education. Some of these are discussed below.

Activities for students

- Invite a foreign exchange student to speak to your class to discuss his or her country and culture.
- Design a history project in which students learn about the history/culture of the community.
- Invite speakers involved in various social studies fields to visit your class.

Activities for parents

- Invite parents to special events in the social studies classroom.
- Create a calendar of social studies activities that families can complete during the summer.
- Tell parents what students are learning in your social studies classroom.

Activities for the community

- Invite the community to a History Day.
- Speak to leading groups in your community about the importance of a social studies education.
- Organize an outreach program in a senior citizen center so students can work with senior members of the community.

HISTORY

Understanding the Concept of Chronology

As part of the discipline of history, chronology locates events in time. Relative chronology is locating related events to each other; for example, the Revolutionary War came before the Civil War. Absolute chronology is attaching these events to specific dates; for example, the Revolutionary War began in 1776 and ended in 1783, and the Civil War began in 1861 and ended in 1865.

By understanding chronology, students get a sense of the past; learn to understand causes and effects; learn about people, events, and periods in history; and can understand their own relationship with the world.

Although the abstract concept of chronology is difficult for elementary students to understand, they can begin by learning about the passing of time with concepts such as "before," "after," and "a long time ago." They can sort events in chronological order and be aware of a time beyond their memory. Later, they can sort events into periods and use dates and terms to describe the past. Eventually, they can write about events in chronological order and understand terminology such as *CE*, *BCE*, *century*, and *decade*.

Methods of Interpreting the Past

Interpreting the past is more than examining past experience. It is a way to establish a connection and provide context to modern life.

As teachers, you will use a wide variety of methods to help your students understand past events and their connections to our lives. Through your guidance and structured activities, students can compare and contrast cultures, examine continuity and change over time, and explore cause-and-effect relationships.

At a basic level, elementary students can tell and write stories that show their understanding of past events and they can connect these events to episodes in their own lives to demonstrate an understanding of cause and effect.

Give students a short primary or secondary document and ask them to discuss the point of view of the writer or speaker.

The National Center for Restructuring Education, Schools, and Teaching (NCREST) advocates role-playing and simulation activities to help students understand historical time and place.

Visiting a museum is an important way for students to experience history.

Analyzing Historical Information

One way to analyze historical events, patterns, and relationships is to focus on specific elements of history. Some of these are described below.

- **Politics and political institutions** can provide information about the prevailing opinions and beliefs of a group of people and how these change over time.
- **Race and ethnicity** is another historical lens. Researching the history of how people of different races have treated one another reflects on many other social aspects of a society, and can be a fruitful line of historical interpretation.
- **Gender** is a lens that focuses on the relative positions men and women hold in a society, and is connected to many other themes such as politics and economics.
- **Economic factors** drive many social activities, such as where people live and work and the relative wealth of nations. As a historical lens, economic factors can connect events to their economic causes.

Historical Research

Formulating meaningful questions is a primary part of any research process. Providing students with a wide variety of resources promotes this ability by making students aware of a wide array of social studies issues. Encouraging the use of multiple resources also introduces diverse viewpoints and different methods of communicating research results. This promotes the ability to judge the value of a resource and the appropriate ways to interpret it, which supports the development of meaningful inquiry skills.

Making a decision based on particular information requires careful interpretation of that information to determine the strength of the evidence supplied and what it means. A chart showing that the number of foreign-born citizens living in the United States has increased annually over the last ten years might allow one to make conclusions about population growth and changes in the relative sizes of ethnic groups in the United States. The chart would not give information about the reason the number of foreign-born citizens increased or address matters of immigration status. Conclusions in these areas would be invalid based on this information alone.

Organizing, using, and communicating information

Historians have created an organized system of time periods within which to classify information. Depending on the area of social science, time is classified in different ways. For example, historians may refer to the Egyptian period or the Roman period. However, one of the main classification systems is the geologic time scale used by geologists, paleontologists, and other earth scientists.

A historian's job is to locate, research, analyze, and interpret artifacts, oral records, and written records from the past.

Archaeologists use existing knowledge of cultures to help them locate resources including fossils, artifacts, and primary documents (such as letters, diaries, speeches, etc.) to find historical information. They sometimes incorporate secondary sources such as books, paintings, and media reports, but they rely more on primary resources. In the event that a culture had no written records, historians attempt to utilize the culture's oral history from resources such as legends, songs, folklore, and traditions.

Historians use the resources available to them to confirm and/or project theories about ideas, events, and people in the past. To report information, geographic material might be best communicated with a map, for instance, while historical material might be best conveyed through writing. Population changes might be displayed in a chart or graph. It is important to make students familiar with appropriate ways to communicate various types of information and to give them several options to keep their interest level high.

Primary and secondary sources

Primary sources

- Documents created during the time period being studied, including diaries, letters, newspapers, books, magazines, legal papers, the manuscript census, etc.
- Objects made and/or used during the time period being studied

According to the TEKS glossary, "Secondary sources are descriptions or interpretations prepared by people who were not involved in the events described. Researchers often use primary sources to understand past events but they produce secondary sources. Secondary sources provide useful background material and context for information gained from primary sources."

Guidelines for the use of primary sources:

- Be certain that you understand both explicit and implicit references
- Read the entire text you are reviewing; do not simply extract a few sentences
- Although anthologies of materials may help you identify primary source materials, the full original text should be consulted

Secondary sources

- Books about the period of time, based on primary materials
- Statistical data on the period
- The conclusions and inferences of other historians
- Multiple interpretations of the ethos of the time

Guidelines for the use of secondary sources:

- Do not rely on only a single secondary source
- Check facts and interpretations against primary sources whenever possible

- Do not accept the conclusions of other historians uncritically
- Place greatest reliance on secondary sources created by the best and most-respected scholars
- Do not use the inferences of other scholars as if they were facts
- Ensure that you recognize any bias the writer brings to his or her interpretation of history
- Understand the primary point of the book as a basis for evaluating the value of the material to your questions

Bias related to various points of view

According to the TEKS glossary, "Participants in events view the action from different points of view, physically and psychologically. Those favoring one side over another tend to be biased in their reporting of the events. Their interests, opinions, and attitudes appear in their descriptions."

Multiple sources of evidence

According to the TEKS glossary, "Geographers, historians, archaeologists, and others rarely rely on one source of evidence to formulate their theories of the social studies. Instead they look for multiple sources of evidence, study them, and search for patterns within the evidence."

Frames of reference

According to the TEKS glossary, "People experience life from a variety of vantage points (frames of reference). Historians and other social scientists also have a frame of reference, one based in the present. Their job is to sort through the evidence, prioritize it, distinguish important information from the less important, and interpret it."

Correlational analyses

According to the TEKS glossary, "The degree to which two sets of data are related is the correlation. Correlational analyses result from the analysis of sets of data to determine relationships."

Qualitative methods of inquiry

According to the TEKS glossary, "Research based on qualitative methods of inquiry uses selected writings or actions which best represent the point to be proven or disproven."

Quantitative methods of inquiry

According to the TEKS glossary, "Research based on quantitative methods of inquiry uses data which was systematically collected to prove or disprove a hypothesis.

Key Points of Interest in the History of the World

The Age of Exploration

The Age of Exploration had its beginnings centuries before exploration actually took place. The rise and spread of Islam in the seventh century and subsequent Muslim control over the city of Jerusalem led to the European Crusades. The Crusades were fought to free Jerusalem and the Holy Land from Muslim control. Although the Crusades were not a success, those who survived and returned to Western Europe brought with them new products such as silks, spices, perfumes, and new and different foods.

The returning Crusaders also brought new ideas, inventions, and methods to Western Europe, and from these new influences came the intellectual stimulation that led to the period now known as the Renaissance. The revival of interest in classical Greek art, architecture, literature, science, astronomy, and medicine increased trade between Europe and Asia, and the invention of the printing press helped spread knowledge and interest in exploration.

The trade routes between Europe and Asia were slow, difficult, dangerous, and expensive. Trade was still controlled by the Italian merchants in Genoa and Venice. It could take months or even years for the exotic luxuries of Asia to reach the markets of Western Europe. A faster, cheaper way had to be found.

The rise of Christianity

The rise of Christianity in early modern Europe was due as much to the iron hand of feudalism as it was to the Church itself. Feudalism, more than any other element, helped the Church get its grip on Europe.

Until the period of the Renaissance, the Church was the only place where people could be educated. The Bible and other books were hand-copied by monks in the monasteries. Cathedrals were built and decorated with art depicting religious subjects.

Like the caste system in India, feudalism kept people under strict control according to their social class. If you were a peasant, you had been born that way and you stayed that way for your entire life. The rich and powerful were the highest class in society, and the friends of the rich and powerful were the clergy.

In a way that governments never could, Christianity unified Europe. The Church was only too happy to capitalize on its power, which increased throughout the Middle Ages until it met a stalwart from Germany named Martin Luther.

The age of revolutions

The period from the 1700s to the 1800s in Western countries was characterized by the opposing political ideas of democracy and nationalism. This resulted in strong nationalistic feelings and people of common cultures asserting their belief in the right to have a voice in their government.

The American Revolution resulted in the successful efforts of the English colonists in America to win their freedom from Great Britain. After more than one hundred years of mostly self-government, the colonists resented the increased British control, declared their freedom, won the Revolutionary War with aid from France, and formed a new independent nation.

The French Revolution was the revolt of the middle and lower classes against the gross political and economic excesses of the rulers and the supporting nobility. Conditions leading to revolt included extreme taxation, inflation, lack of food, and the total disregard for the impossible, degrading, and unacceptable condition of the people on the part of the rulers, nobility, and the Church. It ended with the establishment of the first in a series of French republics.

Nationalism

During the eighteenth century and especially in the nineteenth century, **NATIONALISM** emerged as a powerful force in Europe and elsewhere in the world. Strictly speaking, nationalism is a belief in one's own nation, country, or people. More than in previous centuries, the people of the European nations began to think in terms of a nation of people who had similar beliefs, concerns, and needs. This was partly a reaction to growing discontent with the autocratic governments of the day as well as a general realization that there was more to life than the individual. People wanted to feel like they were a part of something like their nation, making themselves more than just an insignificant soul struggling to survive.

NATIONALISM: a belief in one's own nation, country, or people

Nationalism precipitated several changes in government, most notably in France; it also brought large groups of people together, as with the unifications of Germany and Italy. What it didn't do, however, is provide sufficient outlets for the sudden rise in national fervor. Especially in the 1700s and 1800s, European powers and peoples began looking to Africa and Asia in order to find colonies: rich sources of goods, trade, and cheap labor.

This colonial expansion would come back to haunt the European imperialists, as colonial skirmishes spilled over into alliances that dragged the European powers into World War I. Some of these colonial battles were still being fought as late as the start of World War II.

European imperialism

European imperialism was fueled by the urgent demand for raw materials required to sustain the great **Industrial Revolution**. These resources were not available in the huge quantity so desperately needed, which necessitated (and was a rationale for) the partitioning of the continent of Africa and parts of Asia. In turn, these colonial areas would purchase the finished manufactured goods.

One of the main targets of European imperialist expansion was Africa. Southeast Asia was another area of European expansion at this time, mainly by France. India was colonized by Great Britain. France, Great Britain, and Spain all occupied countries in Latin America. Spain also seized the rich lands of the Philippines.

Agricultural Revolution

The **Agricultural Revolution**, initiated by the invention of the plow six thousand years ago in Mesopotamia, led to a thorough transformation of human society by making large-scale agricultural production possible and facilitating the development of agrarian societies.

Numerous changes in lifestyle and thinking accompanied the development of stable agricultural communities.

Numerous changes in lifestyle and thinking accompanied the development of stable agricultural communities. Instead of people gathering a wide variety of plants as hunter-gatherers, agricultural communities become dependent on a limited number of harvested plants or crops. Subsistence became vulnerable to the weather and dependent upon planting and harvesting times. Agriculture also required a great deal of physical labor and the development of a sense of discipline. Agricultural communities became stable in terms of location; people were now tied to the land. This made the construction of dwellings appropriate. Dwellings tended to be built relatively close together, creating villages or towns.

Advances in agricultural technology and the ability to produce a surplus of produce created two opportunities: first, the opportunity to trade the surplus goods for other desired goods, and second, vulnerability to others who might steal those goods.

Scientific Revolution

The **Scientific Revolution** and the **Enlightenment** were two of the most important movements in the history of civilization, resulting in a new sense of self-examination and a wider view of the world than ever before. The Scientific Revolution was, above all, a shift in focus from belief to evidence. Scientists and philosophers wanted to see proof, not just believe what other people told them. It was an exciting time to be a forward-looking thinker.

For information on the Industrial Revolution, see the Economics section of this domain.

Information Revolution

The Information Revolution refers to the sweeping changes in the latter half of the twentieth century that were a result of technological advances and a new respect for the information provided by trained, skilled, and experienced professionals in a variety of fields. This approach to understanding social and economic changes in global society arose from the ability to make computer technology both accessible and affordable. In particular, the development of the computer chip has led to such technological advances as the Internet, the cell phone, cybernetics, wireless communication, and the related ability to readily disseminate and access a massive amount of information.

Technological innovations

According to the TEKS glossary, "Technological innovations are new ways of doing things which are based in a technology. An example is the telephone, which revolutionized the way people communicated because it allowed people to hear the voices of friends and family living miles away. Travel became easier due to improvements in transportation, which began with systems of canals and railroads and expanded to include automobiles, interstate roadway systems, and airlines with international flights. Computers and software revolutionized the ways people process information and communicate. Computers connected to the Internet allow people to share information and conduct personal and professional business nearly instantaneously and relatively inexpensively. The demands of new technologies and their applications promote further innovation to meet changing needs."

Brief Overview of U.S. History

Causes of the American Revolution

The earliest sign of the coming American Revolution was conflict over the issue of trade and taxation. Tensions between the colonists and England arose over the Quartering Act, the Sugar Act, and the Stamp Act, and were expressed in the Boston Massacre and the Boston Tea Party.

The earliest sign of the coming American Revolution was conflict over the issue of trade and taxation.

Articles of Confederation

The Articles of Confederation were the first political system under which the newly independent colonies tried to organize themselves. They were drafted after the Declaration of Independence in 1776, passed by the Continental Congress on November 15, 1777, ratified by the thirteen states, and took effect on March 1, 1781.

The Articles gave Congress the power to declare war, appoint military officers, and coin money. The Congress was also responsible for foreign affairs. The Articles of Confederation limited the powers of Congress by giving the states final authority. Although Congress could pass laws, at least nine of the thirteen states had to approve a law before it went into effect. Congress could not pass any laws regarding taxes. To get money, Congress had to ask each state for it; no state could be forced to pay.

The serious weaknesses of the Articles were:

- Lack of power to regulate finances over interstate trade
- Lack of power to regulate finances over foreign trade
- Lack of power to enforce treaties
- Lack of power to maintain the military

Within a few months from the adoption of the Articles of Confederation, it became apparent that there were serious defects in the system of government established for the new republic. There was a need for change that would create a national government with adequate powers to replace the Confederation, which was actually only a league of sovereign states.

In 1786, an effort to regulate interstate commerce ended in what is known as the Annapolis Convention. Because only five states were represented, this Convention was not able to achieve definitive results. The debates, however, made it clear that a government with as little authority as the Confederation could not regulate foreign and interstate commerce. Congress was, therefore, asked to call a convention to provide a constitution that would address the emerging needs of the new nation. The convention met under the presidency of George Washington, with fifty-five of the sixty-five appointed members present. A constitution was written in four months.

Constitutional convention

In May of 1787, delegates from all states (except Rhode Island) met in Philadelphia. At first, they met to revise the Articles of Confederation as instructed by Congress, but they soon realized that much more was needed. Abandoning their instructions, they set out to write a new Constitution, the foundation of all government in the United States and a model for representative government throughout the world.

The delegates settled on a republican form of government (sometimes referred to as representative democracy) in which the supreme power was in the hands of the voters who would elect the people who would govern for them.

Several compromises balanced the needs of the different states. They include:

- The Great Compromise: Set up a bicameral legislature. All states had two representatives in the Senate, while representation in the House was based on population.
- The Commerce Compromise: Allowed slaves to be imported for 20 years, with an import tax not to exceed $10 per person. After 1808, Congress would decide whether to prohibit or regulate slave importation.

The separation of powers into three branches of government was a built-in system of checks and balances.

War of 1812

The new nation faced an international crisis in the War of 1812. This resulted from political and economic struggles between France and Great Britain.

The war ended on Christmas Eve, 1814, with the signing of the Treaty of Ghent.

Monroe doctrine

The war proved to be a turning point in American history. European events had profoundly shaped U.S. policies, especially foreign policies. Thus, in President Monroe's message to Congress on December 2, 1823, he delivered a speech now known as the Monroe Doctrine. The United States was informing the powers of the Old World that the American continent was no longer open to European colonization and that any effort to extend European political influence into the New World would be considered by the United States "as dangerous to our peace and safety." The United States would not interfere in European wars or internal affairs and expected Europe to stay out of its affairs.

Westward expansion

In the United States, territorial expansion occurred in the expansion westward under the banner of Manifest Destiny.

The impact of the westward movement resulted in the completion of the borders of the present-day conterminous United States.

Political, economic, and social factors leading up to the Civil War

Slavery in the English colonies began in 1619, when twenty Africans arrived in the colony of Virginia at Jamestown. From then on, slavery had a foothold, especially in the agricultural South, where a large amount of labor was needed for the extensive plantations. Free men refused to work for wages on the plantations when land was available for settling on the frontier.

For a brief period after 1815, the nation enjoyed the "era of good feelings." People were moving into the West; industry and agriculture were growing; and a feeling of national pride united Americans in their efforts and determination to strengthen the country. However, tensions mounted and it appeared to the South that the federal government was siding with Northern industrial interests over the South's agricultural concerns.

In 1819, the United States consisted of twenty-one states: eleven free states and ten slave states.

In 1819, the United States consisted of twenty-one states: eleven free states and ten slave states. The Missouri Territory allowed slavery, and if Missouri were admitted to the Union, it would cause an imbalance in the number of U.S. senators. Alabama had already been admitted as a slave state and that had balanced the Senate, with the North and South each having twenty-two senators.

The first **Missouri Compromise** resolved the conflict by approving admission of Maine as a free state along with Missouri as a slave state, thus maintaining a balance of power in the Senate with the same number of free and slave states. Henry Clay, known as the Great Compromiser, then proposed a second Missouri Compromise, which was acceptable to everyone. His proposal was that the U.S. Constitution guaranteed protections and privileges to citizens of states, and Missouri's proposed constitution could not deny these to any of its citizens. The acceptance in 1820 of this second compromise opened the way for Missouri's statehood—a temporary reprieve only—and brought Maine into the Union as a free state, while Missouri was a slave state.

Lincoln-Douglas debates: In 1858, Abraham Lincoln and Stephen A. Douglas were running for the office of U.S. Senator from Illinois and participated in a series of debates, which directly affected the outcome of the 1860 presidential election.

The slavery issue flared up again, not to be resolved until the end of the Civil War. It was obvious that newly acquired territory would be divided up into territories that would later become states. In 1849, California applied for admission to the Union and the furor began.

The result was the **Compromise of 1850**, a series of laws designed as a final solution to the slavery issue. Concessions made to the North included the admission of California as a free state and the abolition of slave trading in Washington, D.C. The laws also provided for the creation of the New Mexico and Utah territories. As a concession to southerners, the residents there would decide whether to permit slavery when these two territories became states. In addition, Congress authorized implementation of stricter measures to capture runaway slaves.

The Civil War

South Carolina was the first state to secede from the Union, and the first shots of the war were fired on Fort Sumter in Charleston harbor. Both sides quickly prepared for war. The North had more in its favor: a larger population; superiority in finances and transportation facilities; and superior manufacturing, agricultural, and natural resources. The North possessed most of the nation's gold, about 92 percent of all industries, and almost all known supplies of copper, coal, iron, and various other minerals.

Since most of the nation's railroads were in the North and Midwest, men and supplies could be moved wherever needed and food could be transported from the farms of the Midwest to workers in the East and soldiers on the battlefields. Trade with nations overseas could go on as usual due to control of the navy and the merchant fleet. There were twenty-four Northern states, including western (California and Oregon) and border states (Maryland, Delaware, Kentucky, Missouri, and West Virginia).

The Southern states numbered eleven and included South Carolina, Georgia, Florida, Alabama, Mississippi, Louisiana, Texas, Virginia, North Carolina, Tennessee, and Arkansas. Together, these states made up the Confederacy. Although outnumbered in population, the South was confident of victory. The southerners knew that all they had to do was fight a defensive war, protecting their own territory until the North, which had to invade and defeat an area almost the size of Western Europe, tired of the struggle and gave up.

Since cotton was such an important crop, southerners felt that British and French textile mills were so dependent on raw cotton that they would be forced to help the Confederacy in the war.

The South had specific reasons and goals for fighting the war. The major aim of the Confederacy never wavered: to win independence, the right to govern themselves as they wished, and to preserve slavery. The northerners were not as clear in their reasons for conducting war. At the beginning, most believed, along with Lincoln, that preservation of the Union was paramount. Only a few abolitionists looked on the war as a way to end slavery. However, by war's end, more and more northerners had come to believe that freeing the slaves was just as important as restoring the Union.

The Civil War took more American lives than any other war in history, with the South losing one-third of its soldiers in battle compared to about one-sixth for the North. More than half of the total deaths were caused by disease and the horrendous conditions of field hospitals. Both sides paid a tremendous economic price, but the South suffered more severely from direct damages. Destruction was widespread, with towns, farms, trade, industry, lives, and homes of men, women, and children all destroyed. An entire Southern way of life was lost.

The Civil War took more American lives than any other war in history, with the South losing one-third of its soldiers in battle compared to about one-sixth for the North.

Effects of the Civil War

The Civil War has been called the first modern war, and its effects were far-reaching. It changed the methods of waging war: It introduced weapons and tactics that, after later improvements, were used extensively in wars of the late 1800s and 1900s. Civil War soldiers were the first to fight in trenches, the first to fight under a unified command, and the first to wage a defense called "major cordon defense," a strategy of advance on all fronts. They were also the first to use repeating and breech-loading weapons. Observation balloons were first used during the Civil War along with submarines, ironclad ships, and mines. Telegraphy and railroads were first put to use in the Civil War.

The Civil War was considered a modern war because of the vast destruction it created, and it was a "total war," involving the use of all of the resources of the opposing sides.

The Civil War was considered a modern war because of the vast destruction it created, and it was a "total war," involving the use of all of the resources of the opposing sides. There was probably no way it could have ended other than in the total defeat and unconditional surrender of one side or the other.

By executive proclamation and constitutional amendment, slavery was officially and finally ended, although there remained deep prejudice and racism. Also, the Union was preserved, and the states were finally truly united. Sectionalism, especially in the area of politics, remained strong for another hundred years, but not to the degree and with the violence that existed before 1861.

The victory of the North established that no state has the right to end or leave the Union. Because of its newfound unity, the United States became a major global power. Lincoln never proposed to punish the South. He was most concerned with restoring the South to the Union in a program that was flexible and practical rather than punitive and unbending.

Reconstruction

RECONSTRUCTION: the period between 1865 and 1877 when the federal and state governments debated and implemented plans to provide civil rights to freed slaves and to set the terms under which the former Confederate states might once again join the Union

Following the Civil War, the nation was faced with repairing the torn Union and readmitting the Confederate states. **RECONSTRUCTION** refers to the period between 1865 and 1877 when the federal and state governments debated and implemented plans to provide civil rights to freed slaves and to set the terms under which the former Confederate states might once again join the Union.

In 1865, Abraham Lincoln was assassinated, leaving Vice President Andrew Johnson to oversee the beginning of the actual implementation of Reconstruction. Johnson assumed a moderate position and was willing to allow former Confederates to keep control of their state governments. These governments quickly enacted Black Codes that denied the vote to blacks and granted them only limited civil rights.

In 1866, the Radical Republicans won control of Congress and passed the Reconstruction Acts, which placed the governments of the southern states under the control of the federal military. With this backing, the Republicans began to implement their policies, such as granting all black men the vote and denying the vote to former Confederate soldiers. Congress had passed the Thirteenth, Fourteenth, and Fifteenth Amendments, granting citizenship and civil rights to black Americans. Ratification of these amendments was a condition of readmission into the Union by the rebel states.

Federal troops were stationed throughout the South and protected Republicans who took control of southern governments. Bitterly resentful, some white southerners fought the new political system by joining a secret society called the Ku Klux Klan (KKK). It used violence to keep black Americans from voting and was a loose group made up mainly of former Confederate soldiers who opposed the Reconstruction government and espoused a doctrine of white supremacy. KKK members intimidated and sometimes killed their proclaimed enemies.

Between 1866 and 1870, all of the states had returned to the Union, but northern interest in Reconstruction was fading.

Reconstruction was a limited success. Its goals had been both the reunification of the nation granting civil rights to freed slaves. In the eyes of blacks it was considered a failure. Its limited successes and included the establishment of public school systems and expanded legal rights of black Americans.

Life after reconstruction

The rise of the Redeemer governments (Democrats that took control after federal troops and Republicans left at the end of Reconstruction) marked the beginning of the Jim Crow laws and official segregation. Blacks were still allowed to vote, but ways were found to make it difficult for them to do so, such as literacy tests and poll taxes.

The Jim Crow laws were upheld in 1896 when the Supreme Court handed down its decision in the case Plessy *v.* Ferguson.

The Court ruled against Plessy, thereby ensuring that the Jim Crow laws would continue to be enforced. The Court held that segregating races was not unconstitutional as long as the facilities for each racial group were identical. This became known as the separate but equal principle. In practice, facilities were seldom equal. Black schools were not funded at the same level, for instance. Streets and parks in black neighborhoods were not maintained.

Reform movements of the nineteenth and twentieth centuries

Abolition movement

Antislavery sentiment increased in the first half of the 1800s, and numerous organizations took up the cause. The American Anti-Slavery Society was founded by Quaker William Lloyd Garrison, who also started a newspaper called *The Liberator*. The newspaper was an important voice for the abolitionist movement, and Garrison was a controversial figure with both supporters and enemies around the country.

Women also formed some abolitionist organizations when they were denied full access to existing groups. Margaretta Forten, for example, cofounded the Philadelphia Female Anti-Slavery Society, a group of black and white women, because the American Anti-Slavery Society would not grant women full membership.

By the end of the nineteenth century, free public elementary school was available for all children in America.

Education reform

A new understanding of education led to major efforts for public education for all children. By the end of the nineteenth century, free public elementary school was available for all children in America.

Early labor movement

As the nature of work changed in the nineteenth century, workers began their efforts for reform. By the 1830s, many labor organizations began a struggle for a ten-hour workday. In 1844, in Lowell, Massachusetts, female textile employees organized the Lowell Female Labor Reform Association to get shorter hours, higher wages, and better working conditions.

In the 1890s, an economic recession called the Panic of 1893 struck the industrial areas of cities. The Knights of Labor had been formed in 1869 under Uriah Stephens and then Terrence Powderly, and its goal was to organize all workers—whether they were skilled or unskilled, black or white, male or female—into one big union united for the rights of workers. Their goals included:

- An eight-hour workday
- Equal pay for women
- The elimination of child labor
- Cooperative ownership of factories and mines

The Second Great Awakening

SECOND GREAT AWAKENING: an evangelical Protestant revival that preached about how salvation was available to everyone, not just a chosen few

The **SECOND GREAT AWAKENING** was an evangelical Protestant revival that preached about how salvation was available to everyone, not just a chosen few. Inspired by the idea that it was possible to gain salvation, adherents subscribed to a strong work ethic, avoided being wasteful, and abstained from drinking. Further, the idea of creating a more godly society inspired reform efforts aimed at improving living conditions in the United States.

Temperance movement

Closely allied to the Second Great Awakening was the temperance movement. The largest and most influential temperance organization was the Women's

Christian Temperance Union (WCTU), founded in 1874. Under the banner of "home protection," WCTU members advocated not just temperance, but all kinds of reform that would protect women and children from the effects of men who drank alcohol.

The Eighteenth Amendment, known as the Prohibition Amendment, was ratified in 1917 and prohibited the sale of alcoholic beverages throughout the United States. This led to a rise in bootlegging, organized crime, and the creation of speakeasies.

Women's suffrage movement

The American women's rights movement began in the 1840s. Among the early leaders of the movement were Elizabeth Cady Stanton, Lucretia Mott, and Ernestine Rose.

The Seneca Falls Convention, held in the New York mill town of Seneca Falls in 1848, was the first women's rights convention in the United States. Some 300 people attended the convention, which culminated in the publication of a *Declaration of Sentiments*, largely written by Stanton and signed by sixty-eight women and thirty-two men. In 1869, Susan B. Anthony, Ernestine Rose, and Elizabeth Cady Stanton founded the National Women's Suffrage Association.

In 1920, the Nineteenth Amendment, which guaranteed women the right to vote, was ratified.

In 1920, the Nineteenth Amendment, which guaranteed women the right to vote, was ratified.

World War I: 1914 to 1918

The origins of World War I are complex, and drawn mainly along the lines of various alliances and treaties that existed between the world powers. Imperialism, nationalism, and economic conditions of the time led to a series of sometimes shaky alliances among the powerful nations, each wishing to protect its holdings and provide mutual defense against smaller powers.

The United States, under President Woodrow Wilson, declared neutrality and did not enter the war immediately. Not until Germany threatened commercial shipping with submarine warfare in 1917 did the United State get involved. Fighting continued until November 1918, when Germany petitioned for armistice. Peace negotiations began in early 1919, and the Treaty of Versailles was signed in June of that year. One result of the peace negotiations was the establishment of the League of Nations (the precursor to the United Nations), a group of countries that agreed to avoid armed conflict through disarmament and diplomacy.

World War II: 1939 to 1945

The Treaty of Versailles that ended the First World War was in part the cause of the second. Severely limited by the treaty, Germany grew to resent its terms, which required reparations and limited the size of its army, and worked constantly to revise them. This was done through diplomacy and negotiation in the 1920s. In 1933, Adolf Hitler became chancellor of Germany and shortly thereafter was granted dictatorial powers. Hitler was determined to remove all restrictions imposed by the treaty and to unify the German-speaking people of the surrounding countries into a single country. Toward this end, Hitler marched into Austria in 1938 and was welcomed. He later made a claim on the Sudetenland, a German-speaking area of Czechoslovakia, a claim that was supported internationally. However, Hitler continued to march into the rest of Czechoslovakia, to which he had no claim.

France and Britain, which had followed a policy of appeasing Hitler in the hopes he would be content with annexing Austria, pledged to fight Germany if Hitler invaded Poland, which he did in September 1939, after signing a pact with the Soviet Union. Days later, France and Britain declared war on Germany, and the fighting began.

Again, the United States initially stayed out of the conflict. Only when Japan, an ally of Germany, attacked a U.S. naval base in Pearl Harbor, Hawaii, did the U.S. enter the war.

The European theater of WWII ended in 1945, when Allied troops invaded Germany and Hitler committed suicide. In the Pacific, the U.S. dropped two atomic bombs on Japan in August of that year, forcing the Japanese to surrender.

WWII left the British and European economies in ruins, and established the United States and the Soviet Union as the two major powers of the world, laying the foundation for the Cold War.

WWII left the British and European economies in ruins, and established the United States and the Soviet Union as the two major powers of the world, laying the foundation for the Cold War. After the failure of the League of Nations to prevent war, a stronger organization was created, the **United Nations**, with the ability to raise peacekeeping forces. Under the **Marshall Plan**, the United States helped rebuild Europe into an industrial, reliable economy.

Korean War: 1950 to 1953

With the surrender of Japan at the end of WWII, its thirty-five-year occupation of Korea came to an end. The Soviet Union and the United States assumed trusteeship of the country, with the Soviets occupying the northern half and the United States controlling the south. Elections were ordered by the United Nations to establish a unified government, but with each occupying country backing different candidates, the result was the formation of two separate states divided along the thirty-eighth parallel of latitude, each claiming sovereignty over the whole country.

These conflicting claims led to occasional military skirmishes along the common border throughout 1949, with each side aiming to unify the country under its own government. In June 1950, North Korea mounted a major attack across the thirty-eighth parallel, marking what is considered the beginning of the war.

The North Koreans received military aid and backing from the Soviet Union, which aroused fear in the United States that communism and Soviet influence might spread. In August 1950, American troops arrived in South Korea to join the fight, along with British, Australian, and UN forces.

In June 1950, North Korea mounted a major attack across the thirty-eighth parallel, marking what is considered the beginning of the war.

In 1953, peace negotiations resulted in a cease-fire and created a buffer zone between the two countries along the thirty-eighth parallel. This cease-fire has been in effect for more than fifty years. The war has never officially ended. Since the cease-fire, North Korea has become an increasingly isolated communist dictatorship, while South Korea has grown into a major world economy.

U.S. involvement in the Vietnam War: 1957 to 1973

Like Korea, Vietnam became a divided country after WWII, with a Soviet- and Chinese-backed communist government in the north, led by Ho Chi Minh, and a Western-backed government in the south. As the communist-backed north drove out the occupying French and maintained more and more insurgency in the south, the larger powers became increasingly involved, with the United States sending advisors and small numbers of troops between 1955 and 1964.

In 1964, following an attack on U.S. ships by North Vietnamese forces in the Gulf of Tonkin, the United States escalated its military involvement, sending more and more troops over the next four years. As fighting continued with no decisive progress, opposition to the war began to grow among the American public. President Richard Nixon began to reduce the number of troops while trying to assist the South Vietnamese army in building enough strength to fight on its own. In January 1973, the Paris Peace Accords were signed, ending offensive action by the United States in Vietnam. Nixon promised defensive assistance, but in 1974 Congress cut off all funding to the South Vietnamese government after Nixon had resigned the presidency following the Watergate scandal.

The withdrawal of the United States left South Vietnam without economic or military support, and the North Vietnamese army was able to overrun and control the entire country. North Vietnamese forces took Saigon, the southern capital, in April 1975. North and South were unified under one socialist government.

The social impact of the Vietnam War was considerable in the United States. Opposition to the draft and to U.S. involvement in the war led to large protests, particularly among young people, and returning veterans found they were not always treated as heroes, as veterans of other wars had been.

Civil rights movement

The beginning of the modern civil rights movement is usually identified as the Montgomery (Alabama) bus boycott in 1955. The movement used nonviolence to end segregation in public places. Supreme Court rulings, like Brown v. Board of Education, contributed to integrating the South, while laws like the Voting Rights Act of 1965 helped African Americans exercise the rights that the Constitution had guaranteed them one hundred years before. In the late 1960s and the 1970s, the movement grew to include more radical organizations like the Black Panthers.

Communications revolution

At the turn of the twenty-first century, the world witnessed unprecedented strides in communications, a major expansion of international trade, and significant international diplomatic and military activity.

The Internet and World Wide Web continued to grow and connect people all over the world, opening new routes of communication and providing commercial opportunities. The expansion of cell phone usage and Internet access led to a worldwide society that is interconnected as never before.

In Asia, new economies matured and the previously tightly controlled Chinese market became more open to foreign investment, increasing China's influence as a major economic power. The European Union made a bold move to a common currency, the Euro, in a successful effort to consolidate the region's economic strength. African nations, many struggling under international debt, appealed to the international community to assist them in building their economies. In South America, countries such as Brazil and Venezuela showed growth despite political unrest, as Argentina suffered a near complete collapse of its economy. As the technology sector expanded, so did the economy of India, where high-tech companies found a highly educated work force.

Conflict between the Muslim world and the United States increased during the last decade of the twentieth century, culminating in a terrorist attack on New York City and Washington, D.C. in 2001. These attacks, sponsored by the radical group Al-Qaeda, prompted a military invasion of Afghanistan by the United States. Shortly afterwards, the United States, the UK, and several smaller countries addressed further instability in the region by ousting Iraqi dictator Saddam Hussein in a military campaign. In the eastern Mediterranean, tension between Israelis and Palestinians continued to build, regularly erupting into violence.

The threat of the spread of nuclear weapons, largely diminished after the fall of the Soviet Union and the end of the Cold War, reared its head again with North Korea's claims that it had the ability to arm a nuclear missile, and the suspicion that Iran was working toward the creation of weapons-grade nuclear material. As international conflict and tension increased, the role of international alliances such as NATO and the United Nations grew in importance.

Key Points of Reference in the History of Texas

- Settlement and culture of Native American tribes before European contact
- 1528-34: Alvar Nunez Cabeza de Vaca (Spanish explorer) explores Texas for trade
- 1529: Spanish explorer Alonso Alvarez de Pineda maps the Texas coast
- 1685: French explorer Sieur de La Salle establishes Fort St. Louis at Matagorda Bay, providing the basis of the French claim to Texas territory
- 1688: The French colony is massacred
- 1689: The French continue to claim Texas but no longer physically occupy any part of the territory
- 1690: Alonso de Leon establishes San Francisco de los Tejas Mission in East Texas, opening the Old San Antonio Road portion of the Camino Real
- 1700-1799: Spain establishes Catholic missions throughout Texas
- 1762: The French give up their claims to Texas and cede Louisiana to Spain until 1800
- 1800: Much of north Texas is returned to France and later sold to the U.S. in the Louisiana Purchase
- 1823: Stephen Austin begins a colony known as the Old Three Hundred along the Brazos River
- 1832: Battle of Velasco—first casualties of the Texas Revolution
- 1832-33: The Conventions respond to unrest over the policies of the Mexican government
- 1835: The Texas Revolution officially begins in an effort to obtain freedom from Mexico
- 1836: The Convention of 1836 signs the Texas Declaration of Independence
  - The Battle of the Alamo
  - Santa Anna executes nearly 400 Texans in the massacre at Goliad
  - Santa Anna is believed to have ended the Texas rebellion
  - Sam Houston leads an army of 800 to victory by capturing the entire Mexican army at the Battle of San Jacinto
  - The Treaty of Velasco is signed by Santa Anna and Republic of Texas officials

- 1837: Sam Houston moves the capital of Texas five times, ending in Houston in 1837
- 1839: Austin becomes the capital of the Republic of Texas
- 1842: Mexican forces twice capture San Antonio and retreat
- 1845: Texas admitted to the Union as a state
- 1850: The Compromise of 1850 adjusts the state boundary and assumes Texas's debts
- 1861: Texas secedes from the Union and joins the Confederacy
- 1861: A government is organized, replacing Houston because of his refusal to swear allegiance to the Confederacy
- 1865: Union troops land in Galveston and put the Emancipation Proclamation into effect in Texas, thus ending slavery
- 1870: Texas is readmitted to the Union
- 1900: Galveston is destroyed and 8,000 people are killed by a category 4 hurricane
- 1901: The Lucas Gusher comes in, starting the Texas oil boom

Native American Groups in Texas Before European Colonization

Archaeologists have discovered evidence of Native American civilizations in Texas dating back to the Upper Paleolithic period (at least 9200 BCE, in the late Ice Age). These first known inhabitants of the state were connected with the Clovis complex. The Folsom complex dates from around 8800-8200 BCE. The Archaic period of Texas history extended from about 6000 BCE to about 700 CE. Little is known about the Early Archaic period (6000-2500 BCE). Hunting was accomplished by spear throwing. The groups that populated the region were small and nomadic. There are indications that there were some relationships across the regions.

The settlement of villages marks the emergence of agriculture and the beginning of social and political systems.

The Middle Archaic period (2500-1000 BCE) was a time of great population increase and proliferation of the number of occupied sites. Regional differences between the groups began to appear during this period. There is also evidence of some trading of artifacts, sometimes over great distances. The Late Archaic period (1000-300 BCE) continued to be a time of hunting societies. There is abundant evidence that bison became a vital source of food. The Transitional Archaic period (300 BCE–700 CE) was a time of some development in tool making as well as the time of the first appearance of settled villages.

The Late Prehistoric period extends from 700 CE to historic times. It is during this period that the bow and arrow first appeared, as well as new types of stone tools, pottery, and the creation and trade of ornamental items. During this period, the early Caddoan culture began to emerge and mound building began. Agriculture spread and became more complex, and in some areas pithouse dwellings appeared. In particular, the presence of obsidian artifacts demonstrates the participation of these peoples in a north-south system of trade that extended to the Great Plains and to Wyoming and Idaho, in particular.

The Caddo, in the east, were good at farming, trading, and making pottery. The Cherokee and Choctaw had advanced political structures, with an elected chief. The Chickasaw didn't stay in Texas long but were known as good hunters and farmers. The Chickasaw were also good farmers, hunters, tool makers, and house builders. The Comanche were famous horsemen and hunters. The Karankawa were good jewelers and shell makers. The Tonkawa were famous for hunting bison and gathering fruits and nuts.

Some of the Native American tribes that have inhabited the area include the Apache, Comanche, Cherokee, and Wichita tribes. Currently, there are three federally recognized Native American tribes located in Texas: the Alabama-Coushatta Tribe of Texas, the Kickapoo Traditional Tribe of Texas, and the Ysleta Del Sur Pueblo of Texas.

Currently, there are three federally recognized Native American tribes located in Texas: the Alabama-Coushatta Tribe of Texas, the Kickapoo Traditional Tribe of Texas, and the Ysleta Del Sur Pueblo of Texas.

European Colonization of Texas

The colonization of Texas by Europeans affected the Native Americans in many ways, many of them negative. The Spanish approach to occupation of a new region was to plant Catholic missions, which would convert the natives, bring them into conformity with Spanish beliefs and ideas, and teach them subsistence agriculture. One of the negative effects of the arrival of the Spanish was the introduction of a number of diseases to which the native people had not been exposed and to which they had no natural immunities.

The Spanish colonists and missionaries introduced a number of European crops as well as methods of irrigation that greatly improved the agricultural output of the Native Americans. They also introduced methods of animal husbandry.

One major result of the European occupation was a lasting dedication to Spanish culture, especially in the names of towns and foods, which is still reflected in the state. The French influence has by and large disappeared.

Development of Texas

Cattle and livestock and agriculture were important factors in the development of Texas because of its open spaces. Many of the cities began as trading posts and then developed. Railroads and other modes of transportation aided the growth of the cities. Dallas became a focal point for grain and cotton trade and was a stop-off point for western migration. Houston was a center for the sugar trade.

Beginning of twentieth century

Texas became a major oil-producing state, which resulted in the creation of many jobs and the infrastructure to support such an industry. In the 1940s, major companies began to relocate to Texas, providing even more jobs.

GEOGRAPHY AND CULTURE

GEOGRAPHY: the study of places and the way living things and the Earth's features are distributed

GEOGRAPHY is the study of places and the way living things and the Earth's features are distributed. It includes where animals, people, and plants live and the effects of their relationship with Earth's physical features. Geographers also explore the locations of Earth's features, how they got there, and this is important.

Themes of Geography

The five themes of geography are:

- Location: Location includes relative and absolute location. A relative location refers to the surrounding geography, e.g., "on the banks of the Mississippi River." Absolute location refers to a specific point, such as "41 degrees north latitude, 90 degrees west longitude," or "123 Main Street."
- Spatial organization: This is a description of how things are grouped in a given space. In geographical terms, spatial organization can describe people, places, and environments anywhere and everywhere on Earth. The most basic form of spatial organization for people is where they live.
- Place: A place has both human and physical characteristics. Physical characteristics include features such as mountains, rivers, and deserts. Human characteristics are the features created by humans' interaction with their environment, such as canals and roads.
- Human-environmental interaction: The theme of human-environmental interaction has three main concepts: Humans adapt to the environment (e.g., wearing warm clothing in a cold climate); humans modify the environment (e.g., planting trees to block a prevailing wind); and humans depend on the environment (e.g., for food, water, and raw materials).

- Movement: Movement refers to the way humans interact with one another through trade, communications, emigration, and other forms of interaction.

Regions

A **REGION** is an area that has some kind of unifying characteristic such as a common language or a common government. There are three main types of regions:

REGION: an area that has some kind of unifying characteristic such as a common language or a common government

- Formal regions are areas defined by political boundaries, such as cities, counties, or states.
- Functional regions are areas defined by a common function, such as the areas covered by a telephone service.
- Vernacular regions are less formally defined areas that are formed by people's perceptions, e.g., the Middle East or the South.

Geographical Features of the Earth

The Earth's surface is made up of 70 percent water and 30 percent land. Physical features of the land surface include:

- Mountains: Landforms with steep slopes at least 2,000 feet or more above sea level.
- Hills: Elevated landforms rising to an elevation of about 500 to 2,000 feet above sea level.
- Plateaus, or mesas: Elevated landforms usually level on top.
- Plains: Areas of flat or slightly rolling land, usually lower than the landforms next to them. Sometimes called lowlands (and sometimes located along seacoasts), they support the majority of the world's people.
- Valleys: Land areas found between hills and mountains.
- Deserts: Large dry areas of land receiving ten inches or less of rainfall each year.
- Deltas: Areas of lowlands formed by soil and sediment deposited at the mouths of rivers.

Water features

- Oceans: The largest bodies of water on the planet. The four oceans of the Earth are the Atlantic Ocean, the Pacific Ocean, the Indian Ocean, and the ice-filled Arctic Ocean.
- Seas: Bodies of water that are smaller than oceans and surrounded by land.

- Rivers: Considered a nation's lifeblood, usually begin as very small streams, formed by melting snow and rainfall, flowing from higher to lower land, emptying into a larger body of water, usually a sea or an ocean.
- Canals: Man-made water passages constructed to connect two larger bodies of water.

Physical Processes and the Environment

WEATHER: the condition of the atmosphere, including temperature, air pressure, wind, and moisture or precipitation

WEATHER is the condition of the atmosphere, including temperature, air pressure, wind, and moisture or precipitation, which includes rain, snow, hail, or sleet.

World weather patterns are greatly influenced by ocean surface currents in the upper layer of the ocean. These currents continuously move along the ocean surface in specific directions.

World weather patterns are greatly influenced by ocean surface currents in the upper layer of the ocean. These currents continuously move along the ocean surface in specific directions. Ocean currents that flow deep below the surface are called subsurface currents and are influenced by such factors as the location of landmasses in the current's path and the earth's rotation.

CLIMATE: the average weather or daily weather conditions for a specific region or location over a long or extended period of time

CLIMATE is the average weather or daily weather conditions for a specific region or location over a long or extended period of time.

Plate tectonics is a geological theory that explains continental drift, which refers to the large movements of the solid portions of the Earth's crust floating on the molten mantle. There are ten major tectonic plates and several smaller plates. There are three types of plate boundaries: convergent, divergent, and transform. Convergent boundaries exist where plates are moving toward one another. When this happens, the two plates collide and fold up against one another, called continental collision, or one plate slides under the other, called subduction. Continental collision can create high mountain ranges, such as the Andes and the Himalayas. Subduction often results in volcanic activity along the boundary, like the horseshoe-shaped "Ring of Fire" that encircles the basin of the Pacific Ocean.

Erosion is the displacement of solid earth surfaces such as rock and soil.

Weathering is the natural decomposition of the Earth's surface from contact with the atmosphere. It is not the same as erosion, but can be a factor in it.

Transportation is the movement of eroded material from one place to another by wind, water, or ice.

Deposition is the result of transportation, and occurs when the material being carried settles on the surface and is deposited.

Land Use

Geography can also form natural boundaries for settlements and civilizations. Mountain ranges and large bodies of water make effective borders between states and countries.

The greatest influence on land use is population and population growth. A burgeoning population demands a considerable amount from the land it surrounds and eventually incorporates—for food, living, and industrial use.

Types of land use

Land-use patterns vary substantially by region. Factors that influence the use of land include: differences in climate, soil makeup, topography, and population dispersal. There are several different types of land use:

- Cropland: Makes up 20 percent of U.S. land use. This category includes land that is actively being used to grow crops as well as idle cropland.
- Grassland pasture and range: Makes up 26 percent of U.S. land use. This category includes land used for grazing livestock, ranching, and animal husbandry.
- Forestland: Makes up 29 percent of U.S. land use. This category includes land used to grow timber for building and fuel.
- Urban uses: Make up 3 percent of U.S. land use. The Northeast and Southeast have the highest percentage of urban-use land.
- Special uses: Make up 13 percent of U.S. land use. Special uses include land used for national and state parks, roads, and recreational areas.
- Miscellaneous uses: Make up 10 percent of U.S. land use. This category includes most other types of land such as swamps, tundras, bare rock areas, and marshes.

Land-use models

Land-use and development models are theories that attempt to explain the layout of urban areas. Two primary land-use models are generally applied to urban regions:

- The Burgess model (also called the concentric model)
- The Hoyt model (also called the sector model)

In rural areas, land use usually includes agriculture, forestry, and sometimes fishing. In the Von Thunen model, a city is the center of a state or region, from which a series of concentric circles emanates, each devoted to particular rural land-use patterns.

Consequences of various types of land use

There are many environmental, cultural, and economic consequences of various types of land use. Human beings have long been altering their surroundings in order to provide water, food, fiber, and shelter for billions of people.

There are many environmental, cultural, and economic consequences of various types of land use. Human beings have long been altering their surroundings in order to provide water, food, fiber, and shelter for billions of people. However, changes to our natural landscape to create croplands, pastures, plantations, and urban areas have had a significant impact on the earth's natural resources and biodiversity. Some of the consequences of various types of land use are:

- Loss of natural landscape: The conversion of the world's natural landscape (forest, wetlands, waterways, etc.) for agriculture, settlement, and other human uses may soon undermine the capacity of the earth's ecosystems to sustain an ever-growing population.
- Loss of natural resources: By making changes to our natural landscape, humans have been able to allocate a huge portion of Earth's natural resources.
- Loss of biodiversity: By altering the earth's natural makeup, humans have vastly changed the plant and animal diversity on the Earth. By destroying the natural habitat of these life forms, humans have put many of them in peril.
- Climate change: Land-cover change has been a major source of greenhouse gases, gases that accumulate in the atmosphere and increase global temperature.

We face the task of balancing immediate human needs with maintaining the ability of the earth to provide natural resources in the long term. Strategies for maintaining this balance include making agricultural production more efficient, increasing open spaces in urban areas, and using forestry techniques that provide food and fiber yet sustain habitats for threatened plant and animal species.

Policy makers, corporations, and governments must determine how to use and distribute scarce resources. Decision makers must balance the immediate demand for resources with the need for resources in the future.

The main concerns in nonrenewable resource management are conservation, allocation, and environmental mitigation. Policy makers, corporations, and governments must determine how to use and distribute scarce resources. Decision makers must balance the immediate demand for resources with the need for resources in the future. Finally, scientists can attempt to minimize and mitigate the environmental damage caused by resource extraction. Scientists can devise methods of harvesting and using resources that do not unnecessarily affect the environment. After the extraction of resources from a location, scientists can devise plans and methods to restore the environment to as close to its original state as possible.

Migration

According to the TEKS glossary, "Migration is the process of moving from one place to another place intending to stay permanently or at least for a long period of time. Pull factors draw migrants from their original location. These include social, economic, and environmental attractions. Push factors are the social, economic, and environmental forces which drive people from their original location and cause them to seek a new one."

Effect of Geography on Settlement Patterns Around the World

Two things seem to have come together to produce cultures and civilizations: A society/culture based on agriculture and the development of social centers populated with a literate minority and religious organizations. The members of these elite groups managed the functional aspects of society, such as the water supply and irrigation, as well as the religious aspects of society, such as rituals and religious life. They asserted their own right to use a portion of the goods produced by the community in return for their management of the community.

As trade routes developed and travel between cities became easier, trade led to specialization.

Cities and rural areas

Cities are the major hubs of human settlement. Almost half of the population of the world now lives in cities. These percentages are much higher in developed regions. Established cities continue to grow. The fastest growth, however, is occurring in developing areas.

Rural areas tend to be less densely populated due to the needs of agriculture. More land is needed to produce crops or for animal husbandry than is required for manufacturing.

Spatial organization

We can examine the spatial organization of the places where people live. For example, in a city, where are the factories and buildings for heavy industry? Are they near airports or train stations? What about housing developments? Are they near these industries, or are they far away? Where are the schools, hospitals, and parks? How close are homes to each of these things? Towns, and especially cities, are routinely organized into neighborhoods, so that each house or home is close to most things its residents might need on a regular basis.

Patterns of urban development

Before the advent of efficient overland routes of commerce, i.e., railroads and highways, water provided the primary means of transportation of commercial goods. Most large American cities are situated along bodies of water.

The growth of an urban area is often linked to the advantages provided by its geographic location. Before the advent of efficient overland routes of commerce, i.e., railroads and highways, water provided the primary means of transportation of commercial goods. Most large American cities are situated along bodies of water.

As transportation technology advanced, the supporting infrastructure was built to connect cities with one another and to connect remote areas to larger communities. The railroad, for example, allowed for the quick transport of agricultural products from rural areas to urban centers. This newfound efficiency not only further fueled the growth of urban centers, but it changed the economy of rural America. When once farmers had practiced only subsistence farming—growing enough to support one's own family—the new infrastructure meant that farmers could convert agricultural products into cash by selling them at market.

For urban dwellers, improvements in building technology and advances in transportation allowed for larger cities to develop. Growth brought new problems, unique to each location. The bodies of water that had made the development of cities possible in their early days also formed natural barriers to growth. Further infrastructure in the form of bridges, tunnels, and ferry routes was needed to connect central urban areas to outlying communities.

The growth of suburbs had the effect in many cities of creating a type of economic segregation. Working-class people who could not afford new suburban homes and perhaps an automobile to carry them to and from work were relegated to closer, more densely populated areas. Frequently, these areas had to be passed through by those on their way to the suburbs, and rail lines and freeways sometimes bisected these urban communities.

In the modern age, advancements in telecommunications infrastructure may have an impact on urban growth patterns as information can now pass instantly and freely between almost any two points on the globe, providing access to some aspects of urban life to those in remote areas. Flight has made global commerce and goods exchange possible on a level never before seen. Foods from all around the world can be flown literally around the world, and, with the aid of refrigeration techniques, be kept fresh enough to sell in markets nearly everywhere. The same is true of medicine, and, unfortunately, weapons.

Geography lends itself to many other disciplines. Geographical factors have a bearing on problems and solutions in a number of other fields of study.

Influence of Geography in Other Domains

Geography lends itself to many other disciplines. Geographical factors have a bearing on problems and solutions in a number of other fields of study.

One of the foremost examples of this is geography's application to economics. Business owners seeking the best location for a manufacturing plant will naturally consider geographic factors when making their final decision. Will the plant depend on hydroelectric power? If so, should the plant be located near a natural water source like a river, lake, or dam? Will the plant be exporting or importing a large number of products? If so, where is the nearest airport and how far away are the nearest highways and residential areas? If the plant owners will depend heavily on land-based transportation, what is the surrounding terrain like? Can heavy trucks easily connect from plant to highway, and vice versa? Is privacy a concern? How will what the company is doing affect the local community? Strip mining of local hills and mountains could be a source of much friction. If the plant is manufacturing secret products, then the owners will want to situate that plant as far away from the rest of civilization as possible, within the guidelines already mentioned.

Geography's influence also extends to politics. The way an industry or organization treats the land around them can be the source of political debate. So can the treatment of nearby wildlife.

Geography of the United States

The continental United States is bordered by the Pacific Ocean on the west and the Atlantic Ocean on the east. The country is divided into two main sections by the Rocky Mountains, which extend from New Mexico in the south through the Canadian border in the north. The western portion of the country contains forested, mountainous areas in the Pacific Northwest and northern California, including Mt. St. Helens, an active volcano in the Cascade Range. Dryer, warmer regions in the south include the Mojave Desert in the Southwest. The Great Salt Lake in Utah is at the foot of the Wasatch Mountains.

The **Rocky Mountains** slope down in the east to the **Great Plains**, a large, grassy region drained by the **Mississippi River**, the nation's largest river, and one of the largest rivers in the world. The Great Plains give way in the east to hilly, forested regions. The **Appalachian Mountain** chain runs along the eastern coast of the United States. Along the border with Canada between Minnesota and New York are Lake Huron, Lake Ontario, Lake Michigan, Lake Erie, and Lake Superior, known as the **Great Lakes**.

Geography of Texas

Most of Texas is flat farmland, particularly West Texas, where the dominant crops are cotton, wheat, and sorghum. The land is semiarid and, for the most part, flat, with the exception of some hills and one mountain range, the Davis Mountains. Oil can be found in West Texas, near the Midland-Odessa corridor. The antebellum and Civil War-era civilizations in East Texas depended almost entirely on "King Cotton," with the hills and swamps dominated by vast plantations. Cotton's influence can still be felt there, but the dominant crop now is rice.

Houston is very much a port city, capitalizing on an early-twentieth-century canal to the Gulf of Mexico as a way to ship goods to the world. Indeed, only New York City ships more than Houston.

The Gulf Coast is dominated by Houston, the fourth-largest city in the United States. Houston is very much a port city, capitalizing on an early-twentieth-century canal to the Gulf of Mexico as a way to ship goods to the world. Indeed, only New York City ships more than Houston. The lower Rio Grande area has citrus fruits and winter vegetables in abundance. The rest of the Rio Grande valley is dotted with cattle ranches, some of which are very large.

Further north are the backland prairies, a large range of agricultural and ranch land, where large quantities of cotton and grain are grown and cattle are raised. The large cities of Dallas and Fort Worth are in this area. These two cities together form one of the most burgeoning metropolitan areas in the U.S, with big business in oil refining, grain milling, and cotton processing. The high plains have a somewhat varied landscape, although the semiarid climate falls mostly on flat land. Of note is a dry-farming area near Lubbock, one of the larger cities of the region. Oil, grain, wheat, and cotton are the major industries.

The people who live and have lived in Texas have made the land their own, turning flat, sometimes water-starved lands into vast plantations, ranches, and fields.

The people who live and have lived in Texas have made the land their own, turning flat, sometimes water-starved lands into vast plantations, ranches, and fields. Large cities have not been confined to waterways (although the state's largest city, Houston, is on the Gulf Coast). Dirt roads, railroads, and then paved roads have connected the large state's many towns and cities.

The most drastic change to the environment wrought by people has been the sheer number of square miles devoted to living space. Texas still maintains vast areas of agricultural and ranch land, but that area is shrinking by the year as more and more people claim land exclusively for residential use.

Effect of Physical Environment on Early Settlement in Texas

According to the TEKS glossary, "Several factors may influence ongoing development and events in history. Physical factors relate to the physical characteristics of a place such as climate, weather, and landforms. These lead to events, such as tornadoes, hurricanes, or droughts, which influence the chain of events constituting Texas history. Physical factors also influence development. Most early settlement in Texas concentrated in the eastern portion of the state because the soils, climate, and vegetation compared favorably to other parts of the South from which most settlers migrated. Transportation routes developed to link settlements which evolved into cities. Human factors relate to the human characteristics of a place. These also play a role in Texas history. As population pressures in the eastern portion of the state increased, settlement moved west. As technology improved, settlers in the western plains began to irrigate their crop land and the area's economy developed around cotton-based agriculture. This is one way human factors influence development by modifying the environment."

Effect of Geography on Politics in Texas

Politics in Texas have always been contentious. One source of contention is the struggle between the ranch politics of yesterday and the high-tech politics of today. Farmers and ranchers obviously have different interests than atomic scientists, and these interests often clash in the halls of Austin policymakers. Geography contributes to this clash because farmers' and ranchers' concerns are related to their locations, and urbanites' perspectives are influenced by their environments, which are more metropolitan. Oil companies and their lobbyists are also a vocal group.

Oil continues to be a staggeringly large business in Texas, and oil interests often clash with those of other industries.

Basic Concepts of Culture

Humans are social animals who naturally form groups based on familial, cultural, national, and other lines. Conflicts and differences of opinion between these groups are just as natural.

Ethnocentrism: The belief that one's own culture is the central and usually superior culture. An ethnocentric view usually considers different practices in other cultures inferior.

A variety of factors differentiate cultures, including language, customs, dress, food, religious beliefs, and ethnicity. It is these attributes that define a culture and emphasize the differences between cultures. For example, citizens of the United States share a common language, English, whereas in Europe a multitude of languages and dialects are spoken by people from a variety of cultures, including Spanish, French, German, Italian, and Swedish. If you visit various regions of the United States, you will find a variety of accents and cadences—from the slang of New York City natives to the soft drawl of southern Texans to the flat, nasal tones of a Bostonian.

Belief systems are introduced to new societies in a variety of ways: through military and political conquest or through other types of human interaction such as commercial interaction or the identification of common or similar primitive mythologies (e.g., creation and myths). Educational interaction and cultural sharing frequently spread religious belief systems as well.

CULTURAL DIFFUSION: the movement of cultural ideas or materials between populations independent of the movement of those populations

CULTURAL DIFFUSION is the movement of cultural ideas or materials between populations independent of the movement of those populations.

ADAPTATION: the process that individuals and societies go through in changing their behavior and organization to cope with social, economic, and environmental pressures

ACCULTURATION: an exchange or adoption of cultural features when two cultures come into regular direct contact

ASSIMILATION: the process of a minority ethnic group adopting the culture of the larger group in which it exists

EXTINCTION: the complete disappearance of a culture

RACE: a population of people from a common geographic area who share certain physical traits

ETHNIC GROUP: a group of people who identify themselves as having a common social background and set of behaviors

CULTURAL IDENTITY: the identification of individuals or groups as they are influenced by belonging to a particular group or culture

ADAPTATION is the process that individuals and societies go through in changing their behavior and organization to cope with social, economic, and environmental pressures.

ACCULTURATION is an exchange or adoption of cultural features when two cultures come into regular direct contact. An example of acculturation is the adoption of Christianity and western dress by many Native Americans in the United States.

ASSIMILATION is the process of a minority ethnic group adopting the culture of the larger group in which it exists. Immigrants moving to a new country typically assimilate into the larger culture.

EXTINCTION is the complete disappearance of a culture. Extinction can occur suddenly—from disease, famine, or war—when the culture is completely destroyed, or slowly over time as a culture adapts, acculturates, or assimilates to the point where its original characteristic features are lost.

Race, Ethnicity, and Cultural Identity

RACE is a term used most generally to describe a population of people from a common geographic area who share certain physical traits. Skin color and facial features have traditionally been used to categorize individuals by race. The term has generated some controversy among sociologists, anthropologists, and biologists regarding what race and racial variation mean.

An **ETHNIC GROUP** is a group of people who identify themselves as having a common social background and set of behaviors, and who perpetuate their culture by traditions of marriage within their own group. Ethnic groups often share a common language and ancestral background and frequently exist within larger populations.

CULTURAL IDENTITY is the identification of individuals or groups as belonging to a particular group or culture. This refers to the sense of who one is, one's values, and what racial or ethnic characteristics are important in one's self-understanding and manner of interacting with others.

Cross-cultural exchanges can enrich every involved group of persons with the discovery of shared values and needs, as well as an appreciation for the unique cultural characteristics of each group. For the most part, the history of the U.S. has been the story of successful enculturation and cultural enrichment. The notable failures, usually resulting from prejudice and intolerance of one form or another, include oppression of Chinese-, Japanese-, and African-Americans.

The Transmission of Culture

A culture's beliefs and values are reflected in its cultural products, such as literature, art, media, and architecture. These products last from generation to generation, becoming one way that culture is transmitted through time. A common language among all members of a culture makes this transmission possible.

Sociologists have identified five different types of institutions around which societies are structured: family, education, government, religion, and economy. These institutions provide a framework for members of a society to learn about and participate in the society, and allow the society to perpetuate its beliefs and values in succeeding generations.

Sociologists have identified five different types of institutions around which societies are structured: family, education, government, religion, and economy.

The family is the primary social unit in most societies. It is through the family that children learn the most essential skills for functioning in their society such as language and appropriate forms of interaction. The family is connected to ethnicity, which is partly defined by a person's heritage.

Education is an important institution in a society because it allows for the formal passing on of a culture's collected knowledge. Education is connected to the family because that is where a child's earliest education takes place.

A society's governmental institutions often embody its beliefs and values. Laws, for instance, reflect a society's values by enforcing its ideas of right and wrong.

Religion is frequently the institution from which a society's primary beliefs and values stem, and can be closely related to other social institutions.

A society's economic institutions define how an individual can contribute to and receive economic reward from his or her society. The United States has a capitalist economy motivated by free enterprise.

Oral tradition and mythology

Before the time of the written word, cultures transmitted their stories, laws, history, beliefs, and knowledge through the spoken word. This could take the form of ballads, stories, poems, speeches, and chants. The purpose of maintaining an oral tradition is to transmit cultural knowledge from one generation to the next, thus reinforcing cultural norms and cultural identity.

Although each culture has developed its own unique oral traditions, many similarities exist between them. Oral traditions, and culture's the mythologies they may include, often seek to explain the world and our relation to the world. They provide insight into the order and ethics of life and provide explanations for the origin of the universe, the workings of natural phenomena, and the unique story of one's own people.

Major Cultural Regions of the World

- North America
- Latin America
- Europe
- The Middle East and North Africa
- Sub-Saharan Africa
- The region of Russia and Central Asia
- East Asia
- South Asia
- Southeast Asia
- Australia and New Zealand

Major Cultural Regions of the United States

- New England
- The Mid-Atlantic region
- The South
- The Midwest
- The Southwest
- The West

Texas, the Melting Pot

Stretching back through the history of the Mexican Territory, the number of Mexican residents who have migrated to Texas to seek a better life is very large indeed.

Stretching back through the history of the Mexican Territory, the number of Mexican residents who have migrated to Texas to seek a better life is very large indeed. Mexican-Americans work in a variety of capacities throughout the state—in agriculture, at oil fields, on ranches, and in hundreds of other white-collar capacities.

The Latino heritage of many Texas citizens is officially honored by the preservation of early settlements and artifacts such as Ceremonial Cave, Espiritu Santo, and Morhiss Mound.

African-Americans were first brought to Texas as slaves of the early white settlers. They worked both on cattle ranches and in cotton fields. After the Civil War, many African Americans migrated from southern states in search of greater opportunity. In 1966, Curtis Graves and Barbara Jordan became the first African-Americans elected to the state legislature since 1898. The Mansfield School Desegregation Incident in 1956 was a notable turning point in school desegregation in Texas.

ECONOMICS

Basic Economic Concepts

ECONOMICS is the study of how a society allocates its scarce resources to satisfy what are basically unlimited and competing wants. A fundamental fact of economics is that resources are scarce and that wants are infinite. The fact that scarce resources have to satisfy unlimited wants means choices have to be made. If a society uses its resources to produce good A, then it doesn't have those resources to produce good B. More of good A means less of good B. This trade-off is referred to as the opportunity cost, or the value, of the sacrificed alternative.

ECONOMICS: the study of how a society allocates its scarce resources to satisfy what are basically unlimited and competing wants

A market economy answers these questions in terms of demand and supply and the use of markets. Demand is based on consumer preferences and satisfaction and refers to the quantities of a good or service that buyers are willing and able to buy at different prices during a given period of time. Supply is based on costs of production and refers to the quantities that sellers are willing and able to sell at different prices during a given period of time. The determination of market equilibrium price is where the buying decisions of buyers coincide with the selling decisions of sellers. Free enterprise is when business is conducted based on the laws of supply and demand rather than governmental regulations.

The determination of market equilibrium price is where the buying decisions of buyers coincide with the selling decisions of sellers.

Economic systems refer to the arrangements a society has made to answer what are known as the three questions: what goods to produce, how to produce them, and for whom they are being produced, or, put another way, how the allocation of the output is determined.

GOODS: the physical products that can be delivered to, purchased by, owned by, and/or sold to a consumer

The economic term **GOODS** refers to the physical products that can be delivered to, purchased by, owned by, and/or sold to a consumer. **SERVICES**, in contrast, are intangible goods, i.e., things someone can do for someone else that are exchanged

SERVICES: intangible goods, i.e., things someone can do for someone else that are exchanged for money

for money. The factors of production refer to the resources people and businesses use to create goods and supply services.

Consumer economics

Consumers vote for the products they want with their spending. Goods acquiring enough dollar votes are profitable, signaling to the producers that society wants their scarce resources used in this way. This is how the "what" question is answered. The producer then hires inputs in accordance with the goods consumers want, looking for the most efficient or lowest-cost method of production. The lower a firm's costs for any given level of revenue, the higher the firm's profits. This is the way the "how" question is answered in a market economy. The "for whom" question is answered by the determination of the equilibrium price.

MARKET EFFICIENCY: obtaining the most output from the available inputs that are consistent with the preferences of consumers

Price serves to ration the goods to those who can and will transact at the market price or higher. Those who can't or won't are excluded from the market. This mechanism results in **MARKET EFFICIENCY**, obtaining the most output from the available inputs that are consistent with the preferences of consumers. Society's scarce resources are being used the way society wants them to be used.

The interdependence of households and businesses is illustrated by a circular flow diagram. In the two markets, inputs and outputs are exchanged and paid for by households and businesses. Factor owners sell their factors to employers in the input market. Firms use those factors to produce outputs that are sold in the output market. This is where factor owners spend their incomes on goods and services. Receipts for goods and services flow from households to businesses, and factor incomes flow from businesses to households.

The means of payment, whether it is barter, currency, or credit, do not affect the income flows; they are just different ways in which money can flow through the economy. Barter is the exchange of one good for another good.

Loans

The market price of loans is the interest rate.

All markets function to effect an efficient allocation of resources, even financial markets. They also function on the basis of supply and demand and loan funds to those who are willing to transact at the market price. The market price of loans is the interest rate. The supply of loanable funds comes from savings. Since savings represent dollars of postponed spending, households must have some form of inducement to save. This inducement or payment for saving dollars is the interest rate. The higher the interest rate is, the more dollars households will be willing to save.

Loans are needed by businesses and by individuals for investment purposes. Borrowers are willing to pay a price for the funds they borrow. This price is the interest rate. Borrowers borrow more funds at lower interest rates than they do at higher interest rates. This means that the demand for loanable funds curve slopes downward. We now have the downward-sloping demand for loanable funds curve and the upward-sloping supply of loanable funds curve. If we put the two curves together then we have the market equilibrium at the point of intersection of demand and supply.

Types of Economic Systems

Economists identify three types of economic systems:

- Traditional (also known as subsistence)
- Command (also known as planned)
- Market (commercial)

In a traditional economy, goods and services are produced by a family for the family's personal consumption. There is little surplus and little exchange of goods. There is only a limited need for markets (places to buy and sell goods and services). This is the type of economy found in less developed nations, usually in rural areas. The economy reflects the customs, habits, laws, and religious beliefs of the area, and these control decisions. Most less-developed nations today are a mix of traditional and either market or command economies.

In a command economy, the government regulates economic activity, making decisions about what and how much to produce, where to locate economic activities, and what prices to charge for goods and services. These economic decisions are often made to further social goals.

Communism is one example of a command economy; socialism is another. In a command economy, the price of goods, including agricultural products, is controlled by the government, not market forces. Production costs are not reflected in prices. For example, it may cost $1.00 to produce a loaf of bread, but the price may be set at $.25 to ensure that customers are able to afford adequate provisions. The price may also be set over production costs, given demand.

In a market economy, elements of which may be considered a free enterprise economic system, the laws of supply and demand and the market determine decisions about what and how much to produce, where to locate economic activities, and what prices to charge for goods and services. Profit drives decisions in a market economy. A mixed economy combines elements of these three systems.

The U.S. Economic System

The fundamental characteristics of the U.S. economic system are competition and markets. Competition is determined by market structure. Since the cost curves are the same for all firms, the only difference is on the revenue side. The most competitive of all market structures is perfect competition, characterized by numerous buyers and sellers, all with perfect knowledge. No one seller is big enough to influence price. Products are homogenous, so buyers are indifferent about which companies they buy from. The absence of barriers to entry makes it easy for firms to enter and leave an industry. At the other end of the spectrum is monopoly, in which there is only one seller of a particular product or commodity. Barriers to entry are significant enough to keep firms from entering or leaving an industry.

Oligopoly is a market structure in which a few large firms sell heterogeneous or homogenous products in a market structure with varying barriers to entry. Each firm maximizes profits by producing at the point where marginal costs equal marginal revenue. The existence of economic profits, an above-normal rate of return, attracts capital to an industry and results in expansion. Whether or not new firms can enter depends on barriers to entry.

Profit functions as a financial incentive for individuals and firms. The possibility of earning profit is why individuals are willing to undertake entrepreneurial ventures and why firms are willing to spend money on research and development and innovation. Without these kinds of financial incentives, there would be no new product development or technological advancement.

Economic Activities

Economic activities are closely tied to the availability of resources required to support them. Resources include the raw materials required to make a product, the communications and transportation infrastructure needed to provide a service, and a supply of people to create the product or provide service efficiently.

Historically, many towns and cities grew up around a single economic activity. A mill town, for instance, usually located along a river to harness its waterpower, was a central place for grain farmers from the surrounding regions to bring their products for processing. Mining towns and logging towns were organized in a similar way, with most of the economic survival of the community reliant on a local natural resource.

Modern transportation means that economic activities are not as closely tied to particular locations as they were in the past. Oil, for instance, is sometimes transported for thousands of miles to the refineries where it is processed.

Measuring the size of an economy

The size of an economy is typically measured as the **gross domestic product**, or **GDP**. Economic activities can also be measured through one or more of the following methods: gross national product (GNP), GDP per capita, gross domestic income (GDI), consumer spending, stock markets, interest rates, rate of inflation, national debt, and unemployment. All of these measures shed light on the economic state of a nation.

When a society transforms from preindustrial to more organized and mechanized labor, skills, trades, and mass production, it is said to have become industrialized.

The Industrial Revolution

The first phase of the Industrial Revolution (1750-1830), which took place in Great Britain and Europe, saw the mechanization of the textile industry; vast improvements in mining, with the invention of the steam engine; and numerous improvements in transportation, with the development and improvement of turnpikes and canals and the invention of the railroad.

The second phase (1830-1910) resulted in vast improvements in a number of industries that had already been mechanized through such inventions as the Bessemer steel process and the invention of steamships.

Results of the Industrial Revolution

The direct results of the Industrial Revolution, particularly as they affected industry, commerce, and agriculture, included:

- Enormous increases in productivity
- Huge increases in world trade
- Specialization and division of labor
- Standardization of parts and mass production
- Growth of giant business conglomerates and monopolies
- A new revolution in agriculture facilitated by the steam engine, machinery, chemical fertilizers, processing, canning, and refrigeration

Political results

- Growth of complex government by technical experts
- Centralization of government, including regulatory administrative agencies
- Advantages of democratic development, including extension of franchise to the middle class and later to all elements of the population; mass education to meet the needs of an industrial society; and the development of media of public communication, including radio, television, and inexpensive newspapers

- Dangers to democracy, including the risk of manipulation of the media of mass communication; facilitation of dictatorial centralization and totalitarian control; subordination of the legislative function to administrative directives; efforts to achieve uniformity and conformity; and social impersonalization

Economic results

- Conflict between free trade and low tariffs and protectionism
- Issue of free enterprise versus government regulation
- Struggles between labor and capital, including the trade-union movement
- Rise of socialism
- Rise of the utopian socialists

Social results

- Increase in population, especially in industrial centers
- Advances in science applied to agriculture, sanitation, and medicine
- Growth of great cities
- Disappearance of the distinctions between city dwellers and farmers
- Faster tempo of life and increased stress from the monotony of the work routine
- Emancipation of women

Interdependence of Texas Economy with U.S. and Other World Economies

Texas, like all of the other states, is a part of the U.S. economy. Texas engages in trade and commerce with other states and the national government. In today's world, markets are international. Participation in a global economy means that what one nation does affects other nations because economies are linked through international trade, commerce, and finance.

Trade and trade barriers

The relative importance of trade is based on the percentage of a country's gross domestic product that trade constitutes. In a country like the United States, trade represents only a few percent of GDP. In other nations, trade may represent over 50 percent of GDP. For those countries, changes in international transactions can cause many economic fluctuations and problems.

Trade barriers can cause economic problems. Suppose a domestic government is confronted with rising unemployment in a domestic industry due to cheap foreign imports. Consumers are buying the cheaper foreign import instead of the higher-priced domestic good. In order to protect domestic labor, the government imposes a tariff, thus raising the price of the more-cheaply produced foreign good. The result of the tariff is that consumers buy more of the domestic good and less of the foreign good. However, the foreign good is the product of the foreign nation's labor. A decrease in the demand for the foreign good means that foreign producers don't need as much labor, so they lay off workers in the foreign country.

Bretton Woods system (post-World War II)

The United States, along with the Soviet Union, emerged as the new world powers after World War II. The European economies were shattered by the war, as were their infrastructures. The U.S. embarked on a program of massive aid called the Marshall Plan to help the war-devastated economies rebuild. The Bretton Woods system was established to provide stable exchange rates. The General Agreement on Tariffs and Trade (GATT) and other trade organizations were established to help lower trade barriers. This system worked well and the world economies recovered from the war.

Under the Bretton Woods system, the U.S. dollar was expressed in terms of gold, at $35.00 per ounce, and all other world currencies were expressed in terms of the U.S. dollar. Nations were required to keep their currency values within specified ranges and nations would settle their balance of payment imbalances at the end of the year. This system worked well until the 1960s, when the world experienced exchange-rate crises that resulted in the exchange markets closing. The situation continued until 1973, when world exchange rates began to float. This eliminated the need for the settlement of payment imbalances because the exchange rate adjusts to eliminate any payment disequilibrium. A deficit results in currency depreciation and a surplus results in currency appreciation. As firms and traders became more adept at hedging, currency problems were eliminated and international trade continued to grow.

After this time, many industries began to relocate to Texas, and the oil and aeronautics industries, as well as other industries, developed. Houston remains a major international shipping center.

GOVERNMENT AND CITIZENSHIP

Forms of Government

Systems of government vary throughout the world, and the way the government of a society rules the citizen body is called the form, or type, of government.

Form of Government	Description
Anarchism	Political movement advocating the elimination of all government and its replacement by a cooperative community of individuals. Sometimes it has involved political violence such as assassinations of important political or governmental figures. The historical banner of the movement is a black flag.
Communism	A belief as well as a political system, characterized by the ideology of a classless system and commonly controlled property. Communism encourages a one-party state and government ownership of the means of production and the distribution of goods and services.
Dictatorship	The rule by an individual or small group of individuals (oligarchy) that centralizes all political control in itself and enforces its will with a represive police force.
Fascism	A belief as well as a political system, with a one-party state, centralized political control, and a repressive police system. Fascism, however, tolerates private ownership of the means of production, though it maintains tight overall control. Central to its belief is the idolization of the leader, a "cult of personality," and most often an expansionist ideology. Examples have been German Nazism and Italian Fascism.
Monarchy	The rule of a nation by a monarch, (a nonelected, usually hereditary leader), most often a king or queen. Monarchy may or may not be accompanied by some measure of democratic open institutions and elections at various levels.
Democracy	A familiar system to most, the system under which we live in the United States. The term comes from the Greek "for the rule of the people." The two most prevalent types are **direct** and **indirect democracy**. Direct democracy usually involves all of the people in a given area coming together to vote and decide on issues that will affect them. It is used only when the population involved is relatively small; for example, a local town meeting. An **indirect democracy** involves much larger areas and populations and involves sending representatives to a legislative body to vote on issues affecting the people. Such a system can be a **presidential** or **parliamentary** system. In the United States, we have an indirect, or representative, democracy of the presidential type.

Continued on next page

Form of Government	Description
Parliamentary system	A system of government with a legislature, usually involving a number of political parties and often coalition politics. There is a distinction between the head of state and the head of government. The head of government is usually known as a prime minister, who is also usually the head of the largest political party.
Presidential system	A system of government with a legislature, which can involve few or many political parties, with no distinction between the head of state and the head of government.
Socialism	A political belief and system in which the state takes a guiding role in the national economy and provides extensive social services to its population. The state may or may not own outright the means of production, but even when it does not, it exercises tight control.

U.S. Government

There are three branches of government at the U.S. federal level, discussed below.

Legislative branch

Article I of the Constitution establishes the legislative or law-making branch of the government called the Congress. It is made up of two houses, the House of Representatives and the Senate. Voters in each state elect the members who represent them in each respective house of Congress. The legislative branch is responsible for making laws, raising and printing money, regulating trade, establishing the postal service and federal courts, approving the president's appointments, declaring war, and supporting the armed forces. The Congress also has the power to change the Constitution itself, and to impeach (bring charges against) the president. Charges for impeachment are brought by the House of Representatives and then tried in the Senate.

Executive branch

Article II of the Constitution creates the executive branch of the government, headed by the president, who leads the country, recommends new laws, and can veto bills passed by the legislative branch. As the chief of state, the president is responsible for carrying out the laws of the country and the treaties and declarations of war passed by the legislative branch. The president also appoints federal judges and is commander-in-chief of the military. Other members of the executive branch include the vice president, also elected, and various officials appointed by the president: cabinet members, ambassadors, presidential advisors, members of the armed forces, and other civil servants of government agencies, departments, and bureaus. Although the president appoints them, they must be approved by the legislative branch.

Judicial branch

Article III of the Constitution establishes the judicial branch of government, headed by the Supreme Court. The Supreme Court has the power to declare a law passed by the legislature or an act of the executive branch illegal and unconstitutional. Citizens, businesses, and government officials can appeal to the Supreme Court to review a decision made in a lower court if they believe the ruling by a judge is unconstitutional. The judicial branch also includes lower federal courts known as federal district courts that have been established by the Congress. These courts try and review cases referred from other courts.

Powers of the Federal Government	Powers of the States
1. To tax	1. To regulate intrastate trade
2. To borrow and coin money	2. To establish local governments
3. To establish a postal service	3. To protect general welfare
4. To grant patents and copyrights	4. To protect life and property
5. To regulate interstate and foreign commerce	5. To ratify amendments
6. To establish courts	6. To conduct elections
7. To declare war	7. To make state and local laws
8. To raise and support the armed forces	
9. To govern territories	
10. To define and punish felonies and piracy on the high seas	
11. To fix standards of weights and measures	
12. To conduct foreign affairs	

Concurrent powers of the federal government and states

1. Both Congress and the states may tax
2. Both may borrow money
3. Both may charter banks and corporations

4. Both may establish courts
5. Both may make and enforce laws
6. Both may take property for public purposes
7. Both may spend money to provide for the public welfare

Implied powers of the federal government

1. To establish banks or other corporations, implied from delegated powers to tax, borrow, and to regulate commerce
2. To spend money for roads, schools, health, insurance, etc., implied from powers to establish post roads, to tax to provide for general welfare and defense, and to regulate commerce
3. To create military academies, implied from powers to raise and support an armed force
4. To locate and generate sources of power and sell surplus, implied from powers to dispose of government property, commerce, and war powers
5. To assist and regulate agriculture, implied from power to tax and spend for general welfare and to regulate commerce

Declaration of Independence and U.S. Constitution

Many of the core values in the U.S. democratic system can be found in the opening words of the Declaration of Independence, including the belief in equality, and the rights of citizens to "life, liberty and the pursuit of happiness."

The Declaration was a condemnation of the British king's tyrannical government, and these words emphasized the American colonists' belief that a government received its authority to rule from the people, and that its function should not be to suppress the governed, but rather to protect the rights of the governed, including protection from the government itself.

POPULAR SOVEREIGNTY is the idea that citizens should have the ability to directly participate in their own government by voting and running for public office. This ideal is based on the right of all citizens to engage in their own governance, established in the U.S. Constitution. The Constitution also contains a list of specific rights of citizens, upon which the government cannot infringe. Popular sovereignty also includes the idea that citizens can change their government if they feel it is necessary.

POPULAR SOVEREIGNTY: the idea that citizens should have the ability to directly participate in their own government by voting and running for public office

RULE OF LAW: the ideal that the law applies not only to the governed but to the government as well

The **RULE OF LAW** is the ideal that the law applies not only to the governed but to the government as well. This core value gives authority to the justice system, which grants citizens protection from the government by requiring that any accusation of a crime be proved by the government before a person is punished. This principle, called due process, ensures that any accused person has an opportunity to confront his or her accuser(s) and provide a defense.

The process by which laws and regulations can be enacted is defined by the Constitution, with the protection of the balance of powers. Laws are introduced, debated, and passed by the U.S. Congress, with both houses required to pass the same version of the law. Laws must then be signed by the president. Once signed, a law is considered enacted and is enforced. Challenges to the constitutionality of the law and questions of interpretation of the law are handled by the federal court system. Each state has the authority to make laws covering anything not controlled by the federal government. State laws cannot negate federal laws.

Bill of Rights

The first ten amendments to the U.S. Constitution, written mostly by James Madison, constitute the Bill of Rights and deal with civil liberties and civil rights. They are, in brief:

1. Freedom of religion
2. Right to bear arms
3. Security from the quartering of troops in homes
4. Right against unreasonable search and seizure
5. Right against self-incrimination
6. Right to trial by jury, right to legal council
7. Right to jury trial for civil actions
8. No cruel or unusual punishment allowed
9. These rights shall not deny other rights the people enjoy
10. Powers not mentioned in the Constitution shall be retained by the states or the people

AMENDMENT: a change or addition to the U.S. Constitution

Amendments to the U.S. Constitution

An **AMENDMENT** is a change or addition to the U.S. Constitution. Two-thirds of both houses of Congress must propose and then pass an amendment, or two-thirds of the state legislatures must call a convention to propose one and then it must be ratified by three-fourths of the state legislatures. To date, only twenty-seven amendments to the Constitution have passed. An amendment can be used to cancel out a previous one; for example, the Eighteenth Amendment (1919), known as Prohibition, was canceled by the Twenty-first Amendment (1933).

Amending the U.S. Constitution is an extremely difficult thing to accomplish. The final and most difficult step for an amendment is the ratification by the state legislatures. A total of three-fourths of those must approve an amendment. Approvals in the state legislatures only need to be a simple majority, but the number of states that must approve the amendment is thirty-eight.

Hundreds of amendments have been proposed through the years, but only twenty-seven have become part of the Constitution.

A key element in some of those failures has been the time limit Congress has the option to put on amendment proposals. A famous example of an amendment that got close but didn't reach the threshold before the deadline expired was the **Equal Rights Amendment (ERA)**, which was proposed in 1972. It couldn't muster enough support for passage, even though the deadline was extended from seven to ten years.

The first ten amendments are called the Bill of Rights and were approved at the same time, shortly after the Constitution was ratified. The Eleventh and Twelfth Amendments were ratified around the turn of the nineteenth century and, respectively, voided foreign suits against states and revised the method of presidential election. The Thirteenth, Fourteenth, and Fifteenth Amendments were passed in succession after the end of the Civil War. The Thirteenth Amendment outlawed slavery. The Fourteenth and Fifteenth Amendments provided for equal protection and for voting rights, respectively, without consideration of skin color.

The first twentieth-century amendment was the Sixteenth Amendment, which provided for a federal income tax. Providing for direct election to the Senate was the Seventeenth Amendment. Until then, Senators were appointed by state leaders, not elected by the public at large.

The Eighteenth Amendment prohibited the use or sale of alcohol across the country. The long battle for voting rights for women ended in success with the passage of the Nineteenth Amendment. The Twentieth Amendment changed the date for the beginning of political terms from March to January for the president and the Congress. With the Twenty-first Amendment came the only instance in which an Amendment was repealed. In this case, it was the Eighteenth Amendment, the prohibition of the sale or consumption of alcohol.

The Twenty-second Amendment limited the number of terms a president could serve to two. Presidents since George Washington had followed Washington's practice of not running for a third term; this changed when Franklin D. Roosevelt ran for reelection a third time, in 1940. He was reelected that time and a fourth time, too, four years later. He didn't live out his fourth term, but he did convince Congress and most of the state legislatures that some sort of term limit should be put in place.

The little-known Twenty-third Amendment provided for representation of Washington, D.C., in the electoral college. The Twenty-fourth Amendment prohibited poll taxes, which some people—usually African-Americans—had been required to pay in order to vote.

Presidential succession is the focus of the Twenty-fifth Amendment, which provides a blueprint of what to do if the president is incapacitated or killed. The Twenty-sixth Amendment lowered the legal voting age for Americans from twenty-one to eighteen. The Twenty-seventh, and final, Amendment, prohibits members of Congress from substantially raising their own salaries. This amendment was one of twelve originally proposed in the late eighteenth century. Ten of those twelve became the Bill of Rights, and one has yet to become law.

A host of potential amendments have made news headlines in recent years. A total of six have been proposed by Congress and passed muster in both houses, but have not been ratified by enough state legislatures. The aforementioned equal rights amendment is one. Another one, which would grant the District of Columbia full voting rights equivalent to those of the states, has not passed; like the equal rights amendment, its deadline has expired. A handful of others remain on the books without expiration dates, including an amendment to regulate child labor.

How A Bill Becomes Law

Federal laws are passed by the Congress, and can originate in either the House of Representatives or the Senate. The first step in the passing of a law is for the proposed law to be introduced in one of the houses of Congress. A proposed law is called a **bill** while it is under consideration by Congress.

Once a bill is introduced, it is assigned to one of several standing committees of the house in which it was introduced. The committee studies the bill and researches the issues it covers. The committee may gather public comments and call experts to testify about the bill. The committee may revise the bill. Finally, the committee votes on whether to release the bill for a vote by the full body. A committee may also lay aside a bill to eliminate the voting opportunity. Once a bill is released, it can be debated and amended by the full body before the vote occurs. If it passes by a simple majority vote, the bill is sent to the other house of Congress, where the process begins again.

Once a bill has passed both the House of Representatives and the Senate, it is assigned to a conference committee made up of members of both houses. The conference committee resolves differences between the House and Senate versions of a bill, if any, and then sends it back to both houses for final approval. Once a bill receives final approval, it is signed by the speaker of the House and the vice president, who is also the president of the Senate, and sent to the president for consideration. The president can either sign the bill or veto it. If the bill is vetoed, the veto can be overruled if two-thirds of both the Senate and the House vote to do so. Once signed by the president, the bill becomes a law.

Federal laws are enforced by the executive branch and its departments. The Department of Justice, led by the U.S. attorney general, is the primary law enforcement department of the federal government. The Justice Department is aided by other investigative and enforcement departments such as the Federal Bureau of Investigation (FBI) and the U.S. Postal Inspection Service.

Rights and Responsibilities of Citizenship

Citizenship in a democracy bestows on an individual certain rights, the most important of which is the right to participate in one's own government. Along with these rights come responsibilities, including the responsibility of a citizen to participate in his or her government.

The most basic form of participation is **voting**. Citizens who have reached the age of eighteen in the United States are eligible to vote in public elections. With this right comes the responsibility to be informed before voting, and not to sell or otherwise give away one's vote. Citizens are also eligible to run for public office. Along with the right to run for office comes the responsibility to represent the voters as fairly as possible and to perform the duties expected of a representative of the government.

In the United States, citizens are guaranteed the right to **free speech**, the right to express an opinion on public issues. In turn, citizens have the responsibility to allow others to speak freely.

In the United States, citizens are guaranteed the right to free speech, the right to express an opinion on public issues. In turn, citizens have the responsibility to allow others to speak freely.

The U.S. Constitution also guarantees **freedom of religion**. This means that the government cannot impose an official religion on its citizens and that people are free to practice any religion they choose. Citizens are also responsible for allowing those of other religions to practice freely without obstruction.

The U.S. Constitution guarantees that all citizens be treated equally by the law. In addition, federal and state laws make it a crime to discriminate against citizens based on their sex, race, religion, and other factors. To ensure that all people are treated equally, citizens have the responsibility to follow these laws.

State and Local Governments

State governments are mirror images of the federal government, with a few important exceptions: Governors are not technically commanders-in-chief of armed forces; state supreme court decisions can be appealed to federal courts; terms of state representatives and senators vary; judges, even of the state supreme courts, are elected by popular vote; and governors and legislators have term limits that vary by state.

Local governments vary widely across the country, although none of them has a judicial branch *per se*. Some local governments consist of a city council with limited powers, of which the mayor is a member, and in other cities, the mayor is the head of the government and the city council are the chief lawmakers. Local governments also have less strict requirements for people running for office than do the state and federal governments.

Texas Government and the Texas Constitution

The government of Texas is like a miniature U.S. government. Texas has three branches of government: executive, legislative, and judicial. The governor is the head of the executive branch. The legislature has two houses, a House of Representatives with 150 members and a Senate with 31 members, and meets in regular session every two years. The judicial branch has many, sometimes overlapping courts, of which the supreme court (civil cases) and the Texas Court of Criminal Appeals are the highest. Judges are elected, as are many members of the executive branch.

Amending the Texas Constitution requires two-thirds approval by the Texas house and senate followed by a majority vote of the people approving the amendment.

The **Texas constitution** is an extremely long document, full of details for nearly every imaginable eventuality. The overriding idea behind the Texas constitution is the protection of individual rights.

Citizens of the state of Texas have a host of rights and responsibilities. The state constitution protects them from harm, from unfair government and laws, and from violence from outside sources. The state government protects their right to a legal job at a fair wage as well.

Texas residents are expected to obey their state, local, and national laws and to pay their taxes and vote in elections at all three levels of government. They are expected to represent their state well when they travel outside its borders.

Landmark Supreme Court Cases

Marburg* v. *Madison (1803) ruled that the Supreme Court could strike down an act of Congress if it was in conflict with the Constitution.

McCulloch v. *Maryland* (1819) established the doctrine of implied powers. The federal government can use any means not forbidden by the Constitution; the states cannot hinder legal actions by the federal government.

Dred Scott v. *Sanford* (1857) ruled that blacks could not be U.S. citizens or sue in federal courts. Slavery could not be outlawed in western territories before they became states.

Plessey v. *Ferguson* (1896) ruled that "separate but equal" facilities were constitutional; this decision lasted for sixty years and was overturned by *Brown* v. *Board of Education.*

Korematsu v. *United States* (1944) ruled that citizens of Japanese ancestry could be interned and would forfeit constitutional rights.

Brown v. *Board of Education* (1954) ruled that segregated schools were unconstitutional; this decision overturned *Plessey* v. *Ferguson.*

Mapp v. *Ohio* (1961) ruled that evidence obtained illegally is inadmissible in court.

Gideon v. *Wainwright* (1963) ruled that anyone charged with a serious criminal offense has the right to an attorney and the state must provide one if the individual charged cannot afford legal counsel.

Miranda v. *Arizona* (1966) ruled that police must advise suspects of their rights to remain silent, to consult with a lawyer, and to have one appointed; police must stop interrogation if suspect asks to remain silent.

Tinker v. *Des Moines* (1969) ruled that wearing armbands is protected under the First Amendment.

Roe v. *Wade* (1973) ruled that laws restricting abortion are unconstitutional.

U.S. v. *Nixon* (1974) ruled that the president of the United States is not above the law.

Regents of CA v. *Bakke* (1978) ruled that race-based admissions in education violated the Equal Protection Clause of the Constitution.

Hazelwood v. *Kuhlmeier* (1983) ruled that public school newspapers have a lower level of protection under the First Amendment rights of free speech.

Texas v. *Johnson* (1989) ruled that a law prohibiting burning of the American flag is unconstitutional and a violation of the First Amendment.

American Symbols and Celebrations

Symbols

The United States has a variety of symbols that represent the country, including the American bald eagle, the Great Seal, the American flag (and, in general, the colors red, white, and blue), the Statue of Liberty, the national anthem and "America, the Beautiful," the Liberty Bell, the Pledge of Allegiance, and Uncle Sam. Teachers can utilize these symbols in a variety of lesson plans with students.

Celebrations

The United States observes many holidays throughout the calendar year. These include Martin Luther King, Jr. Day, the Fourth of July, Presidents' Day, Labor Day, Memorial Day, Columbus Day, Veterans Day, Flag Day, and Thanksgiving. Some religious holidays are also celebrated, such as Easter, Christmas, Rosh Hashanah, Yom Kippur, and Kwanza.

DOMAIN IV
SCIENCE

PERSONALIZED STUDY PLAN

PAGE		KNOWN MATERIAL/ SKIP IT
179	Theory and practice of science teaching	☐
186	Safe and proper laboratory process	☐
191	Geography and culture	☐
193	Impact of science on daily life/environment	☐
196	Physical science: forces and motion and their relationships	☐
202	Physical science: physical and chemical properties of and changes in matter	☐
205	Physical science: energy and interactions between matter and energy	☐
208	Physical science: energy transformations and the conservation of matter and energy	☐
210	Life science: structure and function of living things	☐
221	Life science: reproduction and the mechanisms of heredity	☐
227	Life science: adaptations of organisms and the thory of evolution	☐
230	Life science: relationships between organisms and the environment	☐
232	Earth and space science: structure and function of earth systems	☐
237	Earth and space science: cycles in earth systems	☐
240	Earth and space science: role of energy in weather and climate	☐
242	Earth and space science: characteristics of the solar system and the universe	☐

THEORY AND PRACTICE OF SCIENCE TEACHING

Influence of Developmental Stages on Learning

Teachers must understand that some techniques will only be effective at certain stages during childhood.

Early-childhood students

Plant growth: Students should plant seeds and take care of plants while the teacher models and explains the process and stages of plant growth (germination, sprouting, seedling, etc.).

Elementary students

Study of rocks and porosity: Students can test the porosity of limestone, shale, slate, sandstone, etc., using droppers filled with water.

Middle-school students

Cells and genetics: Students can learn about their own genetics and cells during this study. One good idea is to include a study of how each student is different in genetic ways; for example, detached/attached earlobes, widow's peak, tongue rolling, swirls in fingerprints, and hair characteristics.

Sequence of Presentation

Generally, science textbooks present an approach to science sequenced to allow basic principles to be taught first and advanced principles to be taught later. Even when curricula are oriented toward specific testable outcomes or objectives, the materials included should be sequenced to support educational progress.

Science courses and principles should be taught using an ordered methodology that allows students to leverage existing knowledge. Concepts should be sequenced in a manner that allows prior material to support current and future materials.

The sequence of presentation must be appropriate for the available instructional hours and period. The sequence should also conform to policy guidelines and optimally align with the organization of textbooks and other course materials in use. The sequence may need to conform to mandated educational outcomes.

Teachers must ensure that students understand foundational principles before moving on to derived principles. When students have mastered principles, it is time to move forward with the sequenced material to maintain a challenging education environment. The sequenced materials should not be pinned to a strict schedule; they should be implemented flexibly to accommodate and challenge students.

Adapting Curricula to Meet Needs of All Students

Students approach the materials with disparate backgrounds and knowledge. The educator must therefore adapt the curricula to a broad audience and attempt to meet the needs of all students.

When it becomes apparent that students are struggling with a particular topic, the teacher should take the time to review underlying principles. Words with specific scientific meanings must be carefully defined so students do not mistakenly assign them broader, popular meanings.

Addressing Common Scientific Misconceptions

Perhaps the most common misconceptions derive from imprecise language: Scientific terminology is often not well understood by students.

It is critical that instructors understand common misconceptions in science so they can not only avoid them but also correct them. Perhaps the most common misconceptions derive from imprecise language: Scientific terminology is often not well understood by students. Also, media reporting about science (particularly on politically sensitive or popular science topics) is often inaccurate or speculative. Finally, generally held public opinions of scientific topics are often incorrect or only partially correct.

Principles of Scientific Ethics

The guiding principles of scientific ethics include:

- Scientific honesty: Not to commit fraud; not to fabricate or misinterpret data for personal gain
- Caution: To avoid errors and sloppiness in all scientific experimentation
- Credit: To give credit where credit is due and not to copy
- Responsibility: To report only reliable information to the public and not to mislead in the name of science
- Freedom: The freedom to criticize old ideas, question new research, and conduct research

Scientists are expected to show good conduct in their scientific pursuits. Conduct here refers to all aspects of scientific activity including experimentation, testing, education, data evaluation, data analysis, data storage, peer review, government funding, staff, etc.

Overview of History of Science

Andreas Vesalius (1514-1564) was a Belgian anatomist and physician whose dissections of the human body and descriptions of his findings helped to correct the misconceptions of science.

Anton van Leeuwenhoek is known as the father of microscopy. In the 1650s, Leeuwenhoek began making tiny lenses that gave magnifications up to 300x. He was the first to see and describe bacteria, yeast, and the microscopic life found in water.

Robert Hooke (1635-1703) was a renowned inventor, natural philosopher, astronomer, experimenter, and cell biologist. He is remembered mainly for Hooke's law, an equation describing elasticity. He devised the compound microscope and illumination system. With it he observed organisms as diverse as insects, sponges, bryozoans, foraminifera, as well as bird feathers.

Carl Von Linnaeus (1707-1778), a Swedish botanist, physician, and zoologist, is well known for his contributions in ecology and taxonomy. Linnaeus is famous for his binomial system of nomenclature in which each living organism has two names, a genus and a species name.

In the late 1800s, Louis Pasteur discovered the role of microorganisms in the cause of disease, invented the process that came to be called pasteurization, and created the rabies vaccine. Robert Koch took Pasteur's observations one step further by formulating the hypothesis that specific diseases are caused by specific pathogens. Koch's postulates are still used as guidelines in the field of microbiology. They state that the same pathogen must be found in every diseased person; that the pathogen must be isolated and grown in culture; that the disease is induced in experimental animals from the culture; and that the same pathogen must be isolated from the experimental animal.

Matthias Schleiden, a German botanist, is famous for his cell theory. He observed plant cells microscopically and concluded that the cell is the common structural unit of all plants. He proposed the cell theory along with Theodor Schwann, a zoologist, who observed cells in animals.

In the eighteenth century, many fields of science like botany, zoology, and geology began to evolve as scientific disciplines in the modern sense.

In the twentieth century, the rediscovery of Gregor Mendel's work led to the rapid development of genetics.

In the 1950s, James Watson and Francis Crick discovered that the structure of a DNA molecule is a double helix. The discovery of this structure made it possible to explain DNA's ability to replicate and to control the synthesis of proteins.

The Scientific Method

SCIENTIFIC METHOD: the basic process of scientific investigation

Good scientific investigation should seek to provide a number of plausible hypotheses for any given phenomenon and then identify the correct hypothesis as established by experimental results.

The **SCIENTIFIC METHOD** is the basic process of scientific investigation. It begins by posing a question and ends by drawing a conclusion based on reproducible experimental results.

Good scientific investigation should seek to provide a number of plausible hypotheses for any given phenomenon and then identify the correct hypothesis as established by experimental results. It is therefore critical that students approach a given scientific phenomenon with an open mind and a willingness to accept logical conclusions, even when they are unanticipated.

Additionally, a variety of explanations may be correct for a given phenomenon if they seek to explain the phenomenon as resulting from different causes.

- Posing a question: Although many discoveries happen by chance, the standard thought process of a scientist begins with forming a question to research. The more limited the question, the easier it is to set up an experiment to answer it.
- Forming a hypothesis: Once the question is formulated, the researcher makes an educated guess about the answer to the problem or question. This "best educated guess" is the hypothesis.
- Conducting the test: Ensuring tests are fair requires that an experiment have a variable or condition that can be changed (such as temperature or mass). A good test manipulates as few variables as possible in order to see which variable is responsible for the results. Depending on the type of research being conducted, a control may be necessary to prove that the results occurred because of the changed conditions and would not have happened otherwise.
- Observing and recording data: Observations and results of the experiment should be recorded. Drawings, graphs, and illustrations should be included to support the gathered information. Observations are objective, whereas analysis and interpretation are subjective. Reporting of the data should include specific information about how the measurements were calculated.
- Drawing a conclusion: After recording the data, it is compared with data from other groups. A conclusion is the judgment derived from the results. A conclusion should explain why the results of the experiment either prove or disprove the hypothesis.

Graphing data

Graphing utilizes numbers to demonstrate patterns. The patterns offer a visual representation of the information, making it easier to draw conclusions.

Communicating results

Conclusions must be communicated by clearly describing the information using accurate data, visual presentations, and other appropriate media such as a PowerPoint presentation. Examples of visual presentations are graphs (bar/line/pie), tables and charts, diagrams, and artwork.

Conclusions must be communicated by clearly describing the information using accurate data, visual presentations, and other appropriate media such as a PowerPoint presentation.

Inquiry Strategies to Elicit Higher-Level Thinking

Deductive inquiry

The main goal of this strategy is to move students from generalized principles to specific instances. The strategy stresses the process of testing general assumptions, applying them, and exploring the relationships between specific elements.

Inductive inquiry

The information-seeking process of the inductive inquiry method helps students establish facts, determine relevant questions, and develop ways to pursue these questions and build explanations. Students are encouraged to develop and support their own hypotheses. Through inductive inquiry, students experience the thought processes which require them to move from specific facts and observations to inferences.

Interactive instruction

This strategy relies heavily on discussion and sharing among participants. Examples of this type of instruction include debates, brainstorming, discussions, and laboratory groups.

Scientific Models

A model is any simplification or substitute for what we are studying, understanding, or predicting.

Types of models

- Scale models: Some models are basically downsized or enlarged copies of their target systems, like models of protein and DNA.

- Idealized models: An idealization is a deliberate simplification of something complicated with the objective of making it easier to understand. Some examples are frictionless planes, point masses, and isolated systems.
- Analogical models: Standard examples of analogical models are the billiard model of a gas, the computer model of the mind, and the liquid-drop model of the nucleus.
- Phenomenological models: These are usually defined as models that are independent of theories.
- Data models: These are corrected, rectified, regimented, and, in many instances, idealized versions of the data gained from immediate observation (raw data).
- Theory models: Any structure is a model if it represents an idea, or theory. An example of this is a flow chart, which summarizes a set of ideas.

Uses of models

Models are crucial for understanding the structure and function of processes in science. They help us visualize the organs or systems they represent, like putting a face to a person. Models are also useful for predicting and foreseeing future events like hurricanes.

Displaying and Communicating Data

Line graphs

Line graphs show two variables represented by one point on the graph. The *x*-axis is the horizontal axis and represents the dependent variable. The *y*-axis is the vertical axis and represents the independent variable.

Graphs should be calibrated at equal intervals. If one space represents one day, the next space cannot represent ten days. A "best-fit" line is drawn to join the points and cannot include all of the points in the data. Axes must always be labeled for the graph to be meaningful. A good title describes both the dependent and the independent variables.

Bar graphs

In bar graphs, the dependent variable is set up as a bar where the *x*-axis intersects the *y*-axis. Each bar is a separate item of data.

Importance of Laboratory Activities

Many simple but profound experiments can be demonstrated with near-complete safety and very little financial outlay; these should always be used because they invite students to engage and interact with the physical world. While some students learn solely from lectures, notes, and reading, most students benefit from personal interaction with scientific processes.

According to the National Science Teachers Association, "Problem-solving abilities are refined in the context of laboratory inquiry. Laboratory activities develop a wide variety of investigative, organizational, creative, and communicative skills. The laboratory provides an optimal setting for motivating students while they experience what science is."

Laboratory activities enhance student performance in the following domains:

- Process skills: Observing, measuring, manipulating physical objects
- Analytical skills: Reasoning, deduction, critical thinking
- Communication skills: Organizing information, writing
- Conceptualization of scientific phenomena

The National Science Teachers Association makes the following recommendations:

Preschool/elementary level

- Classes should include activity-based, hands-on experiences that allow students to discover and construct science concepts; and, after a concept is labeled and developed, activities should allow for application of the concept to the real lives of students. Teachers should also provide activities in which students manipulate one variable while holding others constant and establish experimental and control groups.
- Appropriate hands-on experiences must be provided for children with special needs who are unable to participate in classroom activities.
- A minimum of 60 percent of the science instruction time should be devoted to hands-on activities, in which children are manipulating, observing, exploring, and thinking about science using concrete materials.
- Evaluation and assessment of student performance must reflect hands-on experience.
- Hands-on activities should be revised and adapted to meet student needs and to enhance curricular goals and objectives.
- Enough supplies (e.g., magnets, cells, hand lenses) should be available to allow each child to have hands-on experiences.
- Reasonable and prudent safety precautions should always be taken when teachers and students are interacting with manipulative materials.
- Workspace should include flat, moveable desks or tables/chairs, equipment, and hands-on materials. Computers, software, and other electronic tools should be available.

- Parents, members of the community, and members of parent/teacher organizations should be enlisted to assist.
- There should not be more than twenty-four children assigned to each class.

SAFE AND PROPER LABORATORY PROCESS

Safety in the science classroom and laboratory requires proactive training and regular in-service updates for all staff and students who utilize the science laboratory.

Safety in the science classroom and laboratory requires proactive training and regular in-service updates for all staff and students who utilize the science laboratory. This training should include how to identify and evaluate potential hazards as well as how to prevent or respond to them.

Right-to-know laws state that employees must be informed of potentially toxic chemicals. An inventory must be made available if requested. The inventory must contain information about the hazards and properties of the chemicals. Training must be provided in the safe handling and interpretation of the Material Safety Data Sheet.

Schools should consider the following types of training:

- Right-to-know training (OSHA training on the importance and benefits of properly recognizing and safely working with hazardous materials), along with some basic chemical hygiene and instruction in how to read and understand a Material Safety Data Sheet
- Instruction in how to use a fire extinguisher
- Instruction in how to use a chemical fume hood
- General guidance on when and how to use personal protective equipment (e.g., safety glasses or gloves)
- Instruction in how to monitor activities for potential impact on indoor air quality

Material Safety Data Sheets (MSDS) include information on substances such as physical data (melting point, boiling point, etc.), toxicity, health effects, first aid, reactivity, storage, disposal, protective gear, and spill/leak procedures.

They are particularly important to have available if a spill or other accident occurs. You should have an MSDS in the lab for every item in your chemical inventory. This will assist you in determining how to store and handle your materials.

The National Association of Biology Teachers (NABT) and International Science Education Foundation (ISEF) have set parameters for the science classroom. All science labs must contain the following items of safety equipment (*required by law*):

- Fire blanket that is visible and accessible
- Ground fault circuit interrupters (GFCIs) within two feet of water supplies
- Emergency shower capable of providing a continuous flow of water
- Signs designating room exits
- Emergency eye-wash station which can be activated by the foot or forearm
- Eye protection for every student and a means of sanitizing equipment
- Emergency exhaust fans providing ventilation to the outside of the building
- Master cut-off switches for gas, electric, and compressed air. Switches must have permanently attached handles. Cut-off switches must be clearly labeled.
- An ABC fire extinguisher
- Storage cabinets for flammable materials

Also recommended, but not required by law:

- Chemical spill control kit
- Fume hood with a motor that is spark-proof
- Protective laboratory aprons made of flame-retardant material
- Signs that will alert people to potentially hazardous conditions
- Containers for broken glassware, flammables, corrosives, and waste
- Containers should be labeled

A teacher should never leave a class for any reason without providing alternate supervision. When an accident occurs, two factors are always considered: foreseeability and negligence. Foreseeability is the anticipation that an event may occur under certain circumstances. Negligence is the failure to exercise ordinary or reasonable care.

Handling of Chemicals

All laboratory solutions should be prepared as directed in the lab manual. Students should wear safety goggles while working with glassware in case of an accident.

Chemicals should not be stored on benches or near heat sources; they should be stored in a secure, dry area. They should be stored in accordance with their reactability. Acids should be locked in a separate area from nonacids.

All containers in the lab must be labeled. Suspected and known carcinogens must be labeled as such and segregated within trays to contain leaks and spills.

Used solutions should be disposed of according to local disposal procedures.

Chemical waste should be disposed of in properly labeled containers. Waste should be separated based on its reactivity with other chemicals. All biological waste should be disposed of in biological hazardous waste bags.

The following chemicals are potential carcinogens and are not allowed in school facilities:

- Acrylonitrile
- Arsenic compounds
- Asbestos
- Benzidine
- Benzene
- Cadmium compounds
- Chloroform
- Chromium compounds
- Ethylene oxide
- Ortho-toluidine
- Nickel powder
- Mercury

Handling of Organisms and Specimens

Only animals obtained from recognized sources should be used. Decaying animals or those of unknown origin may harbor pathogens and/or parasites. Specimens should be rinsed before handling, and the teacher and students should wear latex gloves during handling.

Students objecting to dissections for moral reasons should be given an alternative assignment.

Formaldehyde is a carcinogen and should be avoided or disposed of according to district regulations. Students objecting to dissections for moral reasons should be given an alternative assignment.

No dissections can be performed on living mammalian vertebrates or birds. All animals housed and cared for in the school must be handled in a safe and humane manner. Animals are not to remain on school premises during extended vacations unless adequate care is provided. For those students who object to performing dissections, interactive dissections are available online or from software companies.

Use of Equipment

If Bunsen burners are used, the following precautions should be followed:

1. Know the location of fire extinguishers and safety blankets and train students in their use.
2. Make sure students secure long hair and long sleeves to keep them out of the way.
3. Turn the gas all the way on and make a spark with the striker. The preferred method of lighting burners is to use strikers rather than matches.
4. Adjust the air valve at the bottom of the Bunsen burner until the flame shows an inner cone.
5. Adjust the flow of gas to the desired flame height by using the adjustment valve.
6. Do not touch the barrel of the burner (it is hot).
7. Use hot plates whenever possible to avoid the risk of burns or fire.

Light microscopes are commonly used in high school laboratory experiments. Total magnification is determined by multiplying the ocular (usually 10X) and the objective (usually 10X on low, 40X on high) lenses. A few steps should be followed to properly care for this equipment:

- Clean all lenses with lens paper only.
- Carry microscopes with two hands, one on the arm and one on the base.
- Always begin focusing on low power, then switch to high power.
- Store microscopes with the low-power objective down.
- Always use a cover slip when viewing wet-mount slides.
- Bring the objective down to its lowest position, then focus by moving up to avoid breaking or scratching the slide.

Life-science studies often use the following equipment and techniques for measuring small quantities:

- Graduated cylinders are used for precise measurements. They should always be placed on a flat surface. The surface of the liquid forms a meniscus (lens-shaped curve). The measurement is read at the bottom of this curve.
- Electronic balances should always be tared (returned to zero) before measuring and used on a flat surface. Substances should always be placed on a piece of paper to avoid spills and/or damage to the instrument.

- A **buret** is used to dispense precisely measured volumes of liquid. A stopcock is used to control the volume of liquid dispensed at one time.

Lab Procedures

Common laboratory techniques are dissection, preserving, staining and mounting microscopic specimens, and preparing laboratory solutions.

Common laboratory techniques are dissection, preserving, staining and mounting microscopic specimens, and preparing laboratory solutions.

Staining

Specimens have to be stained because they are mostly transparent (except plant cells, which are green) under the microscope and difficult to see against a white background. The stains work by fixing themselves to various structures on or in the cell, making the components of the specimen much easier to see. Some common stains used in laboratories are methylene blue, chlorazol black, lignin pink, and gentian violet.

Mounting of specimens

In order to observe microscopic specimens or minute parts, mounting them on a microscope slide is essential. Water is well suited for temporary mounting. One problem with water mounting, however, is that the water evaporates. Glycerin is nontoxic and remains stable for years. It provides good contrast to the specimens under microscopic examination. The only problem with glycerin as a medium is that it supports mold formation.

Preparation of laboratory solutions

1. Weigh out the required amount of each solute.
2. Dissolve the solute in less than the total desired volume (about 75%).
3. Add enough solvent to get the desired volume.

RANDOM ERRORS: statistical fluctuations in the measured data due to the precision limitations of the measurement device

SYSTEMATIC ERRORS: reproducible inaccuracies that are consistently in the same direction

Accuracy of Measurement with Scientific Instruments

RANDOM ERRORS are statistical fluctuations in the measured data due to the precision limitations of the measurement device. Random errors usually result from the experimenter's inability to take the same measurement in exactly the same way to get exactly the same number.

SYSTEMATIC ERRORS, by contrast, are reproducible inaccuracies that are consistently in the same direction. Systematic errors are often due to a problem that persists throughout the entire experiment.

ACCURACY is the degree of conformity of a measured, calculated quantity to its actual (true) value. **PRECISION** is also called reproducibility or repeatability and is the degree to which further measurements or calculations show the same or similar results.

ACCURACY: the degree of conformity of a measured, calculated quantity to its actual (true) value

PRECISION: the degree to which further measurements or calculations show the same or similar results

Accuracy is the degree of veracity, while precision is the degree of reproducibility.

Potential Sources of Experimental Error

In addition to errors caused by instrument limitations, there are other potential sources of error within almost every experiment:

- Human error (e.g., errors that occur as a result of inexperience)
- Use of the wrong chemical
- External influences (e.g., impure chemical used)
- Unrepresentative sample

ASSESSMENTS IN SCIENCE LEARNING

Teachers should be able to assess students on a daily basis using informal assessments such as monitoring during work time, class discussions, and note taking.

More formal assessments are necessary to ensure that students fully understand selected objectives. Regular grading using selected performance skills is necessary; for example, students could keep a science journal, tracking the progress of their ongoing assignments, projects, and labs. Other tools for observing and evaluating students are rubrics and checklists. Student profiles and checklists are excellent ways to quickly determine whether students are meeting selected objectives.

Student Name	Objective #1	Objective #2	On Task
Joe Student	X	X	X
Jan Student		X	X

When evaluating a child's developmental level, a professional may use a formal adaptive rating scale as well as his or her professional judgment to assess the child's motivation and behavior.

Curriculum-Based Assessment

Curriculum-based assessment is assessment of an individual's performance of objectives within a curriculum such as a reading, math, or science program. The individual's performance is measured in terms of which objectives have been mastered. This type of testing can be verbal, written, or demonstration based. Its general structure may include such factors as amount of time to complete, amount to complete, and whether it is group or individual testing. The level of response may be multiple choice, essay, or recall of facts.

Momentary Time Sampling

Momentary time sampling is a technique used for measuring behaviors of a group of individuals or several behaviors of the same individual. Time samples are usually brief, and can be conducted at fixed or variable intervals. The advantage of using variable intervals is increased reliability, as the students will not be able to predict when the time sample will be taken.

Multiple Baseline Design

Multiple baseline design can be used to test the effectiveness of an intervention in the performance of a skill or to determine if the intervention accounted for the observed changes in a target behavior. First, the initial baseline data is collected, followed by the data during the intervention period. To get the second baseline, the intervention is stopped for a period of time and data is collected again. The intervention is then restarted or reapplied, and data collected on the target behavior.

Group Tests and Individual Tests

When administering an individual test, the tester has the opportunity to observe the individual's responses and to determine how such things as problem solving are accomplished. Within limits, the tester is able to control the pace and tempo of the testing session, and to rephrase and probe responses in order to elicit the individual's best performance. If a child becomes tired, the examiner can give the child a break between parts of the test or end the test; if the child loses his or her place on the test, the tester can help the child regain it; if the child dawdles or loses interest, the tester can encourage or redirect him or her. If the child lacks self-confidence, the examiner can reinforce the child's efforts. In short, individual tests allow the examiner to encourage a child's best efforts and to observe how a student uses his or her skills to answer questions. Thus, individual tests allow the gathering of both quantitative and qualitative information.

On the other hand, with a group test, the examiner can provide oral directions for younger children; beyond the fourth grade, however, directions are usually written. The children write or mark their own responses, and the examiner monitors the progress of several students at the same time. The teacher cannot rephrase questions or probe or prompt responses.

IMPACT OF SCIENCE ON DAILY LIFE/ENVIRONMENT

Human Behaviors That Affect Health

While genetics plays an important role in health, human behaviors can greatly affect short- and long-term health both positively and negatively.

Smoking decreases lung capacity, causes persistent coughing, and limits one's ability to engage in strenuous physical activity. Long-term smoking can cause lung cancer, heart disease, and emphysema.

Excessive comsumption of alcohol can lead to reckless behavior and distorted judgment that can cause injury or death. Extreme alcohol abuse can cause alcohol poisoning which can result in immediate death. The potential effects of long-term alcohol abuse include liver cirrhosis, heart problems, high blood pressure, stomach ulcers, and cancer.

A healthy diet and regular exercise are the cornerstones of a healthy lifestyle. A diet rich in whole grains, fruits, vegetables, polyunsaturated fats, lean protein, and low in saturated fat and sugar can have a positive effect on one's overall health. Such diets can reduce cholesterol levels, lower blood pressure, and help manage body weight. Conversely, diets high in saturated fat and sugar can contribute to weight gain, heart disease, strokes, and cancer.

Exercise increases physical fitness and improves energy levels, overall body function, and mental well-being. Over the long term, exercise helps protect against chronic diseases, maintains healthy bones and muscles, helps one maintain a healthy body weight, and strengthens the body's immune system.

Human Population Growth

POPULATION: a group of individuals of one species that live in the same general area

A **POPULATION** is a group of individuals of one species that live in the same general area. Population size may depend on the total amount of life a habitat can support, or the carrying capacity of the environment. As a population increases, the competition for resources is more intense, and the growth rate declines. This is a density-dependent growth factor. Density-independent factors such as weather and climate affect the individuals in a population regardless of population size. Temperatures that are too hot or too cold may kill many individuals in a population that has not reached its carrying capacity.

While the Earth's ultimate carrying capacity for humans is uncertain, some factors that may limit growth are the availability of food, water, space, and fossil fuels.

The human population increased slowly until 1650. Since 1650, it has grown almost exponentially, reaching the current population of over 6 billion. Factors that have led to this increased growth rate include improved nutrition, sanitation, and health care. In addition, advances in technology, agriculture, and scientific knowledge have made the use of resources more efficient and increased their availability.

Natural Resources

Water

Most uses of water, such as for drinking and crop irrigation, require fresh water. Only 2.5 percent of the water on Earth is fresh water, and more than two-thirds of this fresh water is frozen in glaciers and polar ice caps. Consequently, in many parts of the world, water demand greatly exceeds supply.

Plants

Plant resources are renewable and can be regrown and restocked. Plant resources can be used to make clothing, buildings, and medicines, and can also be directly consumed.

The list of plants grown to provide food for the people of the world is extensive. Major crops include corn, potatoes, wheat, sugar, barley, peas, beans, beets, flax, lentils, sunflowers, soybeans, canola, and rice. These crops can have alternate uses as well. For example, corn is used to manufacture cornstarch, ethanol fuel, high-fructose corn syrup, ink, biodegradable plastics, chemicals used in cosmetics and pharmaceuticals, adhesives, and paper products.

Nonrenewable Resources

Nonrenewable resources, including fossil fuels, cannot be regenerated and do not naturally re-form at a rate that could sustain human use. Nonrenewable resources are therefore depleted and not restored. Presently, nonrenewable resources provide the main source of energy for humans.

Common fossil fuels used by humans are coal, petroleum, and natural gas, which all form from the remains of dead plants and animals through natural processes over millions of years. Because of their high carbon content, when burned these substances generate high amounts of energy as well as carbon dioxide, which is released back into the atmosphere and increases global warming.

Minerals

Mineral resources are concentrations of naturally occurring inorganic elements and compounds located in the Earth's crust that are extracted through mining for human use. Construction and manufacturing rely heavily on metals and industrial mineral resources. These metals include iron, bronze, lead, zinc, nickel, copper, and tin. Bulk rocks, including limestone, clay, shale, and sandstone, are used as aggregate in construction, in ceramics, and in concrete. Common ore minerals include calcite, barite, and gypsum. Mineral resources are also used as fertilizers and pesticides.

Deforestation

Deforestation due to urban development has resulted in the extinction or relocation of many species of plants and animals.

Energy Crisis

The supplies of fossil fuels are limited and rapidly declining. Also, most oil now comes from a politically volatile area of the world. Finally, continuing to produce energy from fossils fuels is unwise given the disruption to the environment necessary to harvest them and the byproducts of their combustion, which cause pollution.

It is important to recognize that a real energy crisis has vast economic implications. Oil, currently the most important fossil fuel, is needed for heating, electricity, and as a raw material for the manufacture of many items, particularly plastics. The gasoline made from oil is important for transporting people and goods, including food and other items necessary for life.

It is important to recognize that a real energy crisis has vast economic implications.

The Role of Science In Resolving Global Challenges

Technological advances may help in the search for alternative fuels. Possible alternative energy sources include biodiesel, nuclear power, biomethanol, hydrogen fuel, and fuel cells. Increasing the efficiency of solar fuel cells, hydroelectricity, and wind energy may also help reduce dependence on fossil fuels.

RECYCLING: the reprocessing of materials into new products

RECYCLING is the reprocessing of materials into new products. Recycling prevents many materials from becoming waste and also avoids the need to harvest new materials. For many materials, recycling requires less energy than new production. The most commonly recycled materials are glass, paper, aluminum, asphalt, steel, textiles, and plastic.

PHYSICAL SCIENCE: FORCES AND MOTION AND THEIR RELATIONSHIPS

Electricity and Magnetism

The electromagnetic spectrum consists of frequency (f), measured in hertz, and wavelength (λ), measured in meters. The frequency times the wavelength of every electromagnetic wave equals the speed of light (3.0×10^9 meters/second).

Roughly, the range of wavelengths in the electromagnetic spectrum is:

	f	λ
Radio waves	$10^5 - 10^{-1}$ hertz	$10^3 - 10^9$ meters
Microwaves	$10^{-1} - 10^{-3}$ hertz	$10^9 - 10^{11}$ meters
Infrared radiation	$10^{-3} - 10^{-6}$ hertz	$10^{11.2} - 10^{14.3}$ meters
Visible light	$10^{-6.2} - 10^{-6.9}$ hertz	$10^{14.3} - 10^{15}$ meters
Ultraviolet radiation	$10^{-7} - 10^{-9}$ hertz	$10^{15} - 10^{17.2}$ meters
X-rays	$10^{-9} - 10^{-11}$ hertz	$10^{17.2} - 10^{19}$ meters
Gamma rays	$10^{-11} - 10^{-15}$ hertz	$10^{19} - 10^{23.25}$ meters

Electricity

Electrically charged objects share these characteristics:

- Like charges repel one another.
- Opposite charges attract each other.
- Charge is conserved. A neutral object has no net charge.

CONDUCTORS are materials through which electric charges flow easily.

An **INSULATOR** is a material through which electric charges do not move easily, if at all.

CONDUCTORS: materials through which electric charges flow easily

INSULATOR: a material through which electric charges do not move easily, if at all

Grounding charge

Charge can be removed from an object by connecting it to the Earth through a conductor. The removal of static electricity by conduction is called **GROUNDING**.

GROUNDING: the removal of static electricity by conduction

Circuits

An **ELECTRIC CIRCUIT** is a path along which electrons flow. A simple circuit can be created with a dry cell, wire, and a bell or lightbulb. When all are connected, the electrons flow from the negative terminal through the wire to the device and back to the positive terminal of the dry cell. If there are no breaks in the circuit, the device will work; the circuit is closed. Any break in the flow will create an open circuit and cause the device to shut off.

ELECTRIC CIRCUIT: a path along which electrons flow

Load and switch

The device (bell or bulb) is an example of a load. A **LOAD** is a device that uses energy. Suppose that you add a buzzer so that the bell rings when you press the buzzer. The buzzer is acting as a switch. A **SWITCH** is a device that opens or closes a circuit. Pressing the buzzer makes the connection complete and the bell rings. When the buzzer is not engaged, the circuit is open and the bell is silent.

LOAD: a device that uses energy

SWITCH: a device that opens or closes a circuit

Circuit types

A series circuit is one in which the electrons have only one path along which they can move. When one load in a series circuit, the circuit is open. An example of this is a set of Christmas tree lights that is missing a bulb. None of the bulbs will work if one bulb is not working.

A parallel circuit is one in which the electrons have more than one path to travel. If a load goes out in a parallel circuit, another load will continue to work because the electrons can find a way to continue moving along the path.

POTENTIAL DIFFERENCE: the work needed to move an electron from one point to another

CURRENT: the number of electrons per second that flow past a point in a circuit

RESISTANCE: the ability of a material to oppose the flow of electrons through it

Potential difference, voltage, and current

When an electron goes through a load, it does work and therefore loses some of its energy. The measure of how much energy is lost is called the **POTENTIAL DIFFERENCE**. The potential difference between two points is the work needed to move an electron from one point to another.

Potential difference is measured in a unit called a volt. Voltage is potential difference. The higher the voltage, the more energy the electrons have.

CURRENT is the number of electrons per second that flow past a point in a circuit.

As electrons flow through a wire, they lose potential energy. Some of the energy is changed to heat energy because of resistance. **RESISTANCE** is the ability of a material to oppose the flow of electrons through it. All substances have some resistance, even if they are good conductors, such as copper. This resistance is measured in units called ohms. A thin wire has more resistance than a thick one because it has less room for electrons to travel. In a thicker wire, there are more possible paths for the electrons. Resistance also depends upon the length of the wire. The longer the wire, the more resistance it will have.

Ohm's law

Potential difference, resistance, and current form a relationship known as Ohm's law. Current (I) is measured in amperes and is equal to potential difference (V) divided by resistance (R).

$$I = V \div R$$

If you have a wire with resistance of 5 ohms and a potential difference of 75 volts, you can calculate the current by:

$$I = 75 \text{ volts} \div 5 \text{ ohms}$$
$$I = 15 \text{ amperes}$$

A current of 10 or more amperes will cause a wire to get hot. The maximum current for a house circuit is about 22 amperes. Current above 25 amperes can start a fire.

Magnetism

MAGNETIC FIELD: the space around a magnet where its force affects objects

Magnetic fields and poles

Magnets have a north pole and a south pole. Like poles repel and opposing poles attract. A **MAGNETIC FIELD** is the space around a magnet where its force affects objects.

Some materials act as magnets and some do not. This is because magnetism is a result of electrons in motion.

The Earth has a magnetic field. In a compass, a tiny, lightweight magnet is suspended and will line its south pole up with the north-pole magnet of the Earth.

Magnetic domains

In an atom of iron, there are four unpaired electrons. The magnetic fields of these electrons are not canceled out. Their fields add up to make a tiny magnet. Their fields exert force on each other, setting up small areas in the iron called **magnetic domains** where atomic magnetic fields line up in the same direction.

Electromagnets

A magnet can be made out of a coil of wire by connecting the ends of the coil to a battery. When the current goes through the wire, the wire acts the same way that a magnet does; this is called an **electromagnet**. The poles of the electromagnet will depend upon which way the electric current runs.

There are three ways to make an electromagnet more powerful:

1. Make more coils
2. Put an iron core (nail) inside the coils
3. Use more battery power

In a **motor**, electricity is used to create magnetic fields that oppose each other and cause the rotor to move. The wiring loops attached to the rotating shaft have a magnetic field opposing the magnetic field caused by the wiring in the housing of the motor that cannot move. The repelling action of the opposing magnetic fields turns the rotor.

An electric motor uses an electromagnet to change electric energy into mechanical energy.

A **generator** is a device that turns rotary, mechanical energy into electrical energy. As a wire, or any other conductor, moves across a magnetic field, an electric current occurs in the wire.

A **transformer** is an electrical device that changes electricity of one voltage into another voltage, usually from high to low. If another wire is close to an electric current that is changing strength, the electric current will also flow into that other wire as the magnetism changes. A transformer takes in electricity at a higher voltage and lets it run through many coils wound around an iron core. An output wire with fewer coils is also around the core. The changing magnetism makes a current in the output wire. Fewer coils means less voltage, so the voltage is reduced.

Measuring and Describing Changes In Motion

Speed is a scalar quantity that refers to how fast an object is moving (i.e., a car traveling 60 mi./hr).

Velocity is a vector quantity that refers to the rate at which an object changes its position. In other words, velocity is speed with direction (i.e., a car traveling 60 mi./hr east).

Instantaneous speed is speed at any given instant in time.

Average speed is the average of all instantaneous speeds, found by a distance/time ratio.

Acceleration is a vector quantity defined as the rate at which an object changes its velocity, where *f* represents the final velocity and *i* represents the initial velocity. Since acceleration is a vector quantity, it always has a direction associated with it. The direction of the acceleration vector depends on whether the object is speeding up or slowing down and whether the object is moving in a positive or negative direction.

Dynamics and Motion

DYNAMICS: the study of the relationship between motion and the forces affecting motion

Weight (W) = mass times acceleration due to gravity (W = mg).

DYNAMICS is the study of the relationship between motion and the forces affecting motion. Force causes motion.

Mass and weight are not the same qualities. An object's mass gives it a resistance to change its current state of motion. It is also the measure of an object's resistance to acceleration. The force that the Earth's gravity exerts on an object with a specific mass is the object's weight on Earth. Weight is a force that is measured in Newtons.

Weight (W) = mass times acceleration due to gravity (W = mg).

Newton's laws of motion

Newton's first law of motion is also called the law of inertia. It states that an object at rest will remain at rest and an object in motion will remain in motion at a constant velocity unless acted upon by an external force.

Newton's second law of motion states that if a net force acts on an object, it will cause the acceleration of the object. The relationship between force and motion is force equals mass times acceleration (F = ma).

Newton's third law of motion states that for every action there is an equal and opposite reaction. Therefore, if an object exerts a force on another object, that second object exerts an equal and opposite force on the first object.

Motion and Resistance to Motion

Surfaces that touch each other have a certain resistance to motion. This resistance is called friction. Some principles of motion and resistance to motion include:

- The materials that make up the surfaces determine the magnitude of the frictional force.
- The frictional force is independent of the area of contact between the two surfaces.
- The direction of the frictional force is the opposite of the direction of motion.
- The frictional force is proportional to the normal force between the two surfaces in contact.

Types of friction and resistance

Static friction describes the force of friction of two surfaces that are in contact with each other but do not have any motion relative to each other, such as a block sitting on an inclined plane. Kinetic friction describes the force of friction of two surfaces in contact with each other when there is relative motion between the surfaces.

Conserving energy

The law of conservation of energy states that energy can neither be created nor destroyed. Therefore, the sum of all energy in a system remains constant.

The law of momentum conservation states that when two objects collide in an isolated system, the total momentum of the two objects before the collision is equal to the total momentum of the two objects after the collision. That is, the momentum lost by object 1 is equal to the momentum gained by object 2.

Circular motion

Circular motion is defined as acceleration along a circle, a circular path, or a circular orbit. Circular motion involves acceleration of the moving object by a centripetal force that pulls the moving object toward the center of the circular orbit. Without acceleration, the object would move in a straight line, according to Newton's first law of motion. Circular motion is accelerated even though the speed is constant, because the object's velocity is constantly changing direction.

Periodic motion

Periodic motion occurs when an object moves back and forth in a regular motion. Periodic motion has three characteristics:

1. Velocity: The rate at which an object changes its position (speed with direction). Both a bouncing ball and a weight on a pendulum have velocity.
2. Period: The time the object takes to go back and forth. The time a ball takes to bounce back can be measured. Sometimes, the word *period* is replaced by the word *frequency*. *Frequency* is the reciprocal of *period*.
3. Amplitude: Half the distance the object goes from one side of the period to the other (the height of the pendulum or bouncing ball). When an object is rotating, the amplitude is the radius of the circle (half the diameter).

PHYSICAL SCIENCE: PHYSICAL AND CHEMICAL PROPERTIES OF AND CHANGES IN MATTER

PHYSICAL PROPERTY: a property that can be observed without changing the identity of a substance

CHEMICAL PROPERTY: the ability of a substance to change into a new substance

PHYSICAL CHANGE: a change that does not produce a new substance

A **PHYSICAL PROPERTY** can be observed without changing the identity of a substance. For instance, you can describe the color, mass, shape, and volume of a book.

A **CHEMICAL PROPERTY** is the ability of a substance to change into a new substance.

A **PHYSICAL CHANGE** is a change that does not produce a new substance. The atoms are not rearranged into different compounds; the material has the same chemical composition that it had before the change. Changes of state such as freezing and melting are examples of physical changes.

A **CHEMICAL CHANGE** (or chemical reaction) is any change of a substance into one or more other substances. Burning materials turn into smoke; a seltzer tablet fizzes into gas bubbles.

Mass is a measure of the amount of matter in an object. Two objects of equal mass will balance each other on a simple balance scale no matter where the scale is located. For example, two rocks with equal mass that are in balance on Earth will also be in balance on the Moon.

CHEMICAL CHANGE: any change of a substance into one or more other substances

Weight is the measure of the Earth's pull of gravity on an object. It can also be defined as the pull of gravity between bodies. The units of weight measurement commonly used are the pound (standard measure) and the kilogram (metric measure).

Volume is the amount of cubic space an object occupies.

Density is the mass of a substance per unit of volume. Density is stated in grams per cubic centimeter (g/cm^3), where the gram is the standard unit of mass. ($D = m/V$).

Specific gravity is the ratio of the density of a substance to the density of water.

A **conductor** is a material that transfers thermal or electrical energy easily. An **insulator** is a material through which electric charges do not move easily, if at all.

Hardness describes how difficult it is to scratch or dent a substance.

Solubility is defined as the amount of substance (referred to as **solute**) that will dissolve into another substance, called the **solvent**.

Melting point refers to the temperature at which a solid becomes a liquid.

Boiling point refers to the temperature at which a liquid becomes a gas.

Solids

- Have a definite shape that can be changed in some way
- Have a definite volume that cannot be changed
- Have mass that can be changed when the physical shape is diminished, e.g., sawing a board into two pieces
- Can be any color and temperature
- Some will melt under high temperatures, in which case they become liquids
- Are very hard

Liquids

- Take the shape of the container into which they are poured

- When a liquid results from melting a solid, it has the same color as the solid
- Flow
- Cannot be compressed and keep the same volume
- Weight may be lighter than that of a solid because of evaporation
- Are soft

Gases

- Do not keep their shape and fill a container
- Flow very quickly
- Are colorless
- Can be compressed and take on a different volume than that of a solid or liquid
- Are of high temperature
- Are extremely light and do not have weight

Properties of Mixtures and Solutions

SOLUTIONS: homogenous mixtures of two or more components

MIXTURE: a material that can be separated by physical means into two or more substances

SOLUTIONS are homogenous mixtures of two or more components. The components of solutions are atoms and molecules, thus the particles are 1 nanometer (nm) or less in diameter. Solutions are transparent and do not usually absorb visible light. An example of a solution is sugar and water.

A **MIXTURE** is a material that can be separated by physical means into two or more substances. Most materials around us are mixtures. A mixture has a variable composition.

Mixtures are classified into two types:

- Heterogeneous mixture: A mixture that consists of physically distinct parts, each with different properties. Example: sugar and salt stirred together
- Homogeneous mixture (solution): A mixture that is uniform in its properties throughout a given sample

Chemical Reactions in Daily Life

- Rusting: An iron nail rusts to form a rusty nail. The rusty nail, however, is not made up of the same iron atoms as a nail that is not rusty. It is now composed of iron (III) oxide molecules that form when the iron atoms combine with oxygen molecules during oxidation.

- Burning of fossil fuels: Coal, petroleum, and natural gas all form from the remains of dead plants and animals through natural processes over millions of years. Because of their high carbon content, when burned, these substances generate large amounts of energy as well as carbon dioxide.
- Cellular respiration: Cellular respiration is the metabolic pathway in which food (glucose, etc.) is broken down to produce energy in the form of ATP. Steps include glycolysis, the Krebs cycle, and the electron transport chain. The net gain from the whole process of respiration is 36 molecules of ATP.

PHYSICAL SCIENCE: ENERGY AND INTERACTIONS BETWEEN MATTER AND ENERGY

Laws of Thermodynamics

The first law of thermodynamics is a restatement of the conservation of energy. The change in heat energy supplied to a system (Q) is equal to the sum of the change in the internal energy (U) and the change in the work done by the system against internal forces ($\Delta Q = \Delta U + \Delta W$).

The second law of thermodynamics is stated in two parts:

1. No machine is 100 percent efficient. It is impossible to construct a machine that only absorbs heat from a heat source and performs an equal amount of work because some heat will always be lost to the environment.
2. Heat cannot spontaneously pass from a colder to a warmer object.

The law of conservation of energy states that energy is neither created nor destroyed. Thus, energy changes form when energy transactions occur in nature.

- Thermal energy is the total internal energy of objects created by the vibration and movement of atoms and molecules. Heat is the transfer of thermal energy.
- Acoustical energy, or sound energy, is the movement of energy through an object in waves. Energy that forces an object to vibrate creates sound.
- Radiant energy is the energy of electromagnetic waves. Light—visible and otherwise—is an example of radiant energy.
- Electrical energy is the movement of electrical charges in an electromagnetic field. Examples of electrical energy are electricity and lightning.
- Chemical energy is the energy stored in the chemical bonds of molecules, for example, the energy derived from gasoline.
- Mechanical energy is the potential and kinetic energy of a mechanical system. Rolling balls, car engines, and body parts in motion demonstrate mechanical energy.
- Nuclear energy is the energy present in the nucleus of atoms. Division, combination, or collision of nuclei release nuclear energy.

Basic Concepts of Heat Energy

The heat of fusion is the amount of heat that it takes to change from a solid to a liquid or the amount of heat released during the change from liquid to solid.

The heat of vaporization is the amount of heat that it takes to change from a liquid to a gaseous state.

Melting takes place when there is sufficient energy available to break the intermolecular forces that hold molecules together in a solid.

Boiling occurs when there is enough energy available to break the intermolecular forces holding molecules together as a liquid.

Evaporation is the change in phase from liquid to gas.

Condensation is the change in phase from gas to liquid.

The colors of visible light are sometimes referred to as ROYGBIV (red, orange, yellow, green, blue, indigo, and violet).

Properties of Light

When we refer to light, we are usually talking about a type of electromagnetic wave that stimulates the retina of the eye, or visible light. Each individual wavelength within the spectrum of visible light represents a particular color. When a particular wavelength strikes the retina, we perceive that color.

Light travels in a straight line.

Reflection, refraction, diffraction

When light hits a surface, it is reflected. The angle of the incoming light (angle of incidence) is the same as the angle of the reflected light (angle of reflection). It is this reflected light that allows you to see objects.

When light enters a different medium, it bends. This bending, or change of speed, is called refraction.

Light can be diffracted, or bent around the edges of an object. Diffraction occurs when light goes through a narrow slit. As light passes through the slit, it bends slightly around the edges of it.

Light and other electromagnetic radiation can be polarized because the waves are transverse. The distinguishing characteristic of transverse waves is that they are perpendicular to the direction of the motion of the wave. Light can be polarized by passing it through special filters that block all vibrations except those in a single plane.

Sound

Sound waves are produced by a vibrating body, which moves forward and compresses the air in front of it. The body then reverses direction, so that the pressure on the air decreases and expansion of the air molecules occurs. One compression and expansion creates one longitudinal wave. Sound can be transmitted through any gas, liquid, or solid. However, it cannot be transmitted through a vacuum (because there are no particles in a vacuum to vibrate and bump into adjacent particles to transmit the wave).

Levels of sound

The pitch of a sound depends on the frequency that the ear receives. High-pitched sound waves have high frequencies. High notes are produced by an object that is vibrating at a greater rate per second than an object that produces a low note.

The intensity of a sound is the amount of energy that crosses a unit of area in a given amount of time. Two tones of the same intensity but different pitches may appear to have different loudness. The intensity level of sound is measured in decibels. Normal conversation is approximately 60 decibels.

The amplitude of a sound wave determines its loudness, with loud sound waves creating larger amplitudes.

DOPPLER EFFECT: the changes in experienced frequency due to the relative motion of the source of the sound

Sound waves

Interference is the interaction of two or more waves that meet. If the waves interfere constructively, the crest of each one meets the crests of the others. They combine into a crest with greater amplitude, creating a louder sound. If the waves interfere destructively, then the crest of one meets the trough of another. They produce a wave with lower amplitude that produces a softer sound.

Doppler effect

The DOPPLER EFFECT is defined as the changes in experienced frequency due to the relative motion of the source of the sound. As a moving sound source approaches a listener, the sound waves are closer together, causing an increase in frequency in the sound that is heard. As the source passes the listener, the waves spread out, and the sound experienced by the listener is lower.

Transverse waves are characterized by particle motion that is perpendicular to the wave motion; longitudinal waves are characterized by particle motion that is parallel to the wave motion.

PHYSICAL SCIENCE: ENERGY TRANSFORMATIONS AND THE CONSERVATION OF MATTER AND ENERGY

Alternative Energy Resources

- Hydroelectric power: Power produced from falling water
- Wind power: Windmills harness the energy of the wind by driving a turbine that generates electricity.
- Tidal power: Electricity generated by deflecting and diverting strong tidal currents through offshore turbines that drive electric generators
- Geothermal energy: Energy is produced from hot igneous rocks within the Earth. Rainwater percolates porous strata near an active magma chamber

and flashes to steam. The steam is captured and routed to turbine-powered electrical generators.

- Solar energy: Solar power can be utilized directly as a source of heat or to produce electricity. The most common use of solar power is to heat water.
- Solar cells produce electricity from the solar radiation. Photons striking the junction between two semiconductors (usually selenium) induce an electrical current that is stored in batteries.
- Biomass: Plant and animal waste (decaying or decayed) can be burned to produce heat for steam turbine electrical generators.
- Fusion power: This technology does not currently exist, but researchers are actively pursuing the means to make fusion power a reality. Unlike fission, the other form of nuclear energy currently in use, fusion does not rely on splitting the atoms of uranium or other radioactive elements. Energy is produced when small atomic nuclei fuse together to form new atoms. In a fusion reaction, two isotopes of hydrogen, deuterium, and tritium combine to make helium.

Heat Transfer

Heat energy that is transferred into or out of a system is **HEAT TRANSFER**. The temperature change is positive for a gain in heat energy and negative when heat is removed from the object or system.

HEAT TRANSFER: heat energy that is transferred into or out of a system

The formula for heat transfer is $Q = mc\Delta T$, where Q is the amount of heat energy transferred, m is the amount of substance (in kilograms), c is the specific heat of the substance, and ΔT is the change in temperature of the substance.

Heat is transferred in three ways:

- Conduction occurs when heat travels through a heated solid. The transfer rate is the ratio of the amount of heat per amount of time it takes to transfer heat from one area of an object to another: the less time, the greater the transfer rate.
- Convection is heat transported by the movement of a heated substance. Warmed air rising from a heat source such as a fire or electric heater is a common example of convection. Convection ovens make use of circulating air to efficiently cook food.
- Radiation is heat transfer as the result of electromagnetic waves. The Sun warms the Earth by emitting radiant energy.

Conservation of Matter and Energy

The principle of conservation of mass states that the total mass of a system is constant. Examples of conservation of mass in nature include the burning of wood, the rusting of iron, and phase changes of matter. When wood burns, the total mass of the products, such as soot, ash, and gases, equals the mass of the wood and the oxygen that reacts with it when it burns. When iron reacts with oxygen, rust is formed. The total mass of the iron-rust complex does not change. Finally, when matter changes phase, mass remains constant. Thus, when a glacier melts because of atmospheric warming, the mass of liquid water formed is equal to the mass of the frozen glacier.

The principle of conservation of charge states that the total electrical charge of a closed system is constant. Thus, in chemical reactions and interactions of charged objects, the total charge does not change.

Matter changes state when energy is added or taken away.

The kinetic theory states that matter consists of molecules, possessing kinetic energy, in continual random motion. The state of matter (solid, liquid, or gas) depends on the speed of the molecules and the amount of kinetic energy the molecules possess. The molecules of solid matter merely vibrate, allowing strong intermolecular forces to hold the molecules in place. The molecules of liquid matter move more freely and quickly, and the molecules of gaseous matter move randomly and at high speeds.

LIFE SCIENCE: STRUCTURE AND FUNCTION OF LIVING THINGS

Physical Processes of Plants

PHOTOSYNTHESIS: the process by which plants make carbohydrates from the energy of the Sun, carbon dioxide, and water

PHOTOSYNTHESIS is the process by which plants make carbohydrates from the energy of the Sun, carbon dioxide, and water. Oxygen is a waste product. Photosynthesis is divided into two major steps:

- Light reactions: Sunlight is trapped, water is split, and oxygen is given off. ATP is made and hydrogens reduce NADP to $NADPH_2$. The light reactions occur in light. The products of the light reactions enter into the dark reactions (Calvin cycle).

- Dark reactions: Carbon dioxide enters during the dark reactions that can occur with or without the presence of light. The energy transferred from $NADPH_2$ and ATP allows for the fixation of carbon into glucose.

The formula for photosynthesis is:

$CO_2 + H_2O$ + energy (from sunlight) becomes $C_6H_{12}O_6 + O_2$

During times of decreased light, plants break down the products of photosynthesis through cellular respiration. Glucose, with the help of oxygen, breaks down and produces carbon dioxide and water as waste.

Water travels up the xylem of the plant. As it evaporates through the stomata of the leaves, the water is pulled up the column from the roots.

Angiosperms are the largest group in the plant kingdom. They are the flowering plants that produce true seeds for reproduction. Angiosperms reproduce through a method of double fertilization. An ovum is fertilized by two sperm. One sperm produces the new plant; the other forms the food supply for the developing plant.

The success of plant reproduction depends on seed dispersal, which involves the seed moving away from the parent plant to decrease competition for space, water, and minerals. Seeds can be carried by wind (maple trees), water (palm trees), or animals (burrs), or ingested by animals and released in their feces in another area (blackberries).

Structures and Functions of Plant Components

Xylem	Transports water
Phloem	Transports food (glucose)
Cortex	Stores food and water
Pith	Storage area in stems
Stomata	Openings on the underside of leaves that let carbon dioxide in and water out (transpiration)
Palisade mesophyll	Contain chloroplasts in leaves; site of photosynthesis

Continued on next page

Spongy mesophyll	Open spaces in the leaves that allow for gas circulation
Endosperm	Food supply in the seed
Apical meristem	An area of cell division allowing for growth
Flowers	The reproductive organs of the plant
Sepals	Green, leaflike parts that cover the flower prior to blooming
Petals	Contain coloration by pigments, whose purpose is to attract insects to assist in pollination
Anther	Male part of the flower that produces pollen
Filament	Supports the anther; the filament and anther make up the stamen
Stigma	Female part of the flower that holds pollen grains that come from the male part
Style	Tube that leads to the ovary (female)
Ovary	Contains the ovules; the stigma, style, and ovary make up the carpel

Life Cycles of Common Organisms

Bacteria reproduce by binary fission. This asexual process simply divides the bacterium in half. As asexual reproduction produces only exact copies of the parent organism, it does not allow for genetic variation, which means that mutations, or weaker qualities, will always be passed on.

Butterflies actually go through four different stages of life. In the first stage, the adult butterfly lays an egg. In the second stage, the egg hatches into a caterpillar, or larva. In the third stage, the caterpillar forms the chrysalis, or pupa. Finally, the chrysalis matures and the adult butterfly emerges.

Frogs also have multiple stages in their life cycle. Initially, an adult frog lays its eggs in the water. In the second stage, tadpoles hatch from the eggs and use gills for breathing. Tadpoles have tails that are used for locomotion. Two to four months after hatching, the tadpole is known as a froglet. You can recognize a froglet because the rim around its tail, which made the tadpole appear more fish-like, has disappeared; its tail is shorter, and its four legs have grown to the extent that its rear legs are bent underneath it. In the final stage, the tail has been entirely reabsorbed.

Basic Requirements for Life

- Food and water: Because all biochemical reactions take place in aqueous environments, all organisms must have access to clean water, if only infrequently. Organisms also require two types of food: a source of energy (fixed carbon) and a source of nutrients. Autotrophs can fix carbon for themselves, but must have access to certain inorganic precursors. These organisms must also be able to obtain other nutrients, such as nitrogen, from their environment. Heterotrophs, on the other hand, must consume other organisms for both energy and nutrients.
- Sunlight and air: Plants require carbon dioxide for photosynthesis and oxygen for cellular respiration. Sunlight is also necessary for photosynthesis and is used by many animals to synthesize essential nutrients (i.e., vitamin D).
- Shelter and space: The need for shelter and space varies greatly among species. Many plants do not need shelter, per se, but must have adequate soil to spread their roots and acquire nutrients. Plants and many animals also require protection from environmental hazards. Some locations may facilitate reproduction (for instance, nesting sites) or provide seasonal shelter (for examples, dens and caves used by hibernating species).

Cell Types

Animal cells have a cell membrane, which lets nutrients in and waste materials out; a cytoplasm, which contains the cellular organelles; and a nucleus, which contains the cellular DNA.

Plant cells are similar to animal cells except they also contain a cell wall, which gives a rigid structure to the cell; and a chloroplast, which contains chlorophyll for photosynthesis.

Prokaryotes Versus Eukaryotes

Prokaryotic cells are found only in bacteria and blue-green algae.

Eukaryotic cells are found in protists (single-celled organisms), fungi, plants, and animals.

Cell Organelles and Their Functions

Parts of eukaryotic cells

1. Nucleus: The brain of the cell. The nucleus contains:
   - Chromosomes: DNA, RNA, and proteins tightly coiled to conserve space while providing a large surface area
   - Chromatin: Loose structure of chromosomes. Chromosomes are called chromatin when the cell is not dividing.
   - Nucleoli: Where ribosomes are made. These are seen as dark spots in the nucleus.
   - Nuclear membrane: Contains pores that let RNA out of the nucleus. The nuclear membrane is continuous with the endoplasmic reticulum, which allows the membrane to expand or shrink if needed.
2. Ribosomes: The site of protein synthesis. Ribosomes may be free-floating in the cytoplasm or attached to the endoplasmic reticulum. There may be up to half a million ribosomes in a cell, depending on how much protein is made by the cell.
3. Endoplasmic reticulum: These are folded and provide a large surface area. They are the "roadway" of the cell and allow for transport of materials. The lumen of the endoplasmic reticulum helps to keep materials out of the cytoplasm and headed in the right direction. The endoplasmic reticulum is capable of building new membrane material. There are two types:
   - Smooth endoplasmic reticulum: Contains no ribosomes on its surface
   - Rough endoplasmic reticulum: Contains ribosomes on its surface. This form of endoplasmic reticulum is abundant in cells that make many proteins, e.g., in the pancreas, which produces many digestive enzymes.
4. Golgi complex or Golgi apparatus: This structure is stacked to increase surface area. The Golgi complex functions to sort, modify, and package molecules that are made in other parts of the cell. These molecules are either sent out of the cell or to other organelles within the cell.
5. Lysosomes: Found mainly in animal cells. Lysosomes contain digestive enzymes that break down food, substances not needed, viruses, damaged cell components, and eventually the cell itself. It is believed that lysosomes are responsible for the aging process.

6. Mitochondria: Large organelles that make ATP to supply energy to the cell. Muscle cells have many mitochondria because they use a great deal of energy. The folds inside the mitochondria are called cristae. They provide a large surface where the reactions of cellular respiration occur. Mitochondria have their own DNA and are capable of reproducing themselves if a greater demand is made for additional energy. Mitochondria are found only in animal cells.

Mitochondria are found only in animal cells.

7. Plastids: Found in photosynthetic organisms only. They are similar to mitochondria due to their double membrane structure. They also have their own DNA and can reproduce if increased capture of sunlight becomes necessary. There are several types of plastids:
   - Chloroplasts: Green; function in photosynthesis. They are capable of trapping sunlight.
   - Chromoplasts: Make and store yellow and orange pigments; they provide color to leaves, flowers, and fruits.
   - Amyloplasts: Store starch and are used as a food reserve. They are abundant in roots like potatoes.

8. Cell Wall: Found in plant cells only, composed of cellulose and fibers. The cell wall is thick enough for support and protection yet porous enough to allow water and dissolved substances to enter. Cell walls are cemented to each other.

9. Vacuoles: Hold stored food and pigments. Vacuoles are very large in plants. This allows them to fill with water in order to provide turgor pressure. Lack of turgor pressure causes a plant to wilt.

10. Cytoskeleton: Composed of protein filaments attached to the plasma membrane and organelles. The cytoskeleton provides a framework for the cell and aids in cell movement. It constantly changes shape and moves about. Three types of fibers make up the cytoskeleton:
    - Microtubules: Largest of the three types of fibers; makes up cilia and flagella for locomotion. Flagella grow from a basal body. Some examples are sperm cells and tracheal cilia. Centrioles are also composed of microtubules. They form the spindle fibers that pull the cell apart into two cells during cell division. Centrioles are not found in the cells of higher plants.
    - Intermediate filaments: Smaller than microtubules but larger than microfilaments. They help the cell to keep its shape.
    - Microfilaments: Smallest of the three types of fibers, made of actin and small amounts of myosin (as in muscle cells). They function in cell

movement such as cytoplasmic streaming, endocytosis, and ameboid movement. This structure pinches the two cells apart after cell division, forming two cells.

Human Body Systems

Groups of related organs are called organ systems. Organ systems consist of organs working together to perform a common function. The commonly recognized organ systems include the reproductive system, the nervous system, the circulatory system, the respiratory system, the lymphatic system (immune system), the endocrine system, the urinary system, the muscular system, the digestive system, the integumentary system, and the skeletal system.

Form and function are closely related properties of organisms and systems. The function of an object usually dictates its form, and the form of an object usually facilitates its function.

One obvious example of the interconnectedness of organ systems is the relationship between the circulatory and respiratory systems. As blood circulates through the organs of the circulatory system, it is reoxygenated in the lungs, which are part of the respiratory system.

Skeletal system

The function of the skeletal system is to provide support. Vertebrates have an endoskeleton, with muscles attached to bones.

Bone is a connective tissue. Parts of the bone include compact bone, which gives strength; spongy bone, which contains red marrow to make blood cells and yellow marrow in the center of long bones to store fat cells; and the periosteum, which is the protective covering on the outside of the bone.

Ligaments attach bone to bone. Tendons attach bone to muscle.

Muscular system

The function of the muscular system is to allow movement.

There are three types of muscle tissue:

- Skeletal muscle is voluntary. Skeletal muscles are attached to bones.
- Smooth muscle is involuntary. It is found in organs and enables functions such as digestion and respiration.
- Cardiac muscle is a specialized type of smooth muscle and is found only in the heart.

Muscles can only contract; therefore, they work in antagonistic pairs to allow back-and-forth movement. Muscle fibers are made up of groups of myofibrils, which are made up of groups of sarcomeres. Actin and myosin are proteins that make up the sarcomere.

Physiology of muscle contraction

A nerve impulse strikes a muscle fiber. This causes calcium ions to flood the sarcomere. Calcium ions allow ATP to expend energy. The myosin fibers creep along the actin, causing the muscle to contract. Once the nerve impulse has passed, calcium is pumped out and the contraction ends.

Nervous system

The neuron is the basic unit of the nervous system. It consists of the cell body, which contains the nucleus; an axon, which carries impulses away from the cell body, and the dendrite, which carries impulses toward the cell body. Synapses are spaces between neurons. Chemicals called neurotransmitters are found close to the synapses.

Some neurotransmitters stimulate while others inhibit action.

Physiology of the nerve impulse

Nerve action depends on depolarization and an imbalance of electrical charges across the neuron. Neurotransmitters turn off the sodium pump, which results in depolarization of the membrane. This wave of depolarization (as it moves from neuron to neuron) carries an electrical impulse. This is actually a wave of opening and closing gates that allows for the flow of ions across the synapse. Nerves have an action potential. There is a threshold of the level of chemicals that must be met or exceeded in order for muscles to respond.

Organization of the nervous system

The somatic nervous system is controlled consciously. It consists of the central nervous system (brain and spinal cord) and the peripheral nervous system (nerves that extend from the spinal cord to the muscles). The autonomic nervous system is unconsciously controlled by the hypothalamus of the brain. Entities and processes controlled by the autonomic nervous system include smooth muscles, the heart, and digestion.

Neurotransmitters

- Acetylcholine: The most common neurotransmitter; controls muscle contraction and heartbeat. The enzyme acetylcholinesterase breaks it down to end the transmission.
- Epinephrine: Responsible for the "fight or flight" reaction. Epinephrine causes an increase in heart rate and blood flow to prepare the body for action. It is also called adrenaline.

- **Endorphins and enkephalins:** These are natural painkillers released during serious injury and childbirth.

Digestive system

The function of the digestive system is to break food down and absorb it into the bloodstream, where it can be delivered to all cells of the body for use in cellular respiration.

The teeth and saliva begin digestion by breaking food down into smaller pieces The food is carried down the pharynx by the process of **peristalsis** (wave-like contractions) and enters the stomach.

Most nutrient absorption occurs in the small intestine.

In the stomach, pepsinogen and hydrochloric acid form **pepsin**, the enzyme that breaks down proteins. The food is broken down further by this chemical action and is turned into chyme, an acid. The pyloric sphincter muscle opens to allow the food to enter the small intestine. Upon arrival into the small intestine, chyme is neutralized to allow the enzymes there to function. Any food left after the trip through the small intestine enters the large intestine. The large intestine functions to reabsorb water and produce vitamin K. Feces, or remaining waste, are passed out through the anus.

Respiratory system

The respiratory system functions in the gas exchange of oxygen and carbon dioxide. It delivers oxygen to the bloodstream and picks up carbon dioxide for release out of the body.

Air enters the mouth and nose. Cilia in the trachea trap unwanted material in mucus. The trachea splits into two bronchial tubes, and the bronchial tubes divide into smaller and smaller bronchioles in the lungs. The internal surface of the lungs is composed of alveoli, which are thin-walled air sacs. These sacs provide a large surface area for gas exchange. The alveoli are lined with capillaries. Oxygen diffuses into the bloodstream and carbon dioxide diffuses out to be exhaled. The oxygenated blood is carried to the heart and delivered to all parts of the body.

Circulatory system

The function of the circulatory system is to carry oxygenated blood and nutrients to all cells of the body and return carbon dioxide waste to be expelled from the lungs.

Unoxygenated blood enters the heart through the inferior and superior vena cava. The first chamber it encounters is the right atrium. It goes through the tricuspid valve to the right ventricle, on to the pulmonary arteries, and then to the lungs, where it is oxygenated. It returns to the heart through the pulmonary vein into the left atrium. It travels through the bicuspid valve to the left ventricle where it is pumped to all parts of the body through the aorta.

Reproductive system

Hormones regulate sexual maturation in humans. Humans cannot reproduce until puberty, about the age of 8-14, depending on the individual. The hypothalamus begins secreting hormones that help mature the reproductive system and develop the secondary sex characteristics. Reproductive maturity in girls occurs with their first menstruation and in boys with the first ejaculation of viable sperm.

Hormones also regulate reproduction. In males, the primary sex hormones are the androgens, testosterone being the most important. The testes produce androgens that dictate the primary and secondary sex characteristics of the male. Female hormone patterns are cyclic and complex. Most women have a reproductive cycle of approximately twenty-eight days. The menstrual cycle is specific to the changes in the uterus. The ovarian cycle results in ovulation and occurs in parallel with the menstrual cycle. Hormones regulate this parallelism. Five hormones participate in this regulation, most notably estrogen and progesterone. Estrogen and progesterone play an important role in signaling to the uterus and in the development and maintenance of the endometrium. Estrogens also dictate the secondary sex characteristics of females.

GAMETOGENESIS is the production of sperm and egg cells.

GAMETOGENESIS: the production of sperm and egg cells

Spermatogenesis begins at puberty in the male. One spermatogonia, the diploid precursor of sperm, produces four sperm. The sperm mature in the seminiferous tubules located in the testes. Oogenesis, the production of egg cells (ova), is usually complete by the birth of a female. Females do not release egg cells until menstruation begins at puberty. Meiosis forms one ovum with all the cytoplasm and three polar bodies that the body reabsorbs. The ovaries store the ovum and release one each month from puberty to menopause.

Seminiferous tubules in the testes house sperm, where they mature. The epididymis, located on top of the testes, contains mature sperm. After ejaculation, the sperm travel up the vas deferens, where they mix with semen made in the prostate and seminal vesicles and travel out the urethra.

Ovulation releases the egg into the fallopian tube, where cilia move it along the length of the tube. Fertilization of the egg by the sperm normally occurs in the fallopian tube. If pregnancy does not occur, the egg passes through the uterus and is expelled through the vagina. Levels of progesterone and estrogen stimulate menstruation. Implantation of a fertilized egg regulates the levels, stopping menstruation.

There are many methods of contraception (birth control) that affect different stages of fertilization. Chemical contraception (birth control pills or injections) prevents ovulation by synthetic estrogen and progesterone. Several barrier methods of contraception are available. Male and female condoms block semen from contacting the egg. Sterilization is another method of birth control. Tubal ligation in women prevents eggs from entering the urethra. A vasectomy in men involves cutting the vas deferens. This prevents the sperm from entering the urethra. The most effective method of birth control is abstinence.

Lymphatic System (Immune System)

Nonspecific defense mechanisms do not target specific pathogens but are a whole-body response. Results of nonspecific mechanisms are seen as symptoms of an infection. These mechanisms include the skin, mucous membranes, and cells of the blood and lymph (i.e., white blood cells, macrophages).

Specific defense mechanisms recognize foreign material and respond by destroying the invader. These mechanisms are specific in purpose and diverse in type. They are able to recognize individual pathogens and differentiate between foreign material and self. Memory of the invaders provides immunity upon further exposure.

ANTIGEN: any foreign particle that invades the body

An **ANTIGEN** is any foreign particle that invades the body. Manufactured by the body, **ANTIBODIES** recognize and latch onto antigens, and attempt to destroy them.

ANTIBODIES: recognize and latch onto antigens, and attempt to destroy them

Excretory System

The function of the excretory system is to rid the body of nitrogenous wastes in the form of urea.

Urine forms in the collecting duct that leads to the ureter, then to the bladder where it is stored. Urine is passed from the bladder through the urethra.

Endocrine System

The function of the endocrine system is to manufacture proteins called hormones. Hormones are released into the bloodstream and carried to a target tissue where they stimulate an action.

Hormones work on a feedback system. The increase or decrease in one hormone may cause the increase or decrease in another.

Hormones fit specific receptors on the target tissue cell surface. The receptor activates an enzyme that converts ATP to cyclic AMP. Cyclic AMP (cAMP) is a second messenger from the cell membrane to the nucleus. The genes found in the nucleus turn on or off to cause a specific response.

Steroid hormones, which come from cholesterol, cause sexual characteristics and mating behavior. These hormones include estrogen and progesterone in females and testosterone in males.

Peptide hormones are made in the pituitary glands, adrenal glands (kidneys), and the pancreas.

LIFE SCIENCE: REPRODUCTION AND THE MECHANISMS OF HEREDITY

Sexual reproduction greatly increases diversity because of the many combinations possible through meiosis and fertilization. All organisms (except twins or clones) are genetically unique and represent a unique combination of genetic heritable variation.

Variation is generated by mutation and, in sexually reproducing species, sexual recombination. Mutations can be errors in replication or spontaneous rearrangements of one or more segments of DNA and—ultimately—mutations are responsible for all innovative heritable variation. Mutations contribute a minimal but constant amount of variation to a population. In sexually reproducing species, the unique recombination of existing alleles causes the majority of genetic difference between individuals. Genetic variability is caused by independent assortment during meiosis, random fertilization, and crossing over during meiosis.

Cell Division

The purpose of cell division is to provide growth and repair in body (somatic) cells and to replenish or create sex cells for reproduction. There are two forms of cell division: **MITOSIS** is the division of somatic cells and **MEIOSIS** is the division of sex cells (eggs and sperm). The table below summarizes the major differences between the two processes.

MITOSIS: the division of somatic cells

MEIOSIS: the division of sex cells (eggs and sperm)

Mitosis	Meiosis
1. Division of somatic cells	1. Division of sex cells
2. Two cells result from each division	2. Four cells or polar bodies result from each division
3. Chromosome number is identical to parent cells	3. Chromosome number is half the number of parent cells
4. Division occurs for cell growth and repair	4. Recombinations provide genetic diversity

Phases of mitosis

1. Interphase: Chromatin is loose; chromosomes are replicated; cell metabolism is occurring. Interphase is technically not a stage of mitosis.
2. Prophase: Once the cell enters prophase, it proceeds through the following steps continuously, with no stopping. The chromatin condenses to become visible chromosomes. The nucleolus disappears and the nuclear membrane breaks apart. Mitotic spindles form, which will eventually pull the chromosomes apart. They are composed of microtubules. The cytoskeleton breaks down and the spindles are pushed to the poles, or opposite ends, of the cell by the action of centrioles.
3. Metaphase: Kinetechore fibers attach to the chromosomes, which causes the chromosomes to line up in the center of the cell (think: *middle* for *metaphase*).
4. Anaphase: Centromeres split in half and homologous chromosomes separate. The chromosomes are pulled to the poles of the cell, with identical sets at either end.
5. Telophase: Two nuclei form, each with a full set of DNA that is identical to that of the parent cell. The nucleoli become visible and the nuclear membrane reassembles. A cell plate is visible in plant cells, whereas a cleavage furrow is formed in animal cells. The cell is pinched into two cells. Cytokinesis, or division, of the cytoplasm and organelles occurs.

Meiosis

Meiosis has the same five stages as mitosis, but is repeated in order to reduce the chromosome number by one half. This way, when the sperm and egg join during fertilization, the haploid number is reached.

Major function of meiosis I: Chromosomes are replicated; cells remain diploid

- Prophase I: Replicated chromosomes condense and pair with homologues. This forms a tetrad. Crossing over (the exchange of genetic material between homologues to further increase diversity) occurs during Prophase I.
- Metaphase I: Homologous sets attach to spindle fibers after lining up in the middle of the cell.
- Anaphase I: Sister chromatids remain joined and move to the poles of the cell.
- Telophase I: Two new cells are formed; chromosome number is still diploid.

Major function of meiosis II: To reduce the chromosome number in half

- Prophase II: Chromosomes condense.
- Metaphase II: Spindle fibers form again; sister chromatids line up in center of cell; centromeres divide; and sister chromatids separate.
- Anaphase II: Separated chromosomes move to opposite ends of the cell.
- Telophase II: Four haploid cells form for each original sperm germ cell. One viable egg cell gets all the genetic information, and three polar bodies with no DNA form. The nuclear membrane reforms and cytokinesis occurs.

DNA Structure

DNA is made of nucleotides, which are composed of a five-carbon sugar, phosphate group, and nitrogen base (either adenine, guanine, cytosine, or thymine). The base consists of a sugar/phosphate backbone that is covalently bonded. The bases are joined down the center of the molecule and attached by hydrogen bonds that are easily broken during replication.

The amount of adenine equals the amount of thymine, and the amount of cytosine equals the amount of guanine.

The shape of DNA is called a double helix and looks like a twisted ladder. The sugar/phosphates make up the sides of the ladder and the base pairs make up the rungs of the ladder.

DNA Replication

The DNA molecule untwists during replication. The hydrogen bonds between the bases break and serve as a pattern for replication. Free nucleotides inside the nucleus join on to form a new strand. Two new pieces of DNA that are identical are formed.

Base-pairing rules are important in determining the sequence of a new strand of DNA. For example, say our original strand of DNA had the following sequence:

A T C G G C A A T A G C

This can be called our sense strand, because it contains a sequence that makes sense, or codes, for something. The complementary strand (or other side of the ladder) would follow base-pairing rules (A bonds with T, and C bonds with G) and would read:

T A G C C G T T A T C G

When the molecule opens up and nucleotides join on, the base-pairing rules create two new identical strands of DNA:

A T C G G C A A T A G C and A T C G G C A A T A G C
T A G C C G T T A T C G   T A G C C G T T A T C G

Protein Synthesis

- Messenger RNA (mRNA): Copies the code from DNA in the nucleus and takes it to the ribosomes in the cytoplasm.
- Transfer RNA (tRNA): Free-floating in the cytoplasm. Its job is to carry and position amino acids for assembly on the ribosome.
- Ribosomal RNA (rRNA): Found in the ribosomes, which make a place for the proteins to be made. rRNA is believed to have many important functions, so much research is currently being done in this area.

There are two stages of protein synthesis:

- Transcription: This phase allows for the assembly of mRNA and occurs in the nucleus where the DNA is found. The DNA splits open and the mRNA reads the code and "transcribes" the sequence onto a single strand of mRNA. For example, if the code on the DNA is T A C C T C G T A C G A, the mRNA will make a complementary strand reading: A U G G A G C A U G C U (remember that uracil replaces thymine in RNA). Each group of three bases is called a codon. The codon will eventually code for a specific amino acid to be carried to the ribosome. "Start" codons begin the building of the protein and "stop" codons end transcription. When the stop codon is reached, the mRNA separates from the DNA and leaves the nucleus for the cytoplasm.
- Translation: This is the assembly of the amino acids to build the protein and occurs in the cytoplasm. The nucleotide sequence is translated to choose the correct amino acid sequence. As the rRNA translates the code

at the ribosome, tRNAs that contain an anticodon seek out the correct amino acid and bring it back to the ribosome. For example, using the codon sequence from the example above:

The mRNA reads: A U G / G A G / C A U / G C U

The anticodons are: U A C / C U C / G U A / C G A

The amino acid sequence would be: Methionine (start) - Glu - His - Ala

This whole process is accomplished through the assistance of activating enzymes. Each of the twenty amino acids has its own enzyme. The enzyme binds the amino acid to the tRNA. When the amino acids get close to each other on the ribosome, they bond together using peptide bonds. The start and stop codons are called nonsense codons. There is one start codon (AUG) and three stop codons (UAA, UGA, and UAG).

Irregularities or interruptions of mitosis and meiosis

Inheritable changes in DNA are called **MUTATIONS**. Mutations can be errors in replication or a spontaneous rearrangement of one or more segments by factors like radioactivity, drugs, or chemicals. The amount of change is not as critical as where the change is.

MUTATIONS: inheritable changes in DNA

Mutations can occur on somatic or sex cells. Usually the ones on sex cells are more dangerous because they contain the basis of all information for the developing offspring. Mutations are not always bad. They are the basis of evolution, and if they make a more favorable variation that enhances the organism's chances of survival, then they are beneficial. But mutations can also lead to abnormalities, birth defects, and even death. There are several types of mutations. Suppose a normal sequence is as follows:

Normal: A B C D E F

Duplication: One gene is repeated (A B <u>C C</u> D E F)

Inversion: A segment of the sequence is flipped around (A <u>E D C B</u> F)

Deletion: A gene is left out (A B <u>C E</u> F)

Insertion or translocation: A segment from another place on the DNA is inserted in the wrong place (A B C <u>R S</u> D E F)

Breakage: A piece is lost (A B C)—DEF is lost

Nondisjunction: This occurs during meiosis when chromosomes fail to separate properly. One sex cell may get both genes and another may get none.

Depending on the chromosomes involved, this may or may not be serious. Offspring end up with either an extra chromosome or a missing one. An example of nondisjunction is Down syndrome, in which there are three copies of chromosome 21 instead of two.

Genetics

Gregor Mendel, recognized as the father of genetics, realized that there were factors (now known as genes) that were transferred from parents to their offspring. He found that two factors governed each trait, one from each parent. Traits, or characteristics, come in several forms, known as alleles.

The law of segregation

The law of segregation states that only one of the two possible alleles from each parent is passed on to the offspring. If the two alleles differ, then one is fully expressed in the organism's appearance (the dominant allele) and the other has no noticeable effect on appearance (the recessive allele).

- Homozygous: Having a pair of identical alleles; for example, *PP* and *pp* are homozygous pairs
- Heterozygous: Having two different alleles; for example, *Pp* is a heterozygous pair
- Phenotype: The organism's physical appearance
- Genotype: The organism's genetic makeup; for example, *PP* and *Pp* have the same phenotype (purple in color), but different genotypes

The law of independent assortment

The law of independent assortment states that alleles sort independently of each other. The law of segregation applies for monohybrid crosses (only one character—in this case, flower color—is varied). In a dihybrid cross, two characters are explored.

Dominant and recessive traits

In Mendel's law of segregation, the F1 generation has either purple or white flowers. This is an example of complete dominance.

Incomplete dominance is when the F1 generation results in an appearance that is a cross between those of the two parents. For example, red flowers are crossed with white flowers, resulting in an F1 generation with pink flowers.

In codominance, the genes form new phenotypes. The ABO blood grouping is an example of codominance. Types A and B are of equal strength and type O is recessive. Therefore, type A blood may have the genotypes of AA or AO; type B blood may have the genotypes of BB or BO; type AB blood has the genotype A and B; and type O blood has two recessive O genes.

LIFE SCIENCE: ADAPTATIONS OF ORGANISMS AND THE THEORY OF EVOLUTION

Theory of Natural Selection

Charles Darwin defined the theory of natural selection in the mid-1800s. Through the study of finches on the Galapagos Islands, Darwin theorized that nature selects the traits that are advantageous to the organism. Those individuals that do not possess the desirable traits die and do not pass on their genes to future generations. Those more fit to survive reproduce, thus increasing the stronger genes in the population.

Certain factors increase the chances of variation in a population, thus leading to evolution. Factors that increase variation include mutations, sexual reproduction, immigration, and large populations.

Biological adaptation

Anatomical structures and physiological processes that evolve over time to increase the overall reproductive success of an organism in its environment are known as biological adaptations. Such evolutionary changes occur through **NATURAL SELECTION**, the process by which individual organisms with favorable traits survive to reproduce more frequently than those with unfavorable traits. The heritable component of such favorable traits is passed down to offspring during reproduction, increasing the frequency of the favorable trait in a population over many generations.

NATURAL SELECTION: the process by which individual organisms with favorable traits survive to reproduce more frequently than those with unfavorable traits

Adaptations increase long-term reproductive success by making an organism better suited for survival under particular environmental conditions and pressures. These biological changes can increase an organism's ability to obtain air, water, food, and nutrients, to cope with environmental variables, and to defend itself. The term adaptation may apply to changes in biological processes which, for example, enable an organism to produce venom or regulate body temperature, and also to structural adaptations, such as organisms' skin color and shape. Adaptations can occur in behavioral traits and survival mechanisms as well.

How Populations and Species Change Through Time

Paleontological evidence

PALEONTOLOGY: the study of the life of past geological time periods based on fossil records

PALEONTOLOGY is the study of the life of past geological time periods based on fossil records.

Petrification is the process by which a dead plant or animal gets fossilized. For this to happen, a dead organism must be buried quickly to avoid weathering and decomposition. When an organism is buried, the organic matter decays. The mineral salts from the mud in which the organism is buried infiltrate the bones and gradually fill up the pores. The bones harden and are preserved as fossils. Besides petrification, organisms can be well-preserved in ice, in the hardened resin of coniferous trees (amber), in tar, or in anaerobic acidic peat. Fossilization can sometimes be only a trace or an impression of a form, e.g., leaves or footprints.

Horizontal layers of sedimentary rocks formed by layers of silt or mud are called strata, and each layer can contain fossils. The oldest layer is the one at the bottom, so the fossils found in this layer are the oldest. This is how paleontologists can determine the relative age of fossils.

Some organisms appear only in certain layers, indicating that they lived only during that period and then became extinct. A succession of animals and plants can also be seen in fossil records, which supports the theory that organisms tend to progressively increase in complexity.

Anatomical evidence

Groups with little in common are supposed to have diverged from a common ancestor much earlier in geological history than groups that have more in common.

Comparative anatomical studies reveal that some structural features of organisms are basically similar, e.g., flowers generally have sepals, petals, stigma, style, and ovaries but the size, color, and number of petals, sepals, etc. may differ from species to species. The degree of resemblance between two organisms indicates how closely they are related.

When a group of organisms shares a homologous structure that has been specialized to perform a variety of functions in order to adapt to different environmental conditions, it is called adaptive radiation.

Under similar environmental conditions, fundamentally different structures in different groups of organisms may undergo modifications to serve similar functions.

This is called convergent evolution.

Organs that are smaller and simpler in structure than corresponding parts in the ancestral species are called vestigial organs. They are usually degenerated or underdeveloped. These organs were functional in the ancestral species but have become nonfunctional, e.g., vestigial hind limbs of whales, vestigial leaves of some xerophytes, and vestigial wings of flightless birds like ostriches.

Geographical evidence

All organisms adapt to their environment to a greater or lesser extent. It is generally assumed that the same type of species would be found in a similar habitat in a similar geographic area.

Comparative embryological evidence

Comparative embryology shows that embryos start off looking the same. As they develop, their similarities slowly decrease until they take the form of their particular class.

Comparative embryology shows that embryos start off looking the same. As they develop, their similarities slowly decrease until they take the form of their particular class.

For example, adult vertebrates are diverse, yet their embryos are quite similar at very early stages. Fishlike structures still form in early embryos of reptiles, birds, and mammals. In fish embryos, a two-chambered heart, some veins, and parts of arteries develop, which persist in adult fish. The same structures form early in human embryos but do not persist in adults.

Physiological and biochemical evidence

Evolution of widely distributed proteins and molecules

All organisms make use of DNA and/or RNA. ATP is the metabolic currency of all organisms. The genetic code is the same for almost every organism. A piece of RNA in a bacterium cell codes for the same protein as in a human cell.

Comparison of the DNA sequence allows organisms to be grouped by sequence similarity, and the resulting phylogenetic trees are typically consistent with traditional taxonomy and are often used to strengthen or correct taxonomic classifications.

The proteomic evidence also supports the universal ancestry of life. Vital proteins such as ribosome, DNA polymerase, and RNA polymerase are found in the most primitive bacteria as well as the most complex mammals.

LIFE SCIENCE: RELATIONSHIPS BETWEEN ORGANISMS AND THE ENVIRONMENT

Response to stimuli is one of the key characteristics of all living things. Any detectable change in the internal or external environment (the stimulus) may trigger a response in an organism. Like physical characteristics, an organism's responses to stimuli are adaptations that allow it to better survive.

Single-celled organisms

Single-celled organisms are able to respond to basic stimuli such as the presence of light, heat, or food. They typically sense changes in the environment via receptors on the cell surface. These organisms may respond to stimuli by making changes in internal biochemical pathways or initiating reproduction or phagocytosis. Those capable of simple mobility—using flagella, for instance—may respond by moving toward food or away from heat.

Plants

Plants typically do not possess sensory organs so individual cells recognize stimuli through a variety of pathways. When many cells respond to stimuli together, a response becomes apparent. Logically, then, the responses of plants occur more slowly than those of animals. Plants are capable of responding to a few basic stimuli including light, water, and gravity. Some common examples include the way plants turn and grow toward the sun, the sprouting of seeds when exposed to warmth and moisture, and the growth of roots in the direction of gravity.

The nervous system, sensory organs (eyes, ears, skin, etc.), and muscle tissue all allow animals to sense and quickly respond to changes in their environment.

Animals

As with other organisms, many animal responses to stimuli are involuntary. For example, pupils dilate in response to the reduction of light. Such reactions are typically called **reflexes**. However, many animals are also capable of voluntary responses. In many animal species, voluntary reactions are instinctual. For instance, a zebra's response to a lion is *voluntary*, but, *instinctually*, it will flee quickly as soon as it senses the lion's presence. Complex responses, which may or may not be instinctual, are typically termed **BEHAVIOR**.

BEHAVIOR: complex responses, which may or may not be instinctual

Relationships Between Organisms

- Parasitism: Two species occupy a similar place; the parasite benefits from the relationship and the host is harmed.
- Commensalism: Two species occupy a similar place; neither species is harmed or benefits from the relationship.
- Mutualism (symbiosis): Two species occupy a similar place; both species benefit from the relationship.
- Competition: Two species occupy the same habitat or eat the same food are said to be in competition with each other.
- Predation: Animals that eat other animals are called predators. The animals they feed on are called prey. Population growth depends upon competition for food, water, shelter, and space. The number of predators determines the amount of prey, which, in turn, affects the number of predators.

Food Chains

TROPHIC LEVELS describe the feeding relationships that determine energy flow and chemical cycling in a food chain. Energy is lost as the trophic levels progress from producer to tertiary consumer. The amount of energy that is transferred between trophic levels is called the ecological efficiency.

TROPHIC LEVELS: the feeding relationships that determine energy flow and chemical cycling in a food chain

Pyramid of productivity

A pyramid of productivity represents the energy flow through trophic levels. Most food chains are more elaborate, becoming food webs.

Pyramid of Productivity

Tertiary
Consumers
Secondary Consumers
Primary Consumers
Producers

Tertiary consumers eat the secondary consumers.

Secondary consumers are carnivores that eat primary consumers.

Primary consumers are herbivores that eat plants or algae.

Producers are mainly autotrophs/plant life.

Decomposers are consumers that feed off animal waste and dead organisms.

A Niche in an Ecosystem

NICHE: the relational position of a species or population in an ecosystem

The term **NICHE** describes the relational position of a species or population in an ecosystem.

According to the competitive exclusion principle, no two species can occupy the same niche in the same environment for a long period of time. The full range of environmental conditions (biological and physical) under which an organism can exist describes its fundamental niche. Because of the pressure from superior competitors, organisms are driven to occupy a niche much narrower than their previous niche. This is known as the "realized niche."

EARTH AND SPACE SCIENCE: STRUCTURE AND FUNCTION OF EARTH SYSTEMS

Structure of the Earth

Core

The outer core of the Earth begins about 3,000 km beneath the surface and is a liquid, though far more viscous than that of the mantle. Even deeper, approximately 5,000 km beneath the surface, is the solid inner core. The inner core has a radius of about 1,200 km. Temperatures in the core exceed 4,000°C.

Scientists agree that the core is extremely dense. It is hypothesized that when the Earth was forming, the densest material sank to the middle of the planet. Thus, it is not surprising that the core is about 80 percent iron.

Mantle

The Earth's mantle begins about 35 km beneath the surface and stretches all the way to 3,000 km beneath the surface, where the outer core begins. Near the boundary with the crust it is approximately 1,000°C, while near the outer core it may reach nearly 4,000°C. Within the mantle there are silicate rocks, which are rich in iron and magnesium. The silicate rocks exist as solids but the high heat means they are ductile enough to "flow" very slowly.

Crust

The crust of the Earth is the outermost layer and continues down between 5 and 70 km beneath the surface. Thin areas generally exist under ocean basins (oceanic crust) and thicker crust underlies the continents (continental crust). Oceanic crust is composed largely of iron magnesium silicate rocks, while continental crust is less dense and consists mainly of sodium potassium aluminum silicate rocks.

It is generally believed that swirling of the iron-rich liquid in the outer core results in the Earth's magnetic field, which is readily apparent on the surface.

Interactions between the layers

It is generally believed that swirling of the iron-rich liquid in the outer core results in the Earth's magnetic field, which is readily apparent on the surface. Heat also moves out from the core to the mantle and crust.

Constructive and Destructive Processes

Erosion and weathering

EROSION is the inclusion and transportation of surface materials by another moveable material, usually water, wind, or ice. The breaking down of rocks at or near the Earth's surface is known as **WEATHERING**.

- Physical weathering is the process by which rocks are broken down into smaller fragments without undergoing any change in chemical composition.
- Chemical weathering is the breaking down of rocks through changes in their chemical composition. Water, oxygen, and carbon dioxide are the main agents of chemical weathering.

EROSION: the inclusion and transportation of surface materials by another moveable material, usually water, wind, or ice

WEATHERING: the breaking down of rocks at or near the Earth's surface

Plate tectonics

PLATES are rigid blocks of Earth's crust and upper mantle. These rigid solid blocks make up the lithosphere and are broken into nine large sections and

PLATES: rigid blocks of Earth's crust and upper mantle

several small ones. The major plates are named after the continents they are "transporting."

The plates float on and move with a layer of hot, plastic-like rock in the upper mantle. Movement of these crustal plates creates areas where the plates diverge as well as areas where they converge. **Convergence** is when the oceanic crust collides with either another oceanic plate or a continental plate. The oceanic crust sinks, forming an enormous trench and generating volcanic activity. Convergence also includes continent-to-continent plate collisions. When two plates slide past one another, a **transform fault** is created.

These movements produce many major features of the Earth's surface, such as mountain ranges, volcanoes, and earthquake zones. Most of these features are located at plate boundaries, where the plates interact by spreading apart, pressing together, or sliding past each other. These movements are very slow, averaging only a few centimeters a year.

Boundaries form between spreading plates where the crust is forced apart in a process called **rifting**. As the seafloor spreading takes place, new material is added to the inner edges of the separating plates. In this way the plates grow larger and the ocean basin widens.

When a plate of ocean crust collides with a plate of continental crust, the denser oceanic plate slides under the lighter continental plate and plunges into the mantle. This process is called **subduction.**

The crustal movement of plates sliding sideways past each other produces a plate boundary characterized by major faults that are capable of unleashing powerful earthquakes.

Earthquakes

The epicenter of an earthquake is the point on the Earth's surface located directly above the earthquake's point of origin within the Earth.

An **earthquake** is the shaking or displacement of the ground at the Earth's surface that results from a sudden release of stored energy in the crust that propagates seismic waves. Earthquakes generally occur along fault lines.

Seismic waves

There are two types of simultaneously generated seismic waves that contribute to the characteristic shaking of an earthquake: body waves and surface waves. **Body waves**, which include P-waves (primary waves) and S-waves (secondary or shear waves), travel through the interior of the Earth along paths determined by the Earth's varying density and composition.

Surface waves travel just under the Earth's surface in the same manner as water waves. They are characterized by low frequency, long duration, slow speed, and large amplitude. For these reasons, surface waves are the more destructive type of seismic wave.

Mountain formation

A mountain is terrain that has been raised high above the surrounding landscape by volcanic action or some form of tectonic plate collision.

Folded mountains (e.g., the Alps and the Himalayas) are produced by the folding of rock layers during their formation.

Fault-block mountains (e.g., mountains in Utah, Arizona, and New Mexico) are created when plate movement produces tension forces instead of compression forces. Rock along these faults is displaced upward.

Dome mountains are formed as magma tries to push up through the crust but fails to break the surface.

Upwarped mountains (e.g., the Black Hills of South Dakota) are created by a broad arching of the crust.

Volcanism

VOLCANISM is the movement of magma through the crust and its emergence as lava onto the Earth's surface.

VOLCANISM: the movement of magma through the crust and its emergence as lava onto the Earth's surface

An active volcano is one that is presently erupting or building to an eruption. A dormant volcano is one that is between eruptions but still shows signs of internal activity that might lead to an eruption in the future. An extinct volcano is said to be no longer capable of erupting. Most of the world's active volcanoes are found along the rim of the Pacific Ocean, which is also a major earthquake zone. This curving belt of active faults and volcanoes is often called the Ring of Fire.

Three types of volcanic mountains are:

- Shield volcanoes are associated with quiet eruptions. Lava emerges from the vent or opening in the crater and flows freely out over the Earth's surface until it cools and hardens into a layer of igneous rock.
- Cinder-cone volcanoes are associated with explosive eruptions during which lava is hurled high into the air in a spray of droplets of various sizes. These droplets cool and harden into cinders and particles of ash before falling to the ground. The ash and cinder pile up around the vent to form a steep, cone-shaped hill.
- Composite volcanoes are built by both lava flows and layers of ash and cinder.

Glaciation

About 12,000 years ago, a vast sheet of ice covered a large part of the northern United States. This huge, frozen mass had moved south from the northern regions of Canada as several large bodies of slow-moving ice, or glaciers.

There are two main types of glaciers: valley glaciers and continental glaciers.

U-shaped erosion is characteristic of erosion by valley glaciers, which produce sharp-peaked mountains such as the Matterhorn in Switzerland. Continental glaciers often ride over mountains in their paths, leaving smoothed, rounded mountains and ridges.

Surface Water and Groundwater

Precipitation that soaks into the ground through small pores or openings becomes groundwater. Gravity causes groundwater to move through interconnected porous rock formations from higher to lower elevations. The upper surface of the zone saturated with groundwater is the water table. A swamp is an area where the water table is at the surface. Sometimes the land dips below the water table, and these areas fill with water, forming lakes, ponds, or streams. Groundwater that flows out from underground onto the surface is called a spring.

Groundwater provides drinking water for 53 percent of the population in the United States and is collected in reservoirs.

Permeable rocks filled with water are called aquifers. An aquifer forms when a layer of permeable rock is trapped between two layers of impermeable rock. Groundwater fills the pore spaces in the permeable rock. Layers of limestone are common aquifers. Confined aquifers are deep in the ground and below the water table. Unconfined aquifers border on the water table.

Composition and Structure of the Atmosphere

The most abundant dry gases in the atmosphere are:

(N_2) Nitrogen	78.09 % (makes up about $\frac{4}{5}$ of gases in atmosphere)
(O_2) Oxygen	20.95 %
(AR) Argon	0.93 %
(CO_2) Carbon dioxide	0.03 %

The atmosphere is divided into four main layers based on temperature:

1. Troposphere: Layer closest to the Earth's surface. All weather phenomena occur here because it is the layer with the most water vapor and dust. The average thickness of the troposphere is 7 miles (11 km).
2. Stratosphere: This layer contains very little water. The ozone layer is located in the upper portions of the stratosphere.
3. Mesosphere: The coldest layer, with temperatures in the range of -100°C at the top.
4. Thermosphere: The thermosphere extends upward into space. Oxygen molecules in this layer absorb energy from the Sun, causing temperatures to increase with height. The lower part of the thermosphere is called the ionosphere in which there are charged particles, or ions, and free electrons. The upper portion of the thermosphere is called the exosphere. Gas molecules are very far apart in this layer.

EARTH AND SPACE SCIENCE: CYCLES IN EARTH SYSTEMS

Rock Cycle

Within the rock cycle, igneous rocks are formed when magma escapes from the mantle as lava during volcanic eruption. Rocks can also be forced back into the mantle, where the high heat and pressure recreate them as metamorphic rocks.

Types of rock

- Sedimentary rocks: When fluid sediments are transformed into solid sedimentary rocks, the process is known as **LITHIFICATION**. A common process that affects sediments is compaction, when the weight of overlying materials compresses and compacts the deeper sediments.

LITHIFICATION: when fluid sediments are transformed into solid sedimentary rocks

- Igneous rocks: Igneous rocks can be classified according to their texture, their composition, and the way they formed. As magma cools, the elements and compounds begin to form crystals. The more slowly the magma cools, the larger the crystals grow. Rocks with large crystals are said to have a coarse-grained texture. Granite is an example of a coarse-grained rock. Rocks that cool rapidly before any crystals can form have a glassy texture like obsidian.
- Metamorphic rocks: Metamorphic rocks are formed by high temperatures and great pressures. The outcome of metamorphic changes includes deformation by extreme heat and pressure, compaction, destruction of the original characteristics of the parent rock, bending and folding while in a plastic stage, and the emergence of completely new and different minerals due to chemical reactions with heated water and dissolved minerals. Metamorphic rocks are classified into two groups: foliated (leaflike) rocks and unfoliated rocks. Foliated rocks consist of compressed, parallel bands of minerals, which give the rocks a striped appearance. Examples of such rocks include slate, schist, and gneiss. Unfoliated rocks are not banded; examples of unfoliated rocks include quartzite, marble, and anthracite.

Minerals

The major groups of minerals are silicates, carbonates, oxides, sulfides, sulfates, and halides.

Minerals must:

- Be nonliving
- Be formed in nature
- Be solid in form
- Have atoms that form a crystalline pattern
- Have a chemical composition fixed within narrow limits

Soils

Soils are composed of particles of sand, clay, various minerals, tiny living organisms, humus, and the decayed remains of plants and animals.

- Sandy soils are gritty, and their particles do not bind together firmly. Sandy soils are porous: Water passes through them rapidly.
- Clay soils are smooth and greasy; their particles bind together firmly. Clay soils are moist and usually do not allow water to pass through easily.
- Loamy soils feel somewhat like velvet and their particles clump together. Loamy soils are made up of sand, clay, and silt. Loamy soils hold water but allow some water to pass through.

Water Cycle

Water that falls to Earth in the form of rain or snow is called **PRECIPITATION**. Precipitation is part of a continuous process in which water at the Earth's surface evaporates, condenses into clouds, and returns to Earth. This process is called the water cycle.

PRECIPITATION: water that falls to Earth in the form of rain or snow

Geochemical Cycles

Carbon cycle

Ten percent of all available carbon in the air (from carbon dioxide gas) is fixed by photosynthesis. Plants fix carbon in the form of glucose. Animals eat the plants and are able to obtain the carbon they need. When animals release carbon dioxide through respiration, the plants have a source of carbon to fix again.

Nitrogen cycle

Eighty percent of the atmosphere is nitrogen gas. Nitrogen must be fixed and taken out of its gaseous form to be incorporated into an organism. Only a few genera of bacteria have the enzymes necessary to break the triple bond between nitrogen atoms. These bacteria live in the roots of legumes (peas, beans, alfalfa) and add bacteria to the soil so the plant can use it. Nitrogen is necessary to make amino acids and the nitrogenous bases of DNA.

Phosphorus cycle

Phosphorus exists as a mineral and is not found in the atmosphere. Fungi and plant roots have structures called mycorrhizae that are able to fix insoluble phosphates into usable phosphorus. Urine and decayed matter return phosphorus to the Earth where it can be fixed in the plant. Phosphorus is needed for the backbone of DNA and for the manufacture of ATP.

EARTH AND SPACE SCIENCE: ROLE OF ENERGY IN WEATHER AND CLIMATE

Wind

Air masses moving toward or away from the Earth's surface are called air currents. Air moving parallel to the Earth's surface is called wind. Weather conditions are generated by winds and air currents carrying large amounts of heat and moisture from one part of the atmosphere to another.

The wind belts in each hemisphere consist of convection cells that encircle the Earth like belts. There are three major wind belts on Earth:

1. Trade winds
2. Prevailing westerlies
3. Polar easterlies

Sea breezes are caused by the unequal heating of the land and an adjacent, large body of water.

Wind-belt formation depends on the differences in air pressure that develop in the Doldrums, the horse latitudes, and the polar regions. The Doldrums surround the equator. Within this belt, heated air usually rises straight up into the Earth's atmosphere. The horse latitudes are regions of high barometric pressure with calm and light winds, and the polar regions contain cold dense air that sinks to the Earth's surface.

Monsoons are huge wind systems that cover large geographic areas and reverse direction seasonally. As denser, cooler air from over the ocean moves inland, a steady seasonal wind called a summer, or wet, monsoon is produced.

Storms

A thunderstorm is a brief, local storm produced by the rapid upward movement of warm, moist air within a cumulonimbus cloud. Thunderstorms always produce lightning and thunder and are accompanied by strong wind gusts and heavy rain or hail.

A severe storm with swirling winds that can reach speeds of hundreds of km per hour is called a tornado. The sky is covered by large cumulonimbus clouds and violent thunderstorms; a funnel-shaped swirling cloud may extend downward from a cumulonimbus cloud and reach the ground.

Hurricanes are storms that develop when warm, moist air carried by trade winds rotates around a low-pressure "eye."

A blizzard is a storm with strong winds, blowing snow, and frigid temperatures.

Weather Instruments

Instruments that forecast weather include the aneroid barometer and the mercury barometer, which measures air pressure. The air exerts varying pressures on a metal diaphragm that reads air pressure. The mercury barometer operates when atmospheric pressure pushes on a pool of mercury in a glass tube. The higher the pressure, the higher up the tube the mercury rises.

RELATIVE HUMIDITY is defined as the ratio of existing amounts of water vapor and moisture in the air to the maximum amount of moisture the air can hold at the same given pressure and temperature.

RELATIVE HUMIDITY: the ratio of existing amounts of water vapor and moisture in the air to the maximum amount of moisture the air can hold at the same given pressure and temperature

Weather vs. Climate

The weather in a region is called the climate of that region. Unlike the weather, which consists of hourly and daily changes in the atmosphere over a region, climate is the average of all weather conditions in a region over a period of time.

Climates are classified into three groups: polar, tropical, and temperate.

EARTH AND SPACE SCIENCE: CHARACTERISTICS OF THE SOLAR SYSTEM AND THE UNIVERSE

Sun

The Sun is the nearest star to Earth that produces solar energy. By the process of nuclear fusion, hydrogen gas is converted to helium gas.

Parts of the Sun include:

- The core: The inner portion of the Sun, where fusion takes place
- The photosphere: Considered the surface of the sun, which produces sunspots
- The chromosphere: Hydrogen gas causes this portion to be red in color
- The corona: The transparent area of the Sun, visible only during a total eclipse

Earth

The Earth orbits the Sun over a period of 365 days. During this orbit, the average distance between the Earth and Sun is ninety-three million miles. The Earth is closest to the Sun at perihelion, occurring around January 2 of each year, and farthest from the Sun at aphelion, occurring around July 2.

Stars

All stars derive their energy from the thermonuclear fusion of light elements into heavy elements. A star that is composed mostly of hydrogen is a young star. As a star gets older, its hydrogen is consumed and tremendous energy and light is released through fusion.

In stars with central temperatures greater than 600-700 million degrees, carbon fusion rather than hydrogen fusion, is thought to play the dominant role. Carbon fusions can produce magnesium, sodium, neon, or helium.

Vast collections of stars are called **GALAXIES**. Galaxies are classified as irregular, elliptical, or spiral. An irregular galaxy has no real structured appearance; most are in their early stages of life. An elliptical galaxy consists of smooth ellipses, containing little dust and gas, but composed of millions or trillions of stars. Spiral galaxies are disk-shaped and have extending arms that rotate around their dense centers. Earth's galaxy is a spiral galaxy called the Milky Way.

GALAXIES: vast collections of stars

Moon

TIDES are changes in the level of the ocean caused by the varying gravitational pull of the Moon as it orbits the Earth.

TIDES: changes in the level of the ocean caused by the varying gravitational pull of the Moon as it orbits the Earth

Seasons

The axis of the Earth is tilted 23.45° from the perpendicular. The tilt of the Earth's axis is known as the obliquity of the ecliptic, and is mainly responsible for the four seasons of the year because it influences the intensity of solar rays received by the northern and southern hemispheres.

The effect of the Earth's tilt on climate is best demonstrated at the solstices, the two days of the year when the Sun is farthest from the Earth's equatorial plane. At the summer solstice (June), the Earth's tilt on its axis causes the northern hemisphere to lean toward the Sun, while the southern hemisphere leans away. At the winter solstice (December), it is the southern hemisphere that leans toward the Sun and thus experiences summer.

Phases of the Moon

As the Earth orbits the Sun over a period of 365 days, the Moon orbits the Earth every twenty-seven days. As the Moon circles the Earth, its shape in the night sky changes. The changes in the appearance of the Moon as seen from Earth are known as lunar phases. At all times, half of the Moon is facing the Sun and is thus illuminated by reflecting the Sun's light. As the Moon orbits the Earth and the Earth orbits the Sun, the half of the Moon that faces the Sun changes. However, the Moon is in synchronous rotation around the Earth, meaning that nearly the same side of the Moon faces the Earth at all times. This side is referred to as the near side of the Moon.

When the Sun and Moon are on opposite sides of the Earth, observers on Earth perceive a "full moon," meaning the Moon appears circular because the entire illuminated half of the Moon is visible. As the Moon orbits the Earth, the Moon "wanes" as the amount of the illuminated half of the Moon that is visible from Earth decreases. A gibbous moon is between a full moon and a half moon, or between a half moon and a full moon. When the Sun and the Moon are on the same side of Earth, the illuminated half of the Moon is facing away from Earth, and the Moon is invisible. This lunar phase is known as the "new moon." The time between each full moon is approximately 29.53 days.

Eclipses

Eclipses are the passing of one object into the shadow of another object. A lunar eclipse occurs when the Moon travels through the shadow of the Earth. A solar eclipse occurs when the Moon positions itself between the Sun and the Earth.

Planets

- Mercury: The closest planet to the Sun. Its surface has craters and rocks. The atmosphere is composed of hydrogen, helium, and sodium. Mercury was named after the Roman messenger god.
- Venus: Has a slow rotation compared to Earth's. Venus and Uranus rotate in opposite directions from the other planets. This opposite rotation is called retrograde rotation. The surface of Venus is not visible due to its extensive cloud cover. The atmosphere is composed mostly of carbon dioxide. Sulfuric acid droplets in the dense cloud cover give Venus a yellow appearance. Venus has a greater greenhouse effect than Earth. The dense clouds combined with the carbon dioxide gas trap heat. Venus was named after the Roman goddess of love.
- Earth: Considered a water planet, 70 percent of its surface is covered by water. Gravity holds the water in place. The different temperatures observed on Earth allow for the different states (solid, liquid, gas) of water to exist. The atmosphere is composed mainly of oxygen and nitrogen. Earth is the only planet known to support life.
- Mars: The surface of Mars contains numerous craters, active and extinct volcanoes, ridges, and valleys with extremely deep fractures. Iron oxide found in the dusty soil makes the surface seem rust-colored and the skies pink. The atmosphere is composed of carbon dioxide, nitrogen, argon, oxygen, and water vapor. Mars has polar regions with ice caps composed of water. Mars has two satellites. Mars was named after the Roman war god.

- Jupiter: The largest planet in the solar system. Jupiter has sixteen moons. The atmosphere is composed of hydrogen, helium, methane, and ammonia. There are white-colored bands of clouds indicating rising gas and dark-colored bands of clouds indicating descending gas on Jupiter's surface. The gas movement is caused by heat resulting from the energy of Jupiter's core. Jupiter has a great red spot that is thought to be a hurricane-type cloud. Jupiter has a strong magnetic field.
- Saturn: The second largest planet in the solar system. Saturn has rings of ice, rock, and dust particles circling it. Saturn's atmosphere is composed of hydrogen, helium, methane, and ammonia. Saturn has more than twenty satellites. Saturn was named after the Roman god of agriculture.
- Uranus: The second largest planet in the solar system; it has retrograde revolution. Uranus is a gaseous planet. It has ten dark rings and fifteen satellites. Its atmosphere is composed of hydrogen, helium, and methane. Uranus was named after the Greek god of the heavens.
- Neptune: Another gaseous planet with an atmosphere consisting of hydrogen, helium, and methane. Neptune has three rings and two satellites. Neptune was named after the Roman sea god because its atmosphere is the same color as the sea.
- Pluto: Once considered the smallest planet in the solar system, it is no longer considered a planet. Pluto's atmosphere probably contains methane, ammonia, and frozen water. Pluto has one satellite. Pluto revolves around the Sun every 250 years. Pluto was named after the Roman god of the underworld.

Comets, Asteroids, and Meteors

Comets are masses of frozen gases, cosmic dust, and small, rocky particles. They consist of a nucleus, a coma, and a tail.

Meteoroids are composed of particles of rock and metal of various sizes. When a meteoroid travels through the Earth's atmosphere, friction causes its surface to heat up and it begins to burn. The burning meteoroid falling through the Earth's atmosphere is called a meteor (also known as a shooting star).

Meteorites are meteors that strike the Earth's surface.

DOMAIN V
FINE ARTS, HEALTH, AND PHYSICAL EDUCATION

PERSONALIZED STUDY PLAN

VISUAL ARTS

Developing Students' Observation Skills

Visual art encompasses many areas. Students are expected to fine-tune their observation skills and be able to identify and recreate their experiences. For example, a group of students may go on a nature hike, and afterward discuss the repetition they see in the leaves on the trees or the bricks in the sidewalk, or the size and shapes of the buildings and how they relate. They may also use such experiences to describe lines, colors, shapes, forms, and textures.

Children begin to notice elements of perspective at an early age. The question of why buildings look smaller at a distance and bigger when they are closer is sure to spark the imagination of early childhood students. Students can then move to a higher level of learning with hands-on activities such as constructing three-dimensional buildings using paper and geometric shapes. Eventually, students should acquire higher-level thinking skills and begin to question artists and analyze many different aspects of visual art.

Exploring Different Mediums

Students should be able to select and use mediums and processes that actively communicate and express the intended meaning of their artworks and exhibits and prove competence in at least two mediums. For example, students should be able to select a process or medium for their intended work of art and describe the reasons for their selection.

Students should create and experience works of art that explore different types of subject matter, themes, and topics. Students need to understand the sensory elements and organizational principles of art and the expression of images.

Students should also be able to use the computer and electronic media to express their visual ideas and demonstrate a variety of different approaches to their selected medium. An excellent example is for students to produce works using mixed media or a work of art that uses the computer, the camera, the copy machine, or another type of electronic equipment.

Teachers can ask students of any age to compile a variety of their best works of art using different types of media. This is typically referred to as a portfolio. The portfolio should begin with an early sample of the student's work, a rough draft or a sketch. The portfolio shows the student's progress and growth in uses of various mediums and techniques. Progress can be tracked through use of a rubric or simply by observation.

Some of the areas that students should master and that the teacher can model include:

- Experimenting using a variety of mediums: drawing, painting, sculpture, ceramics, printmaking, and video
- Producing a collection of artwork (a portfolio) and using a variety of mediums, topics, themes, and subject matter
- Conveying meaning through artwork
- Creating and evaluating different works of art and types of mediums
- Reflecting on one's own and others' work

Critiquing Artwork

The elementary teacher's ability to think critically and solve problems is reflected in her or his teaching in many ways, including the way art is perceived and discussed in the classroom.

The capacity to critique a work of art is an asset for all teachers, especially in classrooms with integrated curricula, where art is taught in conjunction with other subjects, or in classrooms where there is no separate art program.

Critiquing artwork involves using both objective and subjective approaches. Gathering information is the first step. The next step is analyzing and synthesizing the information. The final step is making an evaluation.

Objective information useful to a thoughtful critique includes:

- The artist's name and title of work
- The medium and techniques employed in the work
- The year the work was completed
- Historical information about the work, as well as other aspects of historical relevance
- The period, style, or genre to which the work belongs
- An analysis of the elements of the work, such as color, line, intensity, sense of movement, light, use of space and shape, use of contrast

Subjective information that can contribute to an effective critique includes:

- The observer's emotional reaction to the piece
- Others' feelings and reactions to the work (spoken or observed)
- The subject matter (this may be objectively observed in some work)
- Strengths and weaknesses of the work
- Details that draw one's attention

- Elements that seem most important to the work
- The focal point of the piece
- Elements or aspects of the work that elicit excitement or pleasure

Some useful questions that can bring together objective and subjective information include:

- How does the title of the work inform the viewer's experience of it?
- What does the work say? What is the artist trying to communicate? How do the colors and lines and textures (and other elements) contribute to the message?
- Is the work original? If it is derivative of others' work, does it contribute something by adding to the genre or the subject?
- What do I like about this work overall?
- Where might this piece be effectively displayed? Why?
- Does this piece of work bring beauty to the world?
- Does it make a statement? If so, what kind of statement?
- Do the choice of media and the craftsmanship enhance the basic message or intent of the artist? Do they detract in any way?
- What would improve this piece, if anything? Why?

Teachers should introduce students to the wide range of opportunities to explore art, including exhibits, galleries, museums, libraries, and personal art collections. Opportunities for research include reproductions, art slides, films, print materials, and electronic media. Once students have learned how to effectively research and use these sources, they should be expected to move on to higher-level thinking skills. Students should begin to reflect on, interpret, evaluate, and explain how works of art and various styles of artwork explain social, psychological, cultural, and environmental aspects of life.

Students should be asked to review, respond to, and analyze various types of art.

Purposes of Art

Whether we express ourselves creatively from the theatrical stage, visually through fine art and dance, or musically, recognizing and appreciating the relationships among various art forms is essential to understanding ourselves and our diverse society.

By studying and experiencing works of fine art and literature and understanding their place in our cultural and intellectual history, we can develop an appreciation of the significance of the arts and humanities through history and across cultures.

Literature is the most common means of exposing young students to art, but video and other types of media provide rich art experiences as well.

Through art projects, field trips, and theatrical productions, students learn that all forms of art are a way for cultures to communicate with each other and the world at large. By understanding the concepts, techniques, and materials used in the visual arts, music, dance, and literature, students will begin to appreciate the concept of using art to express oneself. They might begin by writing a short story that gets transformed into a play with costumes, music, and movement to experience the relationships among various art forms.

The arts have played a significant role throughout history. In cultures all over the world, people have expressed feelings, told stories, imitated nature, and persuaded others through artistic expression. The arts bring meaning to ceremonies, rituals, celebrations, and recreation. By creating their own art and examining art made by others, children can learn to make sense of and communicate ideas.

Through the arts and humanities, students realize that, although people are different, they share common experiences and attitudes. They also learn the power of nonverbal communication.

Benefits of Education in the Arts

Teaching in and through the arts within the context of the total school curriculum, especially during the formative years of an elementary K-6 education, is key to maximizing the benefits of the arts in education.

For students, an education in the arts provides:

- The ability to be creative and inventive decision makers
- An enhanced sense of poise and self-esteem
- The confidence to undertake new tasks
- An increased ability to achieve across the curriculum
- A framework that encourages teamwork and fosters leadership skills
- Knowledge of the less-recognized experiences of aesthetic engagement and intuition
- Increased potential for life success
- An enriched quality of life

Guidelines and Strategies for the Classroom

Art-criticism strategies for the classroom include comparing/contrasting works of art; writings based on questions on activity cards; and narratives, poetry, cinquains, and other forms of writing.

Interpretation of works of art may extend to dramatic presentations through reader's theater (students write dialogue for the people in an artwork, then perform the parts with different voices), "living paintings" or tableaux, and sound symphonies (students act out the sounds that are suggested by the artwork). A variety of approaches will help students learn to interpret works of art from multiple perspectives.

Elements of Visual Art

Color: An attribute of an object that is visible. When light is emitted, transmitted, or reflected off an object, the retina in our eye perceives color. The primary colors are red, yellow, and blue. The secondary colors are orange (a combination of red and yellow), purple (a combination of red and blue), and green (a combination of yellow and blue).

Texture: The way something feels.

Shape: A shape is a two-dimensional, enclosed space. An example of a shape is a square.

Form: A form is a three-dimensional, enclosed space. An example of a form is a cube.

Line: A mark or point that travels an identifiable path. It has both length and direction. It can be straight, curvy, horizontal, vertical, jagged, or smooth. It can be thin or thick.

Value: The lightness or darkness of a color.

Principles of Visual Art

Sketch: An image-development strategy; a preliminary drawing

Abstract: An image that reduces a subject to its essential visual elements, such as lines, shapes, and colors

Background: Those areas of composition that are behind the primary, or dominant, subject matter or design areas

Emphasis: Making one or more elements in a work of art stand out in such a way as to appear more significant

Contrast: Juxtaposing one or more elements in opposition to show their differences

Pattern: Also called a motif, a pattern is the repetition of an element. The repeated element can be a shape, line, or color.

Rhythm: The regular repetition of a form or element

Balance: The arrangement of one or more elements in a work of art so that they appear symmetrical or asymmetrical in design and proportion

Proportion: The harmonious relationship of one part to another or of one part to the whole

Unity: The arrangement of one or more elements to create coherence and a feeling of completeness or wholeness

Art in Various Cultures and Periods in History

The greatest works in art, literature, music, theater, and dance all reflect universal themes. Universal themes reflect the human experience, regardless of time period, location, or social standing. Universal themes tend to fall into broad categories, such as man versus society, man versus himself, man versus God, man versus nature, and good versus evil, to name the most obvious.

The list below provides a brief description of art in some of the important cultures and periods throughout history.

Prehistoric period (ca. 1,000,000–ca. 8,000 BCE)

Major themes of this long period center around religious fertility rites and sympathetic magic. Much of the art includes imagery of pregnant animals and faceless, pregnant women.

Mesopotamia (ca. 8,000–400 BCE)

The prayer statues and cult deities of this period point to the theme of polytheism in religious worship.

Ancient Egypt (ca. 3,000–100 BCE)

The predominance of funerary art from ancient Egypt conveys the importance of the preparation for the afterlife and polytheistic worship. Another dominant theme is the divinity of the pharaohs. In architecture, the themes are monumentality and adherence to ritual.

Ancient Greece (800–100 BCE)

Dominant genres from this period are vase paintings, both black-figure and red-figure, and classical sculpture. The sculpture of ancient Greece is replete with human figures, either nude or draped. Most of the sculptures represent athletes and various gods and goddesses. The predominant theme is that of the ideal human. In architecture, scale is based on the ideal human proportions.

Rome (ca. 480 BCE–476 CE)

Major genres of Roman art include frescoes, classical sculpture, funerary art, state propaganda art, and relief work. The emphasis of the Roman arts is on the realistic depiction of human beings. Another major theme of this period is the glory of serving the Roman state. In architecture, the theme is rugged practicality mixed with Greek proportions and elements.

Middle Ages (300–1400 CE)

Significant genres during the Middle Ages include Byzantine mosaics, illuminated manuscripts, ivory reliefs, altarpieces, cathedral sculptures, and frescoes painted in various styles.

Although the Middle Ages covered a long time span, the major themes of this period remained relatively constant. Since the Roman Catholic Church was the primary patron of the arts, most work was religious in nature. The purpose of much of the art was to educate. Specific themes varied from the illustration of Bible stories, to interpretations of theological allegory, to lives of the saints, to the consequences of good and evil. Depictions of the Holy Family were popular. Themes found in secular art and literature centered on chivalric love and warfare. In architecture, the theme is glorification of God and education of the congregation in religious principles.

Renaissance (ca. 1400–1630 CE)

Important genres from the Renaissance include Florentine fresco painting (mostly religious), High Renaissance painting and sculpture, northern oil painting, Flemish miniature painting, and northern printmaking.

Renaissance themes include Christian religious depiction (see Middle Ages), but tend to reflect a renewed interest in all things classical. Specific themes include Greek and Roman mythological and philosophical figures and ancient battles and legends. Dominant themes reflect the philosophical beliefs of humanism, emphasizing individuality, human reason, and the psychological attributes of individuals. In architecture, scale is based on human proportions.

Baroque period (1630–1700 CE)

Important genres in the baroque era include Mannerism, Italian baroque painting and sculpture, Spanish baroque, Flemish baroque, and Dutch portraiture. Genre paintings in still life and landscape appear prominently in this period.

The predominant themes in the arts of the baroque period include the dramatic climaxes of well-known stories, legends, and battles, and the grand spectacle of mythology. Religious themes are common in the art of this period, but drama and insight are emphasized rather than the medieval "salvation factor." Baroque artists and authors incorporated various types of characters into their works, careful to include minute details. Portraiture focuses on the psychology of the subjects. Architecture is characterized by large-scale grandeur and splendor.

Eighteenth century (1700–1800 CE)

Predominant genres of the eighteenth century include rococo painting, portraiture, social satire, romantic painting, and neoclassical painting and sculpture.

Rococo themes of this century focus on religion, mythology, portraiture of aristocrats, pleasure and escapism, and, occasionally, satire. In architecture, artifice and gaiety prevailed, combined with an organic quality of form. Neoclassical themes centered on examples of virtue and heroism, usually in classical settings and historical stories. Architecture focuses on classical simplicity and utility of design.

Nineteenth century (1800–1900 CE)

Important genres of the nineteenth century include romantic painting, academic painting and sculpture, landscape and realistic painting, Impressionism, and many varieties of post-Impressionism.

Romantic themes include human freedom, equality, and civil rights, a love of nature, and a tendency toward the melancholic and mystic. The underlying theme is that the most important discoveries are made within the self, not in the exterior world. In architecture, the theme is fantasy and whimsy, known as the **picturesque style**. Realistic themes included social awareness and a focus on society victimizing individuals. The themes behind Impressionism are the constant flux of the universe and the immediacy of the moment. In architecture, the themes are strength, simplicity, and upward thrust as skyscrapers came on the scene.

Twentieth century (1900–2000 CE)

Major genres of the twentieth century include symbolism, art nouveau, fauvism, expressionism, cubism (both analytical and synthetic), futurism, nonobjective art, abstract art, surrealism, social realism, constructivism in sculpture, pop art, op art, and conceptual art.

Diverse artistic themes of the century reflect a parting with traditional religious values and a painful awareness of man's inhumanity to man. Themes also illustrate a growing reliance on science, while simultaneously expressing disillusionment with man's failure to adequately control science. A constant theme is the quest for originality and self-expression, while seeking to express the universal in human experience. In architecture, "form follows function."

Art History

Art history is a relatively new field in academia. The study of art history relies on the faithful reproduction of artworks as a springboard for discussion and study. The development of new photography techniques after World War II made this possible; however, the appreciation and study of the visual arts has intrigued humanity for hundreds of years. Art history features the study of biographies of individual artists. In the eighteenth century, scholars began arguing that the real emphasis in the study of art should be placed on the views of the learned beholder and not on the unique viewpoint of the charismatic artist.

Art history has enhanced the study of political history by showing how art interacts with power structures in society.

Art predates history: sculptures, cave paintings, and rock paintings have been found that are roughly 40,000 years old. However, the precise meaning of such art is often disputed because we know so little about the cultures that produced it.

Eastern vs. Western Art

There is an obvious difference in aesthetic principles between works created in Eastern and Western cultures. Eastern works of art are more often based on spiritual concerns, while much Western art is secular in nature. Eastern artists portray the human figure with symbolic meaning and little regard for muscle structure, resulting in a mystical view of the human experience. Western artists use the "principle of ponderation," which requires knowledge of human anatomy.

Eastern artists prefer a diagonal projection of eye movement into the picture plane, and often leave large areas of the surface untouched by detail. The result is the illusion of vast space, an infinite view that coincides with the spiritual philosophies of the East. Western artists rely on several techniques, such as overlapping planes, variation of object size, object position on the picture plane, linear and aerial perspective, color change, and various points of perspective to convey the illusion of depth.

MUSIC

Students can explore creating moods with music and analyzing stories and creating musical compositions that reflect or enhance them. Their daily routines can include exploration and interpretation of musical sound. Immersing them in musical conversations as they sing, speak rhythmically, and walk in step stimulates their awareness of the beauty and structure of musical sound.

Involvement in music is thought to teach basic skills such as concentration, counting, and listening and to promote the understanding of language.

As students acquire the skills and knowledge that music brings to their lives, they go through stages similar to the stages of language development. Singing, chanting, and moving; exposing them to many different sources of sound in play, including a variety of styles of music; and reinforcing rhythm through patting, tapping, and moving will enhance students' awareness of musical sound.

Any single strike or series of beats on a percussion instrument creates a rhythmic pattern, sometimes called a beat. Percussion instruments are sometimes referred to as **nonpitched**, or **untuned**, because the sound of the percussion instrument has no pitch that can be heard by the ear.

Music Notation

When music is written down, the composer includes instructions about what he or she wants listeners to hear and how the musician(s) should perform the music. This is referred to as **music notation**. Standard present-day music notation is based on a five-line staff called a **clef**. The upper clef is called the **treble clef**; the lower clef is called the **bass clef**. Pitch is shown by placing notes on the staff. These notes are modified by additional symbols called sharps, flats, and naturals. The duration of a note (the length of time it is held) is shown by different note shapes and additional symbols such as ties, dotted notes, and rests. In addition to the notations developed for human performers, there are also computer-generated representations of music designed to either be turned into conventional notation or be read directly by the computer.

MELODIC MUSIC: music that is characterized by a single, strong melody line

MELODIC MUSIC is music that is characterized by a single, strong melody line. The melody line, or tune, is easy to remember and follow. Melodic music can be performed by a singer, an orchestra, a single instrument, or any combination of the three. Opera is considered to be a classical form; the lighter operetta is considered borderline; and the musical is placed in the popular category.

HARMONIC NOTATION is commonly referred to as the key in which music is written. Keys can be major or minor, depending on the combination of whole and half steps used in the scale, and are indicated by sharp signs and flat signs after the clef signs in the signature. There are twelve pitches in the musical scale, each of which is a degree of the scale. An interval is the relationship between two separate musical pitches. Harmony is the result of more than one note being played simultaneously (e.g., a chord) and is created by the combination of notes making intervals.

HARMONIC NOTATION: the key in which music is written

RHYTHMIC NOTATION refers to the exact rhythm in which the indicated notes or chords are played or sung. The rhythm key is written above the staff. Rhythms are usually arranged by using a time signature, signifying a meter. The top number of the time signature reflects the number of beats in each measure, whereas the bottom number reflects which type of note uses a single beat (e.g., 1 on the bottom reflects a whole note, 2 on the bottom reflects a half note, 4 reflects a quarter note, etc.). The speed of the underlying beat is the tempo (e.g., allegro, allegretto, presto, moderato, lento, largo).

RHYTHMIC NOTATION: the exact rhythm in which the indicated notes or chords are played or sung

Musical Terms

- Accent: Stress of one tone over others, making it stand out; often it is the first beat of a measure
- Accompaniment: Music that goes along with a more important part; often harmony or rhythmic patterns accompanying a melody
- Adagio: Slow, leisurely
- Allegro: Lively, brisk, rapid
- Cadence: The close of a phrase or section of music
- Chord: Three or more tones combined and sounded simultaneously
- Crescendo: Gradually growing louder
- Dissonance: A simultaneous sounding of tones that produces a feeling of tension or unrest
- Harmony: The sound resulting from the simultaneous sounding of two or more tones consonant with each other
- Interval: The distance between two tones
- Melody: An arrangement of single tones in a meaningful sequence
- Phrase: A small section of a composition constituting a musical thought

- Rhythm: The regular occurrence of accented beats that shape the character of music or dance
- Scale: A graduated series of tones arranged in a specified order
- Staccato: Separate; sounded in a short, detached manner
- Syncopation: The rhythmic result produced when a regularly accented beat is displaced onto an unaccented beat
- Tempo: The speed at which a musical composition is performed
- Theme: A short musical passage that states an idea; it often provides the basis for variations, development, etc.
- Timbre: The quality of a musical tone that distinguishes voices and instruments
- Tone: A musical sound or the quality of a musical sound

Musical Instruments

Musical instruments can be divided into four basic categories:

- Stringed instruments: Stringed instruments make their sounds through strings. The sound of the instrument depends on the thickness and length of the strings. The more slowly a string vibrates, the lower the resulting pitch. The way the strings are manipulated varies among string instruments. With some string instruments, the strings are plucked (e.g., guitar) while with others the player uses a bow to make the strings vibrate (e.g., violin). Other common string instruments include the viola, double bass, and cello.
- Percussion instruments: To play a percussion instrument, the musician hits or shakes it. The sound is created from vibrations as a result of shaking or striking the instrument. Many materials, such as metal or wood, are used to create percussion instruments, and different thicknesses or sizes of the material affect the sound. Thicker, heavier materials like drum membranes make deeper sounds, while thinner materials make higher-pitched sounds. Common percussion instruments include the cymbals, tambourine, bells, xylophone, and wood block.
- Wind instruments: The sound of wind instruments is caused by wind vibrating in a pipe or tube. Air blows into one end of the instrument, and, in many wind instruments, it passes over a reed, which causes the air to vibrate. The pitch depends on the air's frequency as it passes through the tube, and the frequency depends on the tube's length or size. Larger tubes create deeper sounds. The pitch is also controlled by holes or valves. As the musician's

fingers cover the holes or press the valves, the pitch changes. Common wind instruments include the pipe organ, oboe, clarinet, and saxophone.

- Brass instruments: Brass instruments are similar to wind instruments because music from brass instruments also results from air passing through an air chamber. Brass instruments, however, are made from metal or brass. Pitch on a brass instrument is controlled by the size or length of the air chamber. Many brass instruments are twisted or coiled, which lengthens the air chamber without making the instrument unmanageably long. As with wind instruments, larger air chambers create deeper sounds, and valves on the instrument control the pitch. In addition, in some brass instruments, the position of the musician's mouth on the mouthpiece controls the pitch. Common brass instruments include the French horn, trumpet, trombone, and tuba.

Arranging Music

Music is written for many different voices, instruments, uses, and settings. Being able to arrange music for specific purposes—for example, for students in a classroom setting or for a group of students performing in a chorale or band—is a valuable asset for all teachers of music, and is often a necessity when working with older or more accomplished students.

Such work entails familiarity with music notation, basic music theory, the range of musical styles, the key signatures of various instruments, transposition, harmony, and the different abilities of students, among other things. It is also extremely helpful to have access to and the ability to use computer software that scores music. This reduces the amount of time and effort involved in arranging music.

At the elementary level, the arrangement of music is often limited to changing the key to make a song easier for students to sing, adding harmonies to simple or familiar melodies, or incorporating instruments that have different key signatures.

Arranging music for use by elementary students should be guided by three factors:

- The content of the instructional activity
- The ability of the student(s)
- The intended outcome

While learning is always the intended outcome to some degree, sometimes there is an additional goal, such as a performance. The audience might be classmates, the whole school, or parents/guardians and the community. Different outcomes may affect how the music is arranged, and should be considered before the musical pieces are selected and arranged.

Critiquing Musical Performances

Teaching basic music terminology is a prerequisite for any critiquing process. Without the necessary language, students will not be able to evaluate a piece of music. Similarly, students must be given the opportunity to develop listening skills so they are able to hear different musical elements, themes, instruments, and tones. They will also benefit from an overview of the sounds of different instruments and a listing of musical styles.

The key steps in critiquing music are: listen, analyze, describe, and evaluate.

While establishing the fundamental skills noted above, teachers can introduce simple rubrics (often called critique sheets) for critiquing a song. A rubric might include elements like tempo changes, use of specific instruments, rhythms, and loudness and softness, as well as the students' personal responses to the music. Students can also develop their own rubrics for evaluating music, including their own vocal or instrumental performances or their own compositions.

Working in pairs or small groups can help students develop the verbal language of critiques and enhance both listening and performance skills. Their peers may point out nuances they have missed or bring a different perspective to a particular piece of music. In a small-group setting, students can discuss likes and dislikes and come to a greater understanding of their own preferences.

As students gain experience and knowledge, they develop more sophisticated critiquing skills. These may involve listening for differences in technique, varied interpretations of the same piece, expressiveness, and the details specific to various musical styles.

Attending live performances by both amateur and professional musicians can be very helpful in enhancing the critiquing skills of all students; it is especially important for older students. There are also a number of online resources for helping students learn to critique music.

When critiquing students' performances, teachers need to be nonjudgmental and respectful when giving feedback. Providing students with the rubric that will be used to assess their performance ahead of time can decrease the sense of judgment that often accompanies critiques. The rubric should describe observable skills with clear parameters, and should be written using standard music terminology. Familiarity with the rubric as well as with the general process of critiquing may decrease students' anxiety about performance evaluations.

Integrating Music with Other Subjects

Music lends itself to integration with many subjects in elementary school. Most obviously, reading music involves *reading*. Learning to read music notation generally follows the development of basic literacy skills. Children's first exposure to reading music usually involves reading the words of a song, not the actual musical notes. Therefore, in many cases, basic reading skills are enhanced as music is taught. All of the elements of reading are present when reading music with words, including comprehension, prosody, fluency, and vocabulary development.

In other subject areas, music can be the focus (e.g., discovering the musical styles of a particular culture in a social studies class) or a tool used to facilitate the learning of subject matter (e.g., a song that teaches science concepts). Creative teachers can develop impromptu songs to help students learn lists or details. Engaging students in music-related activities can increase their motivation to study the history and geography of a region more effectively than a "straight" social studies approach.

The same can be said for studying the mathematics of music. By using music as a way "in," students may discover they enjoy math. Music offers many opportunities for counting as well as exploring more complex math concepts. Furthermore, students who do well in music tend to do well in math. Some people believe that music and math strengthen the same neural pathways between the two hemispheres in the brain.

There are a number of writing activities that can be incorporated with music. Concert or album reviews, interviews with musicians, articles about musical styles or upcoming music-related events, and song lyrics are just a few of the writing opportunities that can be included with music education.

Making use of small chunks of time can also benefit the music curriculum. For example, practicing a recently learned song while waiting in line or during a bus ride on a field trip can augment regular music classes. Similarly, bringing rhythm instruments to the gym during an indoor recess period or sharing one's own skill at playing guitar or piano, for example, can facilitate music education without straining resources. These opportunities also help students see music as an integral part of life rather than a separate subject limited to the classroom or the concert hall.

In an integrated curriculum, whether music is the focus or a tool really doesn't matter. As educators and researchers have learned, schools that incorporate the arts into the broader curriculum have better-performing students and more positive school environments. These schools are more effective at narrowing the achievement gap and enhancing students' social development.

As educators and researchers have learned, schools that incorporate the arts into the broader curriculum have better-performing students and more positive school environments.

Teaching Students to Play or Sing with Expression

While some students may display a special talent for expressiveness, it is important for teachers to teach all students to play or sing with expression. As with prosody and fluency in reading, some of the skill in this area emerges naturally once students have mastered basic skills and techniques. It is a developmental process. Learning to read music notation, stringing notes together in phrases, knowing how to use one's voice or an instrument to make different sounds—all of these are essential to expressiveness.

Teachers can engage students in particular activities that help students develop expressiveness. Further, teachers can encourage musical "intelligence" and creativity; some in the field of music believe that these abilities underlie the development of expressiveness.

Activities to foster expression in music

Some activities that teachers can use with students to foster expression in music include:

- Introduce the concept of "expression" as a distinct element early in the music curriculum
- Invite students to experiment with sounds (via voice and/or instruments) and to notice the many ways they can produce sound
- Provide opportunities for students to compare and contrast recordings of the same piece of music by different artists, ensembles, or orchestras
- Have students listen to each other play or sing music and notice the differences and similarities
- Combine music with visual arts: Have students draw pictures of what they feel when they listen to different pieces of music
- Encourage students to experiment with playing or singing different variations of the same song
- Help students articulate their understanding of a piece of music, its history, and the meaning and feelings associated with the piece
- With longer pieces of music, compare and contrast each section with the other sections

Teaching Examples that Incorporate TEKS

The development of music skills not only provides a well-rounded education for students, but it also can be an entertaining and engaging way for students to make strides in a variety of subjects. The following are teaching examples for the classroom that incorporate the TEKS for children in kindergarten through grade 4.

Identify higher, lower, faster, slower music

The teacher brings various musical recordings into the classroom—an example of fast music, such as "The Flight of the Bumblebee" by Nikolai Rimsky-Korsakov, and an example of slow music, like Brahms's "Lullaby"—and plays one after the other. The teacher directs students to move around the room in a way that reflects the music they hear. After playing each excerpt, the teacher asks the students to explain why they moved the way they did and introduces the concept of slow and fast music. The teacher plays several other examples, allowing the students to move with the music quickly and slowly. Then, when students return to their seats, they are asked to close their eyes. The teacher plays the same examples in a different order and asks students to raise their hands when they hear fast music or raise their hands when they hear slow music. The same format can be followed for high-pitch and low-pitch music.

Sing songs from diverse cultures

Singing songs from diverse cultures develops musical skills such as pitch matching and memory of melodic patterns. For older students, it can also incorporate actual identification and reading of musical notes. In addition, students learn about societies from around the world.

Identify musical instruments visually and aurally

Introducing children to musical instruments can be an exercise in creativity and a reinforcement of math concepts. The teacher can start with students in a circle and introduce a percussion instrument such as a tambourine. The teacher demonstrates different ways to play the tambourine (shaking, flicking, banging like a drum, scraping). Then the instrument is passed from student to student, as each one experiments on his or her own. The teacher lets one student play the instrument and then asks the next student to imitate the first student. After three or four different percussion instruments are introduced, the teacher chooses one student to be the conductor and gives instruments to the remaining students. The teacher allows the conductor to choose a card. The cards are numbered from 1 to 10. If the number chosen is 5, then the student gets to conduct five "beats." The conductor gestures to the students in a pulse or beat five times, and the musicians must play on each beat. This can evolve into the conductor choosing two cards and conducting 2 + 2 beats, gesturing to half the class for two beats and the other half of the class for the remaining two beats. As a followup, the teacher can ask, "How many total beats did you conduct?"

The conductor game also works with concepts of loud and soft. The teacher asks the conductor to gesture in a way that would encourage students to play loudly and then softly. Teachers may be surprised by the creative ways students direct or conduct their fellow musicians and by the ways the musician students play their instruments. After loud and soft conducting, the teacher can introduce the music terms *forte* (meaning *loud*) and *piano* (meaning *soft*).

In this one short lesson, the teacher has given the students new vocabulary words by introducing the names of instruments, reinforced the math concept of addition, and also introduced basic music terminology such as *conductor*, *beat*, *forte*, and *piano*.

Appropriate behavior during a live performance

- No talking after the lights go down/when the performance begins
- Clap at the end of the performance to show appreciation
- No cell phones
- Sit quietly until the performance ends
- Actors and musicians perform with a loud voice so they can be heard from the back row of an auditorium
- Actors and musicians bow at the end of a performance

Careers in Music

Music-based career options are quite varied. The more obvious careers involve music directly, such as performing, composing, teaching, and conducting. Many other music-related careers also exist, such as working as an agent for musicians, making or repairing instruments, and being a disc jockey.

Teachers can inspire students to pursue a career in a music-related field simply by providing information about the kinds of jobs people do that involve music.

Students who love music may seek out such information and inadvertently discover a satisfying occupation—just because a teacher mentioned it in elementary school.

Music-related career choices:

- Soloist
- Band or orchestra member
- Accompanist
- Background vocalist
- Manager or booking agent
- Composer
- Administrator of a music organization
- Music therapist
- Librettist
- Sound technician or engineer
- Musical librarian or archivist
- Music arranger, orchestrator, or transcriber
- Instrument maker or repairer
- Conductor
- Music teacher (in a school, college, or on an individual basis)
- Choir director
- MIDI engineer or technician
- Music critic
- Disc jockey
- Film scorer
- Music historian
- Recording engineer
- Lyricist
- Music promoter or producer
- Entertainment attorney
- Studio director
- Tour manager

Genres of Music

CLASSICAL MUSIC is a type of music based on European secular and religious music from about the ninth century to the present. The term itself is generally understood to refer to the "golden age" of composers from Johann Sebastian Bach (1685-1750) to Ludwig van Beethoven (1770-1827). Classical music often refers to instrumental music in general, although opera is also considered classical.

CLASSICAL MUSIC: a type of music based on European secular and religious music from about the ninth century to the present

A **BALLAD** is a song that contains a story. A ballad usually has simple repeating rhymes and often contains a refrain (or repeating sections) that are played or sung at regular intervals throughout.

BALLAD: a song that contains a story

FOLK MUSIC is music that has endured and been passed down by oral tradition and that emerges spontaneously from ordinary people. A folk song is usually seen as an expression of a way of life now past or about to disappear.

FOLK MUSIC: music that has endured and been passed down by oral tradition and that emerges spontaneously from ordinary people

Call-and-response songs are a form of interaction between a singer and a listener, in which the listener sings a response to the singer. In West African cultures, call-and-response songs were used in religious rituals and gatherings. In certain Native American tribes, call-and-response songs preserve and protect the tribe's cultural heritage and can be seen and heard at modern-day "pow-wows."

The work song is typically a song sung *a cappella* by people working on a physical and often repetitive task. Frequently, the verses of work songs are improvised and sung differently each time.

Jazz is a form of music that grew out of a combination of folk music, ragtime, and big band music. It has been called the first native art form to develop in the United States.

Blues is a vocal and instrumental music form that came from West African spirituals, work songs, and chants. This musical form has been a major influence on later American popular music, finding expression in jazz, rock and roll, and country music.

Rock and roll, in its broadest sense, refers to almost all pop music recorded since the early 1950s. Its main features include an emphasis on rhythm and the use of percussion and amplified instruments like the bass and guitar.

Early American Music

Throughout history, American society has used music to pass on traditions, share stories, celebrate, and grieve. Music reflects the heritage of the United States as a whole, and of Texas in particular.

Music is a terrific historian. Students can trace the popular music of each decade to observe how it comments on events in American history.

Long before European settlers made it to the United States, Native Americans used song and dance to worship, celebrate the harvest, ward off disease, and pass down stories from one generation to the next. Vocal singing dominated the music of Native Americans, who impressed early explorers with their ability to synchronize large groups of singers into one voice.

Beginning in the 1700s and throughout the Civil War, slaves contributed to our musical heritage with the singing of spirituals. These spirituals sprang from the tradition of retelling Old Testament stories, but they also highlighted the profound melancholy and sorrow of the life of the slaves. They are the roots of present-day blues and jazz in the United States.

In the 1800s, American folk music took on a distinct sound and again described the history of a new country. Individuals like Stephen C. Foster were instrumental in providing the country with tunes that reflected everyday American life. Some of these songs include "Oh! Susanna," "Camptown Races," "Old Folks at Home," "My Old Kentucky Home," "Jeanie with the Light Brown Hair," and "Beautiful Dreamer."

Nineteenth-Century Music

Music created around the time of the Civil War reflected a time of conflict and uncertainty in the United States. "Amazing Grace," "The Battle Hymn of the Republic," "My Darling Clementine," "Old Black Joe," and "Go Tell it on the Mountain" described events in a torn country and feelings of loss, fear, hope, patriotism, and religious fervor. This time period also saw the growth of **American gospel music**, which was the first American hymnody. Gospel songs dealt with redemption from sin and were easy and fun to sing in large groups.

Aaron Copeland, one of the best-known American composers of the twentieth century, took many of the cowboy songs popular in the western United States and incorporated them into his classical compositions, which have a uniquely American sound.

Toward the end of the nineteenth century, another American music form was born: **ragtime**. This new music was the direct result of the combining of diverse cultures—namely, European and African—in the southern United States. Ragtime evolved as an informal experiment in combining music traditions from both cultures. It features syncopated rhythms and the piano.

Around the turn of the century in Texas, another clash of cultures produced the Texas-Mexican music called **conjunto**. Working-class musicians from German and Mexican backgrounds combined their talents to produce this folk music, which uses the accordion as its main instrument.

Jazz and Rock 'n' Roll

Gospel and ragtime laid the groundwork for American jazz. It broke down barriers between various groups because the exploration and experimentation involved in the development of jazz pulled from multiple cultural experiences within the United States. Louis Armstrong, Billie Holiday, Duke Ellington, Benny Goodman, and Charlie Parker represent just a few stellar examples of American artists from the golden age of jazz.

Jazz music testifies to the continuous flow of different cultures into a single, uniquely American musical style.

One of America's most popular forms of music today–rock 'n' roll–grew out of the roots of jazz and blues in the 1940s. Once icons like Little Richard, Elvis Presley, and Buddy Holly moved it into the mainstream, it caught fire throughout the country and freedom of expression in music took on new dimensions. Rock 'n' roll lyrics have covered everything from personal relationships to war protests to the freedom of dancing without inhibition.

HEALTH

Wellness

Wellness has two major components:

- Understanding the basic human body functions and how to care for and maintain personal fitness
- Developing an awareness and knowledge of how certain everyday factors, stresses, and personal decisions can affect one's health

Teaching fitness needs to go along with skill and activity instruction. Cross-discipline teaching and teaching thematically with other subject matter in classrooms is an ideal method to teach health to adolescents.

Lifelong fitness and the benefits of a healthy lifestyle need to be part of every physical education teacher's curriculum.

Positive health behaviors can help decrease the risk of illness and disease. Good nutrition and regular exercise can help prevent everyday illnesses such as colds and flu as well as chronic diseases such as heart disease and cancer. Exercise and a healthy diet help maintain a healthy body composition; reduce cholesterol levels; strengthen the heart, lungs, and musculoskeletal system; and strengthen the body's immune system.

Strategies for Positive Behavior Change

Strategies for positive behavior change in students will relate the teaching of new behaviors to the students' perceptions and frames of reference, and will focus on a series of small, incremental changes. Instructors should link new behaviors to existing behaviors, the goal being to gradually modify behavioral patterns.

Instructors should actively involve students in the process of change. The behavioral change should be the student's own goal, not the teacher's goal for the student. In this way, the process of change becomes intrinsically motivated, making it far more likely the student will seriously commit to the process. The instructor should reinforce positive behavior, but not excessively; behavioral change should, for the most part, be intrinsically motivated.

Supporting positive change

Good resources for research include the Internet, local libraries, and fitness and health-care professionals in the community.

Health and fitness education should include an introduction to research skills so students have access to appropriate and relevant information when they need to make decisions about their health.

Positive health choices and behavior also require a layer of economic support, because healthy lifestyle choices may be more expensive than less-healthy alternatives. It is also important for the student's environment to be conducive to positive choices and behaviors regarding health. For example, the availability of resources (educational and practical) and facilities (medical and fitness) in proximity to the individual can have a positive impact on the decision-making process.

Assessing Behavioral-Health Risk Factors

There are various resources available to assess the behavioral-health risk factors of a community. The Centers for Disease Control and Prevention (CDC) annually publishes the Youth Risk Behavior Survey (YRBS). This survey describes national and state-level adolescent health risks. This information is available directly from the CDC. State education agencies compile and maintain statistics on youth health risks. Individual schools or school districts provide data regarding the types of problems seen in the school health room. Individual schools or school districts can also supply information regarding the number of referrals for pregnancy and substance abuse and data on absenteeism, dropouts, and disciplinary actions.

Another source of information is social service agencies, which have data on poverty, unemployment, and child abuse.

Stages of Human Growth and Development

Physical development

Small children (ages 3-5) have a propensity for engaging in periods of intense physical activity, punctuated by a need for a lot of rest. Children at this stage lack fine-motor skills and cannot focus on small objects for very long. Their bones are still developing. At this age, girls tend to be better coordinated and boys tend to be stronger.

The lag in fine-motor skills continues during the early-elementary-school years (ages 6-8).

Preadolescent children (ages 9-11) become stronger, leaner, and taller. Their motor skills improve, and they are able to sit still and focus for longer periods of time. Growth during this period is constant. This is also the time when gender-specific physical predispositions will begin to manifest. Preadolescents are at risk of obesity without proper nutrition and adequate activity.

Young adolescents (ages 12-14) experience dramatic physical growth (girls earlier than boys), and are highly preoccupied with their physical appearance.

As children proceed to the later stages of adolescence (ages 15-17), girls will reach their full height, while boys will continue to grow. The increase in hormone levels may cause acne. At this age, children may begin to initiate sexual activity. There is a risk of teen pregnancy and sexually transmitted diseases.

Cognitive development

Language development is the most important aspect of cognitive development in small children (ages 3-5). Allowing successes, rewarding mature behavior, and allowing the child to explore can improve confidence and self-esteem at this age.

Language development is the most important aspect of cognitive development in small children (ages 3-5).

Early-elementary-school children (ages 6-8) are eager to learn and love to talk. Children at this age have a very literal understanding of rules and verbal instructions and must develop strong listening skills.

Preadolescent children (ages 9-11) display increased logical thought, but their knowledge or beliefs may be unusual or surprising. Differences in cognitive styles develop at this age (e.g., field-dependent or field-independent preferences).

In early adolescence (ages 12-14), boys tend to score higher on mechanical/spatial reasoning, and girls on spelling, language, and clerical tasks. Boys are better with mental imagery, and girls have better access to and retrieval of information from memory. Self-efficacy (the ability to self-evaluate) becomes very important at this stage.

In later adolescence (ages 15-17), children are capable of formal thought but don't always apply it. Conflicts between teens' and parents' opinions and worldviews arise. Children at this age may become interested in advanced political thinking.

Social development

Small children (ages 3-5) are socially flexible. Different children will prefer solitary play, parallel play, or cooperative play. Frequent minor quarrels will occur between children, and boys will tend to be more aggressive (children at these ages are already aware of gender roles).

Early-elementary-school children (ages 6-8) are increasingly selective of friends (usually of the same sex). Children at this age enjoy playing games but are excessively preoccupied by the rules. Verbal aggression becomes more common than physical aggression, and adults should encourage children of this age to solve their own conflicts.

Preadolescent children (ages 9-11) place great importance on the (perceived) opinions of their peers and of their social stature, and will go to great lengths to "fit in." Friendships at this age are very selective, and usually of the same sex.

Young adolescents (ages 12-14) develop greater understanding of the emotions of others, which results in increased emotional sensitivity and affects peer relationships. Children at this age develop an increased need to perform.

In the later stages of adolescence (ages 15-17), peers are still the primary influence on day-to-day decisions, but parents have increasing influence on long-term goals. Girls' friendships tend to be close and intimate whereas boys' friendships are based on competition and similar interests. Many children at this age work part-time, and educators should be alert for signs of potential school dropouts.

Emotional development

Small children (ages 3-5) express emotions freely and have a limited ability to understand how emotions influence behavior. Jealousy at this age is common.

Early-elementary-school children (ages 6-8) have easily bruised feelings and are just beginning to recognize the feelings of others. Children at this age want to please teachers and other adults.

Preadolescent children (ages 9-11) develop a global and stable self-image (self-concept and self-esteem). Comparisons to their peers and the opinions of their peers are important. An unstable home environment at this age contributes to an increased risk of delinquency.

Young adolescence (ages 12-14) can be a stormy and stressful time for children, but, in reality, this is only the case for roughly 20 percent of teens. Boys may have trouble controlling their anger and may display impulsive behavior. Girls may suffer from depression.

Young adolescents are very egocentric and concerned with their appearance, and may feel strongly that "adults don't understand."

In later stages of adolescence (ages 15-17), educators should be alert for signs of surfacing mental health problems (e.g., eating disorders, substance abuse, schizophrenia, depression, and suicide).

Malfunctions of the Body Systems

Respiratory and excretory systems

Emphysema is a chronic obstructive pulmonary disease (COPD), which makes breathing difficult. Partial obstruction of the bronchial tubes limits airflow. The primary cause of emphysema is smoking. There is no cure for emphysema, but there are treatments available. The best prevention against emphysema is to refrain from smoking.

Nephritis usually occurs in children. An antigen-antibody complex that causes inflammation and cell proliferation produces nephritis. Nephritis damages normal kidney tissue and, if left untreated, can lead to kidney failure and death.

Circulatory system

Cardiovascular diseases are the leading cause of death in the United States. Cardiac disease usually results in either a heart attack or a stroke. A heart attack occurs when cardiac muscle tissue dies, usually from coronary artery blockage. A stroke occurs when nervous tissue in the brain dies due to the blockage of arteries in the head.

Atherosclerosis causes many heart attacks and strokes. Plaques form on the inner walls of arteries, narrowing the area in which blood can flow. Atherosclerosis occurs when the arteries harden from the plaque accumulation. A healthy diet low in saturated fats and cholesterol and regular exercise can prevent atherosclerosis. High blood pressure (hypertension) also promotes atherosclerosis. Diet, medication, and exercise can reduce high blood pressure and prevent atherosclerosis.

Immune system

The immune system attacks both microbes and cells that are foreign to the host. This is the problem with skin grafts, organ transplantations, and blood transfusions. Antibodies to foreign blood and tissue types already exist in the body. Antibodies will destroy the new blood cells in transfused blood that is not compatible with the host. There is a similar reaction with tissue and organ transplants.

The immune system attacks both microbes and cells that are foreign to the host.

Autoimmune disease occurs when the body's immune system destroys its own cells. **Lupus**, **Grave's disease**, and **rheumatoid arthritis** are examples of autoimmune diseases. There is no way to prevent autoimmune diseases. Immunodeficiency is a deficiency in either the humoral or cell-mediated immune defenses. **Human immunodeficiency virus (HIV)** is an example of an immunodeficiency disease.

Digestive system

Gastric ulcers are lesions in the stomach lining. Bacteria are the main cause of ulcers, but pepsin and acid can exacerbate the problem if the ulcers do not heal quickly enough.

The blocked appendix can cause bacterial infections and inflammation leading to appendicitis.

Appendicitis is the inflammation of the appendix. The appendix has no known function; however, it is open to the intestine and hardened stool or swollen tissue can block it. The blocked appendix can cause bacterial infections and inflammation leading to appendicitis. The swelling cuts off the blood supply, killing the organ tissue. If left untreated, this leads to rupture of the appendix, allowing the stool and the infection to spill out into the abdomen. This condition is life-threatening and requires immediate surgery. Symptoms of appendicitis include lower abdominal pain, nausea, loss of appetite, and fever.

Nervous and endocrine systems

Diabetes is the best-known endocrine disorder. A deficiency of insulin resulting in high blood glucose is the primary cause of diabetes. Type I diabetes is an autoimmune disorder. The immune system attacks the cells of the pancreas, ending the ability to produce insulin. Treatment for type I diabetes consists of daily insulin injections. Type II diabetes usually occurs with age and/or obesity.

Hyperthyroidism is another disorder of the endocrine system. Excessive secretion of thyroid hormones is the cause. Symptoms are weight loss, high blood pressure, and high body temperature. The opposite condition, **hypothyroidism**, causes weight gain, lethargy, and intolerance to cold.

There are many nervous system disorders. The degeneration of the basal ganglia in the brain causes **Parkinson's disease**. This degeneration causes a decrease in the motor impulses sent to the muscles. Symptoms include tremors, slow movement, and muscle rigidity. Progression of Parkinson's disease occurs in five stages: early, mild, moderate, advanced, and severe. In the severe stage, the person is confined to a bed or chair. There is no cure for Parkinson's disease. Private research with stem cells is currently underway to find a cure.

Types of Disease

Pathogens that enter the body through direct or indirect contact cause communicable, or infectious, diseases. A **PATHOGEN** is a disease-causing organism. Common communicable diseases include influenza, the common cold, chickenpox, pneumonia, measles, mumps, and mononucleosis. To minimize the circulation of pathogens that cause these illnesses, people can follow simple precautions. Individuals who are ill with these diseases should stay away from others during the contagious period of the infection. All people should avoid sharing items such as towels, toothbrushes, and silverware. At home, thorough clothes washing, dishwashing, and frequent hand washing can decrease pathogen transmission. Keeping immunizations up to date is also important in reducing the spread of communicable diseases.

PATHOGEN: a disease-causing organism

Sexual activity is the source of transmission for other communicable diseases. The commonly used terms for these diseases are sexually transmitted diseases (STDs) or sexually transmitted infections (STIs). Common STDs include chlamydia, gonorrhea, syphilis, genital herpes, genital warts, bacterial vaginosis, human papillomavirus (HPV), pediculosis pubis (pubic lice), hepatitis B, and HIV. Certain STDs can result in infertility. HPV can result in a deadly form of cervical cancer. HIV may result in Acquired Immunodeficiency Syndrome (AIDS), which can be fatal. Some of these diseases, such as genital herpes, are incurable.

A **CHRONIC DISEASE** is a disease that is long-lasting. A chronic disease continues for more than three months. Examples of chronic conditions include diseases such as heart disease, cancer, and diabetes. These diseases are currently the leading causes of death and disability in America. Many forms of these widespread and expensive diseases are preventable. Choosing nutritious foods, participating in physical activity, and avoiding tobacco use can prevent or control many of these illnesses.

CHRONIC DISEASE: a disease that is long-lasting. A chronic disease continues for more than three months

A **DEGENERATIVE DISEASE** is a condition in which diseased tissues or organs steadily deteriorate. The deterioration may be due to ordinary wear and tear or to lifestyle choices such as lack of exercise or poor nutrition. In addition, many degenerative diseases are of questionable origin, and may be linked to heredity and environmental factors. Some examples of degenerative diseases include osteoporosis, Alzheimer's disease, ALS (Lou Gehrig's disease), osteoarthritis, inflammatory bowel disease (IBD), and Parkinson's disease.

DEGENERATIVE DISEASE: a condition in which diseased tissues or organs steadily deteriorate

Public Health

Factors that influence public health include:

- Availability of health care in the community
- Pollution levels
- Community resources to promote and facilitate healthy living habits
- Awareness of healthy living habits among adults in the community

Availability of health care in the community that is both accessible and affordable has a critical influence on public health. When health care is not readily available to the community, relatively minor problems will tend to go untreated and develop into bigger problems.

Pollution levels in a community can affect public health by exposing the community to toxic and carcinogenic chemicals that negatively affect systems including (but not limited to) the circulatory and respiratory systems.

Community resources are an important influence on public health. When financing is available to support health education and programs that encourage the development of healthy living habits, the health of the community will benefit. Conversely, if the community does not dedicate resources to this cause, the health of the community will suffer.

Related to this is the issue of awareness of healthy living habits among adults in the community. A strong personal commitment among responsible community members sets an important example for others to follow.

Disease Prevention

One of the most important principles related to disease prevention and control is hygiene. Community members, especially children, should wash their hands frequently, especially when they are ill or interacting with others who are ill.

Characteristics of disease that must be considered in a discussion of public and family health include the extent to which a disease is contagious and the symptoms that a disease causes. Contagious diseases demand special attention and sensitivity, because the integrative nature of communities (especially among children) provides ample opportunity for diseases to spread. The symptoms of a disease must be considered in order to ensure that members of the community are properly diagnosed and treated.

Education in the community should include the concept of germ theory and the ways in which various diseases can and cannot spread. When community members have a solid understanding of the way diseases "work," they are more likely to respond in an effective manner.

Nutrition and Weight Control

Components of nutrition include:

- **Carbohydrates:** The main source of energy (glucose) in the human diet. The two types of carbohydrates are **simple** and **complex**. Complex carbohydrates have greater nutritional value because they take longer to digest, contain dietary fiber, and do not excessively elevate blood sugar levels. Common sources of carbohydrates are fruits, vegetables, grains, dairy products, and legumes.

- Proteins: Necessary for growth, development, and cellular function. The body breaks down consumed protein into component amino acids for future use. Major sources of protein are meat, poultry, fish, legumes, eggs, dairy products, grains, and legumes.
- Fats: A concentrated energy source and important component of the human body. The different types of fats are saturated, monounsaturated, and polyunsaturated. Polyunsaturated fats are the healthiest because they may lower cholesterol levels, while saturated fats increase cholesterol levels. Common sources of saturated fats include dairy products, meat, coconut oil, and palm oil. Common sources of unsaturated fats include nuts, most vegetable oils, and fish.
- Vitamins and minerals: Organic substances that the body requires in small quantities for proper functioning. People acquire vitamins and minerals through their diets and in supplements. Important vitamins include A, B, C, D, E, and K. Important minerals include calcium, phosphorus, magnesium, potassium, sodium, chlorine, and sulfur.
- Water: Makes up 55–75 percent of the human body. It is essential for most bodily functions and can be obtained through foods and liquids.

Nutritional requirements vary from person to person. General guidelines for meeting adequate nutritional needs are: no more than 30 percent total caloric intake from fats (preferably 10 percent from saturated fats, 10 percent from monounsaturated fats, 10 percent from polyunsaturated fats), no more than 15 percent total caloric intake from protein (complete), and at least 55 percent of caloric intake from carbohydrates (mainly complex carbohydrates).

Exercise and diet help maintain proper body weight by equalizing caloric intake and caloric output.

Body Composition Management

The only proven method for maintaining a healthy body composition is following a healthy diet and engaging in regular exercise. A healthy diet consists primarily of fruits, vegetables, whole grains, unsaturated fats, and lean protein, and minimizes saturated fat and sugar consumption. Such a program of nutrition and exercise helps balance caloric intake and output and prevents the production of excessive body fat.

Stress

Sources of stress

Stress has many negative effects. It is important that instructors and students recognize the significance of stress to long-term health. To successfully manage it, instructors and students must understand the sources of stress as well as the signs and symptoms of it.

Signs and Symptoms of Stress

Emotional signs of stress: Depression, lethargy, aggressiveness, irritability, anxiety, edginess, fearfulness, impulsiveness, chronic fatigue, hyperexcitability, inability to concentrate, frequent feelings of boredom, feeling overwhelmed, apathy, impatience, pessimism, sarcasm, humorlessness, confusion, helplessness, melancholy, alienation, isolation, numbness, purposelessness, isolation, self-consciousness, and inability to maintain intimate relationships.

Behavioral signs of stress: Elevated use of substances (alcohol, drugs, tobacco), crying, yelling, insomnia or excessive sleep, excessive TV watching, school/job burnout, panic attacks, poor problem-solving capability, avoidance of people, aberrant behavior, procrastination, being accident-prone, restlessness, loss of memory, indecisiveness, aggressiveness, inflexibility, phobic responses, tardiness, disorganization, and sexual problems.

Physical signs of stress: Pounding heart, stuttering, trembling/nervous tics, excessive perspiration, teeth grinding, gastrointestinal problems (constipation, indigestion, diarrhea, queasy stomach), dry mouth, aching lower back, migraine/tension headaches, stiff neck, asthma attacks, allergy attacks, skin problems, frequent colds or low-grade fevers, muscle tension, hyperventilation, high blood pressure, amenorrhea, nightmares, and cold intolerance.

Stress management

General stress management principles include:

- Regular physical activity
- Exercise
- Physical play
- Proper nutrition

Proper nutrition is a balanced diet, consisting of adequate amounts of lean protein, complex carbohydrates, fruits, vegetables, and unsaturated fats.

Stress management and good nutrition are cornerstones of healthy living. Physical education instructors can introduce students to these important concepts through development of individualized fitness and wellness plans. Fitness and wellness plans should include a concrete exercise plan and a detailed nutritional plan.

There are five health-related components of physical fitness:

1. Cardiovascular endurance: The ability of the body to sustain aerobic activities (activities requiring oxygen utilization) for extended periods
2. Muscle strength: The ability of muscle groups to contract and support a given amount of weight
3. Muscle endurance: The ability of muscle groups to contract continually over a period of time and support a given amount of weight
4. Flexibility: The ability of muscle groups to stretch and bend
5. Body composition: Percentage of body fat and ratio of body fat to muscle

Physical activity improves each of the components of physical fitness. Aerobic training improves cardiovascular endurance. Weight training, body support activities, and calisthenics increase muscular strength and endurance. Stretching improves flexibility. Finally, all types of physical activity improve body composition by increasing muscle and decreasing body fat.

Types and Symptoms of Eating Disorders

Eating disorders are complex, and often there are genetic, behavioral, and societal disturbances involved that further complicate these illnesses. There are two chief categories of eating disorders: bulimia nervosa and anorexia nervosa. Eating disorders often first occur during adolescence but can develop in later adulthood. Young girls are more likely than boys to develop some type of an eating disorder. However, eating disorders are becoming more common in men and boys.

Anorexia nervosa

Anorexia nervosa is characterized by a persistent quest for a thin body. People who display symptoms of anorexia nervosa have a tremendous fear of gaining weight even when their bodies are severely malnourished. They also tend to have a distorted image of their bodies. They often weigh themselves many times during the course of a day. Some people with anorexia lose weight by doing an extreme amount of exercise combined with an extremely low-calorie diet. Others lose weight by abusing laxatives, inducing vomiting, and using diuretics.

Bulimia nervosa

The symptoms of bulimia nervosa include repeated bouts of consuming abnormally large amounts of food, called binge eating, which causes a feeling of lack of control over the eating. After the episodes of binge eating, the need to get rid of the excess food is expressed as purging in the form of vomiting, excessive use of laxatives, water fasting, or even extreme exercising. This cycle is usually repeated several times a week. Like people with anorexia nervosa, people with bulimia nervosa often also suffer from other disorders such as substance abuse or severe depression, and may even have suicidal thoughts.

Substance Abuse

Substance abuse can lead to adverse behaviors and increased risk of injury and disease. All substances affecting the normal functions of the body, illegal or not, are potentially dangerous and students and athletes should avoid them completely.

Substances commonly abused include:

- Anabolic steroids: The alleged benefit is an increase in muscle mass and strength. However, this substance is illegal and produces harmful side effects. Premature closure of growth plates in bones can occur if a teenager abuses steroids, limiting adult height. Other effects include bloody cysts in the liver, increased risk of cardiovascular disease, increased blood pressure, and dysfunction of the reproductive system.
- Alcohol: Alcohol is legal for adults but is commonly abused. Moderate to excessive consumption can lead to an increased risk of cardiovascular disease, nutritional deficiencies, and dehydration. Alcohol also causes ill effects on various aspects of performance such as reaction time, coordination, accuracy, balance, and strength.
- Nicotine: Another legal but often abused substance that can increase the risk of cardiovascular disease, pulmonary disease, and cancers of the mouth and lungs. Nicotine consumption through smoking severely hinders athletic performance by compromising lung function. Smoking especially affects performance in endurance activities.
- Marijuana: This is the most commonly abused illegal substance. Adverse effects include a loss of focus and motivation, decreased coordination, and lack of concentration.
- Cocaine: Another illegal and commonly abused substance. Effects of cocaine abuse include increased alertness and excitability. This drug can give the user a sense of overconfidence and invincibility, leading to a false sense of

one's ability to perform certain activities. An increased heart rate is associated with the use of cocaine, leading to an increased risk of heart attack, stroke, potentially deadly arrhythmias, and seizures.

Alternatives to substance abuse and aspects of treatment and control

Alternatives to substance use and abuse include regular participation in stress-relieving activities like meditation, exercise, and therapy, all of which can have a relaxing effect. For example, a healthy alternative would be to train oneself to substitute exercise for a substance abuse problem. More important, the acquisition of longer-term coping strategies (for example, self-empowerment via practice of problem-solving techniques) is key to maintaining a commitment to alternatives to substance use and abuse.

Limiting access to the addictive substance (opportunities for use) is important, because the symptoms of withdrawal and the experiences associated with the substance can provide a strong impetus to return to using it. Finally, recovering addicts should learn strategies of self-control and self-discipline to help them stay off addictive substances.

Violence and Abuse

There is a wide range of hurtful interpersonal behaviors that students may experience from peers or adults in their lives, including ridicule, sexual abuse, exploitation, dating violence, unwanted sexual contact, discrimination, and harassment.

There is a wide range of hurtful interpersonal behaviors that students may experience from peers or adults in their lives, including ridicule, sexual abuse, exploitation, dating violence, unwanted sexual contact, discrimination, and harassment.

Health instructors can teach students ways of avoiding or confronting these behaviors in a proactive manner. For example, students can learn to refuse to accept the hurtful behavior, negotiate to prevent it, or collaborate to change it.

Violence prevention strategies in the home, school, and community

Violence is a primary concern of educators. Assault, rape, suicide, gang violence, and weapons in school are major issues confronting educators in today's schools.

The fear of violence negatively affects students' growth, development, and ability to learn. In order to create learning and healthy growth and development, schools must be violence-free. In order to accomplish this, schools must enact policies and procedures that promote an environment free from crime, drugs, and weapons. For some schools, this may require locker searches, full-time school security officers, and metal detectors. Some school systems may choose to establish separate alternative schools for students proven to be violent or abusive.

Students should be encouraged to have faith in their feelings about people and situations. If their instincts indicate that a person or situation is potentially dangerous, they should trust that feeling and remove themselves from the situation. They should always pay attention and be aware of the actions of people near them. They should avoid situations that increase the chance that something harmful will happen. Finally, adult mentors can play a vital role in helping young people to stay safe. Educators are in a unique position to mentor young people and to act as a resource to help students avoid violence.

Coping with Child Abuse or Neglect

The term neglect is generally defined as deliberately ignoring a child's needs, which causes that child to experience undue harm or stress. There are several types of child neglect, which can include the following:

- Physical neglect
- Emotional neglect
- Mental neglect
- Educational neglect
- Medical neglect

There are several strategies that can be implemented when cases of suspected child abuse are discovered. These include asking various organizations to step in and assist, support of relatives, parental education, housing assistance, and neighborhood advocacy. However, if the abuse is recurring or cannot be halted, more forceful strategies such as the removal of the child from the home, placement in foster care, and, ultimately, criminal prosecution can be implemented to ensure the safety of the child.

Conflict Management

Interpersonal conflict is a major source of stress and worry. Common sources of interpersonal conflict include family relationships, competition, and disagreement over values or decisions. Teaching students to successfully manage conflict will help them reduce stress levels throughout their lives, thereby limiting the adverse health effects of stress. The following is a list of conflict resolution principles and techniques.

- Think before reacting: In a conflict situation, it is important to resist the temptation to react immediately. Step back, consider the situation, and plan an appropriate response. Also, do not react to petty situations with anger.

- **Listen:** Be sure to listen carefully to the opposing party. Try to understand the other person's point of view.
- **Find common ground:** Try to find some common ground as soon as possible. Early compromise can help ease the tension.
- **Accept responsibility:** In every conflict, there is plenty of blame to go around. Admitting when you are wrong shows you are committed to resolving the conflict.
- **Attack the problem, not the person:** Personal attacks are never beneficial and usually lead to greater conflict and hard feelings.
- **Focus on the future:** Instead of trying to assign blame for past events, focus on what needs to be done differently to avoid future conflict.

Building Healthy Interpersonal Relationships

Teachers' relationships with students and parents

Healthy interpersonal relationships are associated with such behaviors as effective communication and **empathic listening**. By using expressive speaking skills, teachers can discuss their thoughts, emotions, and hopes honestly and respectfully with parents and caregivers without provoking unwanted resentment or hostility.

Teachers should develop empathic listening skills, which involve communicating understanding and acceptance of a student's thoughts, feelings, and requests.

Strategies to reinforce healthy student-teacher relationships:

- Set clear expectations
- Praise students for work accomplished
- Encourage active listening
- Listen to what students are saying
- Keep lines of communication open

Effective communication skills such as controlling facial expressions, maintaining a level tone of voice, using the correct body language, and giving the proper reaction enable teachers to build and maintain strong interpersonal relationships with students and parents/caregivers.

Helping students build healthy relationships

Mutual respect, shared values and interests, and a mutual ability to trust and depend on each other characterize responsible friendship. Genuine respect is vital for a positive and responsible friendship. Shared values are a foundation for mutual respect, and shared interests are necessary for the development of a friendship. Trust and dependability are the cement that holds responsible friendships together.

We can develop positive interpersonal relationships by devoting time to character-building activities to strengthen the traits described above. Individuals can work to become trustworthy and dependable. Specific techniques that one can apply to develop positive interpersonal relationships with others include active listening and considerate respect for the things others value.

We can develop respect for others by actively asking ourselves what others would see as significant in the current scenario we are facing. This is an exercise aimed at placing value and emphasis on the priorities of others.

Social support systems are the networks that students develop with their peers that provide support when students experience challenges and difficulties. The support offered by these systems is often emotional and sometimes logistical. Financial support is generally inappropriate. Social support systems are vital to students (and individuals, in general), especially students who don't have other support mechanisms in place.

The benefits of maintaining healthy peer relationships include having a social support system to assist one in difficult times and the knowledge that that system exists. This gives students the confidence to take greater risks (within reason) and achieve more because they know the support system is there if they need it.

How Personal Differences Affect Communication

There are many personal differences among students that can affect communication. Instructors should consider cultural, economic, and environmental differences when addressing their students.

Cultural differences that affect communication may include different perceptions of what falls into the category of acceptable behavior. For example, depending on his or her cultural background, a child may believe it is appropriate or inappropriate to speak without having been directly spoken to, look an educator in the eye, or speak out in a classroom setting (some cultures view all of these actions as aggressive behavior).

Economic differences can also affect communication. Children from various socioeconomic backgrounds are likely to have different frames of reference. These may include references to "normal" after-school activities (whether the child spends time in front of a television or computer may depend on whether the family is able to afford the equipment—this can be a significant issue when homework requires a computer) and benchmarks of value (what is seen as valuable, both in dollar amounts and in commodities).

Environmental differences also affect communication. The difference between an urban and rural environment is a major cultural difference (depending on context), and often corresponds to differences in economic means.

Fostering Sensitive Interactions with and Among Students

Instructors can foster open communication in the classroom by reminding students that they can and should approach the teacher with issues and concerns. Of course, instructors must make themselves available to students and listen respectfully to the issues that they raise. Teachers should also devote classroom time to open, moderated discussions in which students can air their concerns related to issues between classmates. The instructor can serve as a mediator.

An environment conducive to learning has open lines of communication and a clear sense of respect among students and between teachers and students.

Respect is fundamental; otherwise, students will not bring issues to the attention of the teacher more than once. The teacher must be genuinely respectful of the concerns and backgrounds of students, and demand respect in turn. Instructors must also stress that they will not tolerate disrespectful behavior between students.

Factors That Affect Family Health

The primary factors that affect family health include environmental conditions such as pollution and proximity to industrial areas, smoking and drinking habits of family members, economic conditions that affect nutrition, and level of education of family members related to healthy living habits.

Technology

The technology market is rapidly changing. Consumers are progressively turning to technology for a healthier life. Consumer-focused health care information technology helps individuals handle the significant demands of managing their health care.

Health care information technology is a term describing the wide array of digital resources that are available to promote community health and proper health care for consumers. Health care information technology empowers patients to direct their health care and to advocate for themselves and their families as they use health care services. Health care information technology enables consumers, patients, and informal caregivers to gather facts, make choices, communicate with health care providers, control chronic disease, and participate in other health-related activities.

Peer Pressure

Peer pressure can influence children to make both positive and negative decisions. For example, a child who interacts with other children who use drugs is more likely to use drugs. On the other hand, interacting with children who are committed to exercise may encourage a previously inactive child to become physically active.

Media

Media-based role models often become the benchmarks against which students measure their traits.

Media-based expectations influence the development of children's self-concepts. A child's self-concept is a set of statements describing the child's own cognitive, physical, emotional, and social self-assessment.

Sources of Health Information

State and national initiatives

Important state and national initiatives that influence physical education content and practices include the Texas-based "Eat Smart—Be Active" campaign, and national initiatives like the Centers for Disease Control and Prevention (CDC) National Physical Activity Initiative, programs run by the Office of Safe and Drug-Free Schools (OSDFS) for Health, Mental Health, Environmental Health, and Physical Education, and the National Heart, Lung, and Blood Institute (NHLBI) Obesity Education Initiative (OEI). You can find further information about these initiatives on the following web sites:

- "Eat Smart—Be Active"

  http://www.eatsmartbeactivetx.org

- CDC's National Physical Activity Initiative

  http://www.cdc.gov/nccdphp/sgr/npai.htm

- Office of Safe and Drug-Free Schools (OSDFS)

  http://www.ed.gov/about/offices/list/osdfs/programs.html#health

- National Heart, Lung, and Blood Institute

  http://www.nhlbi.nih.gov/about/oei/oei_pd.htm

Consumer education

We can find information related to physical activity at local public and university libraries and online. Educators should regularly inform themselves about updates in the field, and should periodically search for resources that they can use with their students. Instructors should encourage students to make use of free resources like libraries, and especially the Internet, to expand their own knowledge.

Most schools maintain relationships with other outside health care agencies in order to offer more extensive health care services to students.

There are a variety of health care providers, agencies, and organizations involved with the maintenance of student health. On-site, the school nurse assists ill or injured students, maintains health records, and performs health screenings. School nurses also assist students who have chronic illnesses such as diabetes, asthma, epilepsy, or heart conditions. Most schools maintain relationships with other outside health care agencies in order to offer more extensive health care services to students. These community partnerships offer students services such as vaccinations, physical examinations and screenings, eye care, treatment of minor injuries and ailments, dental treatment, and psychological therapy. These community partnerships may include relationships with the following types of health care professionals: physicians, psychiatrists, optometrists, dentists, nurses, audiologists, occupational therapists, physical therapists, dieticians, respiratory therapists, and speech pathologists.

Relating the Health Curriculum to Other Content Areas

Physical education connects to other subject areas in the following ways:

- Life and physical sciences: Teaching students about the life and physical sciences can greatly reinforce their physical education experience. For example, understanding the physics of force and leverage gives children insight into the mechanics of gymnastic activities. The biology of carbohydrates turning into fuel for the muscles and protein rebuilding muscle tissue shows the value of the study of nutrition.
- Social sciences: Examining styles of interaction within and between groups in competitive team-based games and sports (e.g., soccer, dodge ball), interaction between children in competitive individual activities (e.g., running a race), and interaction between children engaging in noncompetitive individual activities (e.g., gymnastics training) helps children understand concepts of social organization and interaction and helps them draw parallels with their own experiences in physical education.
- Health sciences: Children who are taught the relationship between physical activity and health—not just in a general "exercise is good for you" sort of way, but in a more detailed way (e.g., aerobic fitness training stimulates the cardiovascular system, strengthening the heart)—are much more likely to look to fitness training as a potential response to health problems.
- Mathematics and language arts: These two fields are more peripherally connected to physical education. Math and language arts are generally used to quantify and communicate one's achievements.
- Visual and performing arts: There is considerable overlap between movement activities and visual and performing arts—whether it is the strenuous work of painting a large canvas or the more obviously artistic elements of gymnastics, dance, figure skating, or martial arts. Helping students to see the connections between these disciplines can stimulate crossovers, helping children to broaden their horizons.

PHYSICAL EDUCATION

Naturally, variations in levels of health and fitness exist; no two individuals are exactly alike. These variations are apparent in all areas of physical fitness including body composition, cardiovascular endurance, muscular strength and endurance, and flexibility.

Improvement in each of these categories leads to a decreased risk of injury and disease and allows one to perform normal, everyday activities with greater ease. Strategies for enhancing adherence to these fitness programs include appropriately maintaining facilities/equipment, emphasizing short-term goals, minimizing injuries, encouraging group participation, emphasizing variety and enjoyment, and providing support and motivation from family and friends.

Physical Education Standards

The goal of physical education is to give students the knowledge, skills, and confidence to enjoy a lifetime of healthful activity.

The goal of physical education is to give students the knowledge, skills, and confidence to enjoy a lifetime of healthful activity. Following is a list of standards that students of a physical education program should be able to achieve.

- Standard 1: Demonstrate competency in motor skills and movement patterns needed to perform a variety of physical activities
- Standard 2: Demonstrate understanding of movement concepts, principles, strategies, and tactics as they apply to the learning and performance of physical activities
- Standard 3: Participate regularly in physical activity
- Standard 4: Achieve and maintain a health-enhancing level of physical fitness
- Standard 5: Exhibit responsible personal and social behavior that respects self and others in physical activity settings
- Standard 6: Value physical activity for health, enjoyment, challenge, self-expression, and/or social interaction

TEKS For Physical Education

The TEKS for physical education emphasizes core physical education content that instructors must teach students. Instructors must observe educational best practices to educate students in a way that is safe, achieves goals, and ensures students' continued progress and motivation. For example, instructors must tailor the lessons to a variety of learning styles, implement knowledge-based assessment systems to track students' progress over the course of a semester, advance consideration of potential safety hazards in chosen activities, implement compensatory safety procedures, and create a pleasant, fun educational environment that encourages student involvement.

Emergency Action Plans

The first step in establishing a safe physical education environment is creating an emergency action plan (EAP). A good EAP can make a significant difference in the outcome of an injury situation. To ensure the safety of students during physical activities, an EAP should be easily comprehensible yet detailed enough to facilitate prompt, thorough action.

Communication

Instructors should clearly communicate rules and expectations to students. This information should include pre-participation guidelines, emergency procedures, and proper game etiquette. Instructors should collect emergency information sheets from students at the start of each school year. First-aid kits, facility maps, and incident report forms should also be readily available. Open communication between students and teachers is essential.

Creating a positive environment in the classroom allows students to feel comfortable enough to approach an adult/teacher if they feel they have sustained a potential injury.

Teacher education

At the start of each school year, every student should undergo a pre-participation physical examination. This allows a teacher to recognize the "high-risk" students before activity commences. The teacher should also take note of any student who requires any form of medication or special care.

Facilities and equipment

It is the responsibility of the teacher and school district to provide a safe environment, playing area, and equipment for students. Instructors and maintenance staff should regularly inspect school facilities to confirm that the equipment and location are adequate and safe for student use.

First-aid equipment

It is essential to have a properly stocked first-aid kit in an easy-to-reach location. Instructors may need to include asthma inhalers and special-care items to meet the specific needs of certain students. Instructors should clearly mark these special-care items to avoid a potentially harmful mix-up.

Implementing the emergency plan

The main thing to keep in mind when implementing an EAP is to remain calm. Maintaining a sufficient level of control and activating appropriate medical assistance will facilitate the process and leave less room for error.

Strategies for Injury Prevention

- Participant screenings: Evaluate injury history, anticipate and prevent potential injuries, watch for hidden injuries and reoccurrence of an injury, and maintain communication
- Standards and discipline: Ensure that athletes obey rules of sportsmanship, supervision, and biomechanics
- Education and knowledge: Stay current in knowledge of first aid, sports medicine, sport techniques, and injury prevention through clinics, workshops, and communication with staff and trainers
- Conditioning: Programs should be yearlong and participants should have access to conditioning facilities in and out of season to produce more fit and knowledgeable athletes who are less prone to injury
- Equipment: Perform regular inspections; ensure proper fit and proper use
- Facilities: Maintain standards and use safe equipment
- Field care: Establish emergency procedures for serious injury
- Rehabilitation: Use objective measures such as power output on an isokinetic dynamometer

Injury Followup and Reporting

Responding to accidents and injuries is an important responsibility of physical educators. After an injury occurs, instructors should contact an injured student's parents or guardians as soon as possible and notify school administrators. Instructors must also complete an accident report.

Goal Setting, Problem Solving, and Decision Making

Instructors can give students a clear understanding of the goals they need to attain, problems they need to solve, and decisions they need to make by clearly explaining an entire scenario to them. Instructors should leave students with a clear impression of why they need to take action (analysis/solution/decision), and what the desired outcome should be.

Next, instructors should give students all of the requisite information to take action, including reasonable timelines and the relevant physical and biomechanical principles. For example, if a student is interested in building upper-body strength, the instructor should ensure that he or she understands the biomechanical systems related to upper-body strength development and what actions the student can take to reach his or her goal.

Finally, instructors should emphasize to students that taking action is their responsibility. Whatever their personal training goals may be, it is the role of the physical educator to show students how to achieve their goals but not to force them to take action. The student must provide the motivation. This creates a reciprocal relationship between decision-making and taking action. The more students get accustomed to making decisions and following through, the better equipped they will be to do so in future situations.

Basic Training Principles

The overload principle is exercising at an above-normal level to improve physical or physiological capacity.

The progression principle states that once the body adapts to the original load/stress, no further improvement of fitness component will occur without an additional load.

The specificity principle refers to overloading a particular fitness component. In order to improve a particular component of one's fitness, one must isolate and specifically work on a single component. Metabolic and physiological adaptations depend on the type of overload; hence, specific exercise produces specific adaptations, creating specific training effects.

The reversibility-of-training principle refers to the fact that all gains in fitness are lost with the discontinuance of a training program.

Benefits of an Active Lifestyle

Regular physical activity and proper nutrition can help prevent diseases, illnesses, and injuries. In addition, regular exercise and a proper diet help maintain a healthy body composition, which is important physically and psychologically. Physically fit and healthy individuals are generally more productive at work. Finally, preventing disease and avoiding injury through healthy behaviors can reduce health care costs.

Students who have been through a good physical education program are better able to care for their own health and use nutrition and exercise to prevent long-term health problems.

Physiological benefits of physical activity include:

- Improved cardiovascular fitness
- Improved muscle strength
- Improved muscle endurance
- Improved flexibility
- More lean muscle mass and less body fat
- Quicker rate of recovery from illness and injury
- Improved ability of the body to utilize oxygen
- Lower resting heart rate
- Increased cardiac output
- Improved venous return and peripheral circulation
- Reduced risk of musculoskeletal injuries
- Lower cholesterol levels
- Increased bone mass
- Cardiac hypertrophy and size and strength of blood vessels
- Increased number of red blood cells
- Improved blood-sugar regulation
- Improved efficiency of thyroid gland
- Improved energy regulation
- Increased life expectancy

Psychological benefits of physical activity include:

- Relief of stress
- Improved mental health because of better physical health
- Reduced mental tension (relieves depression, improves sleeping patterns)
- More resistance to fatigue
- Better quality of life
- More enjoyment of leisure
- Improved capability to handle some stressors
- Opportunity for successful experiences
- Better self-concept

- Better ability to recognize and accept limitations
- Improved appearance and sense of well-being
- Better ability to meet challenges
- Better sense of accomplishment

Sociological benefits of physical activity include:

- The opportunity to spend time with family and friends and make new friends
- The opportunity to be part of a team
- The opportunity to participate in competitive experiences
- The opportunity to experience the thrill of victory

Incorporating physical activity into daily life

One of the most important tasks for physical education instructors is to introduce students to strategies to incorporate physical activity into their everyday lives. For example, instructors can recommend that students walk or ride a bike to school rather than drive or ride the bus. In addition, there are a number of everyday activities that promote fitness, including yard work, sports and games, walking, and climbing stairs.

Movement Principles and Concepts

We can use movement concepts and biomechanical principles to analyze movement skills by first examining the movement skill in detail (often with the assistance of recording equipment that allows playback in slow motion), and then breaking down the motions involved. For each motion, we should note the angle through which the joints must move and the direction of force that the muscles must apply. We can then check this information against our knowledge of movement concepts and biomechanical principles. Finally, we can modify the motion to ensure that the joints move and the muscles apply force in the most efficient way.

Concept of body awareness applied to physical education activities

Body awareness is a person's understanding of his or her own body parts and their capacity for movement. Instructors can assess students' body awareness by playing a game of "Simon Says" and asking students to touch different body parts. Instructors can also direct students to make their bodies into various shapes, from straight to round to twisted, and varying sizes, to fit into spaces of different sizes.

In addition, you can instruct children to touch one part of their body to another and to use various body parts to stamp their feet, twist their necks, clap their hands, nod their heads, wiggle their noses, snap their fingers, open their mouths, shrug their shoulders, bend their knees, close their eyes, bend their elbows, or wiggle their toes.

Concept of spatial awareness applied to physical education activities

Spatial awareness is the ability to make decisions about an object's positional changes in space (i.e., awareness of three-dimensional space position changes).

Developing spatial awareness requires:

- Identifying the location of objects in relation to one's own body in space
- Locating more than one object in relation to each object and independent of one's own body

Plan activities using different-size balls, boxes, or hoops and have children move toward and away; under and over; in front of and behind; and inside, outside, and beside the objects.

Concepts of space, direction, and speed related to movement concepts

Research shows that the concepts of **space**, **direction**, and **speed** are interrelated with movement concepts. Such concepts are extremely important for students to understand, because they need to relate movement skills to direction in order to move with confidence and avoid collisions.

A student or athlete in motion must take the elements of space, direction, speed, and vision into consideration in order to perform and understand a sport. A player must decide how to handle space as well as numerous other factors that arise on the field.

For an athlete, the concepts are all interlinked. He or she has to understand how to maintain or change pathways with speed. This ability allows the athlete to change motion and perform well in space (or the area that the athletes occupy on the field).

Locomotor Skills

Locomotor skills move an individual from one point to another.

- Crawling: A form of locomotion in which the person moves in a prone position with the body resting on or close to the ground or on the hands and knees
- Creeping: A slightly more advanced form of locomotion in which the person moves on the hands and knees
- Walking: With one foot in contact with the surface at all times, walking shifts one's weight from one foot to the other while legs swing alternately in front of the body
- Running: An extension of walking that has a phase in which the body is propelled with no base of support (speed is faster, stride is longer, and arms add power)
- Jumping: Projectile movements that momentarily suspend the body in midair
- Vaulting: Coordinated movements that allow one to spring over an obstacle
- Leaping: Similar to running but characterized by greater height, flight, and distance
- Hopping: Using the same foot to take off from a surface and land
- Galloping: Forward or backward advanced elongation of walking combined and coordinated with a leap
- Sliding: Sideward stepping pattern that is uneven, long, or short
- Body rolling: Moving across a surface by rocking back and forth, by turning over and over, or by shaping the body into a revolving mass
- Climbing: Ascending or descending using the hands and feet, with the upper body exerting the most control

Nonlocomotor Skills

Nonlocomotor skills are stability skills that require little or no movement of one's base of support and do not result in a change of position.

- Bending: Movement around a joint where two body parts meet
- Dodging: Sharp change of direction from original line of movement, such as away from a person or object

- Stretching: Extending/hyperextending joints to make body parts as straight or as long as possible
- Twisting: Rotating body/body parts around an axis with a stationary base
- Turning: Circular motion of the body through space, releasing the base of support
- Swinging: Circular/pendular movements of the body/body parts below an axis
- Swaying: Same as swinging, but movement is above an axis
- Pushing: Applying force against an object or person to move it away from one's body or to move one's body away from the object or person
- Pulling: Executing force to cause objects/people to move toward one's body

Manipulative Skills

Manipulative skills use body parts to propel or receive an object, controlling objects primarily with the hands and feet. Two types of manipulative skills are receptive (catch and trap) and propulsive (throw, strike, kick).

- Bouncing/dribbling: Projecting a ball downward
- Catching: Stopping momentum of an object using the hands
- Kicking: Striking an object with the foot
- Rolling: Initiating force to an object to create contact with a surface
- Striking: Giving impetus to an object with the use of the hands or an object
- Throwing: Using one or both arms to project an object into midair away from the body
- Trapping: Receiving and controlling a ball without the use of the hands

Rhythmic Skills

Rhythmic skills include responding and moving the body in time with the beat, tempo, or pitch of music. To develop rhythmic skills, instructors can ask students to clap their hands or stomp their feet to the beat of the music. Dancing and gymnastics require high levels of rhythmic competency. As with all physical skills, development of rhythmic skills is a sequential process.

Skill Development

Motor-development learning theories that pertain to a general skill, activity, or age level are important teacher background information for effective lesson planning. Individuals develop motor skills at different rates, but there is a general sequential pattern of skill development, starting with gross-motor skills and ending with fine-motor skills. Teachers must begin instruction at a level where all children are successful and proceed to the point where frustration for the majority is hindering performance. Students must learn the fundamentals of a skill first, or learning more advanced skills becomes extremely difficult.

Instructors must spend enough time on beginning skills that they become second nature. Teaching in small groups with enough equipment for everyone is essential.

Visualizing and breaking a skill down mentally is another way to enhance the learning of motor movements. Instructors can teach students to "picture" the steps involved and see themselves executing the skill. An example is teaching dribbling in basketball. Start teaching the skill with a demonstration of the steps involved in dribbling. Starting with the first skill, introduce key language terms and have students visualize themselves performing the skill. A sample-progression lesson plan to teach dribbling could begin with students practicing while standing still. Next, add movement while dribbling. Finally, teach students how to control dribbling while being guarded by another student.

Activities for body-management skill development

Locomotor skills

Sequential development = crawl, creep, walk, run, jump, hop, gallop, slide, leap, skip, and step-hop

- Activities to develop walking skills include walking slower and faster in place; walking forward, backward, and sideways with slower and faster paces in straight, curving, and zigzag pathways with various lengths of steps; pausing between steps; and changing the height of the body.
- Activities to develop running skills include having students pretend they are playing basketball, trying to score a touchdown, trying to catch a bus, finishing a lengthy race, or running on a hot surface.
- Activities to develop jumping skills include alternating jumping with feet together and feet apart, taking off and landing on the balls of the feet, clicking the heels together while airborne, and landing with one foot forward and one foot backward.
- Activities to develop galloping skills include having students play a game of Fox and Hound, with the lead foot representing the fox and the back foot the hound trying to catch the fox (alternate the lead foot).

- Activities to develop sliding skills include having students hold hands in a circle and slide in one direction, then slide in the other direction.
- Activities to develop hopping skills include having students hop all the way around a hoop and hop in and out of a hoop, reversing direction. Students can also place ropes in straight lines and hop side to side over the rope from one end to the other and change (reverse) the direction.
- Activities to develop skipping skills include having students combine walking and hopping activities leading up to skipping.
- Activities to develop step-hopping skills include having students practice stepping and hopping activities while clapping hands to an uneven beat.

Nonlocomotor skills

Sequential development = stretch, bend, sit, shake, turn, rock and sway, swing, twist, dodge, and fall

- Activities to develop stretching include lying on the back and stomach and stretching as far as possible; stretching as though one is reaching for a star, picking fruit off a tree, climbing a ladder, shooting a basketball, or placing an item on a high self; waking and yawning.
- Activities to develop bending include touching knees and toes, then straightening the entire body and straightening the body halfway; bending as though picking up a coin, tying shoes, picking flowers/vegetables, and petting animals of different sizes.
- Activities to develop sitting include practicing sitting from standing, kneeling, and lying positions without the use of hands.
- Activities to develop falling skills include first collapsing in one's own space and then pretending to fall like bowling pins, raindrops, snowflakes, a rag doll, or Humpty Dumpty.

Manipulative skills

Sequential development = striking, throwing, kicking, ball rolling, volleying, bouncing, catching, and trapping

- Activities to develop striking begin with the striking of stationary objects by a participant in a stationary position. Next, the person remains still while trying to strike a moving object. Then, both the object and the participant are in motion as the participant attempts to strike the moving object.
- Activities to develop throwing include throwing yarn/foam balls against a wall, then at a big target, and finally at targets decreasing in size.

- **Activities to develop kicking** include alternating feet to kick balloons/ beach balls, then kicking them under and over ropes. Change the type of ball used as proficiency develops.
- **Activities to develop ball rolling** include rolling balls of various sizes to a wall, then to targets decreasing in size.
- **Activities to develop volleying** include using a large balloon and, first, hitting it with both hands, then one hand (alternating hands), and then using different parts of the body. Change the object as students progress (balloon, then beach ball, then foam ball, etc.)
- **Activities to develop bouncing** include starting with large balls, first using both hands to bounce and then using one hand (alternate hands).
- **Activities to develop catching** include using various objects (balloons, beanbags, balls, etc.) to catch; first catching the object the participant has thrown him/herself, then catching objects someone else has thrown, and finally increasing the distance between the catcher and the thrower.
- **Activities to develop trapping** include trapping slow- and fast-rolling balls; trapping balls (or other objects such as beanbags) that are lightly thrown at waist, chest, and stomach levels; trapping balls of various sizes.

Rhythmic skills

Dancing is an excellent activity for the development of rhythmic skills. Any activity that involves moving the body to music can promote rhythmic skill development.

Dancing is an excellent activity for the development of rhythmic skills. Any activity that involves moving the body to music can promote rhythmic skill development.

Integration of Locomotor, Nonlocomotor, and Object-Control Skills in Various Combinations and Activities

Trainers adopt various strategies to incorporate locomotor, nonlocomotor, and object-control skills into their workout schedule. These skills are very effective in making students stronger and healthier.

Combinations of object-control skills

Object-control skills (e.g., run-and-catch, pivot-and-throw) help students remain fit and agile and become better performers. Physical education instructors often combine a number of object-control skills to enhance a child's reflexes.

Object-control skills make all the difference in successful athletic performance. An ideal combination of these skills keeps students healthy and satisfied.

Catch-and-throw is an ideal example of integrating such skills. This type of skill requires a high level of concentration and nimbleness. A combination of object-control skills is at the heart of all physical activity.

Integration strategies

Physical education instructors should develop innovative strategies to help students learn the nuances of locomotor, nonlocomotor, and object-control skills. Instructors should also present these skills in an entertaining manner for students.

A training schedule with simple activities is more likely to keep students interested. Once students develop interest, the teacher can introduce more complex activities such as running and catching, pivoting and throwing, and running and jumping.

The above progression strategy is a widely accepted method for combining locomotor, nonlocomotor, and object-control skills. From the moment students start taking interest in physical activities, the job becomes easier for the teacher as well as the students. Finally, traditional sports activities are a perfect way to practice combined skills.

Sports and games

All sports require the application of motor skills in complex forms. For example, the motor skills required to play tennis include running, jumping, striking, and volleying. For example, a tennis player often has to strike the ball while running or jumping. To play any sport at a high level, athletes must master a number of motor skills and develop the ability to combine those skills to master sport-specific movements.

Improving Students' Performance, Teamwork, and Skills

For most people, the development of social roles and appropriate social behaviors occurs during childhood. Physical play between parents and children, as well as between siblings and peers, serves as a strong regulator in the developmental process. Chasing games, roughhousing, wrestling, or practicing sport skills such as jumping, throwing, catching, and striking, are some examples of childhood play. These activities may be competitive or noncompetitive and are important for promoting the social and moral development of both boys and girls. Unfortunately, fathers often engage in this sort of activity more with their sons than with their daughters. Regardless of the sex of the child, both boys and girls enjoy these types of activities.

Social competence and self-esteem

In addition to the development of social competence, participation in sports can help young people develop self-esteem. Self-esteem is how we judge our worth and indicates the extent to which an individual believes he or she is capable, significant, successful, and worthy. Educators have suggested that one of the biggest barriers to success in the classroom today is low self-esteem.

Children develop self-esteem by evaluating their own abilities and by evaluating the responses of others. Children actively observe their parents' and coaches' responses to their performance, looking for signs of approval or disapproval. Children often interpret feedback and criticism as either a negative or a positive response to the behavior.

In sports, research shows that the coach is a critical influence on the self-esteem of children.

Little League baseball players whose coaches used a positive approach to coaching (e.g., frequent encouragement; positive reinforcement for effort; and corrective, instructional feedback) had significantly higher self-esteem ratings over the course of a season than children whose coaches used these techniques less frequently. Moreover, studies show that 95 percent of children who played for coaches trained to use the positive approach signed up to play baseball the next year, compared with 75 percent of the children who played for untrained coaches.

Positive social behaviors and traits

Physical education activities can promote positive social behaviors and traits in a number of ways. Instructors can foster improved social relations by making students active partners in the learning process and delegating responsibilities in the classroom environment to students. Giving students leadership positions (e.g., team captain) can give them a heightened understanding of the responsibilities and challenges facing educators.

Team sports promote collaboration and cooperation. Students learn to work together, pooling their talents and minimizing the weaknesses of different team members, in order to achieve a common goal. The experience of functioning as a team can be very productive for the development of loyalty between children, and seeing their peers in stressful situations to which they can relate can promote a more compassionate and considerate attitude among students. Similarly, the need to maximize the strengths of each student on a team (who can complement each other and compensate for weaknesses) is a powerful lesson about valuing and respecting diversity and individual differences. Switching students between leading and following positions in a team hierarchy is a good way to help students become comfortable being both followers and leaders.

Fairness is another trait that physical activities, especially rules-based sports, can foster and strengthen. Children are by nature very rules-oriented, and have a keen sense of what they believe is and isn't fair. Fair play, teamwork, and sportsmanship are all values that should be reinforced in physical education classes.

Finally, communication is another skill that improves enormously through participation in sports and games. Students will come to understand that skillful communication contributes to better outcomes, whether winning a game or successfully completing a team project. They will see that effective communication helps one develop and maintain healthy personal relationships, organize and convey information, and reduce or avoid conflict.

Appropriate Behavior in Physical Education Activities

Team sports require individual players to come together, merge individual skill sets, and pool individual strengths and weaknesses to achieve team success.

Rules and etiquette are of great importance to sports and physical activities. Rules help ensure fair play, equity, and safety for all participants. Teamwork is another important aspect of sports. Team sports require individual players to come together, merge individual skill sets, and pool individual strengths and weaknesses to achieve team success.

Appropriate student etiquette and behaviors include: following the rules and accepting the consequences of unfair actions, good sportsmanship, respecting the rights of other students, reporting one's own accidents and mishaps, not engaging in inappropriate behavior as a result of peer pressure, cooperation, paying attention to instructions and demonstrations, moving to assigned places and remaining in one's own space, complying with directions, practicing as instructed, properly using equipment, and not interfering with the practice of others.

Techniques to Maximize Participation

Instructors must remember to deal with each student as an individual, taking into account his or her capabilities. Although implementing strict management practices may benefit the majority of the class, it can have negative effects, too.

Curriculum design, group participation, cooperative work, fitness activities, and learning practices work well and instill exciting learning experiences for most, but there may be some students who are left out and need special care.

Options for maximizing participation include:

- Activity modification: This is simply modifying the type of equipment used or the activity rules. However, the instructor should keep the activity as close to the original as possible (e.g., substitute a yarn ball for a birdie for badminton).
- Multiactivity designs: Multiple activities permit greater diversification of equipment and more efficient use of available facilities (and keep all students involved).
- Homogeneous and heterogeneous grouping: Groupings can be rearranged for the purpose of individualized instruction, enhancing self-concepts, equalizing competition, and promoting cooperation among classmates.

Furthermore, instructors should plan activities that encourage the greatest amount of participation by utilizing all available facilities and equipment, involving students in planning class work/activities, and being flexible. Instructors can also use tangible rewards and praise.

Factors Influencing Students' Development and Fitness

A variety of factors influence a student's motor development and fitness level.

- Societal influences: We cannot separate students from the societies in which they live. The general societal perceptions of the importance of fitness activities will have an effect on their own choices regarding physical activity.

We should consider the "playground to PlayStation®" phenomenon and the rising levels of obesity among Americans as negative societal influences on motor development and fitness.

- Psychological influences: Psychological influences on motor development and fitness include a student's mental well-being, perception of fitness activities, and level of comfort in a fitness-training environment (both alone and in a group). Students experiencing psychological difficulties, such as depression, tend to be apathetic and lack both the energy and inclination to participate in fitness activities. As a result, their motor development and fitness levels suffer. Factors like the student's confidence level and comfort in a group environment, related to both the student's popularity in the group and the student's own personal insecurities, are also significant.

  It is noteworthy, though, that in the case of psychological influences on motor development and fitness levels, there is a more reciprocal relationship than with other influences. While a student's psychological state may negatively affect his or her fitness level, fitness training has the potential to positively affect the student psychologically, thereby reversing a negative cycle.

- Cultural influences: Culture is a significant and sometimes overlooked influence on a student's motor development and fitness, especially in the case of students belonging to minority groups. Students may not feel motivated to participate in certain physical activities, either because the activities are not associated with the student's sense of identity or because the student's culture discourages them. For example, students from cultures with strict dress codes may not be comfortable swimming. Some students (especially older children) may be uncomfortable with physical activities in inter-gender situations. Educators must keep such cultural considerations in mind when planning physical education curricula.

- Economic influences: The economic circumstances of a student's family can affect his or her motor development and fitness. Lack of resources may inpact the parents' ability to provide access to extracurricular activities that promote development, proper fitness-training equipment (ranging from complex exercise machines to team uniforms to something as simple as a basketball hoop), and even adequate nutrition.

- Familial influences: Familial factors that can influence motor development and fitness relate to the student's home environment. A student's feelings about physical activity often reflect the degree to which caregivers and role models (like older siblings) are athletically inclined and have a positive attitude toward physical activity. It isn't necessary for the parents to be athletically inclined; however, it is important for them to encourage their child to explore fitness activities that might suit him or her.

- Environmental and health influences: Genetic makeup (i.e., age, gender, and ethnicity) has a major influence on growth and development. Various physical and environmental factors directly affect one's personal health and fitness. Poor habits, poor living conditions, and living with a disease or disability can have a negative impact on a person. A healthy lifestyle with adequate living conditions and minimal physical or mental stress will enable a person to develop a positive, healthy existence.

Instructors should provide students with rich learning situations, regardless of students' previous experience or personal issues, which provide plenty of positive opportunities to participate in physical activity. For example, prior to playing a game of softball, instructors might have students practice throwing by tossing the ball to each other, progressing to the underhand toss, and later to the overhand toss.

SAMPLE TEST

SAMPLE TEST

Reading, Language, and Literature

(Average)

1. **While standing in line at the grocery store, three-year-old Megan says to her mother in a regular tone of voice, "Mom, why is that woman so fat?" This indicates a lack of understanding of:**

   A. Syntax

   B. Semantics

   C. Morphology

   D. Pragmatics

(Easy)

2. **Oral language development can be enhanced by which of the following?**

   A. Meaningful conversation

   B. Storytelling

   C. Alphabet songs

   D. All of the above

(Rigorous)

3. **Ms. Chomski is presenting a new story to her class of first graders. In the story, a family visits their grandparents' house, where they all gather around a record player and listen to music. Many students do not understand what a record player is, especially some children for whom English is not their first language. Which of the following would be best for Ms. Chomski to do?**

   A. Discuss what a record player is with her students

   B. Compare a record player with a CD player

   C. Have students look up *record player* in a dictionary

   D. Show the students a picture of a record player

(Rigorous)

4. **Reading aloud correlates with all of the following EXCEPT:**

   A. Reader self-confidence

   B. Better reading comprehension

   C. Literacy development

   D. Overall school success

(Rigorous)

5. **Mr. Johns is using an activity that involves having students analyze the public speaking of others. All of the following would be guidelines for this activity EXCEPT:**

   A. The speeches to be evaluated are not given by other students

   B. The rubric for evaluating the speeches includes pace, pronunciation, body language, word choice, and visual aids

   C. The speeches to be evaluated are best presented live to give students a more engaging learning experience

   D. One of Mr. Johns' goals is to help students improve their own public speaking skills

(Average)

6. **All of the following are true about phonological awareness EXCEPT:**

   A. It may involve print

   B. It is a prerequisite for spelling and phonics

   C. Activities can be done by the children with their eyes closed

   D. It starts before letter recognition is taught

(Rigorous)

7. **Which of the following explains a significant difference between phonics and phonemic awareness?**

   A. Phonics involves print, while phonemic awareness involves language

   B. Phonics is harder than phonemic awareness

   C. Phonics involves sounds, while phonemic awareness involves letters

   D. Phonics is the application of sounds to print, while phonemic awareness is oral

(Average)

8. **Theorist Marilyn Jager Adams, who researches early reading, has outlined five basic types of phonemic awareness tasks. Which of the following is NOT one of the tasks noted by Jager Adams?**

   A. Ability to do oddity tasks

   B. Ability to orally blend words and split syllables

   C. Ability to sound out words when reading aloud

   D. Ability to do phonics manipulation tasks

(Average)

9. **Activities that parents can practice at home with their children to improve phonological and phonemic awareness include which of the following?**

   A. Play games with words that sound alike as you experience them in everyday home activities

   B. Demonstrate how sounds blend together in familiar words

   C. Play a game in which the goal is to find objects with names that begin with a certain initial sound

   D. All of the above

(Rigorous)

10. **The alphabetic principle can best be described by which of the following statements?**

   A. Most reading skills need to be acquired through regular teaching of the alphabet

   B. Written words are composed of patterns of letters that represent the sounds of spoken words

   C. Written words are composed of patterns that must be memorized in order to read well

   D. Spoken words (regular and irregular) lead to phonological reading

(Rigorous)

11. **Which of the following is NOT true about multisensory approaches to teaching the alphabetic principle?**

   A. Some children can only learn through multisensory techniques

   B. Multisensory techniques give multiple cues to enhance memory and learning

   C. Quilt book, rhyme time, letter path, and shape game are multisensory strategies

   D. Multisensory techniques require direct teaching and ongoing engagement

(Average)

12. **Activities that facilitate learning the alphabetic principle include:**

   A. Read alouds, alphabet art, concept books, and name sorts

   B. Read alouds, shared reading, concept books, and picture books

   C. Picture books, concept books, and alphabet books

   D. Alphabet art, name sorts, shared reading, and phonics

(Rigorous)

13. **Which of the following is a convention of print that children learn during reading activities?**

   A. The meaning of words

   B. The left-to-right motion

   C. The purpose of print

   D. The identification of letters

(Average)

14. **Alphabet books are classified as:**

    A. Concept books

    B. Easy-to-read books

    C. Board books

    D. Picture books

(Rigorous)

15. **To determine an author's purpose, a reader must:**

    A. Use his or her own judgment

    B. Verify all the facts

    C. Link the causes to the effects

    D. Rely on common sense

(Easy)

16. **To decode is to:**

    A. Construct meaning

    B. Sound out a printed sequence of letters

    C. Use a special code to decipher a message

    D. None of the above

(Rigorous)

17. **Contextual redefinition is a strategy that encourages children to use the context more effectively by presenting them with sufficient vocabulary __________ the reading of a text.**

    A. after

    B. before

    C. during

    D. None of the above

(Average)

18. **What is the best place for students to find appropriate synonyms, antonyms, and other related words to enhance their writing?**

    A. Dictionary

    B. Spell check

    C. Encyclopedia

    D. Thesaurus

(Easy)

19. **Which of the following indicates that a student is a fluent reader?**

    A. Reads texts with expression or prosody

    B. Reads word to word and haltingly

    C. Must intentionally decode a majority of the words

    D. In a writing assignment, sentences are poorly organized structurally

(Average)

20. **Which of the following reading strategies is NOT associated with fluent reading abilities?**

    A. Pronouncing unfamiliar words by finding similarities with familiar words

    B. Establishing a purpose for reading

    C. Formulating questions about the text while reading

    D. Reading sentences word by word

(Rigorous)

21. **Automaticity refers to all of the following EXCEPT:**

    A. Automatic whole-word identification

    B. Automatic recognition of syllable types

    C. Automatic reactions to the content of a paragraph

    D. Automatic identification of graphemes as they relate to four basic word types

(Easy)

22. **Which of the following activities are likely to improve fluency?**

    A. Partner reading and a reading theater

    B. Phrased reading

    C. Both A and B

    D. None of the above

(Average)

23. **Students are about to read a text that contains words that will need to be understood for them to understand the text. When should the vocabulary be introduced to students?**

    A. Before reading

    B. During reading

    C. After reading

    D. It should not be introduced

(Average)

24. **Which of the following is an important feature of vocabulary instruction, according to the National Reading Panel?**

    A. Repetition of vocabulary items

    B. Keeping a consistent task structure at all times

    C. Teaching vocabulary in more than one language

    D. Isolating vocabulary instruction from other subjects

(Rigorous)

25. **A sixth-grade science teacher has given her class a paper to read on the relationship between food and weight gain. The writing contains signal words and phrases such as "because," "consequently," "this is how," and "due to." This paper has which text structure?**

    A. Cause and effect

    B. Compare and contrast

    C. Description

    D. Sequencing

(Rigorous)

26. **Which of the following is NOT a strategy of teaching reading comprehension?**

    A. Asking questions

    B. Utilizing graphic organizers

    C. Focusing on mental images

    D. Manipulating sounds

(Easy)

27. **The children's literature genre came into its own in the:**

    A. Seventeenth century

    B. Eighteenth century

    C. Nineteenth century

    D. Twentieth century

(Rigorous)

28. **When evaluating reference sources, students should do all of the following EXCEPT:**

    A. Look for self-published books by the author as evidence of expert status

    B. Examine the level of detail provided by the source

    C. Review the references at the end of the book or article

    D. See if the author presents both sides of an argument or viewpoint

(Average)

29. **Graphic organizers:**

    A. Are used primarily in grades K-3

    B. Work better with poetry than other forms of writing

    C. Help readers think critically by pulling out the main idea and supporting details

    D. Generally aren't helpful to ELL students

(Average)

30. **Which of the following helps students in a way that is similar to using a glossary?**

    A. Information in the text such as charts, graphs, maps, diagrams, captions, and photos

    B. Prewriting

    C. Classroom discussion of the main idea

    D. Paired reading

(Rigorous)

31. **Which of these describes the best way to teach spelling?**

    A. At the same time that grammar and sentence structure are taught

    B. Within the context of meaningful language experiences

    C. Independently, so that students can concentrate on spelling

    D. In short lessons, because students pick up spelling almost immediately

(Rigorous)

32. **Which of the following sentences contains an error in agreement?**

    A. Jennifer is one of the women who writes for the magazine.

    B. Each one of their sons plays a different sport.

    C. This band has performed at the Odeum many times.

    D. The data are available online at the listed Web site.

(Rigorous)

33. **All of the following sentences are correctly punctuated EXCEPT:**
    A. "The airplane crashed on the runway during takeoff."
    B. I was embarrassed when Ms. White said, "Your slip is showing!"
    C. "The middle school readers were unprepared to understand Bryant's poem 'Thanatopsis.'"
    D. The hall monitor yelled, "Fire! Fire!"

(Average)

34. **Which of the following is NOT a technique of prewriting?**
    A. Clustering
    B. Listing
    C. Brainstorming
    D. Proofreading

(Average)

35. **Which of the following is NOT a prewriting strategy?**
    A. Analyzing sentences for variety
    B. Keeping an idea book
    C. Writing in a daily journal
    D. Writing down whatever comes to mind

(Easy)

36. **A student has written a paper with the following characteristics: written in first person; characters, setting, and plot; some dialogue; and events organized in chronological sequence with some flashbacks. In what genre has the student written?**
    A. Expository writing
    B. Narrative writing
    C. Persuasive writing
    D. Technical writing

(Rigorous)

37. **Exposition occurs within a story:**
    A. After the rising action
    B. After the denouement
    C. Before the rising action
    D. Before the setting

(Average)

38. **Which of the following messages provides the most accessibility to the most learners?**
    A. Print message
    B. Audiovisual message
    C. Graphic message
    D. Audio message

(Easy)

39. **Which of the following advertising techniques is based on appealing to our desire to think for ourselves?**
    A. Celebrity endorsement
    B. Intelligence
    C. Independence
    D. Lifestyle

(Average)

40. **Which of the following is NOT useful in creating visual media for the classroom?**

 A. Limit your graph to just one idea or concept and keep the content simple

 B. Balance substance and visual appeal

 C. Match the information to the format that will fit it best

 D. Make sure to cite all references to copyrighted material

(Rigorous)

41. **All of the following are examples of ongoing informal assessment techniques used to observe student progress EXCEPT:**

 A. Analysis of student work product

 B. Collection of data from assessment tests

 C. Effective questioning

 D. Observation of students

(Easy)

42. **Which of the following is a formal reading-level assessment?**

 A. A standardized reading test

 B. A teacher-made reading test

 C. An interview

 D. A reading diary

(Easy)

43. **Which of the following is NOT considered a reading level?**

 A. Independent

 B. Instructional

 C. Intentional

 D. Frustrational

(Rigorous)

44. **Which of the following are good choices for supporting a thesis?**

 A. Reasons

 B. Examples

 C. Answer to the question, "why?"

 D. All of the above

(Rigorous)

45. **Which of the following should NOT be included in the opening paragraph of an informative essay?**

 A. Thesis sentence

 B. Details and examples supporting the main idea

 C. A broad general introduction to the topic

 D. A style and tone that grabs the reader's attention

Mathematics

(Average)

46. **Which of the following is NOT a true statement regarding manipulatives in mathematics instruction?**

 A. Manipulatives are materials that students can physically handle

 B. Manipulatives help students make concrete concepts abstract

 C. Manipulatives include fingers, tiles, paper folding, and ice cream sticks

 D. Manipulatives help students make abstract concepts concrete

(Easy)

47. **All of the following are tools that can strengthen students' mathematical understanding EXCEPT:**

    A. Rulers, scales, and protractors

    B. Calculators, counters, and measuring containers

    C. Software and hardware

    D. Money and software

(Average)

48. **Which of the following is NOT a good example of helping students make connections between the real world and mathematics?**

    A. Studying a presidential election from the perspective of the math involved

    B. Using weather concepts to teach math

    C. Having student helpers take attendance

    D. Reviewing major mathematical theorems on a regular basis

(Rigorous)

49. **Which of the following is an example of the associative property?**

    A. $a(b + c) = ab + bc$

    B. $a + 0 = a$

    C. $(a + b) + \mathrm{c} = a + (b + c)$

    D. $a + b = b + a$

(Easy)

50. **What is the greatest common factor of 16, 28, and 36?**

    A. 2

    B. 4

    C. 8

    D. 16

(Rigorous)

51. **Mathematical operations are done in the following order:**

    A. Simplify inside grouping characters such as parentheses, brackets, square roots, fraction bars, etc.; multiply out expressions with exponents; do multiplication or division from left to right; do addition or subtraction from left to right

    B. Do multiplication or division from left to right; simplify inside grouping characters such as parentheses, brackets, square roots, fraction bars, etc.; multiply out expressions with exponents; do addition or subtraction from left to right

    C. Simplify inside grouping characters such as parentheses, brackets, square roots, fraction bars, etc.; do addition or subtraction from left to right; multiply out expressions with exponents; do multiplication or division from left to right

    D. None of the above

(Rigorous)

52. **Which of the following is an irrational number?**

    A. .36262626262…

    B. 4

    C. 8.2

    D. -5

(Rigorous)

53. **The number 0 is a member of all of the following groups of numbers EXCEPT:**

    A. Whole numbers

    B. Real numbers

    C. Natural numbers

    D. Integers

(Easy)

54. **4,087,361: What number represents the ten thousands place?**

A. 4

B. 6

C. 0

D. 8

(Average)

55. **Two mathematics classes have a total of 410 students. The 8:00 a.m. class has 40 more students than the 10:00 a.m. class. How many students are in the 10:00 a.m. class?**

A. 123.3

B. 370

C. 185

D. 330

(Easy)

56. **Three-dimensional figures in geometry are called:**

A. Solids

B. Cubes

C. Polygons

D. Blocks

(Easy)

57. **Volume is:**

A. The area of the faces excluding the bases

B. The total area of all the faces, including the bases

C. The number of cubic units in a solid

D. The measure around the object

(Average)

58. **If a right triangle has legs with measurements of 3 cm and 4 cm, what is the measure of the hypotenuse?**

A. 6 cm

B. 1 cm

C. 7 cm

D. 5 cm

(Rigorous)

59. **If the radius of a right circular cylinder is doubled, how does its volume change?**

A. No change

B. Is doubled

C. Is four times the original

D. Is π times the original

(Rigorous)

60. **What is the area of a rectangle if you know that the length of the base is 8 cm and the diagonal of the rectangle is 8.5 cm?**

A. 24 cm^2

B. 30 cm^2

C. 18.9 cm^2

D. 24 cm

(Average)

61. **An item that sells for $375.00 is put on sale for $120.00. What is the percentage of discount?**

A. 25%

B. 28%

C. 68%

D. 34%

(Rigorous)

62. **What is a translation?**

    A. To turn a figure around a fixed point

    B. When two objects have the same shape and same size, but face in different directions

    C. To "slide" an object a fixed distance in a given direction

    D. The transformation that shrinks or makes a figure bigger

(Easy)

63. **What measures could be used to report the distance traveled when walking around a track?**

    A. Degrees

    B. Square meters

    C. Kilometers

    D. Cubic feet

(Average)

64. **Corporate salaries are listed for several employees. Which would be the best measure of central tendency?**

$24,000	$24,000	$26,000
$28,000	$30,000	$120,000

    A. Mean

    B. Median

    C. Mode

    D. No difference

(Rigorous)

65. **Given a drawer with 5 black socks, 3 blue socks, and 2 red socks, what is the probability that you will draw two black socks in two draws in a dark room?**

    A. $\frac{2}{9}$

    B. $\frac{1}{4}$

    C. $\frac{17}{18}$

    D. $\frac{1}{18}$

(Average)

66. **Suppose you have a bag of marbles that contains 2 red marbles, 5 blue marbles, and 3 green marbles. If you replace the first marble chosen, what is the probability you will choose 2 green marbles in a row?**

    A. $\frac{2}{5}$

    B. $\frac{9}{100}$

    C. $\frac{9}{10}$

    D. $\frac{3}{5}$

(Average)

67. **In probability, the sample space represents:**

    A. An outcome of an experiment

    B. A list of all possible outcomes of an experiment

    C. The number of times you must flip a coin

    D. The amount of room needed to conduct an experiment

(Average)

68. **Deduction is:**

    A. Logical reasoning

    B. The process of arriving at a conclusion based on other statements that are known to be true

    C. Both A and B

    D. Neither A nor B

(Rigorous)

69. **Find the inverse of the following statement: If I like dogs, then I do not like cats.**

    A. If I like dogs, then I do like cats.

    B. If I like cats, then I like dogs.

    C. If I like cats, then I do not like dogs.

    D. If I do not like dogs, then I like cats.

(Average)

70. **Find the converse of the following statement: If I like math, then I do not like science.**

    A. If I do not like science, then I like math.

    B. If I like math, then I do not like science.

    C. If I do not like math, then I do not like science.

    D. If I like math, then I do not like science.

(Easy)

71. **Which of the following is the basic language of mathematics?**

    A. Symbolic representation

    B. Number lines

    C. Arithmetic operations

    D. Deductive thinking

(Easy)

72. **The mass of a cookie is closest to:**

    A. 0.5 kg

    B. 0.5 grams

    C. 15 grams

    D. 1.5 grams

History and Social Science

(Average)

73. **Using graphics can enhance the presentation of social science information because:**

    A. They can explain complex relationships among various data points

    B. Charts and graphs summarize information well

    C. Maps can describe geographic distribution or historical information

    D. All of the above

(Rigorous)

74. **All of the following are key elements in planning a child-centered curriculum EXCEPT:**

A. Referring students who need special tutoring

B. Identifying students' prior knowledge and skills

C. Sequencing learning activities

D. Specifying behavioral objectives

(Average)

75. **The Texas Assessment of Knowledge and Skills (TAKS) test is an example of:**

A. Criterion-referenced assessment

B. Norm-referenced assessment

C. Performance-based assessment

D. Other type of assessment

(Easy)

76. **Ms. Gomez has a number of ELL students in her class. In order to meet their specific needs as second-language learners, which of the following would NOT be an appropriate approach?**

A. Pair students of different ability levels for English practice

B. Focus most of her instruction on teaching English rather than content

C. Provide accommodations during testing and with assignments

D. Use visual aids to help students make word links with familiar objects

(Rigorous)

77. **Which one of the following is NOT a reason why Europeans came to the New World?**

A. To find resources in order to increase wealth

B. To establish trade

C. To increase a ruler's power and importance

D. To spread Christianity

(Easy)

78. **Which of the following were results of the Age of Exploration?**

A. More complete and accurate maps and charts

B. New and more accurate navigational instruments

C. Proof that the Earth is round

D. All of the above

(Easy)

79. **The belief that the United States should control all of North America was called:**

A. Westward expansion

B. Pan-americanism

C. Manifest Destiny

D. Nationalism

(Rigorous)

80. **Nationalism can be defined as the division of land and resources according to which of the following?**

A. Religion, race, or political ideology

B. Religion, race, or gender

C. Historical boundaries, religion, or race

D. Race, gender, or political ideology

(Average)

81. **The study of the social behavior of minority groups is part of the field of:**
   A. Anthropology
   B. Psychology
   C. Sociology
   D. Cultural geography

(Rigorous)

82. **Participant observation is a method of study most closely associated with and used in:**
   A. Anthropology
   B. Archaeology
   C. Sociology
   D. Political science

(Rigorous)

83. **For the historian studying ancient Egypt, which of the following would be least useful?**
   A. The record of an ancient Greek historian on Greek-Egyptian interaction
   B. Letters from an Egyptian ruler to his/her regional governors
   C. Inscriptions on stele of the fourteenth Egyptian dynasty
   D. Letters from a nineteenth-century Egyptologist to his wife

(Easy)

84. **The term *sectionalism* refers to:**
   A. Different regions of the continent
   B. Issues between the North and South
   C. Different regions of the country
   D. Different groups of countries

(Rigorous)

85. **Which political group pushed the Reconstruction measures through Congress after Lincoln's death?**
   A. The Radical Republicans
   B. The Radical Democrats
   C. The Whigs
   D. The Independents

(Average)

86. **As a result of the Missouri Compromise:**
   A. Slavery was not allowed in the Louisiana Purchase
   B. The Louisiana Purchase was nullified
   C. Louisiana separated from the Union
   D. The Embargo Act was repealed

(Easy)

87. **Which country was the Cold War foe of the United States?**
   A. Soviet Union
   B. Brazil
   C. Canada
   D. Argentina

(Average)

88. **The international organization established to work for world peace at the end of the Second World War was the:**
   A. League of Nations
   B. United Federation of Nations
   C. United Nations
   D. United World League

(Average)

89. What event triggered World War I?

A. The fall of the Weimar Republic

B. The resignation of the czar

C. The assassination of Austrian Archduke Ferdinand

D. The assassination of the czar

(Rigorous)

90. What is the most significant environmental change in Texas over the last century?

A. The number of square miles devoted to living space

B. Continued exploration for oil and gas

C. Development along the Gulf Coast

D. Changes in agricultural practices

(Average)

91. The end to hunting, gathering, and fishing of prehistoric people was due to:

A. Domestication of animals

B. Building crude huts and houses

C. Development of agriculture

D. Organized government in villages

(Average)

92. Which of the following is most useful for showing differences in variables at a specific point in time?

A. Histogram

B. Scatter plot

C. Pie chart

D. Bar graph

(Easy)

93. Capitalism and communism are alike in that they are both:

A. Organic systems

B. Political systems

C. Centrally planned systems

D. Economic systems

(Rigorous)

94. During the 1920s, the United States stopped nearly all immigration. One of the reasons was:

A. Plentiful, cheap unskilled labor was no longer needed by industrialists

B. War debts from World War I made it difficult to render financial assistance

C. European nations were reluctant to allow people to leave since there was a need to rebuild populations and economic stability

D. The United States did not become a member of the League of Nations

(Average)

95. In the 1800s, the era of industrialization and growth was characterized by:

A. Small firms

B. Public ownership

C. Worker-owned enterprises

D. Monopolies and trusts

(Rigorous)

96. **Which one of the following would NOT be considered a result of World War II?**

    A. Economic depression and slow resumption of trade and financial aid

    B. Western Europe was no longer the center of world power

    C. The beginnings of new power struggles, not only in Europe but in Asia as well

    D. Territorial and boundary changes for many nations, especially in Europe

(Average)

97. **The New Deal was:**

    A. A trade deal with England

    B. A series of programs to provide relief during the Great Depression

    C. A new exchange rate regime

    D. A plan for tax relief

(Average)

98. **Which of the following is an example of a direct democracy?**

    A. Elected representatives

    B. Greek city-states

    C. The Constitution

    D. The Confederate states

(Average)

99. **Many governments in Europe today have which of the following types of government?**

    A. Absolute monarchies

    B. Constitutional governments

    C. Constitutional monarchies

    D. Another form of government

Science

(Easy)

100. **Accepted procedures for preparing solutions include the use of:**

    A. Alcohol

    B. Hydrochloric acid

    C. Distilled water

    D. Tap water

(Average)

101. **Laboratory activities contribute to student performance in all of the following domains EXCEPT:**

    A. Process skills such as observing and measuring

    B. Memorization skills

    C. Analytical skills

    D. Communication skills

(Average)

102. **Which is the correct order of methodology in the scientific method?**

    1. **Collecting data.**
    2. **Planning a controlled experiment.**
    3. **Drawing a conclusion.**
    4. **Hypothesizing a result.**
    5. **Revisiting a hypothesis to answer a question.**

    A. 1, 2, 3, 4, 5

    B. 4, 2, 1, 3, 5

    C. 4, 5, 1, 3, 2

    D. 1, 3, 4, 5, 2

(Rigorous)

103. In an experiment measuring the growth of bacteria at different temperatures, what is the independent variable?

A. Number of bacteria

B. Growth rate of bacteria

C. Temperature

D. Size of bacteria

(Average)

104. Which of the following is a misconception about the task of teaching science in elementary school?

A. Teach facts as a priority over teaching how to solve problems

B. Involve as many senses as possible in the learning experience

C. Accommodate individual differences in pupils' learning styles

D. Consider the effect of technology on people rather than on material things

(Rigorous)

105. Which of the following is the most accurate definition of a nonrenewable resource?

A. A nonrenewable resource is never replaced once used

B. A nonrenewable resource is replaced on a time scale that is very long relative to human life spans

C. A nonrenewable resource is a resource that can only be manufactured by humans

D. A nonrenewable resource is a species that has already become extinct

(Average)

106. All of the following are hormones in the human body EXCEPT:

A. Cortisol

B. Testosterone

C. Norepinephrine

D. Hemoglobin

(Rigorous)

107. Models are used in science in all of the following ways EXCEPT:

A. Models are crucial for understanding the structure and function of scientific processes

B. Models help us visualize the organs/systems they represent

C. Models create exact replicas of the items they represent

D. Models are useful for predicting and foreseeing future events such as hurricanes

(Rigorous)

108. There are a number of common misconceptions that claim to be based in science. All of the following are misconceptions EXCEPT:

A. Evolution is a process that does not address the origins of life

B. The average person uses only a small fraction of his or her brain

C. Raw sugar causes hyperactive behavior in children

D. Seasons are caused by the Earth's elliptical orbit

(Rigorous)

109. One characteristic of electrically charged objects is that their charge is conserved. This means that:

A. Because of the financial cost, electricity should be conserved

B. A neutral object has no net charge

C. Like charges repel and opposite charges attract

D. None of the above

(Easy)

110. Which of the following describes a state of balance between opposing forces of change?

A. Equilibrium

B. Homeostasis

C. Ecological balance

D. All of the above

(Average)

111. Which of the following describes the amount of matter in an object?

A. Weight

B. Mass

C. Density

D. Volume

(Easy)

112. Sound waves are produced by:

A. Pitch

B. Noise

C. Vibrations

D. Sonar

(Average)

113. The Doppler effect is associated most closely with which property of waves?

A. Amplitude

B. Wavelength

C. Frequency

D. Intensity

(Rigorous)

114. The energy of electromagnetic waves is:

A. Radiant energy

B. Acoustical energy

C. Thermal energy

D. Chemical energy

(Average)

115. Photosynthesis is the process by which plants make carbohydrates using:

A. The Sun, carbon dioxide, and oxygen

B. The Sun, oxygen, and water

C. Oxygen, water, and carbon dioxide

D. The Sun, carbon dioxide, and water

(Rigorous)

116. What is the correct sequence of organization of living things from lower to higher order?

A. Cell, organelle, organ, tissue, system, organism

B. Cell, tissue, organ, organelle, system, organism

C. Organelle, cell, tissue, organ, system, organism

D. Organelle, tissue, cell, organ, system, organism

(Rigorous)

117. **What cell organelle contains the cell's stored food?**

    A. Vacuoles

    B. Golgi apparatus

    C. Ribosomes

    D. Lysosomes

(Rigorous)

118. **Enzymes speed up reactions by:**

    A. Utilizing ATP

    B. Lowering pH, allowing reaction speed to increase

    C. Increasing volume of substrate

    D. Lowering energy of activation

(Rigorous)

119. **Which of the following is a correct explanation for scientific evolution?**

    A. Giraffes need to reach higher for leaves to eat, so their necks stretch. The giraffe babies are then born with longer necks. Eventually there are more long-necked giraffes in the population.

    B. Giraffes with longer necks are able to reach more leaves, so they eat more and have more babies than other giraffes. Eventually there are more long-necked giraffes in the population.

    C. Giraffes want to reach higher for leaves to eat, so they release enzymes into their bloodstream, which in turn causes fetal development of longer-necked giraffes. Eventually there are more long-necked giraffes in the population.

    D. Giraffes with long necks are more attractive to other giraffes, so they get the best mating partners and have more babies. Eventually, there are more long-necked giraffes in the population.

(Rigorous)

120. **The theory of seafloor spreading explains:**

    A. The shapes of the continents

    B. How continents collide

    C. How continents move apart

    D. How continents sink to become part of the ocean floor

(Average)

121. **Weather occurs in which layer of the atmosphere?**

  A. Troposphere

  B. Stratosphere

  C. Mesosphere

  D. Thermosphere

(Average)

122. **Which of the following type of rocks are made from magma?**

  A. Fossils

  B. Sedimentary

  C. Metamorphic

  D. Igneous

(Rigorous)

123. **What is the most accurate description of the water cycle?**

  A. Rain comes from clouds, filling the ocean. The water then evaporates and becomes clouds again.

  B. Water circulates from rivers into groundwater and back, while water vapor circulates in the atmosphere.

  C. Water is conserved except for chemical or nuclear reactions, and any drop of water could circulate through clouds, rain, groundwater, and surface water.

  D. Weather systems cause chemical reactions to break water into its atoms.

(Easy)

124. **Which of the following is the best definition of *meteorite*?**

  A. A meteorite is a mineral composed of mica and feldspar

  B. A meteorite is material from outer space that has struck the Earth's surface

  C. A meteorite is an element that has properties of both metals and nonmetals

  D. A meteorite is a very small unit of length measurement

Fine Arts, Health, and Physical Education

(Easy)

125. **The process of critiquing artwork is:**

  A. An asset for all teachers

  B. Beyond the scope of the elementary teacher

  C. Fairly complex and requires specific training

  D. Limited to art historians and professional artists

(Rigorous)

126. **All of the following are examples of useful art tools for early childhood students EXCEPT:**

  A. Color wheel

  B. Oversized crayons and pencils

  C. Fine-tipped brushes

  D. Clay

(Average)

127. **The Renaissance period was concerned with the rediscovery of the works of:**

   A. Italy

   B. Japan

   C. Germany

   D. Classical Greece and Rome

(Rigorous)

128. **Which of the following statements is most accurate?**

   A. Most artists work alone and are rarely affected by the work of other artists

   B. Artists in every field are influenced and inspired by the works of others in the various disciplines in the humanities

   C. It is rare for visual arts to be influenced by literature or poetry

   D. The political climate of an era affects the art of the period only on specific occasions throughout history

(Average)

129. **A combination of three or more tones sounded at the same time is called a:**

   A. Harmony

   B. Consonance

   C. Chord

   D. Dissonance

(Average)

130. **A series of single tones that add up to a recognizable sound is called a:**

   A. Cadence

   B. Rhythm

   C. Melody

   D. Sequence

(Average)

131. **The term *conjunto* in music refers to:**

   A. Two instruments playing at the same time

   B. A tempo a little faster than allegro

   C. A musical style that involves playing with great feeling

   D. A type of Texas-Mexican music

(Rigorous)

132. **All of the following apply to critiquing music EXCEPT:**

   A. The keys steps are to listen, analyze, describe, and evaluate

   B. Avoid the use of musical terminology in order to facilitate students' enjoyment of music

   C. Have students develop their own rubrics for critiques

   D. Encourage students to work in pairs

(Easy)

133. **Which of the following is NOT a type of muscle tissue?**

   A. Skeletal

   B. Cardiac

   C. Smooth

   D. Fiber

(Average)

134. **Which of these is a type of joint?**

   A. Ball and socket

   B. Hinge

   C. Pivot

   D. All of the above

(Average)

135. **A physical education instructor anticipates and prevents potential injuries, watches for hidden injuries, and takes an injury evaluation of the entire class. Which of the following strategies to prevent injuries is the teacher demonstrating?**

A. Maintaining hiring standards

B. Proper use of equipment

C. Proper procedures for emergencies

D. Participant screening

(Average)

136. **All of the following are signs of anorexia nervosa EXCEPT:**

A. Malnutrition

B. Behavior regression

C. No outward signs

D. Recognizable weight loss

(Rigorous)

137. **Which of the following refers to a muscle's ability to contract over a period of time and maintain strength?**

A. Cardiovascular fitness

B. Muscle endurance

C. Muscle fitness

D. Muscle force

(Average)

138. **A game of "Simon Says" is an opportunity for the teacher to asses which of the following?**

A. Concept of body awareness

B. Concept of spatial awareness

C. Concept of direction and movement

D. Concept of speed and movement

(Average)

139. **Bending, stretching, and turning are examples of which type of skills?**

A. Locomotor skills

B. Nonlocomotor skills

C. Manipulative skills

D. Rhythmic skills

(Rigorous)

140. **Which of the following statements is NOT true?**

A. Children's motor development and physical fitness are affected by a range of factors, including social, psychological, familial, genetic, and cultural factors

B. Motor development is complete by the time a student reaches sixth grade

C. A family's economic status can affect a student's motor development

D. A physical education program can have a positive impact on a student's level of physical fitness

Answer Key

ANSWER KEY								
1. D	17. B	33. B	49. C	65. A	81. C	97. B	113. C	129. C
2. D	18. D	34. D	50. B	66. B	82. A	98. B	114. A	130. C
3. D	19. A	35. A	51. A	67. B	83. D	99. C	115. D	131. D
4. A	20. D	36. B	52. A	68. C	84. B	100. C	116. C	132. B
5. C	21. C	37. C	53. C	69. D	85. A	101. B	117. A	133. D
6. A	22. C	38. B	54. D	70. A	86. A	102. B	118. D	134. D
7. D	23. A	39. D	55. C	71. A	87. A	103. C	119. B	135. D
8. C	24. A	40. D	56. A	72. C	88. C	104. A	120. C	136. C
9. D	25. A	41. B	57. C	73. D	89. C	105. B	121. A	137. B
10. B	26. D	42. A	58. D	74. A	90. A	106. D	122. D	138. A
11. A	27. B	43. C	59. C	75. B	91. C	107. C	123. C	139. B
12. A	28. A	44. D	60. A	76. B	92. D	108. A	124. B	140. B
13. B	29. C	45. B	61. C	77. B	93. D	109. B	125. A	
14. A	30. A	46. D	62. C	78. D	94. A	110. D	126. C	
15. A	31. B	47. C	63. C	79. C	95. D	111. B	127. D	
16. A	32. A	48. D	64. B	80. A	96. A	112. C	128. B	

Rigor Table

RIGOR TABLE	
Rigor level	**Questions**
Easy 20%	2, 16, 19, 22, 27, 36, 39, 42, 43, 47, 50, 54, 56, 57, 63, 71, 72, 76, 78, 79, 84, 87, 93, 100, 110, 112, 124, 125, 133
Average 40%	1, 6, 8, 9, 12, 14, 18, 20, 23, 24, 29, 30, 34, 35, 38, 40, 46, 48, 55, 58, 61, 64, 66, 67, 68, 70, 73, 75, 81, 86, 88, 89, 91, 92, 95, 97, 98, 99, 101, 102, 104, 106, 111, 113, 115, 121, 122, 127, 129, 130, 131, 134, 135, 136, 138, 139
Rigorous 40%	3, 4, 5, 7, 10, 11, 13, 15, 17, 21, 25, 26, 28, 31, 32, 33, 37, 41, 44,45, 49, 51, 52, 53, 59, 60, 62, 65, 69, 74, 77, 80, 82, 83, 85, 90, 94, 96, 103, 105, 107, 108, 109, 114, 116, 117, 118, 119, 120, 123, 126, 128, 132, 137, 140

Sample Test with Rationales

Reading, Language, and Literature

(Average)

1. **While standing in line at the grocery store, three-year-old Megan says to her mother in a regular tone of voice, "Mom, why is that woman so fat?" This indicates a lack of understanding of:**

   A. Syntax

   B. Semantics

   C. Morphology

   D. Pragmatics

   Answer: D. Pragmatics

   Pragmatics is the development and understanding of the social relevance of conversations and topics. It develops as children age. In this situation, Megan simply does not understand, as an adult would, how that question could be viewed as offensive.

(Easy)

2. **Oral language development can be enhanced by which of the following?**

   A. Meaningful conversation

   B. Storytelling

   C. Alphabet songs

   D. All of the above

   Answer: D. All of the above

   Effective oral language development can be encouraged by many different activities including storytelling, rhyming books, meaningful conversation, alphabet songs, dramatic playtime, listening games, and more.

(Rigorous)

3. **Ms. Chomski is presenting a new story to her class of first graders. In the story, a family visits their grandparents' house, where they all gather around a record player and listen to music. Many students do not understand what a record player is, especially some children for whom English is not their first language. Which of the following would be best for Ms. Chomski to do?**

   A. Discuss what a record player is with her students

   B. Compare a record player with a CD player

   C. Have students look up *record player* in a dictionary

   D. Show the students a picture of a record player

   Answer: D. Show the students a picture of a record player

   The most effective method for ensuring adequate comprehension is through direct experience. Sometimes this cannot be accomplished, and therefore it is necessary to utilize pictures or other visual aids to provide students with experience in another mode besides oral language.

(Rigorous)

4. **Reading aloud correlates with all of the following EXCEPT:**

   A. Reader self-confidence

   B. Better reading comprehension

   C. Literacy development

   D. Overall school success

   Answer: A. Reader self-confidence

   Reading aloud promotes language acquisition and correlates with literacy development, better reading comprehension, and overall success in school. It may or may not promote reader self-confidence, depending on the reader and his or her skills and personality.

(Rigorous)

5. **Mr. Johns is using an activity that involves having students analyze the public speaking of others. All of the following would be guidelines for this activity EXCEPT:**

   A. The speeches to be evaluated are not given by other students

   B. The rubric for evaluating the speeches includes pace, pronunciation, body language, word choice, and visual aids

   C. The speeches to be evaluated are best presented live to give students a more engaging learning experience

   D. One of Mr. Johns' goals is to help students improve their own public speaking skills

   Answer: C. The speeches to be evaluated are best presented live to give students a more engaging learning experience

   Analyzing the speech of others is an excellent technique for helping students improve their own public speaking abilities. In most circumstances, students cannot view themselves as they give speeches and presentations, so when they get the opportunity to critique, question, and analyze others' speeches, they begin to learn what works and what doesn't work in effective public speaking. However, an important word of warning: *do not* have students critique each other's public speaking skills. It could be very damaging to a student to have his or her peers point out what did not work in a speech. Instead, video is a great tool teachers can use. Any appropriate source of public speaking can be used in the classroom for students to analyze and critique.

(Average)

6. **All of the following are true about phonological awareness EXCEPT:**

   A. It may involve print

   B. It is a prerequisite for spelling and phonics

   C. Activities can be done by the children with their eyes closed

   D. It starts before letter recognition is taught

   Answer: A. It may involve print

   All of the options are aspects of phonological awareness except the first one, A, because phonological awareness does not involve print.

(Rigorous)

7. **Which of the following explains a significant difference between phonics and phonemic awareness?**

   A. Phonics involves print, while phonemic awareness involves language

   B. Phonics is harder than phonemic awareness

   C. Phonics involves sounds, while phonemic awareness involves letters

   D. Phonics is the application of sounds to print, while phonemic awareness is oral

   Answer: D. Phonics is the application of sounds to print, while phonemic awareness is oral

   Both phonics and phonemic awareness involve sounds, but phonics applies these sounds to print. Phonemic awareness is an oral activity.

(Average)

8. **Theorist Marilyn Jager Adams, who researches early reading, has outlined five basic types of phonemic awareness tasks. Which of the following is NOT one of the tasks noted by Jager Adams?**

   A. Ability to do oddity tasks

   B. Ability to orally blend words and split syllables

   C. Ability to sound out words when reading aloud

   D. Ability to do phonics manipulation tasks

   Answer: C. Ability to sound out words when reading aloud

   The tasks Jager Adams has outlined do not include the ability to sound out words when reading aloud. Her five tasks are: 1) The ability to hear rhymes and alliteration, 2) The ability to do oddity tasks (recognize the member of a set that is different, or odd, among the group), 3) The ability to orally blend words and split syllables, 4) The ability to orally segment words, and 5) The ability to do phonics manipulation tasks.

(Average)

9. **Activities that parents can practice at home with their children to improve phonological and phonemic awareness include which of the following?**

   A. Play games with words that sound alike as you experience them in everyday home activities

   B. Demonstrate how sounds blend together in familiar words

   C. Play a game in which the goal is to find objects with names that begin with a certain initial sound

   D. All of the above

   Answer: D. All of the above

   Games and demonstrations that help children distinguish sounds are all useful in improving phonological and phonemic awareness.

(Rigorous)

10. **The alphabetic principle can best be described by which of the following statements?**

    A. Most reading skills need to be acquired through regular teaching of the alphabet

    B. Written words are composed of patterns of letters that represent the sounds of spoken words

    C. Written words are composed of patterns that must be memorized in order to read well

    D. Spoken words (regular and irregular) lead to phonological reading

Answer: B. Written words are composed of patterns of letters that represent the sounds of spoken words

The alphabetic principle is sometimes called graphophonemic awareness. This technical reading foundation term describes the understanding that written words are composed of patterns of letters that represent the sounds of spoken words.

There are basically two parts to the alphabetic principle: 1) An understanding that words are made up of letters and that each letter has a specific sound, and 2) The correspondence between sounds and letters leads to phonological reading. This consists of reading regular and irregular words and doing advanced analysis of words.

(Rigorous)

11. **Which of the following is NOT true about multisensory approaches to teaching the alphabetic principle?**

    A. Some children can only learn through multisensory techniques

    B. Multisensory techniques give multiple cues to enhance memory and learning

    C. Quilt book, rhyme time, letter path, and shape game are multisensory strategies

    D. Multisensory techniques require direct teaching and ongoing engagement

Answer: A. Some children can only learn through multisensory techniques

Although some children may learn more effectively when multiple senses are involved, there is no evidence to suggest that this is the only way some students can learn. Multisensory techniques enhance learning and memory and provide more solid grounding when students later learn to apply phonics skills to print. Such activities demand teacher engagement with students to directly teach the concepts related to the alphabetic principle.

(Average)

12. **Activities that facilitate learning the alphabetic principle include:**

    A. Read alouds, alphabet art, concept books, and name sorts

    B. Read alouds, shared reading, concept books, and picture books

    C. Picture books, concept books, and alphabet books

    D. Alphabet art, name sorts, shared reading, and phonics

Answer: A. Read alouds, alphabet art, concept books, and name sorts

Read alouds, alphabet art, concept books, name sorts, and shared reading are all activities that help young children learn the alphabetic principle. Picture books and phonics develop other aspects of reading skills and literacy development.

(Rigorous)

13. **Which of the following is a convention of print that children learn during reading activities?**

    A. The meaning of words

    B. The left-to-right motion

    C. The purpose of print

    D. The identification of letters

Answer: B. The left-to-right motion

During reading activities, children learn conventions of print. Children learn the way to hold a book, where to begin to read, the left-to-right motion, and how to continue from one line to another.

(Average)

14. **Alphabet books are classified as:**

    A. Concept books

    B. Easy-to-read books

    C. Board books

    D. Picture books

Answer: A. Concept books

Concept books combine language and pictures to show concrete examples of abstract concepts. One category of concept books is alphabet books, which are popular with children from preschool through grade 2.

(Rigorous)

15. **To determine an author's purpose, a reader must:**

    A. Use his or her own judgment

    B. Verify all the facts

    C. Link the causes to the effects

    D. Rely on common sense

Answer: A. Use his or her own judgment

An author may have more than one purpose for writing. Verifying all the facts, linking causes to effects, and relying on common sense can all help a reader in identifying the author's purpose, but the reader must use his or her own judgment to determine the author's purpose for writing.

(Easy)

16. **To decode is to:**

    A. Construct meaning

    B. Sound out a printed sequence of letters

    C. Use a special code to decipher a message

    D. None of the above

Answer: A. Construct meaning

Word analysis (phonics or decoding) is the process readers use to figure out unfamiliar words based on written patterns. Decoding is the process of constructing the meaning of an unknown word.

(Rigorous)

17. **Contextual redefinition is a strategy that encourages children to use the context more effectively by presenting them with sufficient vocabulary __________ the reading of a text.**

    A. after

    B. before

    C. during

    D. None of the above

Answer: B. before

Contextual redefinition is a strategy that encourages children to use the context more effectively by presenting them with sufficient context before they begin reading. To apply this strategy, the teacher should first select unfamiliar words for teaching. No more than two or three words should be selected for direct teaching.

(Average)

18. **What is the best place for students to find appropriate synonyms, antonyms, and other related words to enhance their writing?**

    A. Dictionary

    B. Spell check

    C. Encyclopedia

    D. Thesaurus

Answer: D. Thesaurus

Students need plenty of exposure to new words. A thesaurus is an excellent resource to use when writing. Students can use a thesaurus to find appropriate synonyms, antonyms, and other related words to enhance their writing.

(Easy)

19. **Which of the following indicates that a student is a fluent reader?**

    A. Reads texts with expression or prosody

    B. Reads word to word and haltingly

    C. Must intentionally decode a majority of the words

    D. In a writing assignment, sentences are poorly organized structurally

Answer: A. Reads texts with expression or prosody

The teacher should listen to the children read aloud, but there are also clues to reading levels in their writing.

(Average)

20. **Which of the following reading strategies is NOT associated with fluent reading abilities?**

    A. Pronouncing unfamiliar words by finding similarities with familiar words

    B. Establishing a purpose for reading

    C. Formulating questions about the text while reading

    D. Reading sentences word by word

Answer: D. Reading sentences word by word

Pronouncing unfamiliar words by finding similarities with familiar words, establishing a purpose for reading, and formulating questions about the text while reading are all strategies fluent readers use to enhance their comprehension of a text. Reading sentences word by word is a trait of a nonfluent reader. It inhibits comprehension, because the reader focuses on each word separately rather than the meaning of the whole sentence and how it fits into the text.

(Rigorous)

21. **Automaticity refers to all of the following EXCEPT:**

    A. Automatic whole-word identification

    B. Automatic recognition of syllable types

    C. Automatic reactions to the content of a paragraph

    D. Automatic identification of graphemes as they relate to four basic word types

Answer: C. Automatic reactions to the content of a paragraph

Automaticity is the ability to automatically recognize words, graphemes, word types, and syllables. This ability progresses through various stages and facilitates reading fluency and prosody. Automaticity is not related to the content of a paragraph or the student's reactions to the content.

(Easy)

22. **Which of the following activities are likely to improve fluency?**

    A. Partner reading and a reading theater

    B. Phrased reading

    C. Both A and B

    D. None of the above

Answer: C. Both A and B

Partner reading, tutors, a reading theater, modeling fluent reading, and opportunities for phrased reading are all strategies designed to enhance fluency.

(Average)

23. **Students are about to read a text that contains words that will need to be understood for them to understand the text. When should the vocabulary be introduced to students?**

    A. Before reading

    B. During reading

    C. After reading

    D. It should not be introduced

Answer: A. Before reading

Vocabulary should be introduced before reading if there are words in the text that are necessary for reading comprehension.

(Average)

24. **Which of the following is an important feature of vocabulary instruction, according to the National Reading Panel?**

    A. Repetition of vocabulary items

    B. Keeping a consistent task structure at all times

    C. Teaching vocabulary in more than one language

    D. Isolating vocabulary instruction from other subjects

    Answer: A. Repetition of vocabulary items

    According to the National Reading Panel, repetition and multiple exposures to vocabulary items are important. Students should be given vocabulary items that are likely to appear in many contexts.

(Rigorous)

25. **A sixth-grade science teacher has given her class a paper to read on the relationship between food and weight gain. The writing contains signal words and phrases such as "because," "consequently," "this is how," and "due to." This paper has which text structure?**

    A. Cause and effect

    B. Compare and contrast

    C. Description

    D. Sequencing

    Answer: A. Cause and effect

    Cause and effect is the relationship between two things when one thing makes something else happen. Writers use this text structure to show order, inform, speculate, and change behavior. This text structure identifies potential causes of a problem or issue in an orderly way.

(Rigorous)

26. **Which of the following is NOT a strategy of teaching reading comprehension?**

    A. Asking questions

    B. Utilizing graphic organizers

    C. Focusing on mental images

    D. Manipulating sounds

    Answer: D. Manipulating sounds

    Comprehension means that the reader can ascribe meaning to text. Teachers can use many strategies to teach comprehension, including questioning, asking students to paraphrase or summarize, utilizing graphic organizers, and focusing on mental images.

(Easy)

27. **The children's literature genre came into its own in the:**

    A. Seventeenth century

    B. Eighteenth century

    C. Nineteenth century

    D. Twentieth century

Answer: B. Eighteenth century

Children's literature is a genre of its own that emerged as a distinct and independent form in the second half of the eighteenth century. *The Visible World in Pictures*, by John Amos Comenius, a Czech educator, was one of the first printed works of children's literature and the first picture book.

(Rigorous)

28. **When evaluating reference sources, students should do all of the following EXCEPT:**

   A. Look for self-published books by the author as evidence of expert status

   B. Examine the level of detail provided by the source

   C. Review the references at the end of the book or article

   D. See if the author presents both sides of an argument or viewpoint

Answer: A. Look for self-published books by the author as evidence of expert status

Anyone can self-publish a book or pamphlet. Experience and background in the subject area have not been reviewed by anyone in many of these cases. Therefore, more research needs to be done to determine whether a source document is based on reliable, expert information when it has been published by the author.

(Average)

29. **Graphic organizers:**

   A. Are used primarily in grades K-3

   B. Work better with poetry than other forms of writing

   C. Help readers think critically by pulling out the main idea and supporting details

   D. Generally aren't helpful to ELL students

Answer: C. Help readers think critically by pulling out the main idea and supporting details

Graphic organizers help readers think critically about an idea, concept, or story by pulling out the main idea and supporting details. These pieces of information can then be depicted graphically through the use of connected geometric shapes. Readers who develop this skill can use it to increase their reading comprehension. Graphic organizers are useful for all ages and types of students and for many forms for literature and writing.

(Average)

30. **Which of the following helps students in a way that is similar to using a glossary?**

   A. Information in the text such as charts, graphs, maps, diagrams, captions, and photos

   B. Prewriting

   C. Classroom discussion of the main idea

   D. Paired reading

Answer: A. Information in the text such as charts, graphs, maps, diagrams, captions, and photos

Charts, graphs, maps, diagrams, captions, and photos in text can work in the same way as looking up unknown words in a glossary. They can provide more insight into and clarification of the concepts and ideas the author is conveying. Students may need to develop these skills to interpret the information accurately.

(Rigorous)

31. **Which of these describes the best way to teach spelling?**

   A. At the same time that grammar and sentence structure are taught

   B. Within the context of meaningful language experiences

   C. Independently, so that students can concentrate on spelling

   D. In short lessons, because students pick up spelling almost immediately

Answer: B. Within the context of meaningful language experiences

Spelling should be taught within the context of meaningful language experiences. Giving a child a list of words to learn to spell and then testing the child on the words every Friday will not aid in the development of spelling. The child must be able to use the words in context and they must have some meaning for the child. The assessment of how well a child can spell or where there are problems also has to be done within a meaningful context.

(Rigorous)

32. **Which of the following sentences contains an error in agreement?**

   A. Jennifer is one of the women who writes for the magazine.

   B. Each one of their sons plays a different sport.

   C. This band has performed at the Odeum many times.

   D. The data are available online at the listed Web site.

Answer: A. Jennifer is one of the women who writes for the magazine.

Women is the plural subject of the verb. The verb should be *write.*

(Rigorous)

33. **All of the following sentences are correctly punctuated EXCEPT:**

   A. "The airplane crashed on the runway during takeoff."

   B. I was embarrassed when Ms. White said, "Your slip is showing!"

   C. "The middle school readers were unprepared to understand Bryant's poem 'Thanatopsis.'"

   D. The hall monitor yelled, "Fire! Fire!"

Answer: B. I was embarrassed when Ms. White said, "Your slip is showing!"

B is incorrectly punctuated because, in exclamatory sentences, the exclamation point should be positioned outside the closing quotation marks if the quote itself is a statement, command, or cited title. The exclamation point is correctly positioned in choice D because the sentence is declarative but the quotation is an exclamation.

(Average)

34. **Which of the following is NOT a technique of prewriting?**

    A. Clustering

    B. Listing

    C. Brainstorming

    D. Proofreading

    Answer: D. Proofreading

    Proofreading cannot be a method of prewriting because it is done only on texts that have already been written.

(Average)

35. **Which of the following is NOT a prewriting strategy?**

    A. Analyzing sentences for variety

    B. Keeping an idea book

    C. Writing in a daily journal

    D. Writing down whatever comes to mind

    Answer: A. Analyzing sentences for variety

    Prewriting strategies assist students in a variety of ways. Common prewriting strategies include keeping an idea book for jotting down ideas, writing in a daily journal, and writing down whatever comes to mind, which is also called "free writing." Analyzing sentences for variety is a revising strategy.

(Easy)

36. **A student has written a paper with the following characteristics: written in first person; characters, setting, and plot; some dialogue; and events organized in chronological sequence with some flashbacks. In what genre has the student written?**

    A. Expository writing

    B. Narrative writing

    C. Persuasive writing

    D. Technical writing

    Answer: B. Narrative writing

    These are all characteristics of narrative writing. Expository writing is intended to give information such as an explanation or directions, and the information is logically organized. Persuasive writing gives an opinion in an attempt to convince the reader that a point of view is valid, or tries to persuade the reader to take a specific action. The goal of technical writing is to clearly communicate particular information to a targeted reader or group of readers.

(Rigorous)

37. **Exposition occurs within a story:**

    A. After the rising action

    B. After the denouement

    C. Before the rising action

    D. Before the setting

Answer: C. Before the rising action

Exposition is when characters and their situations are introduced. *Rising action* is the point at which conflict starts to occur and is often a turning point. *Denouement* is the final resolution of the plot.

(Average)

38. **Which of the following messages provides the most accessibility to the most learners?**

A. Print message

B. Audiovisual message

C. Graphic message

D. Audio message

Answer: B. Audiovisual message

An audiovisual message is the most accessible for learners. It has the advantages of both mediums, the graphic and the audio. Learners' eyes and ears are engaged. Nonreaders get significant access to content. On the other hand, viewing an audiovisual presentation is an even more passive activity than listening to an audio message because information is coming to learners effortlessly through two senses.

(Easy)

39. **Which of the following advertising techniques is based on appealing to our desire to think for ourselves?**

A. Celebrity endorsement

B. Intelligence

C. Independence

D. Lifestyle

Answer: D. Independence

Celebrity endorsements associate product use with a well-known person. Intelligence techniques are based on making consumers feel smart and like they cannot be fooled. Lifestyle approaches are designed to make consumers feel like they are part of a particular way of living.

(Average)

40. **Which of the following is NOT useful in creating visual media for the classroom?**

A. Limit your graph to just one idea or concept and keep the content simple

B. Balance substance and visual appeal

C. Match the information to the format that will fit it best

D. Make sure to cite all references to copyrighted material

Answer: D. Make sure to cite all references to copyrighted material

Although it may be important to acknowledge copyright and intellectual property ownership of some materials used in visual media, this factor is not a guideline for creating useful visual media for the classroom.

(Rigorous)

41. **All of the following are examples of ongoing informal assessment techniques used to observe student progress EXCEPT:**

A. Analysis of student work product

B. Collection of data from assessment tests

C. Effective questioning

D. Observation of students

Answer: B. Collection of data from assessment tests

Assessment tests are formal progress-monitoring measures.

(Easy)

42. **Which of the following is a formal reading-level assessment?**

    A. A standardized reading test

    B. A teacher-made reading test

    C. An interview

    D. A reading diary

Answer: A. A standardized reading test

If the assessment is standardized, it has to be objective, whereas B, C, and D are all subjective assessments.

(Easy)

43. **Which of the following is NOT considered a reading level?**

    A. Independent

    B. Instructional

    C. Intentional

    D. Frustrational

Answer: C. Intentional

Intentional is not a reading level. Reading levels for the purpose of assessment and planning instruction are as follows:

Independent. This is the level at which the child can read text totally on his or her own. When reading books at the independent level, students will be able to decode between 95 and 100 percent of the words and comprehend the text with 90 percent or better accuracy.

Instructional. This is the level at which the student should be taught because it provides enough difficulty to increase his or her reading skills without providing so much that it is too cumbersome to finish the selection. Typically, the acceptable range of accuracy is between 85 and 94 percent, with 75 percent or greater comprehension.

Frustrational. Books at a student's frustrational level are too difficult for the child and should not be used. The frustrational level is any text with less than 85 percent word accuracy and/or less than 75 percent comprehension.

(Rigorous)

44. **Which of the following are good choices for supporting a thesis?**

    A. Reasons

    B. Examples

    C. Answer to the question, "why?"

    D. All of the above

Answer: D. All of the above

The correct answer is D. When answering the question "why?" you are giving reasons, but those reasons need to be supported with examples.

(Rigorous)

45. **Which of the following should NOT be included in the opening paragraph of an informative essay?**

    A. Thesis sentence

    B. Details and examples supporting the main idea

    C. A broad general introduction to the topic

    D. A style and tone that grabs the reader's attention

Answer: B. Details and examples supporting the main idea

The introductory paragraph should introduce the topic, capture the reader's interest, state the thesis, and prepare the reader for the main points in the essay. Details and examples, however, should be given in the second part of the essay to help develop the thesis.

Mathematics

(Average)

46. **Which of the following is NOT a true statement regarding manipulatives in mathematics instruction?**

    A. Manipulatives are materials that students can physically handle

    B. Manipulatives help students make concrete concepts abstract

    C. Manipulatives include fingers, tiles, paper folding, and ice cream sticks

    D. Manipulatives help students make abstract concepts concrete

Answer: D. Manipulatives help students make concrete concepts abstract

Manipulatives are materials that students can physically handle and move, such as fingers and tiles. Manipulatives allow students to understand mathematic concepts by allowing them to see concrete examples of abstract processes. Manipulatives are attractive to students because they appeal to the their visual and tactile senses.

(Easy)

47. **All of the following are tools that can strengthen students' mathematical understanding EXCEPT:**

    A. Rulers, scales, and protractors

    B. Calculators, counters, and measuring containers

    C. Software and hardware

    D. Money and software

Answer: C. Software and hardware

Students' understanding of mathematical concepts is strengthened when they use tools to help make the abstract concepts become concrete realities. Teachers have a wide variety of tools available to help students learn mathematics. These include all of the above except for hardware. Hardware is technically not a tool but part of the infrastructure of the classroom.

(Average)

48. **Which of the following is NOT a good example of helping students make connections between the real world and mathematics?**

   A. Studying a presidential election from the perspective of the math involved

   B. Using weather concepts to teach math

   C. Having student helpers take attendance

   D. Reviewing major mathematical theorems on a regular basis

   Answer: D. Reviewing major mathematical theorems on a regular basis

   Theorems are abstract math concepts, and reviews, while valuable, are not an example of using everyday events to teach math. Teachers can increase student interest in math by relating mathematical concepts to familiar events in their lives and using real-world examples and data whenever possible. Instead of presenting only abstract concepts and examples, teachers should relate concepts to everyday situations to shift the emphasis from memorization and abstract application to understanding and applied problem-solving. This will not only improve students' grasp of math ideas and keep them engaged, it will also help answer the perennial question, "Why do we have to learn math?"

(Rigorous)

49. **Which of the following is an example of the associative property?**

   A. $a(b + c) = ab + bc$

   B. $a + 0 = a$

   C. $(a + b) + \mathrm{c} = a + (b + c)$

   D. $a + b = b + a$

   Answer: C. $(a + b) + c = a + (b + c)$

   The associative property is when the parentheses of a problem are switched.

(Easy)

50. **What is the greatest common factor of 16, 28, and 36?**

   A. 2

   B. 4

   C. 8

   D. 16

   Answer: B. 4

   The smallest number in this set is 16; its factors are 1, 2, 4, 8, and 16. 16 is the largest factor, but it does not divide into 28 or 36. Neither does 8. Four does factor into both 28 and 36.

(Rigorous)

51. **Mathematical operations are done in the following order:**

A. Simplify inside grouping characters such as parentheses, brackets, square roots, fraction bars, etc.; multiply out expressions with exponents; do multiplication or division from left to right; do addition or subtraction from left to right

B. Do multiplication or division from left to right; simplify inside grouping characters such as parentheses, brackets, square roots, fraction bars, etc.; multiply out expressions with exponents; do addition or subtraction from left to right

C. Simplify inside grouping characters such as parentheses, brackets, square roots, fraction bars, etc.; do addition or subtraction from left to right; multiply out expressions with exponents; do multiplication or division from left to right

D. None of the above

Answer: A. Simplify inside grouping characters such as parentheses, brackets, square roots, fraction bars, etc.; multiply out expressions with exponents; do multiplication or division from left to right; do addition or subtraction from left to right

When facing a mathematical problem that requires all mathematical properties to be performed first, do the math within the parentheses, brackets, square roots, or fraction bars. Then multiply out expressions with exponents. Next, do multiplication or division. Finally, do addition or subtraction.

(Rigorous)

52. **Which of the following is an irrational number?**

A. .36262626262...

B. 4

C. 8.2

D. -5

Answer: A. .362626262626...

Irrational numbers are numbers that cannot be made into fractions. This number cannot be made into a fraction.

(Rigorous)

53. **The number 0 is a member of all of the following groups of numbers EXCEPT:**

A. Whole numbers

B. Real numbers

C. Natural numbers

D. Integers

Answer: C. Natural numbers

The number zero is a whole number, real number, and an integer, but the natural numbers (also known as the counting numbers) start with the number one, not zero.

(Easy)

54. **4,087,361: What number represents the ten thousands place?**

A. 4

B. 6

C. 0

D. 8

Answer: D. 8

The ten thousands place contains the number 8 in this number.

(Average)

55. **Two mathematics classes have a total of 410 students. The 8:00 a.m. class has 40 more students than the 10:00 a.m. class. How many students are in the 10:00 a.m. class?**

    A. 123.3

    B. 370

    C. 185

    D. 330

Answer: C. 185

Let $x =$ the number of students in the 8:00 a.m. class and $x - 40 =$ the number of students in the 10:00 a.m. class. There are 225 students in the 8:00 a.m. class, and $225 - 40 = 185$ in the 10:00 a.m. class, which is answer C.

(Easy)

56. **Three-dimensional figures in geometry are called:**

    A. Solids

    B. Cubes

    C. Polygons

    D. Blocks

Answer: A. Solids

Three-dimensional figures are referred to as solids.

(Easy)

57. **Volume is:**

    A. The area of the faces excluding the bases

    B. The total area of all the faces, including the bases

    C. The number of cubic units in a solid

    D. The measure around the object

Answer: C. The number of cubic units in a solid

Volume refers to how much "stuff" can be placed in a solid. Cubic units are one of many things that can be placed in a solid to measure its volume.

(Average)

58. **If a right triangle has legs with measurements of 3 cm and 4 cm, what is the measure of the hypotenuse?**

    A. 6 cm

    B. 1 cm

    C. 7 cm

    D. 5 cm

Answer: D. 5 cm

If you use the Pythagorean theorem, you will get 5 cm for the measure of the hypotenuse.

(Rigorous)

59. **If the radius of a right circular cylinder is doubled, how does its volume change?**

    A. No change

    B. Is doubled

    C. Is four times the original

    D. Is π times the original

Answer: C. Is four times the original

If the radius of a right circular cylinder is doubled, the volume is multiplied by four because in the formula, the radius is squared. Therefore, the new volume is 2×2, or four, times the original.

(Rigorous)

60. **What is the area of a rectangle if you know that the length of the base is 8 cm and the diagonal of the rectangle is 8.5 cm?**

    A. 24 cm^2

    B. 30 cm^2

    C. 18.9 cm^2

    D. 24 cm

Answer: A. 24 cm^2

The answer is A because the base of the rectangle is also one leg of the right triangle formed by the diagonal, and the diagonal is the hypotenuse of the triangle. To find the other leg of the triangle, you can use the Pythagorean theorem. Once you get the other leg of the triangle, that is also the height of the rectangle. To get the area, you multiply the base by the height. The reason the answer is A and not D is because area is measured in centimeters squared, not just centimeters.

(Average)

61. **An item that sells for $375.00 is put on sale for $120.00. What is the percentage of discount?**

    A. 25%

    B. 28%

    C. 68%

    D. 34%

Answer: C. 68%

In this problem, you must set up a cross-multiplication problem. You begin by placing $\frac{x}{100}$ to represent the variable you are solving for over 100%, and then you place $\frac{120}{375}$ to represent the new price over the original price. When you cross-multiply, you get 68, which is the percentage of the discount.

(Rigorous)

62. **What is a translation?**

    A. To turn a figure around a fixed point

    B. When two objects have the same shape and same size, but figures face in different directions

    C. To "slide" an object a fixed distance in a given direction

    D. The transformation that shrinks or makes a figure bigger

Answer: C. To "slide" an object a fixed distance in a given direction

A translation is when you slide an object a fixed distance but do not change the size of the object.

(Easy)

63. What measures could be used to report the distance traveled when walking around a track?

A. Degrees

B. Square meters

C. Kilometers

D. Cubic feet

Answer: C. Kilometers

Degrees measure angles; square meters measure area; cubic feet measure volume; and kilometers measure length or distance.

(Average)

64. Corporate salaries are listed for several employees. Which would be the best measure of central tendency?

$24,000	**$24,000**	**$26,000**
$28,000	**$30,000**	**$120,000**

A. Mean

B. Median

C. Mode

D. No difference

Answer: B. Median

The median provides the best measure of central tendency in this case, because the mode is the lowest number and the mean would be disproportionately skewed by the outlier, $120,000.

(Rigorous)

65. Given a drawer with 5 black socks, 3 blue socks, and 2 red socks, what is the probability that you will draw two black socks in two draws in a dark room?

A. $\frac{2}{9}$

B. $\frac{1}{4}$

C. $\frac{17}{18}$

D. $\frac{1}{18}$

Answer: A. $\frac{2}{9}$

In this example of conditional probability, the probability of drawing a black sock on the first draw is $\frac{5}{10}$. It is implied in the problem that there is no replacement, therefore the probability of obtaining a black sock in the second draw is $\frac{4}{9}$. Multiply the two probabilities and reduce to lowest terms.

(Average)

66. Suppose you have a bag of marbles that contains 2 red marbles, 5 blue marbles, and 3 green marbles. If you replace the first marble chosen, what is the probability you will choose 2 green marbles in a row?

A. $\frac{2}{5}$

B. $\frac{9}{100}$

C. $\frac{9}{10}$

D. $\frac{3}{5}$

Answer: B. $\frac{9}{100}$

When performing a problem in which you replace the item, multiply the first probability fraction by the second probability fraction and replace the item when finding the second probability.

(Average)

67. **In probability, the sample space represents:**

    A. An outcome of an experiment

    B. A list of all possible outcomes of an experiment

    C. The number of times you must flip a coin

    D. The amount of room needed to conduct an experiment

    Answer: B. A list of all possible outcomes of an experiment

    The sample space is the list of all possible outcomes for an experiment.

(Average)

68. **Deduction is:**

    A. Logical reasoning

    B. The process of arriving at a conclusion based on other statements that are known to be true

    C. Both A and B

    D. Neither A nor B

    Answer: C. Both A and B

    Deductive reasoning moves from a generalization or set of examples (such as numbers) to a specific conclusion or solution.

(Rigorous)

69. **Find the inverse of the following statement: If I like dogs, then I do not like cats.**

    A. If I like dogs, then I do like cats.

    B. If I like cats, then I like dogs.

    C. If I like cats, then I do not like dogs.

    D. If I do not like dogs, then I like cats.

    Answer: D. If I do not like dogs, then I like cats.

    When you take the inverse of a statement, you negate both statements. By negating both statements you take the opposite of the original statement.

(Average)

70. **Find the converse of the following statement: If I like math, then I do not like science.**

    A. If I do not like science, then I like math.

    B. If I like math, then I do not like science.

    C. If I do not like math, then I do not like science.

    D. If I like math, then I do not like science.

    Answer: A. If I do not like science, then I like math.

    When finding the converse of a statement, you take the second part of the statement and replace it with the first part of the statement. In other words, you reverse the statements.

(Easy)

71. **Which of the following is the basic language of mathematics?**

    A. Symbolic representation

    B. Number lines

    C. Arithmetic operations

    D. Deductive thinking

    Answer: A. Symbolic representation

    Symbolic representation is the basic language of mathematics. Converting data to symbols allows for easy manipulation and problem solving. Students should have the ability to recognize what the symbolic notation represents and to convert information into symbolic form.

(Easy)

72. **The mass of a cookie is closest to:**

    A. 0.5 kg

    B. 0.5 grams

    C. 15 grams

    D. 1.5 grams

    Answer: C. 15 grams

    A common estimation of mass used in elementary schools is that a paperclip has a mass of approximately one gram, which eliminates choices B and D, because they are very close to 1 gram. A common estimation of one kilogram is equal to one liter of water. Half of one liter of water is still much more than one cookie, eliminating choice A. Therefore, the best estimation for one cookie is narrowed to 15 grams, or choice C.

History and Social Science

(Average)

73. **Using graphics can enhance the presentation of social science information because:**

    A. They can explain complex relationships among various data points

    B. Charts and graphs summarize information well

    C. Maps can describe geographic distribution or historical information

    D. All of the above

    Answer: D. All of the above

    Social science reporting can be interesting and exciting without graphics; however, visual presentations can aid in bringing the data to life. Any idea presented visually in some manner is easier to understand than simply getting an idea across verbally.

(Rigorous)

74. **All of the following are key elements in planning a child-centered curriculum EXCEPT:**

    A. Referring students who need special tutoring

    B. Identifying students' prior knowledge and skills

    C. Sequencing learning activities

    D. Specifying behavioral objectives

Answer: A. Referring students who need special tutoring

Although referring students who need specialized services is an ongoing task, it is not a central element of the overall planning and organization of a curriculum. Well-thought-out planning includes specifying behavioral objectives, identifying students' entry behavior (knowledge and skills), selecting and sequencing learning activities to move students from entry behavior to objective, and evaluating the outcomes of instruction in order to improve planning.

(Average)

75. **The Texas Assessment of Knowledge and Skills (TAKS) test is an example of:**

A. Criterion-referenced assessment

B. Norm-referenced assessment

C. Performance-based assessment

D. Other type of assessment

Answer: B. Norm-referenced assessment

Norm-referenced tests (NRTs) are used to classify student learners for homogenous groupings based on ability levels or basic skills. In many school communities, NRTs are used to classify students into AP (Advanced Placement), honors, regular, or remedial classes that can significantly affect the student's future educational opportunities or success.

TAKS measures statewide curriculum in reading for grades 3–9; writing for grades 4 and 7; English language arts for grades 10 and 11; mathematics for grades 3–11; science for grades 5, 10, and 11; and social studies for grades 8, 10, and 11. The Spanish TAKS is given to grades 3–6. Satisfactory performance on the TAKS at grade 11 is prerequisite for a high school diploma.

(Easy)

76. **Ms. Gomez has a number of ELL students in her class. In order to meet their specific needs as second-language learners, which of the following would NOT be an appropriate approach?**

A. Pair students of different ability levels for English practice

B. Focus most of her instruction on teaching English rather than content

C. Provide accommodations during testing and with assignments

D. Use visual aids to help students make word links with familiar objects

Answer: B. Focus most of her instruction on teaching English rather than content

In working with ELL students, different approaches should be used to ensure that students (a) Get multiple opportunities to learn and practice English, and (b) Learn content. Content should not be given short shrift or be "dumbed down" for ELL students.

(Rigorous)

77. **Which one of the following is NOT a reason why Europeans came to the New World?**

  A. To find resources in order to increase wealth

  B. To establish trade

  C. To increase a ruler's power and importance

  D. To spread Christianity

Answer: B. To establish trade

The Europeans came to the New World for a number of reasons; they often came to find new natural resources to extract for manufacturing. The Portuguese, Spanish, and English were sent over to increase the monarch's power and to spread influences such as religion (Christianity) and culture. Therefore, the only reason given that Europeans didn't come to the New World was to establish trade.

(Easy)

78. **Which of the following were results of the Age of Exploration?**

  A. More complete and accurate maps and charts

  B. New and more accurate navigational instruments

  C. Proof that the Earth is round

  D. All of the above

Answer: D. All of the above

The importance of the Age of Exploration was not only the discovery and colonization of the New World, but also better maps and charts; new, accurate navigational instruments; increased knowledge; great wealth; new and different foods and items not previously known in Europe; a new hemisphere as a refuge from poverty and persecution and as a place to start a new and better life; and proof that Asia could be reached by sea and that the Earth was round.

(Easy)

79. **The belief that the United States should control all of North America was called:**

  A. Westward expansion

  B. Pan-americanism

  C. Manifest Destiny

  D. Nationalism

Answer: C. Manifest Destiny

The belief that the United States should control all of North America was called Manifest Destiny. This idea fueled much of the violence and aggression toward the Native Americans. Manifest Destiny was certainly driven by sentiments of (D), nationalism and gave rise to (A), westward expansion.

(Rigorous)

80. **Nationalism can be defined as the division of land and resources according to which of the following?**

    A. Religion, race, or political ideology

    B. Religion, race, or gender

    C. Historical boundaries, religion, or race

    D. Race, gender, or political ideology

    Answer: A. Religion, race, or political ideology

    Religion, race, and political ideology are some of the characteristics that determine national entity. Tribal membership, language, ethnic affiliation, and even treaty demarcations can dictate national boundaries. Historical boundaries may contribute to conflicts among people, but they are generally secondary to another affiliation. To date, gender has not been a determining factor, although the treatment of women, for example, may be a contributing factor in some nationalistic conflicts.

(Average)

81. **The study of the social behavior of minority groups is part of the field of:**

    A. Anthropology

    B. Psychology

    C. Sociology

    D. Cultural geography

    Answer: C. Sociology

    The study of social behavior in minority groups would be primarily in the field of sociology, because it is the discipline most concerned with social interaction. However, it could be argued that anthropology, psychology, and cultural geography would have some interest in the study of social behavior as well.

(Rigorous)

82. **Participant observation is a method of study most closely associated with and used in:**

    A. Anthropology

    B. Archaeology

    C. Sociology

    D. Political science

    Answer: A. Anthropology

    Participant observation is a method of study most closely associated with and used in anthropology, the study of human cultures. Archaeologists typically study the remains of people, animals, or other physical things. Sociology is the study of human society and usually involves surveys, controlled experiments, and field studies. Political science is the study of political life, including justice, freedom, power, and equality, using a variety of methods.

(Rigorous)

83. **For the historian studying ancient Egypt, which of the following would be least useful?**

    A. The record of an ancient Greek historian on Greek-Egyptian interaction

    B. Letters from an Egyptian ruler to his/her regional governors

    C. Inscriptions on stele of the fourteenth Egyptian dynasty

    D. Letters from a nineteenth-century Egyptologist to his wife

Answer: D. Letters from a nineteenth-century Egyptologist to his wife

Historians use primary sources from the actual time they are studying whenever possible. Ancient Greek records of interaction with Egypt, letters from an Egyptian ruler to regional governors, and inscriptions from the fourteenth Egyptian dynasty are all primary sources created at or near the actual time being studied. Letters from a nineteenth-century Egyptologist would not be considered primary sources, because they were created thousands of years after the time period being studied and may not even be about the subject being studied.

(Easy)

84. **The term *sectionalism* refers to:**

    A. Different regions of the continent

    B. Issues between the North and South

    C. Different regions of the country

    D. Different groups of countries

Answer: B. Issues between the North and South

The term *sectionalism* referred to slavery and related issues before the Civil War. The Southern economy was agricultural and used slave labor. The North was antislavery and industrial.

(Rigorous)

85. **Which political group pushed the Reconstruction measures through Congress after Lincoln's death?**

    A. The Radical Republicans

    B. The Radical Democrats

    C. The Whigs

    D. The Independents

Answer: A. The Radical Republicans

In 1866, the Radical Republicans won control of Congress and passed the Reconstruction Acts, which placed the governments of the southern states under the control of the federal military. With this backing, the Republicans began to implement their policies, such as granting all black men the vote and denying the vote to former Confederate soldiers. Congress had passed the Thirteenth, Fourteenth, and Fifteenth Amendments, granting citizenship and civil rights to blacks. Ratification of these amendments was a condition of readmission into the Union for the rebel states.

(Average)

86. **As a result of the Missouri Compromise:**

   A. Slavery was not allowed in the Louisiana Purchase

   B. The Louisiana Purchase was nullified

   C. Louisiana separated from the Union

   D. The Embargo Act was repealed

Answer: A. Slavery was not allowed in the Louisiana Purchase

The Missouri Compromise was the agreement that eventually allowed Missouri to enter the Union. It did not nullify the Louisiana Purchase or the Embargo Act or separate Louisiana from the Union. As a result of the Missouri Compromise, slavery was specifically banned north of the boundary 36° 30'.

(Easy)

87. **Which country was the Cold War foe of the United States?**

   A. Soviet Union

   B. Brazil

   C. Canada

   D. Argentina

Answer: A. Soviet Union

The Soviet Union was a Cold War superpower and foe of the United States, which was determined to fight the spread of Communism.

(Average)

88. **The international organization established to work for world peace at the end of the Second World War was the:**

   A. League of Nations

   B. United Federation of Nations

   C. United Nations

   D. United World League

Answer: C. United Nations

The international organization established to work for world peace at the end of the Second World War was the United Nations. From the ashes of the failed League of Nations, established following World War I, the United Nations continues to be a major player in world affairs today.

(Average)

89. **What event triggered World War I?**

   A. The fall of the Weimar Republic

   B. The resignation of the czar

   C. The assassination of Austrian Archduke Ferdinand

   D. The assassination of the czar

Answer: C. The assassination of Austrian Archduke Ferdinand

There were regional conflicts and feelings of intense nationalism prior to the outbreak of World War I. The precipitating factor was the assassination of Austrian Archduke Ferdinand and his wife while they were in Sarajevo, Serbia.

(Rigorous)

90. **What is the most significant environmental change in Texas over the last century?**

    A. The number of square miles devoted to living space

    B. Continued exploration for oil and gas

    C. Development along the Gulf Coast

    D. Changes in agricultural practices

Answer: A. The number of square miles devoted to living space

The most drastic change to the environment wrought by people has been the number of square miles devoted to living space. Texas still maintains vast areas of agricultural and ranch land, but that area is shrinking by the year, as more and more people claim and put stakes down on land designed exclusively for residential use. The farmers of the past lived on their land but also lived off it. Their houses were part of their farms and their jobs were working the land. Today, skyscrapers dot the skylines of large cities along with high-rise apartment buildings, which serve the sole function of providing living areas for the people who work in the large cities.

(Average)

91. **The end to hunting, gathering, and fishing of prehistoric people was due to:**

    A. Domestication of animals

    B. Building crude huts and houses

    C. Development of agriculture

    D. Organized government in villages

Answer: C. Development of agriculture

Although the domestication of animals, the building of huts and houses, and the first organized governments were all important steps made by early civilizations, it was the development of agriculture that ended the once-dominant practices of hunting, gathering, and fishing among prehistoric people. The development of agriculture provided a more efficient use of time and, for the first time, a surplus of food. This greatly improved the quality of life and contributed to early population growth.

(Average)

92. **Which of the following is most useful for showing differences in variables at a specific point in time?**

    A. Histogram

    B. Scatter plot

    C. Pie chart

    D. Bar graph

Answer: D. Bar graph

Bar graphs are simple and basic, showing a difference in variables at a specific point in time. Histograms are good for summarizing large sets of data in intervals. Pie charts show proportions, and scatter plots demonstrate correlations, or relationships between variables.

(Easy)

93. **Capitalism and communism are alike in that they are both:**

    A. Organic systems

    B. Political systems

    C. Centrally planned systems

    D. Economic systems

    Answer: D. Economic systems

    While economic and political systems are often closely connected, capitalism and communism are primarily economic systems. Capitalism is a system of economics that allows the open market to determine the relative value of goods and services. Communism is an economic system in which the market is planned by a central state. While communism is a centrally planned system, this is not true of capitalism. Organic systems are studied in biology, a natural science.

(Rigorous)

94. **During the 1920s, the United States stopped nearly all immigration. One of the reasons was:**

    A. Plentiful, cheap unskilled labor was no longer needed by industrialists

    B. War debts from World War I made it difficult to render financial assistance

    C. European nations were reluctant to allow people to leave since there was a need to rebuild populations and economic stability

    D. The United States did not become a member of the League of Nations

    Answer: A. Plentiful, cheap unskilled labor was no longer needed by industrialists

    The United States stopped nearly all immigration during the 1920s because the once much-needed cheap, unskilled labor jobs, made available by the once-booming industrial economy, were no longer needed. This had much to do with the increased use of machines to do the work once done by cheap, unskilled laborers.

(Average)

95. **In the 1800s, the era of industrialization and growth was characterized by:**

    A. Small firms

    B. Public ownership

    C. Worker-owned enterprises

    D. Monopolies and trusts

    Answer: D. Monopolies and trusts

    The era of industrialization and business expansion was characterized by big businesses and monopolies that merged into trusts. There were few small firms and there was no public ownership or worker-owned enterprises.

(Rigorous)

96. **Which one of the following would NOT be considered a result of World War II?**

   A. Economic depression and slow resumption of trade and financial aid

   B. Western Europe was no longer the center of world power

   C. The beginnings of new power struggles, not only in Europe but in Asia as well

   D. Territorial and boundary changes for many nations, especially in Europe

   Answer: A. Economic depressions and slow resumption of trade and financial aid

   Following World War II, the economy was vibrant and flourished from the stimulus of war and the world's increased dependence on U.S. industries. Therefore, World War II didn't result in economic depression and slow resumption of trade and financial aid. Western Europe was no longer the center of world power. New power struggles arose in Europe and Asia, and many European nations experienced changing territories and boundaries.

(Average)

97. **The New Deal was:**

   A. A trade deal with England

   B. A series of programs to provide relief during the Great Depression

   C. A new exchange rate regime

   D. A plan for tax relief

   Answer: B. A series of programs to provide relief during the Great Depression

   The New Deal consisted of a myriad of different programs aimed at providing relief during the Great Depression. Many of the programs were public works programs building bridges, roads, and other infrastructure.

(Average)

98. **Which of the following is an example of a direct democracy?**

   A. Elected representatives

   B. Greek city-states

   C. The Constitution

   D. The Confederate states

   Answer: B. Greek city-states

   The Greek city-states are an example of a direct democracy, because their leaders were elected directly by the citizens, and the citizens themselves were given a voice in government.

(Average)

99. **Many governments in Europe today have which of the following types of government?**

   A. Absolute monarchies

   B. Constitutional governments

   C. Constitutional monarchies

   D. Another form of government

Answer: C. Constitutional monarchies

Over the centuries, absolute monarchies were modified and constitutional monarchies emerged. This form of government recognizes a monarch as leader but invests most of the legal authority in a legislative body such as a Parliament.

Science

(Easy)

100. **Accepted procedures for preparing solutions include the use of:**

A. Alcohol

B. Hydrochloric acid

C. Distilled water

D. Tap water

Answer: C. Distilled water

Alcohol and hydrochloric acid should never be used to make solutions unless one is instructed to do so. All solutions should be made with distilled water because tap water contains dissolved particles that can affect the results of an experiment.

(Average)

101. **Laboratory activities contribute to student performance in all of the following domains EXCEPT:**

A. Process skills such as observing and measuring

B. Memorization skills

C. Analytical skills

D. Communication skills

Answer: B. Memorization skills

Laboratory activities develop a wide variety of investigative, organizational, creative, and communicative skills. The laboratory provides an optimal setting for motivating students while they experience what science is. Such learning opportunities are not focused on memorization but on critical thinking and doing. Laboratory activities enhance student performance in the following domains:

- Process skills: Observing, measuring, and manipulating physical objects
- Analytical skills: Reasoning, deduction, and critical thinking
- Communication skills: Organizing information and writing
- Conceptualization of scientific phenomena

(Average)

102. **Which is the correct order of methodology in the scientific method?**

1. **Collecting data.**
2. **Planning a controlled experiment.**
3. **Drawing a conclusion.**
4. **Hypothesizing a result.**
5. **Revisiting a hypothesis to answer a question.**

A. 1, 2, 3, 4, 5

B. 4, 2, 1, 3, 5

C. 4, 5, 1, 3, 2

D. 1, 3, 4, 5, 2

Answer: B. 4, 2, 1, 3, 5

The correct methodology for the scientific method is first to make a meaningful hypothesis (educated guess) and then to plan and execute a controlled experiment to test that hypothesis. Using the data collected in the experiment, the scientist then draws conclusions and attempts to answer the original question related to the hypothesis.

(Rigorous)

103. **In an experiment measuring the growth of bacteria at different temperatures, what is the independent variable?**

A. Number of bacteria

B. Growth rate of bacteria

C. Temperature

D. Size of bacteria

Answer: C. Temperature

To answer this question, recall that the independent variable in an experiment is the entity that the scientist changes in order to observe the effects. In this experiment, temperature is changed in order to measure growth of bacteria, so (C) is the answer. Note that choice (A) is the dependent variable, and neither (B) nor (D) is directly relevant to the question.

(Average)

104. **Which of the following is a misconception about the task of teaching science in elementary school?**

A. Teach facts as a priority over teaching how to solve problems

B. Involve as many senses as possible in the learning experience

C. Accommodate individual differences in pupils' learning styles

D. Consider the effect of technology on people rather than on material things

Answer: A. Teach facts as a priority over teaching how to solve problems

Prioritizing facts over problem solving is a common misconception in elementary schools. Often, teachers focus on requiring students to learn and recall facts and information alone, rather than teaching them how to apply the learned facts when solving real scientific problems. In fact, problem solving is a vital skill that students need to learn and utilize in all classroom settings, as well as in the real world. Choices B, C, and D all describe effective teaching strategies that exceptional teachers use in their science classrooms.

(Rigorous)

105. **Which of the following is the most accurate definition of a nonrenewable resource?**

A. A nonrenewable resource is never replaced once used

B. A nonrenewable resource is replaced on a time scale that is very long relative to human life spans

C. A nonrenewable resource is a resource that can only be manufactured by humans

D. A nonrenewable resource is a species that has already become extinct

Answer: B. A nonrenewable resource is replaced on a time scale that is very long relative to human life spans

Renewable resources are renewed, or replaced, in time for humans to use more of them. Examples include fast-growing plants, animals, and oxygen gas. (Note that while sunlight is often considered a renewable resource, it is actually a nonrenewable, but extremely abundant, resource.) Nonrenewable resources renew themselves only on very long time scales, usually geologic time scales. Examples include minerals, metals, and fossil fuels.

(Average)

106. **All of the following are hormones in the human body EXCEPT:**

A. Cortisol

B. Testosterone

C. Norepinephrine

D. Hemoglobin

Answer: D. Hemoglobin

Hemoglobin is a component of red blood cells. Cortisol and norepinephrine are stress-related hormones. Testosterone is a sex-related hormone.

(Rigorous)

107. **Models are used in science in all of the following ways EXCEPT:**

A. Models are crucial for understanding the structure and function of scientific processes

B. Models help us visualize the organs/ systems they represent

C. Models create exact replicas of the items they represent

D. Models are useful for predicting and foreseeing future events such as hurricanes

Answer: C. Models create exact replicas of the items they represent

One of the limitations of models is that they *cannot* be exact replicas of real objects or processes. However, they are very useful for conceptualization, visualization, and prediction.

(Rigorous)

108. **There are a number of common misconceptions that claim to be based in science. All of the following are misconceptions EXCEPT:**

   A. Evolution is a process that does not address the origins of life

   B. The average person uses only a small fraction of his or her brain

   C. Raw sugar causes hyperactive behavior in children

   D. Seasons are caused by the Earth's elliptical orbit

Answer: A. Evolution is a process that does not address the origins of life

The theory of evolution presupposes existing life, but does not explain the *origins* of life. This is a good example of a truth that can easily be misconstrued. Most people holding misconceptions are not aware that their beliefs are erroneous. It is critical that instructors understand common misconceptions in science so that they can not only avoid them but also correct them. Some of the most common misconceptions are derived from imprecise language—students often do not understand scientific terminology very well and words with precise scientific meaning are sometimes interpreted in a nonscientific, more general way. Also, media reporting on scientific subjects (particularly politically sensitive issues or popular science topics) is sometimes inaccurate or speculative. Finally, widely held public opinions of scientific topics are often incorrect or only partially correct.

(Rigorous)

109. **One characteristic of electrically charged objects is that their charge is conserved. This means that:**

   A. Because of the financial cost, electricity should be conserved

   B. A neutral object has no net charge

   C. Like charges repel and opposite charges attract

   D. None of the above

Answer: B. A neutral object has no net charge

A plastic rod that is rubbed with fur will become electrically charged and will attract small pieces of paper. The charge on the plastic rod rubbed with fur is negative. If the plastic rod and fur are initially neutral, when the fur charges the rod a negative charge is transferred from the fur to the rod. The net negative charge on the rod is equal to the net positive charge on the fur. This is an example of the charge being conserved.

(Easy)

110. **Which of the following describes a state of balance between opposing forces of change?**

   A. Equilibrium

   B. Homeostasis

   C. Ecological balance

   D. All of the above

Answer: D. All of the above

Homeostasis and ecological balance are specific examples of equilibrium, a state of balance between opposing forces of change.

(Average)

111. **Which of the following describes the amount of matter in an object?**

   A. Weight

   B. Mass

   C. Density

   D. Volume

Answer: B. Mass

Mass is a measure of the amount of matter in an object. Two objects of equal mass will balance each other on a simple balance scale, no matter where the scale is located. For instance, two rocks with the same mass that are in balance on Earth will also be in balance on the Moon. They will feel heavier on Earth than on the Moon because of the gravitational pull of the Earth. So, although the two rocks have the same mass, they will have different weights. Weight is the measure of the Earth's pull of gravity on an object. It can also be defined as the pull of gravity between other bodies. Volume is the amount of cubic space an object occupies, and density is the mass of a substance per unit of volume.

(Easy)

112. **Sound waves are produced by:**

   A. Pitch

   B. Noise

   C. Vibrations

   D. Sonar

Answer: C. Vibrations

Sound waves are produced by a vibrating body. The vibrating object moves forward and compresses the air in front of it; it then reverses direction so pressure on the air decreases and the air molecules expand. The vibrating air molecules move back and forth, parallel to the direction of motion of the wave as they pass the energy from adjacent air molecules closer to the source to air molecules farther away from the source.

(Average)

113. **The Doppler effect is associated most closely with which property of waves?**

   A. Amplitude

   B. Wavelength

   C. Frequency

   D. Intensity

Answer: C. Frequency

The Doppler effect accounts for an apparent increase in frequency when a wave source moves toward a wave receiver or apparent decrease in frequency when a wave source moves away from a wave receiver. (Note that the receiver could also be moving toward or away from the source.) As the wave fronts are released, motion toward the receiver mimics more frequent wave fronts, while motion away from the receiver mimics less frequent wave fronts. Meanwhile, the amplitude, wavelength, and intensity of the wave are not as relevant to this process (although moving closer to a wave source makes it seem more intense).

(Rigorous)

114. The energy of electromagnetic waves is:

A. Radiant energy

B. Acoustical energy

C. Thermal energy

D. Chemical energy

Answer: A. Radiant energy

Radiant energy is the energy of electromagnetic waves. Light, visible and otherwise, is an example of radiant energy. Acoustical energy, or sound energy, is the movement of energy through an object in waves. Energy that forces an object to vibrate creates sound. Thermal energy is the total internal energy of objects created by the vibration and movement of atoms and molecules. Heat is the transfer of thermal energy. Chemical energy is the energy stored in the chemical bonds of molecules. For example, the energy derived from gasoline is chemical energy. Other forms of energy include electrical, mechanical, and nuclear energy.

(Average)

115. Photosynthesis is the process by which plants make carbohydrates using:

A. The Sun, carbon dioxide, and oxygen

B. The Sun, oxygen, and water

C. Oxygen, water, and carbon dioxide

D. The Sun, carbon dioxide, and water

Answer: D. The Sun, carbon dioxide, and water

Photosynthesis requires the energy of the Sun, carbon dioxide, and water. Oxygen is a waste product of photosynthesis.

(Rigorous)

116. What is the correct sequence of organization of living things from lower to higher order?

A. Cell, organelle, organ, tissue, system, organism

B. Cell, tissue, organ, organelle, system, organism

C. Organelle, cell, tissue, organ, system, organism

D. Organelle, tissue, cell, organ, system, organism

Answer: C. Organelle, cell, tissue, organ, system, organism

Organelles are parts of the cell; cells make up tissue, which makes up organs. Organs work together in systems (e.g., the respiratory system), and the organism is the living thing as a whole.

(Rigorous)

117. What cell organelle contains the cell's stored food?

A. Vacuoles

B. Golgi apparatus

C. Ribosomes

D. Lysosomes

Answer: A. Vacuoles

In a cell, the subparts are called organelles. Of these, the vacuoles hold stored food (and water and pigments). The Golgi apparatus sorts molecules from other parts of the cell; the ribosomes are sites of protein synthesis; and the lysosomes contain digestive enzymes.

(Rigorous)

118. **Enzymes speed up reactions by:**

A. Utilizing ATP

B. Lowering pH, allowing reaction speed to increase

C. Increasing volume of substrate

D. Lowering energy of activation

Answer: D. Lowering energy of activation

Because enzymes are catalysts, they work the same way: They cause the formation of activated chemical complexes, which require a lower activation energy. Therefore, the answer is D. ATP is an energy source for cells, and pH or volume changes may or may not affect reaction rate, so these choices can be eliminated.

(Rigorous)

119. **Which of the following is a correct explanation for scientific evolution?**

A. Giraffes need to reach higher for leaves to eat, so their necks stretch. The giraffe babies are then born with longer necks. Eventually there are more long-necked giraffes in the population.

B. Giraffes with longer necks are able to reach more leaves, so they eat more and have more babies than other giraffes. Eventually there are more long-necked giraffes in the population.

C. Giraffes want to reach higher for leaves to eat, so they release enzymes into their bloodstream, which in turn causes fetal development of longer-necked giraffes. Eventually there are more long-necked giraffes in the population.

D. Giraffes with long necks are more attractive to other giraffes, so they get the best mating partners and have more babies. Eventually, there are more long-necked giraffes in the population.

Answer: B. Giraffes with longer necks are able to reach more leaves, so they eat more and have more babies than other giraffes. Eventually, there are more long-necked giraffes in the population.

Organisms with a life/reproductive advantage produce more offspring. Over many generations, this changes the proportions of the population. In any case, it is impossible for a stretched neck (A) or a fervent desire (C) to result in a biologically mutated baby. Although there are traits that are naturally selected because of mate attractiveness and fitness (D), this is not the primary situation here, so choice B is the answer.

(Rigorous)

120. **The theory of seafloor spreading explains:**

   A. The shapes of the continents

   B. How continents collide

   C. How continents move apart

   D. How continents sink to become part of the ocean floor

   Answer: C. How continents move apart

   According to the theory of seafloor spreading, the movement of the ocean floor causes continents to spread apart from one another. This occurs because crust plates split apart and new material is added to the plate edges. This process pulls the continents apart, or it may create new separations, and is believed to have caused the formation of the Atlantic Ocean.

(Average)

121. **Weather occurs in which layer of the atmosphere?**

   A. Troposphere

   B. Stratosphere

   C. Mesosphere

   D. Thermosphere

   Answer: A. Troposphere

   The atmosphere is divided into four main layers based on temperature.

   The troposphere is the layer closest to the Earth's surface and all weather phenomena occur here, because it is the layer with the most water vapor and dust. Air temperature decreases with increasing altitude. The average thickness is 7 miles (11 km). The stratosphere is a layer that contains very little water so clouds in this layer are very rare. The ozone layer is located in the upper portions of the stratosphere. Air temperature is fairly constant but does increase somewhat with height due to the absorption of solar energy and ultraviolet rays by the ozone layer. Air temperature decreases with height again in the mesosphere, which is the coldest layer, with temperatures in the range of -100°C at the top. The thermosphere extends upward into space. Oxygen molecules in this layer absorb energy from the Sun, causing temperatures to increase with height.

(Average)

122. **Which of the following type of rocks are made from magma?**

   A. Fossils

   B. Sedimentary

   C. Metamorphic

   D. Igneous

Answer: D. Igneous

Metamorphic rocks are formed by high temperatures and great pressures. Fluid sediments are transformed into solid sedimentary rocks. Only igneous rocks are formed from magma.

(Rigorous)

123. **What is the most accurate description of the water cycle?**

   A. Rain comes from clouds, filling the ocean. The water then evaporates and becomes clouds again.

   B. Water circulates from rivers into groundwater and back, while water vapor circulates in the atmosphere.

   C. Water is conserved except for chemical or nuclear reactions, and any drop of water could circulate through clouds, rain, groundwater, and surface water.

   D. Weather systems cause chemical reactions to break water into its atoms.

Answer: C. Water is conserved except for chemical or nuclear reactions, and any drop of water could circulate through clouds, rain, groundwater, and surface water.

All natural chemical cycles, including the water cycle, depend on the principle of conservation of mass. Any drop of water may circulate through the hydrologic system, ending up in a cloud, as rain, or as surface or groundwater. Although choices A and B describe parts of the water cycle, the most comprehensive answer is C.

(Easy)

124. **Which of the following is the best definition of *meteorite*?**

   A. A meteorite is a mineral composed of mica and feldspar

   B. A meteorite is material from outer space that has struck the Earth's surface

   C. A meteorite is an element that has properties of both metals and nonmetals

   D. A meteorite is a very small unit of length measurement

Answer: B. A meteorite is material from outer space that has struck the Earth's surface

Meteoroids are pieces of matter in space composed of particles of rock and metal. If a meteoroid travels through the Earth's atmosphere, friction causes burning and creates a "shooting star" or meteor. If the meteor strikes the Earth's surface, it is known as a meteorite. Note that although the suffix *-ite* often means a mineral, choice A is incorrect. Choice C refers to a *metalloid* rather than a meteorite, and choice D is simply a misleading pun on *meter*.

Fine Arts, Health, and Physical Education

(Easy)

125. **The process of critiquing artwork is:**

A. An asset for all teachers

B. Beyond the scope of the elementary teacher

C. Fairly complex and requires specific training

D. Limited to art historians and professional artists

Answer: A. An asset for all teachers

The elementary teacher's ability to think critically and problem-solve is reflected in his or her teaching in many ways, including the way art is perceived and discussed in the classroom. The capacity to critique a work of art is an asset for all teachers, especially in classrooms with integrated curricula, where art is taught in conjunction with other subjects, or in classrooms where there is no separate art program. Many people in various settings can learn to critique art.

(Rigorous)

126. **All of the following are examples of useful art tools for early childhood students EXCEPT:**

A. Color wheel

B. Oversized crayons and pencils

C. Fine-tipped brushes

D. Clay

Answer: C. Fine-tipped brushes

Many prekindergarten and kindergarten students use oversized pencils and crayons for the first semester. Typically, after this first semester, children gradually develop the ability to use smaller-sized materials. However, they usually do not use fine-tipped brushes until the middle grades due to the lack of adequate fine-motor skills. The color wheel is an excellent lesson for young children, and students begin to learn the uses of primary and secondary colors. Clay is also a valuable medium for children; it offers many opportunities for learning about texture, shape, line, and form and provides a good opportunity to be creatively expressive.

(Average)

127. **The Renaissance period was concerned with the rediscovery of the works of:**

A. Italy

B. Japan

C. Germany

D. Classical Greece and Rome

Answer: D. Classical Greece and Rome

The Renaissance period was concerned with the rediscovery of the works of classical Greece and Rome. The art, literature, and architecture of this period (ca. 1400–1630 CE) was inspired by classical order and style, which tended to be formal, simple, and concerned with the ideal human proportions.

(Rigorous)

128. **Which of the following statements is most accurate?**

A. Most artists work alone and are rarely affected by the work of other artists

B. Artists in every field are influenced and inspired by the works of others in the various disciplines in the humanities

C. It is rare for visual arts to be influenced by literature or poetry

D. The political climate of an era affects the art of the period only on specific occasions throughout history

Answer: B. Artists in every field are influenced and inspired by the works of others in the various disciplines in the humanities

The history of the humanities is replete with examples of artists in every field being influenced and inspired by the works of others. Influence and inspiration continuously cross the lines between the various disciples in the humanities.

(Average)

129. **A combination of three or more tones sounded at the same time is called a:**

A. Harmony

B. Consonance

C. Chord

D. Dissonance

Answer: C. Chord

A chord is three or more tones combined and sounded simultaneously. Dissonance is the simultaneous sounding of tones that produce a feeling of tension or unrest. Harmony is the sound resulting from the simultaneous sounding of two or more tones consonant with one another.

(Average)

130. **A series of single tones that add up to a recognizable sound is called a:**

A. Cadence

B. Rhythm

C. Melody

D. Sequence

Answer: C. Melody

A melody is an arrangement of single tones in a meaningful sequence. Cadence is the closing of a phrase or section of music. Rhythm is the regular occurrence of accented beats that shape the character of music or dance.

(Average)

131. **The term *conjunto* in music refers to:**

A. Two instruments playing at the same time

B. A tempo a little faster than allegro

C. A musical style that involves playing with great feeling

D. A type of Texas-Mexican music

Answer: D. A type of Texas-Mexican music

Around the turn of the century in Texas, a clash of cultures produced the Texas-Mexican music called *conjunto*. Working-class musicians from German and Mexican backgrounds combined their talents to produce this folk music, which uses the accordion as its main instrument. Musicians could easily transport accordions, making them the perfect accompaniment for dancing, eating, gambling, and other social events.

(Rigorous)

132. **All of the following apply to critiquing music EXCEPT:**

A. The keys steps are to listen, analyze, describe, and evaluate

B. Avoid the use of musical terminology in order to facilitate students' enjoyment of music

C. Have students develop their own rubrics for critiques

D. Encourage students to work in pairs

Answer: B. Avoid the use of musical terminology in order to facilitate students' enjoyment of music

Teaching basic music terminology is a prerequisite for any critique process. Without the necessary language, it is not effective to try to evaluate a piece of music. Similarly, students must be given the opportunity to develop listening skills so they are able to hear different musical elements, themes, instruments, and tones. They will also benefit from an overview of the sounds of different instruments and musical styles.

(Easy)

133. **Which of the following is NOT a type of muscle tissue?**

A. Skeletal

B. Cardiac

C. Smooth

D. Fiber

Answer: D. Fiber

The main function of the muscular system is movement. There are three types of muscle tissue: skeletal, cardiac, and smooth. Fiber is unrelated to muscle.

(Average)

134. **Which of these is a type of joint?**

A. Ball and socket

B. Hinge

C. Pivot

D. All of the above

Answer: D. All of the above

A joint is where two bones meet. Joints enable movement. Hinge, ball and socket, and pivot are types of joints.

(Average)

135. A physical education instructor anticipates and prevents potential injuries, watches for hidden injuries, and takes an injury evaluation of the entire class. Which of the following strategies to prevent injuries is the teacher demonstrating?

A. Maintaining hiring standards

B. Proper use of equipment

C. Proper procedures for emergencies

D. Participant screening

Answer: D. Participant screening

In order for the instructor to know each student's physical status, he or she takes an injury evaluation. Such surveys are one way to know the physical status of an individual. Injury evaluations chronicle past injuries, activities, and diseases an individual may have or have had. It helps the instructor know the limitations of each individual. Participant screening covers all forms of surveying and anticipation of injuries.

(Average)

136. All of the following are signs of anorexia nervosa EXCEPT:

A. Malnutrition

B. Behavior regression

C. No outward signs

D. Recognizable weight loss

Answer: C. No outward signs

There are significant outward signs displayed when a person is struggling with anorexia.

(Rigorous)

137. Which of the following refers to a muscle's ability to contract over a period of time and maintain strength?

A. Cardiovascular fitness

B. Muscle endurance

C. Muscle fitness

D. Muscle force

Answer: B. Muscle endurance

Cardiovascular fitness relates to the ability to perform moderate-to-high-intensity exercise for a prolonged period. Muscular fitness relates to how much force a muscle group can generate (strength) and how effectively the muscle group can sustain that force over a period of time (endurance).

(Average)

138. A game of "Simon Says" is an opportunity for the teacher to asses which of the following?

A. Concept of body awareness

B. Concept of spatial awareness

C. Concept of direction and movement

D. Concept of speed and movement

Answer: A. Concept of body awareness

Instructors can assess body awareness by playing and watching a game of "Simon Says" and asking the students to touch different body parts. Instructors can also instruct students to make their bodies into various shapes, from straight to round to twisted, and varying sizes, to fit into different sized spaces.

(Average)

139. **Bending, stretching, and turning are examples of which type of skills?**

A. Locomotor skills

B. Nonlocomotor skills

C. Manipulative skills

D. Rhythmic skills

Answer: B. Nonlocomotor skills

Locomotor skills move an individual from one point to another. Nonlocomotor skills are stability skills in which the movement requires little or no movement of one's base of support and does not result in change of position. Manipulative skills use body parts to propel or receive objects, controlling them primarily with the hands and feet. Rhythmic skills include responding and moving the body in time with the beat, tempo, or pitch of music.

(Rigorous)

140. **Which of the following statements is NOT true?**

A. Children's motor development and physical fitness are affected by a range of factors, including social, psychological, familial, genetic, and cultural factors

B. Motor development is complete by the time a student reaches sixth grade

C. A family's economic status can affect a student's motor development

D. A physical education program can have a positive impact on a student's level of physical fitness

Answer: B. Motor development is complete by the time a student reaches sixth grade

Motor development continues until adulthood. Furthermore, many factors have an impact on children's motor development and physical fitness.

CPSIA information can be obtained at www.ICGtesting.com
Printed in the USA
LVOW030339090612

285310LV00003B/24/P

9 781607 871132